D1327353

Slavery and Freedom

Slavery and Freedom in Delaware 1639–1865

William H. Williams

A Scholarly Resources Inc. Imprint
Wilmington, Delaware

6 by Scholarly Resources Inc.
All rights reserved
First published 1996
Printed and bound in the United States of America

Scholarly Resources Inc.
104 Greenhill Avenue
Wilmington, DE 19805-1897

Cover Photo: Courtesy of the Delaware State Archives, Dover (see page 55).

Library of Congress Cataloging-in-Publication Data

Williams, William Henry, 1936–
    Slavery and freedom in Delaware, 1639–1865 / William H.
    Williams.
        p.   cm.
    Includes bibliographical references and index.
    ISBN 0-8420-2594-4 (alk. paper)
    1. Slavery—Delaware—History. 2. Afro-Americans—Delaware
—History. 3. Freedmen—Delaware. 4. Delaware—Race relations.
I. Title.
E445.D3W55   1996
975.1'00496073—dc20   96-13735
                                                                                          CIP

♾The paper used in this publication meets the minimum requirements of the American National Standard for permanence of paper for printed library materials, Z39.48, 1984.

To John A. Munroe,

my teacher and friend

About the Author

William H. Williams is southern coordinator of the University of Delaware's Master of Arts in Liberal Studies Program and professor of history in the Del Tech/University of Delaware Parallel Program in Georgetown, Delaware. His other publications include *Anglo-America's First Hospital: The Pennsylvania Hospital, 1751–1840* (1976), *The Garden of American Methodism: The Delmarva Peninsula, 1769–1820* (1984), and *The First State: An Illustrated History of Delaware* (1985).

Contents

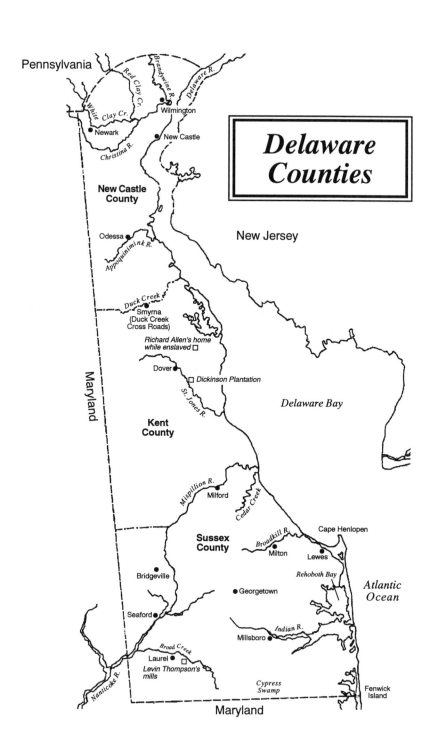

Pennsylvania

Red Clay Cr.

Brandywine R.

White Clay Cr.

Delaware R.

Wilmington

Newark

New Castle

Christina R.

New Castle County

Odessa

New Jersey

Appoquinimink R.

Duck Creek

Smyrna (Duck Creek Cross Roads)

Richard Allen's home while enslaved □

Dover

□ *Dickinson Plantation*

St. Jones R.

Maryland

Delaware Bay

Kent County

Mispillion R.

Milford

Cedar Creek

Broadkill R.

Cape Henlepen

Sussex County

Milton

Lewes

Bridgeville

Rehoboth Bay

Atlantic Ocean

Georgetown

Seaford

Indian R.

Millsboro

Broad Creek

Laurel □

Levin Thompson's mills

Nanticoke R.

Cypress Swamp

Fenwick Island

Maryland

Delaware Counties

Acknowledgments

I am indebted to four colleagues who read, in its entirety, a rough manuscript of this study and offered advice and encouragement. They include John Munroe, to whom this book is dedicated; John Kern, whose support for this project at its earliest stages was crucial; Carol Hoffecker, who urged me to sharpen many of my observations; and Peter Kolchin, who gave both the rough manuscript and a more polished version an exceptionally close reading and then offered constructive suggestions. These four readers, of course, bear no responsibility for any factual or interpretative errors that may appear in the final version.

Among the staff at the Delaware State Archives who were generous with their time and knowledge were Joanne Mattern, Russell McCabe, Susan Evans, Bruce Hass, and Randy Goss. Madeline Dunn Thomas of the Delaware State Museums was supportive of this study from its inception. Others who have contributed to the completion of this work include Jack Murray, Charles Kopay, Bruce Bendler, Brenda Baker, Peter Dalleo, Loren Schweninger, Adrienne Berney, and Helen Williams. I am particularly grateful to the late Harold B. Hancock for his pioneering scholarship on early blacks in Delaware and for encouraging me to work in Delaware history.

Connie Cooper and the staff of the Historical Society of Delaware served my research needs in a particularly professional manner as did the staffs of the Steven Betz Library at Delaware Technical and Community College, Georgetown, and the Hugh Morris Library at the University of Delaware, Newark. Ann M. Aydelotte and Carolyn Travers, editors at Scholarly Resources, patiently guided me through the final stages of turning the manuscript into a book. The Delaware Humanities Forum provided a summer research grant. The University of Delaware generously backed this study with two summer research grants, an expense account, a sabbatical leave, and a year's appointment as a Fellow in the University's Center for Advanced Study.

Delaware Hundreds in 1800

Brandywine

Mill Creek

Christiana

White Clay Creek

New Castle

Pencader

New Castle County

Red Lion

St. Georges

Appoquinimink

Duck Creek

Little Creek

St. Jones

Murderkill

Kent County

Delaware Bay

Mispillion

Cedar Creek

Broadkill

Lewes & Rehoboth

North West Fork

Nanticoke

Indian River

Sussex County

Dagsboro

Broad Creek

Little Creek

Baltimore

Introduction

In 1984, while writing a short history of Delaware, I noticed how little had been published on the state's African-Americans or on black-white race relations.[1] Since then, not much has changed. Indeed, of the fifteen southern slave states, Delaware remains the only one without a published study of slavery and freedom as it existed prior to 1865.[2] This book attempts to fill that void.

Delaware's records concerning slavery and freedom are not numerous, detailed, or complete for four reasons: 1) the state's small size limited the total number of its slaveholders and therefore the number of its record keepers; 2) slave units were smaller than in the rest of the South, and masters with only a few slaves were less inclined to keep detailed accounts of their bondspeople; 3) once blacks were free, literate whites rarely wrote about them in personal or business accounts; and 4) since the overwhelming majority of slaves and free African-Americans was illiterate, they left few written records of their own.

Despite the limited primary source materials, this study attempts to be as developmental (by tracing change over time in the condition of slavery and freedom in Delaware) and as comparative (by juxtaposing slavery and freedom in Delaware with other states) as the records permit. My main purpose, however, is not to create developmental models or to provide comparative statistics. Rather, it is to describe and analyze slavery and freedom, and their impact on the lives of the state's whites as well as its African-Americans, within the peculiar context of Delaware's economic, social, and political history. To some, this focus may seem too provincial; but to those who believe that many of the developments and events of early American history are best understood when studied in a primarily local context, such a focus may strike a certain resonance.

Today, racial fears and tensions are still central to the Delaware experience. Education, housing, jobs, welfare, and crime are only some of the troubled sectors of public life that are seen through the prism of one's own racial sensibilities. The attitudes and perceptions that dominate contemporary relations between blacks and whites have their roots in an "assumed" past—that is, many people, both blacks and whites, base their image of the other race on "assumptions" concerning past developments that may not be accurate. For example, it has been said that all white masters were brutal psychopaths with little interest in the lives of their slaves. It has also been said that, for the most part, African-Americans were well treated and slavery was not all that bad. My hope is that this study of more than two centuries of slavery and freedom will make a small contribution to a more accurate depiction of past race relations within this small state.

Delaware is located on the periphery of the Old South, and that fact is central to understanding the state's past. Even today, the southern mystique continues to cast a spell over the culture and thought patterns of many of its residents. Not long ago an article in the *New York Times* suggested that Sussex, the southernmost of the state's three counties, was "the northernmost county in Mississippi."[3] The primary factor that has traditionally linked the history of Sussex and the rest of Delaware with the other southern states was the presence, at a very early period, of large numbers of enslaved African-Americans.

White concern about this large black population led to the passage of state laws and to the development of specific traditions concerning race that forced a certain uniformity on the life experiences of African-Americans, whether they lived in Delaware or elsewhere in the South. However, because of the state's peripheral geographic location and its singular history, at least some aspects of the lives of its blacks, in both slavery and freedom, more closely resembled those of blacks in the mid-Atlantic states to the immediate north or took on a uniquely Delaware configuration.

Although the Swedes brought the first African to the Delaware Valley in 1639, it was not until the Dutch seized the area in 1655 that African slaves became relatively numerous. Slavery declined dramatically, however, after the English took control of New Netherland in the fall of 1664. During the early eighteenth century, it experienced a strong revival in Delaware as large numbers of blacks were brought in from Maryland's Eastern Shore or were purchased in Philadelphia and elsewhere. But even at its high point, in the decade prior to the American Revolution, only 20 to 25 percent of the colony's population was enslaved. This percentage was far higher than could be found in any northern colony but lower than in any other colony in the South.

The Revolution marked the simultaneous convergence of certain political, religious, and economic forces that produced a stronger manumission movement in Delaware than in any other state with significant numbers of slaves. A state law banning the exportation of slaves for sale was passed in 1787. In subsequent years it was further expanded and defined, helping to make slaveowning increasingly unprofitable and contributing to the freeing of a majority of Delaware blacks by the end of the eighteenth century. Before freedom, however, the state's blacks were subject to a cultural cleansing that more successfully eradicated the celebration of African customs and mores than anywhere else in the South. Moreover, because Delaware slave families faced particularly trying conditions, they were less complete and less viable than were slave families in other southern states.

On a number of occasions the General Assembly came very close to abolishing the "peculiar institution," but it took the Thirteenth Amendment in 1865 to finally end black bondage in Delaware. Earlier, however, in the debate over whether or not to end slavery, members of the General Assembly and the public at large reflected the manumission sentiments popular in such mid-Atlantic states as Pennsylvania and New York as well as the stubborn resistance to ending slavery that characterized attitudes in such Upper South states as Maryland and Virginia.

Once freed, black laborers continued to be crucial to the success of the Delaware economy and were sought after by white employers despite the fact that the latter constantly complained that many blacks refused employment, while the rest were undependable when hired. Responding to white concerns, the General Assembly passed a very coercive labor law in 1849 that threatened to sell free African-Americans into servitude for a year if they remained unemployed. Only Maryland approached Delaware in the coercive nature of its policy toward free black laborers during the antebellum era.

The need to keep free black laborers in Delaware was balanced by the growing white fear of what was, proportionally at least, the largest free African-American population in the United States. The latter concern led to a series of harsh black codes that so restricted the liberties of free African-Americans that Delaware became the least hospitable place in the Union for freedmen prior to the Civil War. This increasingly hostile environment led to an escalation in black emigration to the North in the late antebellum period.

In response to both the harsh black codes and the increased autonomy that accompanied freedom from slavery, there developed an indigenous free African-American culture in antebellum Delaware that was clearly black but not very African. Based largely on a foundation provided by the reconstituted black family and the increasingly independent black church, this evolving culture helped sustain the state's black community even after hopes for racial justice, raised by the Civil War, were dashed.

White resistance to racial justice was dictated by a growing racism that had become so deeply rooted and inflexible, by the late antebellum period, that it would shape much of the state's political and social life for at least another century. Even as late as the midtwentieth century, white racism remained such a powerful legacy in Delaware that it took the intervention of the federal government to ensure equal treatment before the law for African-Americans.

Notes

1. In writing about slavery and freedom, I have decided to use "African-American" and "black" interchangeably because, according to the *Washington Post*, 1/23/1994, these terms are the two most preferred by African-Americans. I have chosen to keep the hyphen in "African-American" because I agree with Professor Henry Louis Gates of Harvard that the hyphen shows "the very complexity of being of African descent in the world." See *Newsweek* 118 (September 23, 1991): 47.

2. The publication of Randolph B. Campbell's *An Empire of Slavery: The Peculiar Institution in Texas, 1821–1865* (Baton Rouge, LA, 1989) left Delaware the only antebellum slave state without a history of slavery. See the review of Campbell's *Empire of Slavery* in *Journal of the Early Republic* 10 (Spring 1990): 100.

3. *New York Times*, 3/8/1992.

Chronology

1638	New Sweden is founded at present-day Wilmington.
1639	Black Anthony, the first African, arrives in New Sweden.
1655	The Dutch conquer New Sweden and add it to New Netherland.
1664	African slaves make up 20 percent of the colony's total population as the English take control from the Dutch.
1700	Slaves make up less than 5 percent of the colony's total population.
1704	The Lower Counties separate from Pennsylvania and are granted their own legislature.
1713	A dramatic increase in slave imports into Delaware begins.
1726	Delaware adopts black codes similar to Pennsylvania's revised black codes.
1750	Tobacco is no longer a significant cash crop in the colony.
1760	Richard Allen, founder of the African Methodist Episcopal Church, is born.
1770	Slaves make up 20 to 25 percent of Delaware's total population. More than 95 percent of its blacks are enslaved.
1775-1783	The American Revolution, the rise of Methodism, and the dramatic increase in manumissions all take place.
1776	The Philadelphia Yearly Meeting directs Delaware Quakers to free their slaves.

1787	Selling Delaware slaves to the Carolinas, Georgia, and the West Indies is banned by law.
1788–89	Abolition societies are established in Dover and Wilmington.
1789	Selling Delaware slaves to Maryland and Virginia is banned by law.
1790	Slaves make up 70 percent of the state's black population and 15 percent of its total population.
1790–1810	Delaware's slave population declines more rapidly, in percentage terms, than that of any other state.
1792	An attempt to have the new state constitution abolish slavery is unsuccessful.
1797	All Delaware slaves sold out of state are declared automatically free.
1803	A bill in the General Assembly to abolish slavery gradually in Delaware fails by one vote in the state House of Representatives.
1805	Ezion Methodist Episcopal Church, the first all-black church in the state, is established in Wilmington by Peter Spencer and others.
1813	African Union Church is established in Wilmington by Peter Spencer and others. It was the first independent black Methodist church in the United States and formed the nucleus of the nation's first independent black denomination.
1814	Big Quarterly begins in Wilmington and becomes the first major black religious festival in the United States.
1816	Levin Thompson, a very successful black landowner in southwestern Sussex County, dies.
1821	Blacks are barred from state-aided schools.
1824	Delaware's first African Methodist Episcopal congregation is established near Smyrna.
1831	Nat Turner's Rebellion takes place in Southampton County, Virginia.
1832	The General Assembly passes the first of a series of restrictive black codes to control freedmen.

1840 Slaves represent only 13 percent of the state's black population and only 3 percent of its total population.

1847 A bill to abolish slavery gradually in Delaware fails by one vote in the state Senate.

1849 The General Assembly declares that idle and poor free blacks will be sold into servitude for up to one year at a time.

1850 The number of free blacks leaving Delaware for the North rises.

1850–60 Property ownership by free blacks increases dramatically.

1861 President Abraham Lincoln's plan to end slavery in Delaware barely fails in the General Assembly.

1861–65 The Civil War divides the nation.

1865 Despite the state's refusal to ratify it, the Thirteenth Amendment abolishes slavery in Delaware.

I

The Dutch Legacy and Its Aftermath

I solicite most seriously that it may please your honor [Peter Stuyvesant] to accomodate me with a company of negroes, as I am very much in want of them in many respects.
—Vice Director William Beekman, Altena (Fort Christina), 1662*

In Delaware, as in much of the New World, slavery was encouraged by the convergence of three factors: virgin land, the desire to grow cash crops, and a great scarcity of free agricultural laborers. During the seventeenth and eighteenth centuries, the largely virgin soil stimulated an interest in cultivating such staple crops as tobacco, corn, and wheat. But throughout most of the colonial period the supply of European men and women willing to cross the Atlantic and toil in Delaware's tobacco, corn, and wheat fields fell considerably short of the labor needs of its planters. Although Sweden, the Netherlands, and England—the three European powers to control colonial Delaware consecutively—could have enslaved portions of their own populations to provide a permanent labor force large enough to meet the needs of Delaware and certain other American colonies, the three nations and their possessions in the New World turned to a different source of enslaved labor.[1]

To meet the manpower shortage, a few Delaware planters looked to Native Americans. The Indians of the lower Delaware Valley were a partly agrarian people, well versed in the mysteries of making the soil productive; but for a number of reasons they proved to be an unsatisfactory source of either free or unfree labor. Europeans preferred male to female slaves on the assumption that men were superior to women in the performance of physical labor. However, because male Indians generally left the responsibility of growing field crops to their wives and daughters, they lacked both the skill and interest to work land that was once their ancestors' but was now controlled by

Europeans. In addition, Native Americans of both sexes had no historical experience with livestock herding because cattle, pigs, and horses were recent imports from Europe. And when they did not like the nature of their work, even those who were slaves would often slip away and hide among their own people. Moreover, by the late seventeenth century, the ravages wreaked by European microbes, alcohol, white population growth, and the resulting westward migration of many Native Americans combined to strip Delaware of most of its Indian people.[2]

Nevertheless, several planters did use enslaved Native Americans. In Kent County, for example, Peter Groenendyke owned a Spanish-Indian slave in 1688, while Evan Jones of the same county listed an Indian woman among his six slaves in 1720. A restrictive provision in the state constitution of 1776, which prohibited the further importation of enslaved Native Americans, indicates that at least a few had been imported, perhaps from the Carolinas. But this handful fell far short of meeting the growing labor needs of colonial Delawareans.[3] Indeed, so unimportant was Indian slavery in Delaware that even its existence was forgotten by the late eighteenth century. In 1796 a state court incorrectly maintained that local laws and customs had always dictated that only blacks could be held as slaves.[4]

While not opposed to Indian slavery, the nearby colonies of Maryland and Virginia met a similar shortage in field hands by importing indentured Englishmen from the home country. During much of the seventeenth century, these indentured servants poured into both Chesapeake colonies to meet labor needs generated by the remarkable expansion of tobacco cultivation. Only after the immigration of English indentured servants dramatically declined in the late seventeenth century did first Virginia and then Maryland turn to the importation of large numbers of unfree Africans.[5] Unlike the Chesapeake colonies, Delaware became dependent on African labor almost from the start.

In 1638 two Swedish ships made their way up what is now called the Delaware River and then turned west into the mouth of the Christina (Christiana) River. Along the north bank, some two miles from the Delaware, the Swedes landed and built Fort Christina, the first permanent European settlement in the Delaware Valley. In subsequent years the settlers of New Sweden, who included many Finns, pushed north along the west bank of the Delaware into present-day Pennsylvania, and a few crossed the river into present-day New Jersey, building their distinctive log cabins as they cleared virgin forests.[6]

In April 1639 one of the two ships, the *Vogel Grip*, returned to Fort Christina from the Caribbean with a black slave named Anthony, who had been purchased in the West Indies. Very little is known about him except that for a number of years Anthony served one of New

Sweden's governors, the extraordinarily porcine and authoritarian Johan Printz. While in office from 1643 to 1653, Printz moved the seat of government northward from Fort Christina to Tinicum Island, near the present site of the Philadelphia Airport. While on Tinicum Island, Anthony cut hay for the governor's cattle and worked on Printz's "little sloop." The last extant record of Anthony indicates that he was still in New Sweden in 1654 and that he made several purchases that year from the commercial company that ran the settlement. His freedom to buy goods for himself probably indicates that he had become a free man.[7] Although he remains an elusive and mysterious figure, Anthony's arrival at Fort Christina in 1639 marked the beginning of the African-American slave experience in Delaware.

From its inception, New Sweden suffered from a shortage of laborers. Despite repeated pleas to Sweden for additional immigrants to clear and cultivate farmland in the Delaware Valley, few were sent. Among Europeans already in New Sweden were a handful of unfree white laborers, but these and the small number of free white laborers fell far short of meeting its needs. By 1647 the colony's total population numbered only 183.[8] Frustrated by the paucity of European immigrants, New Sweden looked elsewhere for field hands. Spain and Portugal had met similar labor shortages in their New World possessions by importing African slaves, but how could the Swedes procure Africans when they lacked both the naval power and the tropical experience to become seriously involved in the Atlantic slave trade? Although a Swedish African company was organized "for the purpose of trade and territorial acquisition" and received its charter in 1649, it did not engage in much slave trading and soon lost its African holdings along the Gold Coast (modern Ghana) to first the Danish and then the Dutch.[9] A few additional Africans may have been imported by New Sweden after Anthony's arrival, but their number was not nearly large enough to energize the economy of the Swedish holdings along the Delaware.[10]

~

Dutch imperial ambitions in the Delaware Valley date back to 1609, when Henry Hudson claimed the region for the Netherlands. In 1631, Dutch investors established an ill-fated settlement called Zwaanendael at the mouth of the Delaware Bay, just north of modern-day Lewes. Within a year its entire population of thirty or so Europeans was massacred by local Indians. Although the Dutch made a few subsequent attempts to reestablish a trading and whaling base at Zwaanendael, by 1633 they had abandoned the area. For two decades after the Zwaanendael disaster, the Dutch did not establish a permanent presence in the Delaware Valley. However, they did remain commercially active in the region by engaging in the fur trade with the Lenni Lenape (Delaware) Indians.[11]

Directing and controlling most of this presence in America was the Dutch West India Company. Organized in 1621, the company was granted monopoly rights by the Dutch government over its commercial and colonizing activities in Africa and the New World. Along the west coast of Africa, in North and South America, and in the islands of the Caribbean, the Dutch West India Company operated in many ways as the military and political arm of the government of the Netherlands.[12] This powerful commercial trading firm, with its monopolistic economic power and considerable political prerogatives, was a formidable colonizing instrument for Dutch expansion across the Atlantic. By the time New Sweden was established in the Delaware Valley in 1638, the Dutch West India Company controlled the Hudson Valley, or New Netherland. Anchoring the Dutch colony at the southern tip of Manhattan Island was the small but growing community of New Amsterdam (now New York). Living in New Amsterdam and serving as the director-general of New Netherland from 1647 to 1664 was the peg-legged and strong-willed Peter Stuyvesant.

Stuyvesant wished to expand New Netherland by annexing New Sweden, but Sweden and the Netherlands were at peace in Europe, and thus Stuyvesant's hands were tied. He could not act against the Swedish colony on the Delaware unless the Swedes could be goaded into initiating hostilities. In 1651 he established the first permanent Dutch settlement on the west bank of the Delaware by building Fort Casimir at the present site of the town of New Castle, a few miles downriver from Fort Christina. As Stuyvesant intended, the new Dutch fort was seen by the Swedes as a provocative challenge to their hegemony on the Delaware. Determined to protect their holdings, the Swedes launched a successful attack against Fort Casimir in 1655. Stuyvesant responded by leading a military expedition to the Delaware, which easily defeated the outnumbered Swedes.[13]

From 1655 to 1664 the present state of Delaware and most of the rest of the lower Delaware Valley were ruled by the Dutch. Although lasting only a decade, Dutch control was long enough to establish the institution of slavery as a central feature in the history of early Delaware. While the Swedes had imported Anthony and perhaps a few other Africans, it was the Dutch who first made slavery an integral part of the region's economic and social life.

Like the Swedes, the Dutch were not very successful in attracting large numbers of free or indentured Europeans to labor in the fields of their New World possessions.[14] But, unlike the Swedes, the Dutch West India Company had a large, ocean-going fleet with considerable commercial experience in the tropics that successfully challenged the initial monopoly of the African slave trade enjoyed by the Portuguese. By 1637 the Dutch West India Company had conquered most of the Portuguese trading centers along the West African coast and controlled the important sources of that region's slaves.

Slavery and the slave trade had existed in Africa long before the Portuguese, the Dutch, and other Europeans began transporting unfree blacks to the New World. Prior to A.D. 700, a trans-Sahara trade in Africans was under way. Over the next thirteen centuries, millions of captives from south of the Sahara were delivered to the Mediterranean Basin and to the Middle East by sophisticated commercial networks run by black Africans.[15] When European sea captains sailed south along the West African coast during the fifteenth century, they found these networks in place and able to provide Europe with gold, sugar, ivory, hides, palm products, and, most important, slaves. The subsequent forced emigration of enslaved Africans to North and South America and the Caribbean began in the early sixteenth century and continued through the midnineteenth century. An estimated ten to eleven million blacks actually survived the 5 to 15 percent mortality rate of the Middle Passage to set foot on the soil of the New World. As Donald R. Wright points out, this involuntary westward movement of Africans was "the greatest intercontinental migration in world history to that time."[16]

During much of the seventeenth century, the Dutch played a central role in this huge transatlantic African diaspora. They purchased slaves from merchants or agents of local rulers at ports or forts along the West African coast, from the Senegal River in the north to the southern boundaries of present-day Angola in the south. The Dutch then shipped these slaves across the Atlantic to such destinations as Brazil, which was captured from Portugal in 1630, or the island of Curaçao, which was seized from Spain in 1634. Initially, Brazil served as the main slave-trading center of the Dutch West India Company until the Portuguese recaptured Brazil in 1654 and the center of the company's slave-trading activities was shifted to Curaçao. From Brazil and then Curaçao, the Dutch West India Company dispatched enslaved Africans to its other American colonies as well as to the New World holdings of Spain, England, and France.[17]

Director-General Stuyvesant of New Netherland knew Curaçao. He had briefly served as the island's chief administrator in 1643–44, and the leg he lost during the latter year at the siege of the French-held Caribbean island of Saint Martin was buried there. When Stuyvesant was appointed director-general in 1647, he found that Curaçao and some other Dutch Caribbean islands were also under his jurisdiction.

In view of the shortage of laborers in New Netherland and Stuyvesant's past and present contacts, it is not surprising that New Netherland subsequently imported hundreds of African slaves from Curaçao.[18]

The Dutch West India Company was sending black slaves to the port of New Amsterdam as early as 1626, but it was not until midcentury that large numbers of Africans began to arrive. This influx of unfree blacks reflected a change in the colony's economic priorities. Initially founded to anchor the Dutch fur trade in North America, New Netherland proved progressively less profitable as the seventeenth century advanced. To give new economic vitality and some substance to its colony along the Hudson, the Dutch West India Company decided to emphasize agricultural productivity so that New Netherland first could become self-sufficient in foodstuffs and then serve as a breadbasket for such other company colonies as Curaçao and Brazil.[19]

Few Dutchmen, however, were willing to brave the uncertainties of an Atlantic crossing and life in the New World to clear and cultivate New Netherland's virgin land. And why should they? As officials of the Dutch West India Company observed, Dutchmen were reluctant to leave their native land where "those inclined to do any sort of work . . . procure enough to eat without any trouble."[20] Lacking a large labor pool, the company turned to African slaves to help make New Netherland economically viable.

In 1646, just a year prior to Stuyvesant's tenure, the then director-general and the colony's governing council were ordered to notify the Dutch West India Company whenever more slaves were needed. Increasing numbers of Africans were imported in subsequent years, but the supply still seemed to fall short of demand. In fact, New Netherlanders were so in need of more slaves that Stuyvesant, in 1659, asked the company to allow local residents to import Africans. It responded by making some concessions, but the company did retain control of the bulk of the slave trade. In 1660 it sent word to Curaçao to ship boatloads of slaves to New Netherland at every opportunity. Although never quite able to satisfy the demand, the supply of Africans imported from Curaçao was enough to exert a profound impact on the economic and social development of New Amsterdam, western Long Island, and much of the Hudson Valley. By 1660, according to some estimates, 12 to 14 percent of the non-Indian population of the Dutch settlements in present-day New York State were African. Indeed, one historian maintains that the survival and the transformation of New Netherland "from a shaky commercial outpost into a permanent settlement" were made possible by unfree African labor.[21]

After being conquered by the Dutch in 1655, New Sweden on the Delaware became part of the Dutch West India Company's expanding colony of New Netherland under Stuyvesant's autocratic rule. In 1656, however, the company sold its holdings south of the Christina River to the City of Amsterdam while retaining the land north of the Christina. For all but the last year of the Dutch period, there would be two Dutch colonies on the west bank of the Delaware: the Company Colony to the north with Altena (formerly Fort Christina) as its center, and the City Colony to the south with New Amstel (modern-day New Castle) as its focus.[22]

Both Dutch colonies naturally followed the Hudson Valley's example and turned to African slaves to meet their labor shortfall. By 1657 an unspecified number of Africans were already in the City Colony. From Altena, on the north bank of the Christina, Company Colony official William Beekman sent a request to Stuyvesant in 1662 for "a company of negroes, as I am very much in want of them in many respects." The next year the immediate need of the City Colony for fifty Africans who were "particularly adapted" to clearing land and to other heavy work was presented to the Amsterdam directors. If the slaves were not sent post haste, preferably via the Dutch West India Company, another entire year would be "lost, which would tend to the serious disadvantage of agriculture" in the City Colony.[23]

These urgent requests from both the Company Colony and the City Colony must have brought a number of enslaved Africans to the Delaware in the early 1660s, but the only surviving record of slave deliveries concerns part of the cargo of the *Gideon* in 1664. The ship was originally scheduled to pick up three hundred slaves from Loango, a small African kingdom just north of the mouth of the Congo River and an important source of Dutch slaves during the midseventeenth century, and then set sail across the Atlantic to Curaçao. After resupplying at Curaçao, the *Gideon* was to deliver its human cargo to New Amsterdam, where one-fourth of its Africans were to be sent on to New Amstel on the Delaware.[24] After a more extensive voyage along the West African coast than planned, the ship finally reached Curaçao with most of its enslaved Africans suffering from scurvy. After sending the sick ashore and filling their places with "seasoned" blacks already in Curaçao, the *Gideon* sailed for New Amsterdam. In mid-August 1664, after a three-week passage in which nine slaves died, the *Gideon* unloaded a mixed cargo of 290 "seasoned" and "green" Africans at New Amsterdam. Despite the last-minute substitutions, the slaves that reached New Netherland were described as a "very poor lot," in part because so many were beyond their prime laboring years.[25]

Peter Alrichs, a City Colony official, traveled from New Amstel to New Amsterdam prior to the arrival of the *Gideon* in order to purchase cows, oxen, and horses for the colony and to receive the one-fourth portion of the slave cargo. Complicating the situation, however, was the outbreak of war between the Netherlands and England in 1664.

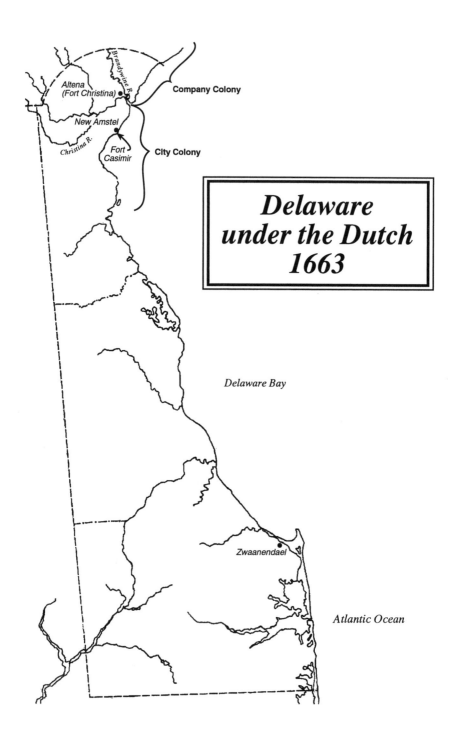

Altena
(Fort Christina)

Brandywine R.

Company Colony

New Amstel

Christina R.

Fort
Casimir

City Colony

Delaware
under the Dutch
1663

Delaware Bay

Zwaanendael

Atlantic Ocean

A shortage of provisions and the appearance off New Amsterdam on August 26 of an English fleet bent on conquering New Netherland caused Alrichs to send off hastily the City Colony's share of the *Gideon*'s Africans in separate gangs to New Amstel by an overland route through New Jersey. By early September, thirty-eight male and thirty-four female Africans—one-third of them more than thirty-six years old—had arrived at New Amstel.[26]

There was no escaping the English. On September 8, Stuyvesant formally surrendered New Amsterdam, Long Island, and the Hudson Valley to the British fleet. Less than a month later, a victorious landing party proceeded to plunder New Amstel and the expanded holdings of the City Colony. (With the blessings of the Dutch West India Company, the City Colony had absorbed the Company Colony the preceding year.) Among the properties seized by the English were sixty to seventy slaves, some of whom were promptly sold to Maryland planters for beef, pork, corn, salt, and other provisions. The eleven additional slaves taken from Alrichs, however, were returned four years later by Governor Francis Lovelace.[27]

Although the property of the City Colony's officials was largely confiscated by the English, most accounts agree that the victors left untouched the property of independent farmers and craftsmen. Therefore, those Africans owned by colonists who were not officials in the City Colony were most likely left alone. Although no extant record indicates the number of slaves in this category, the one hundred or so farms that existed along the west bank of the Delaware just prior to the English conquest probably contained a number of unfree Africans. Because the Swedes and Finns, who were mostly found north of the Christina River, were less likely to own slaves than the Dutch, slavery was more concentrated south of the Christina where most of the Dutch lived.[28]

The exact number of Africans living in Delaware on the eve of the English conquest in September 1664 is impossible to determine because there are no extant census records. An estimate based on incomplete and scattered sources indicates that there was a minimum of 125 Africans in the future state of Delaware, and they represented approximately 20 percent of the total population.[29] By contrast, admittedly rough figures for the same year put the African populations of Maryland and Virginia at only 9 and 5 percent, respectively. As late as 1670 blacks represented only 6 percent of the total population for the entire Chesapeake region.[30] In 1664 the future slave colonies of North and South Carolina, as well as Georgia, had yet to experience significant settlement, white or black. By the early fall of 1664 the Dutch-controlled west bank of the Delaware joined the Dutch-controlled Hudson Valley to become the first regions of the future Thirteen

Colonies to be heavily dependent on African slave labor. In other words, the future states of New York and Delaware were the first significant homes of American slavery north of Spanish Florida.

~

    The English conquest of the Hudson and Delaware valleys in the fall of 1664 marked the beginning of a new era in slavery and in the African-American experience in Delaware. The English victory also made it possible for James, duke of York and Albany, to take posses-sion of a large land grant given to him only a few months before by his brother, King Charles II. Although the duke of York's grant included the Hudson Valley and all of the present state of New Jersey, it did not include the west bank of the Delaware; but this small technical matter did not deter the English from seizing and then adding the west bank to the duke's holdings.[31]

    A temporary decline in slavery followed the English takeover. One contributing factor was the age of some of the seventy-two Africans brought to New Amstel from New Amsterdam in 1664. Although this large group was unusually gender balanced for a seventeenth-century slave shipment—thirty-eight males to thirty-four females—it included "many above the age of 36 years" and thus not as likely as younger adults to produce large numbers of offspring.[32] When the English con-querors seized sixty to seventy Dutch slaves on the west bank and promptly sold a substantial, although unspecified, number to Mary-land planters, no doubt healthy young adults of both sexes were cho-sen for sale because they commanded the highest prices.[33] Left behind on the west bank were the old and the sickly, the least fertile cohorts imaginable.

    Although no census was taken in Delaware until 1790, circum-stantial evidence points to a decline in the number of black Delawar-eans during the late seventeenth century. A tax list for the court at New Castle in 1677, for example, lists only eight slaves. While the actual number on the west bank was considerably higher in 1677, the total number of blacks must have been well under one hundred. The seizure and sale of so many slaves of prime child-bearing age to Maryland planters, the resulting drop in black births among the older cohort left behind, and a concurrent increase in white immigration probably caused African-Americans to decline to less than 5 percent of the total population of the future state of Delaware by the end of the seventeenth century.[34]

    Soon after the English takeover, Governor Richard Nicholls sounded a familiar refrain when he reported that the Delaware Valley needed more European settlers. He made it very clear that where the

Swedes and Dutch had failed, the English must succeed. To attract new immigrants to the west bank, the duke of York's government established a liberal land-grant policy that caused some Swedes, Finns, and Dutch who were already living along the west bank to move inland. This policy also attracted Anglo-Saxon residents of Maryland's Eastern Shore to the unworked soil of present-day central and southern Delaware. Eastern Shore farmers were encouraged to bring their slaves with them when, in 1675, Governor Sir Edmund Andros instructed the high sheriff of the west bank to grant newcomers land in proportion to "their capacity and number of hands they shall bring for clearing it."[35] Andros was so interested in giving "all manner of encouragement to planters of all nations, but especially Englishmen," that he offered to remit the first three years of quitrents to new settlers. So successful were the combined attractions of virgin soil and the liberal land-grant policies of the duke of York and, after 1682, William Penn, that one source estimates that the population of Delaware increased by more than three times between 1670 and 1700.[36]

Although most of the newcomers were from the Eastern Shore, only a handful were black. In fact, few enslaved Africans from any source entered Delaware from 1665 to 1713. Under Dutch rule, the Dutch West India Company provided slaves for both the Hudson and Delaware valleys. By contrast, the duke of York's government did not assume responsibility for supplying the proprietorship with new slaves. At first, this policy created a significant problem for farmers and planters because Dutch slave ships were barred by the Navigation Acts from trading with the English colonies, and no commercial English trading company was as yet either interested in or capable of supplying Africans to the labor-starved west bank of the Delaware.

Predictably, after 1664 colonists on the west bank were frustrated by the shortage of slaves and by their own inability to procure additional Africans. In 1678 the magistrates of the town of New Castle responded by seeking permission for Delawareans to buy slaves from Maryland,[37] but seventeenth-century Maryland was a poor source. The Chesapeake region's early reliance on white indentured labor, the inability of English commercial companies to provide many slaves for any of their mainland colonies until almost the end of the seventeenth century, and the low reproduction rate of its predominantly male African population combined to produce only a few Maryland slaves for export.[38]

Most of the few blacks who arrived in Delaware from 1665 to 1713 accompanied their Maryland masters who, initially at least, wished to grow tobacco on their new lands. The attractions of Delaware to Chesapeake tobacco planters were obvious. During most of the seventeenth century, the Eastern Shore had offered inexpensive virgin land at a time of relatively high tobacco prices. Consequently, the Eastern Shore drew large numbers of ambitious young white males eager to make quick profits by growing the "noxious weed." But, during the late seventeenth century, tobacco prices went into a significant decline.[39]

To add to the woes of Eastern Shore planters, war in Europe broke out in 1689, and the interruption of Atlantic commerce created further downward pressures on tobacco prices. In addition, the decline in productivity of some farmland on the Eastern Shore, now played out from years of repeated corn and tobacco cultivation, created a new hunger for virgin soil. Only a short distance to the east and northeast, at the headwaters of the Nanticoke, Choptank, and regions beyond, lay untouched fields and forests. This undeveloped sector of the future state of Delaware acted as a beacon, guiding to it Eastern Shore men and women who understood, in an era of falling tobacco prices, that their economic salvation depended on the increased productivity that only virgin soil could provide.

Surprisingly, very few gentry were among the first whites to move into Delaware from Maryland's Eastern Shore. Rather, the new immigrants were predominantly the "middling and lesser sorts" who were laborers, tenants, or owners of modest farms. Most Eastern Shore gentry were able to survive the economic hard times of the late seventeenth and the first decade of the eighteenth century, but many of the "middling and lesser sorts" found that falling tobacco prices left them no alternative except to leave the developed areas at home to take advantage of the liberal land policies that characterized the west bank of the Delaware.[40] Because these migrants of limited means usually did not own slaves, they brought only a few blacks with them.

Unlike the early years of English rule, the six decades that followed the end of Queen Anne's War in 1713 brought significant numbers of African-Americans to Delaware from Maryland's Eastern Shore and beyond. In part, this immigration was caused by dramatic changes in the racial makeup of the land to the west and south of Delaware. In the late seventeenth century, despite a modest increase in slave imports, blacks represented less than 10 percent of the population of the Eastern Shore. As late as 1712 the figure was still only 12 percent, but subsequently a substantial increase in slave imports and a rise in the African-American birth rate, partly caused by a balancing out of the once overwhelmingly male-dominated sex ratio, led to a dramatic rise in the region's black population that would continue through most of the eighteenth century. By 1790 approximately 40 percent of the Eastern Shore population was African-American.[41] After 1713 increasing numbers of slaves from the region spilled over into Delaware.

With the end of Queen Anne's War, relatively prosperous times returned to the tobacco farms of the Eastern Shore. Increased profits from tobacco enabled many of the gentry to add significantly to the number of slaves they owned. But, by the second quarter of the eighteenth century, many Maryland planters recognized the finite nature of real estate on the Eastern Shore. There was enough underdeveloped land left to build sizable plantations for themselves and perhaps their children, but what about the generations to come? After all, as Richard L. Bushman has pointed out, these were men who felt responsible not only for their children's economic success but also for the well-being of their grandchildren and great-grandchildren.[42]

The seeming abundance of land in colonial America discouraged the traditional English practice of primogeniture, which left the entire estate to the eldest son, and encouraged the practice of partible inheritance, which divided real estate among all of the sons. (Although daughters might inherit land, they were instead often left movable property such as slaves.) As long as the supply of new land was infinite, partible inheritance did not threaten the future economic and social status of gentry families. However, once the supply became finite, the implications of partible inheritance were unsettling. On the face of it, a 3,600-acre plantation might seem more than enough to ensure the prospects of an Eastern Shore family, but if three sons survived to adulthood and each had three sons, then the nine grandsons individually would inherit no more than 400 acres—sufficient to support an ordinary family but hardly at the level to which the colonial gentry aspired.[43] Although many Eastern Shore gentry looked to the west side of the Chesapeake to satisfy their hunger for more land, still others recognized additional opportunities in Delaware, where considerable stands of forest and stretches of meadow remained unscarred by ax or plow.

The magnetic attraction of cheap virgin land in Delaware was further strengthened by the development of Philadelphia as a major market for agricultural commodities. By 1728 southern Delawareans were routinely sending their surplus agricultural products north to Philadelphia, where they were purchasing "such European or West Indian commodities as they want for their family use."[44] During the first half of the eighteenth century, merchants moved inland from the Delaware River to construct a commercial network that tied most of present-day Delaware and much of Maryland's upper Eastern Shore to Philadelphia's growing demand for wheat and corn. By midcentury it was clear that wheat and corn were more profitable to grow in the region than tobacco.[45]

Among the slave masters drawn to Delaware in the eighteenth century was Samuel Dickinson of Talbot County, Maryland. In 1739 this tobacco planter's holdings amounted to nine thousand acres. By that year he had also accumulated some three thousand acres in Kent County, stretching from Dover southeast to almost the mouth of the St. Jones River. In 1741, Dickinson turned over his Maryland holdings to his son and daughter by his first marriage and moved an unspecified number of slaves and his own family by a second marriage to Jones Neck, southeast of Dover. In moving to the banks of the St. Jones, Dickinson assured, as much as a man could, the economic well-being of the offspring of his second marriage for "at least two generations." Easy access to the growing grain port of Philadelphia, via the St. Jones, and the fact that the sandy soil of eastern Kent was better suited to grain than tobacco caused Dickinson, although nominally a tobacco planter, to follow the general pattern of most eighteenth-century Delaware slaveholders who, by midcentury, generally substituted corn and wheat for large-scale tobacco production.[46]

Unlike Dickinson, some Eastern Shore gentry took up land in Delaware while simultaneously maintaining and supervising their Maryland holdings. Thomas White, for example, moved his slaves back and forth from his Caroline County, Maryland, and Kent County holdings as need dictated.[47] Still others brought their slaves with them from as far away as Maryland's Western Shore and Virginia's Eastern Shore. Significant examples were Samuel Chew of Anne Arundel County, Maryland,[48] and Warner Mifflin of Accomack County, Virginia.[49]

An unspecified number of African-Americans entered Delaware in the eighteenth century after being purchased from Eastern Shore slaveholders. A seventeenth-century precursor was Black Will, sold in 1682 by Captain John Osborne of Somerset County, Maryland, to William Clark of Sussex County.[50] Still other Delaware slaves were purchased in Annapolis's thriving import slave market, providing planters along the upper Nanticoke and its tributaries with additional blacks; most had not been "seasoned" in the West Indies, but came directly from Africa and included a heavy concentration of Ibos and Angolans.[51] Philadelphia, however, was the primary source of new Africans for northern and eastern Delaware. As early as December 1684, only three years after Pennsylvania's founding, a shipload of 150 Africans had arrived in Philadelphia and was quickly purchased by the predominantly Quaker population in commercial transactions that seemed to exhaust much of the colony's available specie. Some Quaker involvement with slavery and the slave trade continued into the mideighteenth century with Swedish visitor Peter Kalm noting that Friends owned "as many negroes as other people."[52]

The French and Indian War (1754–1763) marked a dramatic decline in the immigration of white indentured servants to Pennsylvania, thus causing the colony to turn increasingly to African slaves to meet local labor needs. After the flow of indentured servants recommenced in 1763, the number of imported Africans declined. An average of ninety-one imported slaves per year during the early part of the French and Indian War gave way, by 1770, to fewer than thirty per year. For all intents and purposes, the importation of slaves by Philadelphia merchants had nearly ended during the decade prior to the American Revolution.[53] Before the city's slave traffic ended, however, it provided Delaware with hundreds of bondsmen fresh from Africa or, in lesser numbers, seasoned blacks from the West Indies.

Some Delawareans were involved in the Philadelphia slave trade. Among the first were Hercules and James Coutts from the town of New Castle, who were part owners of the ship *Constant Alice*, which brought nineteen slaves from Barbados to Philadelphia in 1701. Many Delawareans desiring to purchase Africans were drawn to Philadelphia by advertisements in the *Pennsylvania Gazette* or other Quaker City newspapers. In 1765, for example, the *Gazette* announced the arrival of the ship *Granby* with seventy Gold Coast slaves to be sold aboard the docked vessel of city merchant William Plumstead.[54]

Often Delawareans did not have to make the trip north to purchase Africans. From time to time Philadelphia merchants sent slave cargoes south for public sale or to fulfill previously negotiated contracts. In 1762, for example, Willing, Morris, and Company announced in the *Gazette* that 175 newly imported Gold Coast blacks, who were advertised as preferable to other Africans "on account of their natural good dispositions and being better capable of hard labor," would be sold in Wilmington. In the fall of 1763 the schooner *Africa* landed in Wilmington with 80 to 100 slaves. However, thirty-three others had died of "the flux" on the long voyage from Africa and some of those waiting to be purchased were very ill.[55] These alien newcomers left indelible impressions on the memories of some of Wilmington's whites. One older resident recalled "when he was young [probably about 1760] . . . seeing a vessel of two masts anchored in the Christiana Creek with the deck full of negro slaves from Africa." Another Wilmingtonian remembered "a gang or drove of slaves, numbering twenty or thirty, . . . passing by my father's door, driven by owners for sale" in 1761.[56]

Smaller shipments were occasionally routed to specific sites in southern Delaware, such as the sixteen Africans sent in 1738 by Philadelphia merchant Richard Ellis to Lewes, where they were to be sold by his son-in-law Jacob Kollock. These merchants liked shipping newly imported Africans directly to the three Lower Counties (modern-day Delaware) because they levied no import tax on slaves. Pennsylvania, by contrast, taxed imported slaves throughout most of the colonial period and increased the tariff from £2 to £10 per slave in 1761.[57]

By the mideighteenth century, a dramatic increase had taken place in the number of Africans in Delaware. Slave purchases from Annapolis, Philadelphia, and some Eastern Shore plantations, the immigration of Eastern Shore gentry with their bondsmen and bondswomen, and the natural increase among blacks already in the colony all contributed to this remarkable change in the racial makeup of the Lower Counties. The evident decline in numbers of African-Americans that had marked the late seventeenth century began to reverse itself significantly during the second decade of the eighteenth century. By 1728 the number of blacks in eastern Sussex County was on the rise and had already reached an estimated 10 percent of the overall population. A year earlier, one-third of the population of southern New Castle County was reported to be black. From central Kent County in 1751 came the observation that African-Americans were "very numerous."[58]

Slavery's renewed vigor was also reflected in the slaveholding patterns of the members of the eighteenth-century legislature. By the late colonial period, a majority owned African-Americans, with John Dickinson of St. Jones Neck, southeast of Dover, leading the way with at least thirty-seven in 1775. However, none of the other slaveholding colonial legislators owned more than nineteen. The new centrality of slavery is further demonstrated by a random sample representing 16 percent of Kent County inventories filed between 1727 and 1775. About one-third of the decedents in the sample owned slaves, with the estate of Samuel Chew of near Dover leading the list with sixty-three in 1746.[59]

Can we be more exact about how many African-Americans were in Delaware by the end of the colonial period? Although Delaware had to wait for the Federal Census of 1790 for the first real counting of blacks and whites, by projecting the 1790 census figures backward in time we can arrive at an approximation of the African-American population on the eve of the Revolution. In 1790 slaves or descendants of slaves numbered 12,876, or about 22 percent of the state's total population.[60] Twenty years earlier, the main sources of new slaves for the colony had nearly dried up. Philadelphia ceased being a significant importer after the mid-1760s, and Annapolis imported few slaves after 1760. On the eve of hostilities with England, far fewer Eastern Shore gentry than in earlier years considered moving to Delaware with their slaves because most of the virgin land already had been claimed by preceding generations of immigrant Marylanders and Virginians. Now, the unclaimed or very cheap land of the rolling Piedmont west of the Chesapeake, and not flat Delaware, beckoned Eastern Shore masters and their slaves.

With slave imports ending prior to the Revolution, the continued increase in Delaware's African-American population became dependent on the fecundity of blacks already in the state. With declining economic opportunities dramatically decreasing the number of whites willing to move to Delaware at the end of the colonial era, the growth of the state's white population also become dependent on its birth rate. By 1770 the fecundity rate of blacks and whites had probably reached a rough equality that would continue during the late eighteenth century, causing the proportion of blacks to whites to remain about the same over the next twenty years. In short, Delaware's African-Americans, almost all of whom were enslaved on the eve of the Revolution, made up approximately the same 22 percent of its population in 1770 as in 1790. This number was far more than the estimated 2.4 percent for Pennsylvania and 4.4 percent for all of the northern colonies in 1770, but it was considerably less than Maryland's estimated 32.5 percent, Virginia's 42 percent, South Carolina's 60.5 percent, and the entire South's 40 percent in 1770.[61] In the late colonial period, slavery was a far more significant part of the social and economic life of Delaware than of any northern colony including New York; however, it was not as significant in Delaware as in the rest of the colonial South.

~

In 1664 the duke of York gave what is now New Jersey to a group of English proprietors, leaving the west bank of the Delaware an isolated appendage more than one hundred miles southwest of his other holdings.[62] The Duke of York's Laws, a legal code for his physically divided proprietorship, were approved in 1665. But it was not until 1678, under the administration of Governor Andros, that a copy of the Duke's Laws finally reached the magistrates of the town of New Castle.[63] Lacking a code of prescribed English law, the west bank's inhabitants turned to English common law for legal guidance in dealing with slavery.

English common law maintained that once slaves converted to Christianity, they were to be freed. There is some indication that this precedent may have been initially honored in some Anglo-American colonies. In early seventeenth-century Virginia, for example, a black slave probably could sue for freedom if he could document his conversion.[64] But in this era, slavery was not yet very important to the Chesapeake economy, and English common law's linkage of freedom to conversion drew little legal or legislative attention. In the second half of the seventeenth century, however, as Virginia planters gradually became more dependent on unfree African labor and the House of Burgesses in Williamsburg began to pass specific laws defining the nature of black servitude, the linkage of conversion and slavery became an increasing concern to white Virginians. In 1667 the colony's legislature rejected English common law by declaring that conversion and baptism "doth not alter the condition of a person as to his bondage or freedom."[65] Maryland enacted a similar law four years later.

In the Hudson and Delaware valleys, where slavery was more vital to the economy than in the Chesapeake, there was even more concern about conversion leading to freedom. In 1665, two years prior to Virginia's stand on the issue, the Duke of York's Laws specifically denied freedom based on conversion to any enslaved blacks or Indians.[66] In the future, the renunciation of heathenism for Christianity would not help Delaware blacks cross the great divide that separated the enslaved from the free.

As the African-American population of Delaware increased during the eighteenth century, so, too, did government regulations aimed at more specifically defining slavery and then exercising control over this vital but seemingly alien work force. Because many whites had no previous experience with slavery or with Africans, the development of legal and social guidelines for the treatment of blacks was a gradual process shaped by practical considerations and the accepted values of the eighteenth-century Anglo-Saxon world. Although the Dutch were the real fathers of slavery in Delaware, the short time period between the first significant Dutch importation of slaves to the colony and the subsequent English conquest explains why the Dutch did not develop a systematic slave code for the west bank.

During the duke of York's era (1664–1682), slavery in Delaware was a declining institution. Except for denying slaves the right to turn conversion into freedom, the duke's government paid little attention to enacting laws and codes to regulate slavery and the slave trade. When William Penn added the Lower Counties to Pennsylvania in 1682, there followed an attitude toward slavery by his government that can best be labeled ambiguous. This ambiguity caused at least some people in the Lower Counties and in the rest of Pennsylvania to turn to English common law for guidance.

As in the relationship of conversion to freedom, it did not take Anglo-Americans long to decide that unique American conditions often made English legal traditions irrelevant. An important principle of English common law addressed the inherited status of both black and white children when it argued that the social and economic condition of the father, not the mother, was inherited by the offspring. But in the New World it soon became obvious that in dealing with the slave population an emphasis on paternal provenance was less practical than focusing on maternal origins. Because marriage was encouraged and legally sanctioned in colonial white society, most white fathers were fairly easy to identify. Slaves, by contrast, were denied legal marriage by their Anglo-Saxon masters. The unwillingness of whites to recognize and give legitimacy to black marriages helped give most of Delaware's colonial black families a certain tenuous nature. Unstable family ties, in turn, often made fathers of slave children far more difficult than mothers to identify.

For this reason, Delawareans joined other colonial Anglo-Americans in choosing to emphasize maternal rather than paternal provenance in establishing the legal status of black and mulatto children. They justified this rejection of English common law by citing the development of custom over time as well as specific legislation in the other English colonies.[67] In 1662, Virginia decreed that a mother's free or slave status was inherited by her children, and a similar law was passed by New York in 1702. Maryland was the only continental English colony to favor paternal provenance when dealing with the status of black and mulatto children, and then only from 1664 to 1681. Subsequently, the practice of recognizing maternal status as the key factor in deciding the fate of Maryland's black or mulatto children simply evolved by custom. In Pennsylvania, because custom also prevailed, no clear official statement on the issue was necessary until 1786, when the state Supreme Court declared that the principle of maternal provenance for black and mulatto children was and always had been the law.[68]

Although the Lower Counties were subject to Pennsylvania law from only 1682 to 1704, economic, political, and legal patterns in Pennsylvania continued to exercise considerable influence on Delaware's development for at least the next 160 years. But just as significant were the customs and attitudes brought from Maryland to Kent, Sussex, and southern New Castle counties by slaveholding Eastern Shore gentry. Shaped by external example, internal experience, Pennsylvania developments, and Maryland traditions, eighteenth-century Delaware's custom and law proclaimed that the status of the offspring of slaves reflected the condition of the mother rather than that of the father. One example was a Kent County slave girl, who, it was noted in 1766, was "born of the body of a Negro [slave] woman but supposed to be begotten by a white man" and, therefore, "according to the custom of this land," was "held in slavery and bondage."[69]

To make the point further that it was only the mother's status that counted, a manumission document issued in 1786 in the Dover area declared that slave William was "to be as free from slavery as if his mother had been a white woman," but it was ten years later before a written legal decision supported what was already custom. In 1796, Phillis petitioned the Kent County Court of Common Pleas for freedom on the grounds that, despite being illegally held in bondage, her mother and grandmother had been free blacks. Clearly, it was contrary to local custom to hold Phillis in bondage if she was the issue of two generations of legally free women. The court upheld the principle of maternal provenance and freed her.[70]

Evolving custom also dictated that Delaware's unfree African-Americans be enslaved for life. In the late seventeenth century, at least some slaves were freed after a certain number of years in bondage. One example was the same Black Will who had been bought by William Clark in 1682. Although Black Will was purchased "for and during his natrill life," his new master promised, "for the encouragement of the said neagor servant," that if Black Will would "well and truly serve" him for five years, he would have his freedom. At the end of the seventeenth century, Charles, a Kent County mulatto, was serving his master for a fixed number of years. And, as late as 1723, Rachel, a mulatto, was serving her master and mistress in the Lewes area for a limited number of years.[71]

By 1723, however, black servitude for only a limited number of years was very uncommon. To dispel any doubts that might linger because of earlier practices, many slaveholders pointedly used the word "forever" in their wills when speaking of the years that their black bondspersons would serve their heirs. By the middle of the century, the earlier practice of limited bondage had been so long abandoned that even its memory had disappeared. In 1766, for example, a Kent County planter explained that his slave Thomas was to serve for life because that was "the custom of this land."[72] In moving from ambiguity to certainty on the issue of lifetime servitude for African-Americans, Delaware lagged three or four decades behind the Chesapeake Bay colonies.[73]

During the early eighteenth century, laws passed by Pennsylvania and then by Delaware provided further clarification of the legal status of Delaware's slaves. Prior to 1700 slaves on the west bank of the Delaware shared some legal rights with whites. Evidently, all blacks were tried before the same courts and were judged by the same juries as whites. Peter, for example, was a slave indicted by the Kent County Grand Jury on suspicion of murdering a white man but was found not guilty in 1699. Prior to the eighteenth century, blacks and mulattoes were not singled out for especially harsh physical punishment, nor was there a specific ban on interracial sexual relationships; mixed-race marriages were tolerated as long as the African-American partner was free. During the late seventeenth century, for instance, free black

John Johnson of Kent County was married to Elizabeth, who was white.[74]

In 1700 a series of acts passed by the Pennsylvania legislature distinguished between indentured servitude and slavery by mandating that slaves be tried by separate "negro" courts for serious crimes. (The term "negro" in the early and mideighteenth century was often a synonym for slave.) The few free blacks in Pennsylvania, which then still included the Lower Counties, were also subject to these special courts for "negroes."[75] Such courts were a logical response to the white-perceived need to establish tighter controls over the growing and therefore potentially troublesome African-American population.[76] Soon after Delaware was granted its own legislature in 1704, these "negro" courts disappeared from the Lower Counties. With the dramatic increase in the slave population after the end of Queen Anne's War in 1713, the issue of control became increasingly important. In 1726, in some ways closely following the Pennsylvania model, Delaware's colonial assembly officially set up a special negro court in each county, made up of two justices of the peace and six of the county's most substantial freeholders.[77]

As in Pennsylvania, Delaware's negro courts tried slaves charged with major offenses such as murder, manslaughter, buggery, burglary, robbery, rape, attempted rape, or "other high and heinous crimes." To encourage the cooperation of slaveholders, masters were compensated with two-thirds of the value of any of their slaves sentenced to death after 1726; the compensation provision was copied from a Pennsylvania law of 1706. Delaware continued to try slaves before the special negro courts until those courts were temporarily abolished in 1789. But, unlike the situation in Pennsylvania, Delaware's few free blacks were not tried in negro courts but in the same ones as whites. Special courts for slaves were common elsewhere in the Anglo-American colonies as far north as New York. As Philip J. Schwarz has observed, "The more any society was based on slavery, the greater the chance that legislators would develop an independent set of laws and courts for slaves alone."[78]

Colonial Anglo-America's slave courts were not necessarily kangaroo courts. Although black defendants were denied the right to trial by jury by their peers, court decisions in Delaware and elsewhere often upheld their innocence.[79] From 1766 to 1767, for example, twelve slaves were charged and tried before the Dover slave court, but only seven were found guilty; and even when slaves were found guilty by the special negro courts in Dover, Lewes, or the town of New Castle, there was still the possibility of a pardon. Darby, owned by Vincent Loockerman of Dover, was found guilty of "felony and burglary" in

1768 and was sentenced to be executed, only to have the court recommend a reprieve, which was soon issued by Lieutenant Governor John Penn.[80] The limited number of slaves brought before the Dover negro court indicates that other bondspeople charged with crimes were dealt with informally, probably by the master in conjunction with civil authorities.

For those found guilty, criminal punishment was harsh by modern standards. The lack of a prison system for extended incarceration and the era's general insensitivity to physical pain and suffering made execution, dismemberment, and whippings the punishments of choice. The general acceptance of brutality as an integral part of not only the criminal justice system but also of the very social fabric of eighteenth-century life is reflected in the *Delaware Gazette*'s laconic report in 1791 that "Thomas Daniel was killed in a bare-fisted boxing match with James Smith."[81] An example of the period's brutal standards was the punishment of Catherine Bevan, a white woman. In 1731 in New Castle County, Mrs. Bevan and her white, male indentured servant together murdered her husband. Convicted and sentenced to death by burning, Mrs. Bevan was first hung by her neck over the fire so that she would be dead, or at least unconscious, by the time the flames reached her body. However, the flames "instantly" burned through the rope around her neck, and she "fell alive into the fire and was seen to struggle" by a crowd anxious to take in the barbaric scene.[82]

The execution of Catherine Bevan is instructive for two reasons: it exemplifies the insensitivity of colonial Delawareans to the infliction of considerable physical pain; and, in its savage denouement, it reflects the urgent need of a male-dominated society to make an unforgettable public example of what awaited any white woman who murdered her husband. After all, killing a husband represented the ultimate revolt against patriarchal control over both family and society. When black slaves refused to obey the rules promulgated by a white, male-dominated society, or when blacks went so far as to threaten white males or their families, like Catherine Bevan they, too, could expect little mercy.

Prior to 1700 there is no indication that convicted slaves were subjected to harsher physical punishment than were white indentured servants or other convicted members of colonial Delaware's white community. The first convincing evidence of discriminatory punishment is found in the criminal codes passed by Pennsylvania in 1700 and in the additional ones of 1706. Despite its separation from Pennsylvania in 1704, Delaware subsequently patterned most of its criminal codes after Pennsylvania's. When, for example, the former formally adopted its own criminal codes in 1726, they were taken almost verbatim from the latter's codes of 1706.[83]

In 1700, English common law was invoked to protect Pennsylvania and the Lower Counties' African-Americans from castration for the attempted rape of white women, but this was the last time that common law would be used to shield slaves from mutilation or from any other harsh or excessive punishment. By 1726, when Delaware proclaimed that any slave found guilty of attempted rape of a white woman was to stand with his ears nailed to a pillory for four hours and then, before being taken down, to have "both ears cut off close to the head," it was obvious that slaves were subject to more brutal physical punishment than were others. Indeed, Delaware's whites were guaranteed, in 1742, that the brutality of their court-directed punishments would be kept within the limits prescribed by "the laws and statutes of that part of Great Britain called England."[84] In general, however, the surviving laws of the colony do not lend themselves to a close comparison of the punishments of slaves, free blacks, and whites for similar crimes.[85] An exception is the punishment for the "unseasonable firing of woodlands and marshes." According to a Delaware law of 1740, convicted free blacks or free whites were to pay a fine of £5, while slaves were to be publicly whipped with up to thirty-one lashes for setting the countryside on fire.[86]

In contrast to the physical punishment meted out to slaves during the eighteenth century, white indentured servants were commonly sentenced to an increase in their years of servitude, while free blacks and free whites were often subjected only to fines. Clearly, some of the extra brutality that seemed to characterize the public punishment of slaves was really a product of their servile condition: adding years of servitude, or demanding the payment of fines, was futile because slaves had neither to give. Death, dismemberment, or lashes "well laid on" were the only options available to Delaware's lawmakers and courts. In short, at this stage, separate criminal codes for slaves were as much a product of the peculiar nature of slavery as they were a legal expression of racism. As if to drive home this point, Delaware proclaimed in 1752 that slaves who assaulted whites would stand in the public pillory for two hours and then receive up to thirty-nine lashes, while free blacks and free mulattoes convicted of the same crime would be fined between £5 and £10. Free whites found guilty of a similar offense were to be fined "according to the heinousness of the offense."[87]

~

By the eve of the Revolution, Delaware's slave-owning gentry presided over a mature slave society, dependent for much of its economic vitality on the forced labor of unfree blacks. Between one-fourth and one-fifth of its population was made up of enslaved African-

Americans who understood that a lifetime of servitude awaited them and their children. They also knew that their fate and their children's destiny had been partially sealed by a code of laws, a court system, and evolving custom that had grown increasingly oppressive during the eighteenth century. But the colonial government represented only one player on the stage. Taking an even more significant role were slave owners, because their interaction with their bondsmen and bondswomen set the tone and shaped much of the immediate environment within which unfree black Delawareans played out their lives.

Notes

*Samuel Hazard, *Annals of Pennsylvania, 1609–1682* (Philadelphia, 1850), 331.

1. David Eltis, in "Europeans and the Rise and Fall of African Slavery in the Americas: An Interpretation," *American Historical Review* 98 (December 1993): 1399–1423, argues that it would have been much cheaper for European nations to enslave white people who were in penal institutions or prisoner-of-war camps there and send them to the Americas than it was to purchase Africans. What stopped them from enslaving their own was the "insider" versus "outsider" perception then common. To leaders of European political units, it was all right to kill, imprison, or impress their own nationals or citizens of other states on the Continent, but it was not acceptable to enslave them because, as Europeans, they were seen as fellow "insiders"; Africans might be enslaved, however, because they were seen as "outsiders." Africans themselves, by contrast, were willing to enslave other Africans and sell them to Europeans because they perceived "insiders" in a much narrower range. (The tribal concept, as a number of historians remind us, is inappropriate when speaking of Africa prior to European colonization.) Quite simply, one group of black Africans could capture and place in bondage members of another group or nation of black Africans because the latter were seen as "outsiders."

Eltis's point is that Africans were brought to the New World as slaves for more than merely economic reasons. It was the broad, Continent-wide perception of "insiders" held by Europeans rather than the result of careful cost-accounting that explains the willingness of European colonists to meet their labor needs in the New World with enslaved Africans. And it was the much narrower perception of "insiders" held by Africans that made those enslaved blacks available.

2. John A. Munroe, *Colonial Delaware: A History* (Millwood, NY, 1978), 93; C. A. Weslager, *The Delaware Indians, A History* (New Brunswick, NJ, 1972), 120, 134, 150, 152; Charles T. Gehring, ed., *New York Historical Manuscripts: Dutch; Volumes XVIII–XIX, Delaware Papers, 1648–1664* (Baltimore, 1981), 205, 317.

3. Craig W. Horle and Marianne S. Wokeck, eds., *Lawmaking and Legislators in Pennsylvania* (Philadelphia, 1991), 380; Kent County Will Book D, 50–51, Kent County Court House (hereafter KCCH), Dover, Delaware; "Delaware Constitution of 1776," *Laws of the State of Delaware* 1:Appendix. Peter Wood, *Black Majority: Negroes in Colonial South Carolina* (New York, 1975), 39, main-

tains that "Carolina was more active than any other English Colony" during the late seventeenth century in the exportation of Indian slaves.

4. Daniel J. Boorstin, ed., *Delaware Cases, 1792–1830*, 2 vols. (St. Paul, MN, 1943), 1:418–19.

5. Peter Kolchin, *Unfree Labor: American Slavery and Russian Serfdom* (Cambridge, MA, 1987), 24. For a discussion of the change in the Chesapeake's labor pool see Russell R. Menard, "From Servants to Slaves: The Transformation of the Chesapeake Labor System," *Southern Studies* 16 (1977): 355–90. For a specific Virginia county see Darrett B. Rutman and Anita H. Rutman, *A Place in Time: Middlesex County, Virginia, 1650–1750* (New York, 1984), 164–66.

6. Actually, the New Sweden Company, which sponsored the settlement at Fort Christina in 1638, was a Dutch-Swedish enterprise. It was not until 1641 that Dutch interests in the company were totally bought out by the Swedes. Munroe, *Colonial Delaware*, 20.

7. Amandus Johnson, *The Swedish Settlements on the Delaware*, 2 vols. (Baltimore, 1969), 2:Appendix, 699, 706, 710, 722, 722n; C. A. Weslager, *The Swedes and Dutch at New Castle, 1638–1664* (Wilmington, DE, 1987), 34–35; Munroe, *Colonial Delaware*, 18. Blacks were to be sent to the South (Delaware) River in 1639 to serve the Dutch West India Company. However, the Dutch trading posts on the Delaware in the 1630s were temporary and on the east bank, in the present state of New Jersey. Hazard, *Annals of Pennsylvania*, 49.

8. Munroe, *Colonial Delaware*, 25; Johnson, *The Swedish Settlements*, 2:711. Unfree white laborers were generally granted their freedom after a number of years of service in New Sweden.

9. Johnson, *The Swedish Settlements*, 2:49.

10. Ibid., 2:722n, indicates that at least one other resident of New Sweden, Black Lars, may have been African. F. T. Odhner, "The Founding of New Sweden, 1637–1642," *Pennsylvania Magazine of History and Biography* 3 (1879): 38n.

11. Weslager, *The Swedes and Dutch at New Castle*, 6–7; Munroe, *Colonial Delaware*, 3–12.

12. Weslager, *The Swedes and Dutch at New Castle*, 7–8.

13. Ibid., 51–155; Munroe, *Colonial Delaware*, 29–39.

14. Edgar J. McManus, *A History of Negro Slavery in New York* (Syracuse, NY, 1966), 3–4, 7.

15. Donald R. Wright, *African Americans in the Colonial Era* (Arlington Heights, IL, 1990), 16–17.

16. J. D. Fage, *A History of Africa* (New York, 1986), 266, 254–55; Philip D. Curtin, *The Atlantic Slave Trade: A Census* (Madison, WI, 1969), Tables 33, 34, 65, 67, 77; Peter Kolchin, *American Slavery, 1619–1877* (New York, 1993), 22; Wright, *African Americans in the Colonial Era*, 17–33. For a detailed account of slavery in Africa see Paul S. Lovejoy, *A History of Slavery in Africa* (New York, 1983). For a brief, more recent account see Roland Oliver, *The African Experience* (New York, 1991), 116–29.

17. Joyce D. Goodfriend, "Burghers and Blacks: The Evolution of a Slave Society in New Amsterdam," *New York History* 59 (April 1978): 134–37.

18. Ibid., 138–39; McManus, *A History of Negro Slavery in New York*, 3–4, 6, 10; Vidor H. Paltsits, "Petrus Stuyvesant," in Dumas Malone, ed., *Dictionary of American Biography*, 18 vols. (New York, 1936), 9:187–88.

19. E. B. O'Callaghan, ed., *Voyages of the Slavers St. John and Arms of Amsterdam, 1659, 1663* (Albany, NY, 1867), xvi; B. Fernow, trans. and comp., *Documents Relating to the Colonial History of New York*, 12 vols. (Albany, NY,

1888), 1:146; Thomas J. Condon, *New York Beginnings: The Commercial Origins of New Netherland* (New York, 1968), 77.

20. John B. Linn and William H. Egle, eds., *Pennsylvania Archives, Second Series* (Harrisburg, PA, 1870), 5:24–25; McManus, *A History of Negro Slavery in New York*, 4.

21. J. Franklin Jameson, ed., *Narratives of New Netherland, 1609–1664* (New York, 1909), 129n; O'Callaghan, ed., *Voyages of the Slavers*, xiii; Goodfriend, "Burghers and Blacks," 127–28; *Historical Statistics of the United States, Part II* (Washington, DC, 1975), 1168; Arthur Zilversmit, *The First Emancipation: The Abolition of Slavery in the North* (Chicago, 1967), 4; McManus, *A History of Negro Slavery in New York*, 4.

22. Munroe, *Colonial Delaware*, 43–57; Weslager, *The Swedes and Dutch at New Castle*, 157–96.

23. Hazard, *Annals of Pennsylvania*, 239–331; Patience Essah, "Slavery and Freedom in the First State" (Ph.D. diss., UCLA, 1985), 16–17.

24. Fage, *A History of Africa*, 302–3; O'Callaghan, ed., *Voyages of the Slavers*, 198–201, 208.

25. O'Callaghan, ed., *Voyages of the Slavers*, 213, 221–24.

26. Fernow, trans. and comp., *Documents Relating to the Colonial History of New York*, 2:434, 438, 495; O'Callaghan, ed., *Voyages of the Slavers*, 222.

27. Michael Kammen, *Colonial New York* (New York, 1975), 71–72; Weslager, *The Swedes and Dutch at New Castle*, 192–93; C. A. Weslager, *Peter Alrichs, New Castle Merchant, Indian Trader, and Politician* (Radnor, PA, 1987), 7; Munroe, *Colonial Delaware*, 61–62.

28. Munroe, *Colonial Delaware*, 62–63, 56, 77. Peter S. Craig of Washington, DC, who has done considerable research on the early Swedes in the Delaware Valley, maintains that, in general, the Swedes and Finns owned few slaves during the seventeenth century. See also H. Clay Reed, ed., *Delaware: A History of the First State*, 2 vols. (New York, 1947), 2:572n. The greater Dutch propensity for slaveholding, when compared to other European ethnic groups in the mid-Atlantic region during the seventeenth century, is noted in David S. Cohen, "In Search of Carolus Africanus Rex: Afro-Dutch Folklore in New York and New Jersey," *Journal of the Afro-American Historical and Genealogical Society* 5 (Fall-Winter 1984): 150. When John Jay ran for governor of New York in 1792, he was accused of wanting to rob every Dutchman of his slaves, "the property he possesses most dear to his heart." Quoted from Zilversmit, *The First Emancipation*, 165.

29. Although the total population for the Delaware Valley at the end of the Dutch period may have been in excess of 1,000 people (as stated in Weslager, *Peter Alrichs*, 6), that figure included colonists living in modern-day Pennsylvania, New Jersey, and Delaware. When only the area of modern Delaware is included, a population of 640, based on the figures for 1660 and 1670 in *Historical Statistics of the United States, Part II*, 1168, is realistic. For New Amstel and its immediate hinterland, a total population of 400 might be a realistic estimate because a majority of the population of what is now Delaware lived south of the Christina River in 1664.

By adding the unspecified number of slaves already present in 1657 with the 50 slaves asked for by the City Colony in 1663 and probably delivered, and then including the 72 slaves who arrived in New Amstel in early September 1664, a base figure of 125 Africans in what is now Delaware, just prior to the English conquest, represents a conservative estimate. The greatest concentration of Africans was in the New Amstel area. (It should be noted, therefore, that my statistics for Africans in Delaware are at considerable variance with those found in *Historical Statistics of the United States, Part II*, 1168.)

30. Based on figures found in *Historical Statistics of the United States, Part II*, 1168; John J. McCusker and Russell Menard, *The Economy of British North America* (Chapel Hill, NC, 1985), 136.

31. Munroe, *Colonial Delaware*, 59–63.

32. O'Callaghan, *Voyage of the Slavers*, 222.

33. Hazard, *Annals of Pennsylvania*, 366.

34. Reed, ed., *Delaware*, 2:572n; Munroe, *Colonial Delaware*, 75.

35. Essah, "Slavery and Freedom in the First State," 26–28; Hazard, *Annals of Pennsylvania*, 415; Munroe, *Colonial Delaware*, 74.

36. Linn and Egle, eds., *Pennsylvania Archives, Second Series*, 5:671; Hazard, *Annals of Pennsylvania*, 414–16; *Historical Statistics of the United States, Part II*, 1168.

37. Essah, "Slavery and Freedom in the First State," 28–29; Hazard, *Annals of Pennsylvania*, 455–56.

38. Darold D. Wax, "Black Immigrants: The Slave Trade in Colonial Maryland," *Maryland Historical Magazine* 73 (Spring 1978): 30–45; Paul G. Clemens, *The Atlantic Economy and Colonial Maryland's Eastern Shore* (Ithaca, NY, 1980), 54, 59, 60–61, 120n.

39. Clemens, *The Atlantic Economy*, 106, 74.

40. Ibid., 54, 99, 102, 214; Munroe, *Colonial Delaware*, 94, 152.

41. Munroe, *Colonial Delaware*, 94, 152; Carol Hoffecker, *Delaware, A Bicentennial History* (New York, 1977), 90; Clemens, *The Atlantic Economy*, 60–61, 63, 120n, 144. J. Thomas Scharf, *History of Maryland* (Hatboro, PA, 1879), 1:377, provides the figures on which the 1712 estimate is based. Darold D. Wax, "Black Immigrants," 30–45; Barbara J. Fields, *Slavery and Freedom on the Middle Ground* (New Haven, CT, 1985), 11. According to Fields, 13, free blacks represented 9 percent of all blacks on the Eastern Shore of Maryland in 1790.

42. Clemens, *The Atlantic Economy*, 120, 120n; Richard L. Bushman, *The Refinement of America: Persons, Houses, Cities* (New York, 1993), 450 n.16.

43. Richard L. Bushman, "The Gentrification of Kent County, Delaware, 1740–1776" (copy of unpublished paper in my possession), 12; Bushman, *The Refinement of America*, 14; Allan Kulikoff, *Tobacco and Slaves: The Development of Southern Cultures in the Chesapeake, 1680–1800* (Chapel Hill, NC, 1986), 199–201.

44. C. H. B. Turner, ed., *Some Records of Sussex County, Delaware* (Philadelphia, 1909), 224.

45. Clemens, *The Atlantic Economy*, 169–77, 196.

46. Milton E. Flower, *John Dickinson, Conservative Revolutionary* (Charlottesville, VA, 1983), 3–9; Bushman, "The Gentrification of Kent County," 13; Bushman, *The Refinement of America*, 450 n.16.

47. Edward C. Papenfuse et al., eds., *A Biographical Dictionary of the Maryland Legislature, 1635–1789*, 2 vols. (Baltimore, 1985), 2:883; Thomas White, Kent County Wills, Delaware State Archives (hereafter DSA), Dover, Delaware. Thomas White's will was brought to my attention by Allen Clark of North Bowers Beach, Delaware.

48. J. Thomas Scharf, *History of Delaware, 1609–1888*, 2 vols. (Philadelphia, 1888) 1:526, 537; Robert Barns, ed., *Maryland Genealogies*, 2 vols. (Baltimore, 1980), 1:262; Gary B. Nash and Jean Soderlund, *Freedom by Degrees* (New York, 1991), 146; Richard L. Bushman and Anna L. Hawley, eds., "A Random Sample of Kent County, Delaware, Estate Inventories, 1727–1775" (typed copy

in Special Collections, Morris Library, University of Delaware), 61–. Samuel Chew's probate inventory was dated 1746, but his year of death is generally given as 1743.

49. Hilda Justice, *Life and Ancestry of Warner Mifflin* (Philadelphia, 1905), 14, 38–39, 58, 69.

50. Turner, ed., *Some Records of Sussex County*, 75–76.

51. Kulikoff, *Tobacco and Slaves*, 320, 327.

52. *Peter Kalm's Travels in North America*, ed. Adolph B. Benson, 2 vols. (New York, 1964), 1:206.

53. Gary B. Nash, *Race, Class, and Politics; Essays on American Colonial and Revolutionary Society* (Urbana, IL, 1986), 92–96.

54. Munroe, *Colonial Delaware*, 186; Walter A. Powell, *A History of Delaware* (Boston, 1928), 239.

55. *Pennsylvania Gazette*, 5/6/1762; Wade P. Catts, "Slaves, Free Blacks, and French Negroes" (Master's thesis, University of Delaware, 1988), 39–40.

56. Elizabeth Montgomery, *Reminiscences of Wilmington* (Wilmington, DE, 1851), 164–65.

57. Darold D. Wax, "The Negro Slave Trade in Colonial Pennsylvania" (Ph.D. diss., University of Washington, 1962), 20–50; Zilversmit, *The First Emancipation*, 47–48.

58. The estimate for eastern Sussex is based on information in Turner, ed., *Some Records of Sussex County*, 20, 224, 225. For other estimates on the black population of specific parts of Delaware during the late colonial era see Harold B. Hancock, "The Black American in Delaware," 57–58 (unpublished paper in my possession).

59. Bruce Bendler, *Colonial Delaware Assemblymen, 1682–1776* (Westminster, MD, 1989), 1–127; Bushman and Hawley, eds., "A Random Sample," 61.

60. *Negro Population in the United States, 1790–1915* (New York, 1968), 57.

61. In America, during the second half of the eighteenth century, white birth rates were probably at least as high as black birth rates. There is no reason to believe that in Delaware the pattern was any different. See, for example, Herbert S. Klein and Stanley L. Engerman, "Fertility Differentials in the United States and the British West Indies," *William and Mary Quarterly* 35 (April 1978): 374. Comparative statistics on black populations (almost all enslaved) in the Anglo-American colonies in 1770 are in Kolchin, *American Slavery*, 240. The figure that Kolchin gives for Delaware in 1770 is wrong because it is based on erroneous figures in *Historical Statistics of the United States: Colonial Times to 1957*. See my brief comment on black population statistics for Delaware during the colonial period in note 29.

62. Kammen, *Colonial New York*, 77.

63. Ibid.; Munroe, *Colonial Delaware*, 66–74.

64. Philip S. Foner, *History of Black Americans* (New York, 1975), 192; Timothy H. Breen and Stephen Innes, *Myne Own Ground: Race and Freedom on Virginia's Eastern Shore, 1640–1676* (New York, 1980), 9.

65. Quoted from Foner, *History of Black Americans*, 192.

66. A. Leon Higginbotham, Jr., *In the Matter of Color: Race and the American Legal Process, the Colonial Period* (New York, 1978), 270.

67. Jeffrey R. Brackett, *The Negro in Maryland: A Study of the Institution of Slavery* (1889; reprint, New York, 1969), 32–33.

68. Ira Berlin, *Slaves without Masters: The Free Negro in the Antebellum South* (New York, 1976), 33; Higginbotham, *In the Matter of Color*, 43; Zilversmit,

The First Emancipation, 13; Brackett, *The Negro in Maryland*, 37; Edward R. Turner, *The Negro in Pennsylvania: Slavery, Servitude, Freedom* (Washington, DC, 1911), 24.

69. *Laws of the State of Delaware, 1700–1792* (New Castle, DE, 1797), 1:380–83; Deed Book R, Kent County, 85, DSA; Kent County Will Book M, 125, KCCH.

70. Treasa, 1783, Petitions for Freedom, Slavery Material, 1701–1799, DSA; Boorstin, ed., *Delaware Cases*, 1:417–18.

71. C. H. B. Turner, ed., *Some Records of Sussex County*, 76; Leon de Valinger, ed., *Court Records of Kent County, Delaware, 1680–1705* (Washington, DC, 1959), 283–84; Sussex County Will Book No. 1, 176, Sussex County Court House (hereafter SCCH), Georgetown, Delaware; Craig W. Horle, ed., *Records of the Courts of Sussex County, Delaware, 1677–1710* (Philadelphia, 1991), 170.

72. Sussex County Will Book No. 1, 175–76, 47–48, 135–36, 157, SCCH; Deed Book R, Kent County, 207, KCCH.

73. In Virginia in 1661, and in Maryland in 1664, legislation specifically assigned blacks in servitude to their lifetime. See, for example, Kolchin, *Unfree Labor*, 35. For Pennsylvania, note E. R. Turner, *The Negro in Pennsylvania*, 22.

74. E. R. Turner, *The Negro in Pennsylvania*, 26; Higginbotham, *In the Matter of Color*, 272; de Valinger, ed., *Court Records of Kent County*, 151.

75. E. R. Turner, *The Negro in Pennsylvania*, 26, 29; Higginbotham, *In the Matter of Color*, 280–82; *Statutes at Large of Pennsylvania from 1682–1801*, 2:77–79.

76. Higginbotham, *In the Matter of Color*, 281.

77. Introduction, Court for Trial of Negroes, Delaware Agency Histories, DSA; *Laws of the State of Delaware, 1700–1792*, 1:102–4. Higginbotham, *In the Matter of Color*, 281–82, maintains that the special courts for blacks functioned in Pennsylvania from 1700 to 1780. By contrast, Zilversmit, in *The First Emancipation*, 16, argues that these courts did not begin operating there until 1706, when new legislation creating them was judged acceptable by the Crown. The special courts were in place in Delaware by 1706, because both William Rodney and John Brinckloe were members of a court presiding over the trials of negroes by that date according to Horle and Wokeck, eds., *Lawmaking and Legislators in Pennsylvania*, 651.

78. *Laws of the State of Delaware, 1700–1792*, 1:103; Court for Trial of Negroes, Delaware Agency Histories, DSA; Philip J. Schwarz, *Twice Condemned: Slaves and the Criminal Laws of Virginia, 1705–1865* (Baton Rouge, LA, 1988), 6. For an example of the distinction between the legal treatment of slaves and free blacks see *Laws of the State of Delaware, 1700–1792*, 1:306.

79. Schwarz, *Twice Condemned*, 38–49.

80. Folder, Court Trials, 1766–1773, Slavery Material, DSA; Deed Book S, Kent County, 232, DSA.

81. *Delaware Gazette*, 7/9/1791.

82. *Pennsylvania Gazette*, 8/26/1731, 9/2/31, 9/23/31.

83. E. R. Turner, *The Negro in Pennsylvania*, 22; *Laws of the State of Delaware, 1700–1792*, 1:102–4. Higginbotham, *In the Matter of Color*, 276–80, disputes Turner.

84. *Laws of the State of Delaware*, 1:226.

85. Ibid., 104; Essah, "Slavery and Freedom in the First State," 40.

86. *Laws of the State of Delaware*, 1:217.

87. Ibid., 306.

II

The Land and Labor

The cattle . . . are thin but beginning to thrive as the grass on the
marsh is pretty good—and old Charles and one of the boys is constantly with them.
—Thomas Rodney to Caesar Rodney, April 26, 1776*

Despite government regulations, the personal relationship between
black slave and white master was the primary factor in shaping slavery in Delaware. Through constant interaction in the home and in the
fields, there developed a psychological intimacy between slave and
master that inevitably led to the development of some of the same
strong emotions that commonly characterize family ties. Despite attempts by both parties to maintain a psychic distance, deeply held feelings of loyalty, respect, and affection surfaced, along with feelings of
defiance, contempt, and hatred.

The range of emotional responses by Delaware's slaves to this
sometimes symbiotic relationship may be seen in two specific incidents. In 1757, John Dickinson returned to his family's plantation on
Jones Neck, southeast of Dover, after four years of studying law at the
Middle Temple in London. Upon his arrival, "Old Pompey kissed his
hand," and the other slaves warmly welcomed home the young master.[1] By contrast, in 1827, Maria, who was about eighteen years old
and owned by Lewis Prettyman of Little Creek Hundred, Kent County,
reacted to her master in a dramatically different fashion. She did her
best to burn down his home while his entire family was inside. After a
second unsuccessful attempt at torching the house, Maria was forced
to sleep in the same bedroom with Prettyman and his wife so that they
could keep an eye on her. Subsequently, Prettyman discovered that
Maria had previously "attempted to poison her former master." Not
surprisingly, he was now "afraid to have Maria in the house."[2]

Just as remarkable was the range of emotions expressed by masters for their slaves. In a will written in 1674 and probated in 1682, Joseph Jones of western Kent County not only gave Sherry and Freegift Wansey their freedom but also left Sherry 200 acres of land, all of his "chattel and their increase forever [other slaves?]," as well as all movable goods and all outstanding debts owed to Jones. Finally, he made Sherry his full and sole executor.[3] Again, quite different was the attitude of the mistress from "one of the best families" of Lewes in Sussex County during the 1820s. The unnamed lady flew into a rage over the slightest mistake by her slave girls and then had them brutally flogged. Sometimes she "would vary her fashionable pastimes by whipping her house girls with her own hands, tying a coarse bag about their heads to smother their outcries."[4]

The feelings that marked this most private of human relationships were played out against the backdrop of a shared physical world. Not only was the natural world a significant factor to be faced every morning by a basically agricultural people, but Delaware's topography, plant and animal life, and its disease environment also had a considerable impact on the overall nature of slavery in the state. But, just as slavery was shaped by the physical environment, so, too, was the natural world altered by the economic activities of slaves and their masters for 226 years. The result was a changing landscape that reflected the gradual destruction of forest and marsh and the more rapid depletion of wildlife.

At the beginning of European settlement, stands of virgin timber covered most of present-day Delaware from the Piedmont in the extreme north through the Atlantic Coastal Plain, which comprised the remaining 95 percent of the state. Rising in southeastern Pennsylvania, fast-flowing streams cut ravines in the hills of the Piedmont as they rushed southeastward to join with the Delaware River. South of the Piedmont stretched the flat Delaware plain, where sluggish streams generally flowed from west to east as they carved out shallow marshy valleys before emptying into the Delaware Bay or the Atlantic Ocean. The only major exception was the Nanticoke River, which meandered southwestward across Sussex County and Maryland's lower Eastern Shore before finally joining the Chesapeake Bay. It was on Delaware's Coastal Plain that the Piedmont forest met and then grudgingly gave way to the flora of the southern forest and swamp.[5]

The cutting and clearing of virgin forests, the decline in the Native American presence, and the impact of hoe, plow, and livestock produced a remarkable change in the landscape by the late eighteenth century. But unlike the pristine and bucolic scenes of rural America portrayed in Currier and Ives's prints during the nineteenth century, Delaware's farms, fields, and woods had a rather scruffy, unkempt appearance for most of the colonial and early national periods. Played-out fields sprouted shrubbery and saplings, while nearby forests were missing their best and most mature timber, long since harvested for profit. Indeed, timber of any sort was increasingly scarce in many parts of the state by the late eighteenth century.[6]

Yet, by 1790, Delaware's landscape was not totally devoid of mature woodlots or, in a few places such as Cypress Swamp in southern Sussex County, of extensive old-growth forests. But it was increasingly apparent that the constant hunger for new agricultural land, the need for fuel (each family hearth may have consumed up to thirty cords of wood per year),[7] and the demands for lumber had almost exhausted the supply of old-growth trees and placed in immediate jeopardy the remaining maturing stands of new-growth timber.

The gradual destruction of woodland and the draining of marshland, which began with the Swedes in 1638, posed a serious threat to the natural habitat of Delaware's wildlife. Posing just as serious a threat was the fact that, from the very outset of European colonization, many animals were systematically hunted or trapped. During the Swedish period, the settlement's economy was dependent on deer skins and beaver, bear, otter, and muskrat furs. By the end of the Dutch period, however, much of the fur-bearing wildlife had been trapped out, and the west bank settlements, by necessity, were increasingly turning to agriculture.

The devastation of fur-bearing animals and of other wildlife continued throughout the next two centuries. By 1800 the endemic beaver,[8] wolf,[9] elk, and buffalo[10] were gone, while the numbers of bears and deer were nearing extinction in most parts of the state. By 1841 deer sightings were so rare that the General Assembly made it illegal "to shoot, kill or chase any wild deer."[11] Smaller mammals, such as raccoons, foxes, otters, muskrats, and opossum, did survive, although in diminished numbers. Moreover, by 1800 the previously abundant marine life was seriously depleted, with whales now absent from the Delaware Bay and oysters in short supply in Rehoboth Bay. Large runs of herring and shad, however, continued to provide protein for slaves and their masters until the Civil War.[12]

It was against this scruffy and unkempt landscape, depleted of much of its wildlife, that Delaware slaves and masters played out their lives. Fields were cleared, plowed, planted, cultivated, and harvested for a few years and then were temporarily or permanently abandoned. Tobacco, for example, could be grown on the same plot for only four years before the soil was drained of most of its nutrients. To renourish the soil, farmers allowed their fields to lie fallow. In the case of wheat, the land was probably rested for no more than a year at a time; but with corn, and particularly tobacco, the drain on the soil generally demanded a longer rest period which, in the case of tobacco, might last for twenty years. The visual impact of fallow farming was predictable. Most of the landscape was dominated by a mottled combination of fallow or abandoned fields which, to the modern eye, would seem aesthetically displeasing and agriculturally dysfunctional. Fallow land never regained all of its lost fertility before its young growth was cleared away and its soil made ready for planting in yet one more round of Delaware's soil-depleting agricultural cycle.[13]

Fallow land, furthermore, was not only unattractive to the eye but also dangerous to everyone's health. Its immature and random root system tended to hold standing water longer in late summer than did either cultivated fields or mature forests. Standing water, in turn, contributed to an already serious mosquito problem endemic to the entire Atlantic Coastal Plain. The bite of American mosquitoes seemed particularly bothersome to European settlers and caused many Delawareans to turn from knee breeches to trousers by the end of the colonial era.[14] But far more significant than discomfort from the insect's bite was its role in spreading malaria.

In 1739, *Poor Richard's Almanac* noted the prevalence of malaria, or "ague," in Delaware.[15] The residents of the southern part of the colony were particularly susceptible. An Anglican rector in Lewes wrote in 1782 that the inhabitants of Sussex County "are remarkably subject to ague and fever, always in the fall of the year." August, September, and October were the fever months, which unfortunately coincided with much of the harvest season. Malaria did not necessarily kill its victims, but it did render survivors too weak to ward off other diseases or to be effective field hands at a time when they were most needed. Because of centuries of exposure to malaria in Africa many, but not all, enslaved blacks brought with them to Delaware some genetic immunity to the various strains of the disease.[16] Although neither slaves nor their masters understood the relationship of the mosquito to the spread of malaria, it must have been evident to slave owners in Delaware and elsewhere in Anglo-America that many African-Americans seemed less susceptible than whites to the fever and were therefore desirable as field hands in malaria-infested regions.[17]

Unfortunately for recently imported slaves, their new homeland harbored other diseases to which they had little genetic or conditioned resistance. Upon arrival, Africans found themselves at great risk, in part because of the alien climate they encountered in New Castle, Kent, and Sussex counties. In West Africa or in the West Indies, where some slaves had been "seasoned" before coming to Delaware, temperatures were continually in the tropical or semitropical range and never dropped to freezing. By contrast, Delaware's rivers were generally iced over before Christmas, and its winters lasted for three months.[18] Because of this dramatic change in climate and the exposure to new strains of infectious microbes, slaves directly imported from Africa and, to a lesser degree, from the West Indies were far more susceptible than whites to respiratory diseases. In all probability bronchitis, pneumonia, and other debilitating bronchial and pulmonary infections caused Delaware to match the mortality rate of the nearby Chesapeake, where one in four imported slaves died during the first year.[19]

~

What sort of men and women purchased Africans and then maintained them and their offspring in slavery? Were they driven by values and motives that were primarily paternalistic, or were they simply rural businessmen with a constant eye on the bottom line? On initial examination they seem to be a little of each. In the early and mideighteenth century, slave owners demonstrated considerable sensitivity to the profit implications of changing commercial networks by switching from tobacco to corn and wheat. But all through Delaware's slave era, a number of masters exhibited certain paternalistic traits in dealing with their slaves that seem alien to the stereotype of the profit-driven entrepreneur.

One way to gain a better understanding of slaveholders is to enter into their world of aspiration and self-perception. In the eighteenth century the main north-south route in Delaware was the King's Road, which connected Wilmington and the town of New Castle in the north with Lewes in the south. The King's Road cut right through the heart of a fertile stretch of Kent that had the very small county seat of Dover at its core. This strip of fertile land, which extended no more than eleven miles north and south of Dover and five to ten miles from east to west,[20] was home to the largest slaveholders in Delaware during the mideighteenth century. Here, from 1740 to the American Revolution, the Dickinsons, Loockermans, Chews, Rodneys, Ridgelys, Mifflins, and many other families with significant numbers of slaves built a series of imposing two-and-one-half-story brick houses that made important statements about the ambitions of the area's gentry and its mimetic yeomanry.

These impressive red-brick structures stood out boldly in the landscape because of their color, size, and architectural style. They contrasted dramatically with the much smaller log or planked homes of the "middling and lesser sorts" that were unpainted and quickly took on the drab grays or browns of the winter countryside. The houses of

The Allee House in northeastern Kent County is representative of the brick homes built in the mideighteenth century by the Delaware gentry. *Courtesy of Delaware State Archives, Dover.*

the gentry represented only one dimension of a movement by Kent County's elite, during the late colonial period, to set themselves off from the lower orders of society by adopting the values and tastes of England's rural gentry. Even the practice of some English squires of keeping domesticated deer was emulated by Caesar Rodney and others. So successful were these efforts to recreate at least some of the admired aspects of the English countryside, and so quickly did this movement envelop much of New Castle County and parts of Sussex, that it is not surprising that Thomas Jefferson was moved to compare Delaware to a county in England.[21]

This slave-owning gentry wanted a hierarchical society, similar to that found in England, marked by clear social distinctions ranging from the refined and genteel at the top to the vulgar and crude at the bottom. Thus, in keeping with English traditions, they were willing to exploit dependent people.[22] On the much-admired English manor the exploited labor force was white; in Delaware the shortage of white labor dictated that it be black. Obviously, status as a member of Delaware's Anglicized gentry depended heavily on the acquisition and control of black slaves.

The desire of Delawareans to own slaves rested on more than the wish to mimic the social order of the English countryside. Colonial historian Jack Greene maintains that "perhaps the most powerful drive in the early American experience was the desire for personal independence." Quite simply put, "independence meant freedom from the will of others." Because one's independence rested primarily on one's economic success, in England such a possibility was open to only a small minority at the top of the socioeconomic pyramid. But in Delaware, as well as in the rest of Anglo-America, vast tracts of undeveloped land offered economic opportunities far greater than those found across the Atlantic.[23] Economic success in Anglo-America, however, depended on the presence of enough cheap labor to clear and cultivate undeveloped land. Because cheap labor was usually synonymous with slavery, the slaveholder was the one with the best shot at economic success and thus at becoming independent. It was clear to most Delawareans that slavery could produce the profits that allowed a man to pursue the Anglo-American ideal of personal freedom.

Economic success based on slaveholdings and considerable land also qualified one to become a member of the rural gentry. Indeed, it was assumed in much of early America that slavery was a necessary precondition to the existence of a gentry class. It was particularly self-evident in Delaware that if members of the gentry wished to have free time to devote to public service, then slaves were necessary "to support that mode of life."[24] This perception, combined with obstinacy of custom, family tradition, and the simple visceral pleasure taken in dominating and controlling the lives of other men and women, partly explains why slaveholding continued in some Delaware households well into the midnineteenth century after other families had long since abandoned the practice for moral, religious, or economic reasons.

Only a few families in the state continued to hold slaves on the eve of the Civil War. But when slavery was at its height, in the late colonial period, perhaps as many as 30 percent of white households owned slaves. Due to a wave of manumissions during and after the Revolution, that figure dropped to 22 percent in 1800 and to about 8 percent by 1837. (Nearly 36 percent of all American families living south of Pennsylvania owned slaves in 1830.[25]) The declining percentage of Delaware households owning slaves reflected, in part, growing doubts about the profitability of the institution. These doubts were finally summarized in 1864 by a downstate newspaper that concluded that the profit from slave labor "was greatly exaggerated. . . . By contrast, free compensated labor is much more efficient and energetic."[26] However, free compensated labor was not always available in earlier times. During most of the eighteenth century, using unfree labor was the only option open to most landowners because in Delaware, as in much of the colonial South, land was cheap but free labor was expensive.

~

Although the English conquest of the west bank in 1664 may have temporarily halted the external slave trade, it also opened up Delaware to the importation of another form of unfree labor: indentured Englishmen. The number who came in the decade and one-half after 1664 must have been significant, but statistics are not available. The dramatic decline in the immigration of English indentured servants to America in the late seventeenth century, however, limited the number who arrived in the Delaware Valley after 1680.[27] In the 1720s, when African-Americans increasingly were entering Delaware, a second and much larger wave of white indentured servants began disembarking at the towns of New Castle and Wilmington. Unfree white laborers continued coming until the eve of the Revolution, and they joined with slaves to become members of an interchangeable work force for the remainder of the colonial period. Indeed, according to John A. Munroe, "statistics suggest that unfree white servants were at least as numerous as black slaves in Delaware in the mideighteenth century."[28] In the Chesapeake region, by contrast, a dramatic increase in imported black slaves coincided with a dramatic decline in indentured white servants during the late seventeenth and early eighteenth centuries.

Unlike the predominantly English servants who came to Delaware in the late seventeenth century, the second wave of white indentured servants was predominantly Scots-Irish, with a significant admixture of southern Irish along with a few English, Scots, and Germans. In 1727 at the town of New Castle, for example, almost one thousand Scots-Irish and Irish disembarked. Sometimes against their will, these indentured servants had been forced to cross the Atlantic to the Delaware Valley on ships where conditions "often rivaled in horror those that prevailed in the African slave trade." Mortality rates aboard these vessels continued to be very high up to the Revolution and may have equaled the 5 to 15 percent death rate on slave ships.[29] Delaware's practice probably paralleled the Pennsylvania pattern, where many disembarking white servants, like so many domestic animals, were driven through the countryside to be sold at public fairs. Then it was on to the fields, mills, and craft shops of their new masters where for the next three to seven years they experienced temporary slavery.[30]

There is some indication that the predominantly English servants of the late seventeenth century were better treated than the predominantly Scots-Irish and Irish ones who arrived in Delaware in the eighteenth century. In part this disparity may have been a product of the ethnic makeup of the colony. The English servants of the late seventeenth century were ethnically and culturally similar to their English or Anglicized Dutch and Swedish masters, but the largely Scots-Irish and Irish ones of the next century represented a clearly alien people.[31] Although the latter generally spoke English, it was "much Scotchified" with a "little" or "strong brogue."[32] Moreover, unlike their largely Anglican masters, the Scots-Irish servants were Presbyterian, and the southern Irish servants were Roman Catholic. In addition, because of Old World grievances, neither the Scots-Irish nor the southern Irish had much use for English secular institutions or laws. Not surprisingly, after freedom from servitude, both ethnic groups became strong supporters of the Revolution, and their numbers formed a major part of the anti-English Democratic-Republican party that appeared in Delaware some years after the end of the war.[33]

The ethnic and cultural differences that separated eighteenth-century masters from their white servants, and the generally pervasive view that it was acceptable to live off the unfree labor of others, helped to shape an indenture system in Delaware that was oppressive. More than three hundred white indentured servants made that point when they ran away from their masters between 1730 and 1775. Indeed, almost six times as many white servants as black slaves were listed in newspapers as fugitives during the last forty-five years of the colonial period.[34] These white indentured servants often became fugitives because of the brutal punishment that they received from their masters and mistresses. An example of physical abuse was experienced in 1737 by Scots-Irish servant Elizabeth Riley of central Kent County at the hands of her mistress, who beat Riley "on her bare buttocks with a switch" while pinning her to the floor with a foot on her neck. Riley had complained on several previous occasions of abusive treatment. After the beating, she declared that she "had rather die than be so badly used." She got her wish. The switch cuts on her body became infected and, after being denied care by her mistress, Riley died.[35]

To discourage white servants from running away, during the late colonial period Delaware required them to carry special passes signed by their masters whenever they traveled through the countryside. If a servant went abroad without a pass, he or she was promptly arrested and thrown into jail until the master could be located. If the master was not found within six weeks, the servant was sold to a new master to pay for jail costs.[36] Although their white skin made them less noticeable than black fugitives, escaping indentured servants were often given away by their Celtic accents or even by a particular style of dress.[37]

Masters usually offered rewards for the apprehension of their fugitive indentured servants because many of them, particularly the Scots-Irish, were highly skilled and well educated by the standards of the day and therefore were quite valuable. In the late summer of 1752, for example, a ship from Ireland arrived at the town of New Castle with "a parcel of likely men and women servants," among whom were "tradesmen of different sorts." Losing a skilled craftsman such as shoemaker Henry Shafter of Wilmington, or weaver James Reiley and blacksmith David Finley of Sussex,[38] was a serious economic blow to any master. Because many indentured servants could read and write, they were able to produce counterfeit passes. One example was John Powell, "a very good scholar" who "will undoubtedly write himself and his fellow runaway a pass, . . . posing as a miller or a school teacher."[39]

The need to produce counterfeit passes declined after the colonial period because the Revolution and the subsequent independence of the United States brought a halt to the importation of all but a few indentured servants. With most servants who were already in Delaware completing their terms of indenture, unfree white laborers, with the exception of teenage apprentices, ceased being a significant part of the labor force during the last two decades of the eighteenth century. This dramatic decline was reflected in the number of runaway white servants reported in the newspapers. From 1786 to 1795 only five white servants but fifty-two black slaves were listed as runaways. Now, whites escaping from their masters were outnumbered by black fugitives by ten to one.[40]

Obviously, there were a number of similarities between white servitude and black slavery in Delaware during the eighteenth century, but there were also two overwhelming differences. First, unlike black slaves, white indentured servants were not bound to unfree labor for life nor were their children; and second, unlike all black slaves, most white indentured servants voluntarily left their homeland to come to America. Yet, together, both types of unfree labor—black and white—demonstrated that white skin alone did not guarantee free participation in the colony's economic and social life.

The peculiar ethnic nature of white servitude in the late colonial period may have done much to delay the development of extreme white racism in Delaware. The arrival of so many indentured Scots-Irish and Irish created ethnic tensions that expressed themselves in individual cases of exploitation by Anglo-Saxon masters, often followed by escape attempts by many of the Celtic servants. For those of Anglo-Saxon stock and culture, the Scots, Scots-Irish, and Irish were a troublesome, inferior people who needed to be kept in their place. Typical of this prejudice against the newcomers was the will of a southern New Castle County farmer written in 1751, which forbade his heirs from renting any of his fields "to any Irishman whatsoever."("Irishman" was used during the eighteenth century to designate both Scots-Irish and southern Irish.) Moreover, if the farmer's wife were to marry "an Irishman or any of that extraction," she was to lose her entire inheritance.[41]

With so much of their attention focused on the troublesome Celts, Delawareans of English ancestry perceived the division of their state's population as far more complicated a matter than simply categorizing people as white or black. With wary Anglo-Saxon eyes on the Scots, Scots-Irish, and Irish, building white racial solidarity against African-Americans seemed both less essential and less possible. This situation may partly explain why, until the late eighteenth century, public discourse in Delaware seemed to lack most of the extreme racial diatribes that characterized public discourse in the state in the nineteenth century. (Ethnic divisions among whites in other places—Pennsylvania, Virginia, and North Carolina are only a few possibilities—also may have contributed to a less-developed form of racism in the eighteenth century than would develop in the antebellum era.) However, by the early nineteenth century, the absorption of most of the Scots-Irish and Irish into the state's dominant Anglo-Saxon culture momentarily eased ethnic tensions among whites. Thus, the way was paved for the building of white solidarity and the accompanying popular expression of intense racism that would continue to be a central factor in Delaware life long after the end of slavery.

~

Prior to 1755 more than 50 percent of Delaware's growing slave population was African-born; by contrast, the estimated figure for the Chesapeake in 1755 was only 33 percent. The figure was higher for Delaware because it was a few decades later than Virginia and Maryland in developing a large domestic slave population that reproduced itself.[42] After 1755, however, African-born slaves became a significantly decreasing percentage of the colony's unfree blacks.

Because there are so few extant records, we know almost nothing of the lives led by seventeenth-century slaves. But primary sources do allow us a few brief glimpses of the first generation of eighteenth-century Africans who, shackled in chains in the holds of slave ships, crossed the Atlantic from such places as the Ivory Coast, Gold Coast, Guinea, Gambia, and Angola to find themselves eventually in Delaware. (For a few, their native land may have been even farther away than West Africa, as in the case of Madagascar Jenny, owned by Samuel Chew of Kent County in the 1740s.[43])

For the newly arrived Africans, understanding and speaking the strange language of their masters was a formidable challenge. In 1740, eighteen-year-old Betty arrived at New Castle on a slave ship. After a month in the town she still spoke "very little English." Although most blacks were conversant in English within two or two-and-one-half years after disembarking in Anglo-America, their age at arrival, the intensity of their contact with whites, and the nature of their job all were important variables that controlled the speed with which they picked up the new language. For those who worked at least a few hours each day in craft shops or in the homes of whites, fluency came more quickly than for those who primarily labored in the fields. Runaway slave notices give us some insight into the continuing language difficulties of many Africans. In 1746, for example, Ned of White Clay Creek, New Castle County, was described as speaking "very abruptly and broken" English. By contrast, Greg of Red Lion Hundred in central New Castle County, who was also African-born, was said to speak "pretty good" English in 1752. The tendency of fugitive slave notices to focus right up until the Revolution on how well or how poorly blacks spoke English and whether or not they were "this country born" reflects the continued, although rapidly diminishing, presence of African-born slaves in Delaware.[44]

Difficulty in mastering English was not the only language problem. Because they came from a variety of places in West Africa, the African-born slaves spoke languages that were often unintelligible to each other. Out of the common need to communicate with their masters and with one another, they developed a distinct patois that was initially based on pidgin English and some shared elements in West African speech patterns and then modified over time by repeated exposure to the English spoken by white Delawareans. In 1748 in southern New Castle County, an Anglican cleric commented that blacks had "a language peculiar to themselves, a wild confused medley of Negro and corrupt English." Near the town of New Castle, Dick was speaking this jargon in 1764 when he talked "in the Negro way."[45]

Often regional identity and style of dress, ritual scarification, or even the expression of nostalgia for their homeland joined with difficulties in mastering English in setting apart the African-born from their children and grandchildren. Group distinctions among the former were hard for whites to ignore. In 1748 in northern Delaware, for example, one observer pointed out some differences between the Keromantees and other Africans, but it was the characteristics that separated the African-born from their children that were particularly noticed. In 1764 a male slave in New Castle County who spoke "little or no English" wrapped a blanket around himself in what must have been a traditional African manner. Seventeen years earlier, Cesar from Kent County was missing two foreteeth and carried a scar above each temple from what was probably ritual scarification. And then in 1769 there was the case of Congamochu, alias Squingal, of the town of New Castle, who not only kept his two African names but also continued to bear "many large [ceremonial] scars on his belly and arms in his country fashion," spoke "very bad English," and had "a hole through one of his ears." Congamochu talked much of his homeland and of the wives he had left behind. As late as the end of the eighteenth century, African-born slaves were still in evidence. In 1795, for example, fifty-year-old Bosan was easily identifiable not only because he had trouble speaking English but also because "his face was cut in flowers, after the manner of his country."[46]

On their arrival in Delaware, the African-born were forced by their white masters to apply skills learned while growing up in the agricultural societies of West Africa and, in some cases, subsequently honed on the sugar plantations of the West Indies or in the corn and tobacco fields of the Eastern Shore. Almost all were practiced in the use of the hoe—the single, most important agricultural instrument of West Africa, the West Indies, the Chesapeake region, and early Delaware. Many had raised corn in Africa prior to being shipped to Delaware. In addition, African-born men and women brought with them a host of other skills essential to clearing land, raising grain, and herding cattle.[47]

In the seventeenth century, in the Lower Counties, both slave women and free and unfree white women worked in the fields. As the eighteenth century progressed, however, Delaware probably emulated the pattern in other English colonies where even female indentured servants worked less and less in the fields on a regular basis. Thus, by the late colonial era, most of the women doing field work, except at harvest time, were African-Americans.[48] Early childhood may have seemed a relatively idyllic time for some slaves of both sexes, but black children were working in the fields by the time they were ten or eleven.

As elsewhere in early America, the typical workday of a Delaware slave depended a great deal on his or her own skills and personality, the size and location of the farm or plantation, the cash crop being grown, and the season of the year. In short, the day was subject to so many variables that generalizations are difficult. Like most whites of the eighteenth century, slaves rose early and worked a long day regulated in part by the hours of sunlight. Winter was the time to clear new land, repair and construct buildings and fences, dig ditches, split firewood, shell corn, and slaughter livestock. By contrast, spring, summer, and fall were primarily devoted to plowing, planting, cultivating, and harvesting. Still another variable was the fact that some masters and mistresses worked their slaves harder than others. Mary Parker Welch, for example, who grew up in central Sussex County in the early nineteenth century, described her father's slaves as "laboring languorously" in the fields, but she observed that on other farms "it was far from uncommon to see dwarf slaves, and it was generally admitted that their meager physique was due to grinding labor."[49] As grinding as any labor was the work in the tobacco fields.

Tobacco lent itself well to slavery because it required constant attention for most of the calendar year. In February or early March the cycle began, with slaves planting seeds in flats or in specially prepared ground chosen to catch the rays of the late winter sun. To protect them from late frosts, the seedbeds might be covered with brush or straw. In April or May the seedlings were transplanted to the fields. Most of Delaware's tobacco fields were not plowed but were prepared in Indian fashion by hoe-wielding whites and their slaves, who first pulverized the soil in a circle and then drew the loose soil to the middle to make a hill. One tiny plant was set by hand in each hill, watered, and then watched closely. Generally speaking, tobacco required so much intense labor that one farmhand could handle no more than three acres of the "noxious weed" per year. As a result, farmers with three or fewer fieldhands annually devoted no more than five to ten acres of their land to tobacco. Throughout the summer, the maturing plants had to be hand-cleaned of worms and other pests; then, excess leaves and suckers were pruned back, plants were topped to prevent the development of seeds, and each hill was repeatedly hoed to control the weeds. In August the leaves were cut and then taken to curing barns. Finally, in late fall, the heat-cured tobacco leaves were packed into four-foot-high hogsheads for shipment across the Atlantic.[50]

In contrast with bread grains such as wheat and rye, which did not require much labor during their growing seasons, tobacco demanded almost daily attention in the form of stoop labor under a blazing summer sun. No wonder Auyuba ("Job") Suleiman, brought from Africa to the Eastern Shore of Maryland in 1730, found that work in the tobacco fields made him so ill that his master "was obliged to find easier work for him, and therefore put him to tend cattle."[51]

Cattle, pigs, and corn together provided an almost perfect complement to tobacco. Compared to northern Europe or New England, Delaware had relatively short winters. This meant that livestock could be turned loose all year long to graze and forage in fallow fields and nearby woods and marshes. Corn required intensive labor on those days that corresponded with the few slack times in the tobacco calendar. Moreover, corn, like tobacco, could be grown by the hill-and-hoe method of agriculture so prevalent in much of Delaware until at least the mideighteenth century. Particularly appealing to tobacco farmers was the fact that corn could be picked, husked, and shelled at leisure during the winter when most of the tobacco activity had ceased.[52]

The importance of tobacco was reflected in its occasional use as currency. In 1680, for example, New Castle County farmers asked to pay quitrents to the duke of York in tobacco. Two years later, in Sussex, a decedent's will specified that a surveyor be paid in tobacco, which continued to be Delaware's chief cash crop well into the early eighteenth century. As late as 1754 a tobacco plantation of eight hundred acres was offered for sale some four miles from Dover, which included a plantation house, tobacco houses, stables, and "quarters for negroes."[53]

By 1754, however, very few of Delaware's African-Americans were working and living on farms and plantations that were primarily committed to raising tobacco. This dramatic decline in production was dictated not only by the proximity of the grain port of Philadelphia but also by the growing perception that the quality of Delaware Valley tobacco was generally inferior to that of the Chesapeake Bay.[54] The abandonment of commercial tobacco production in Delaware by the mideighteenth century is confirmed by examinations of wills and inventories. Even wealthy planter Samuel Chew was hedging his bets by the early 1740s by raising considerable amounts of wheat in addition to tobacco and corn on his Kent County holdings. Among the last slaveholders producing tobacco as a cash crop were John Johnson of Kent County in 1746 and Ebenezer Hearn of Sussex in 1785. By 1788, according to one observer, tobacco was no longer commercially grown in Delaware, although some slaveholders continued to grow small amounts for their own use well into the midnineteenth century.[55] In moving from tobacco to grain prior to 1750, Delaware planters pioneered a crop change that later became popular in many sections of the nearby Chesapeake region.[56]

Corn and wheat thus became Delaware's primary cash crops. New Castle County, where wheat and other grains had been significant from the early days of colonization, became a prime wheat-producing region. In Kent, slaveholders and other farmers concentrated on growing both wheat and corn. In Sussex, with a less developed landscape, corn became the primary cash crop, but other grains and timbering also occupied the energies of many masters and their slaves. The nature of the cash crop had a considerable impact on the work patterns of slaves and on the future of slavery in each of the three counties. As James Tilton pointed out in 1788, grains such as wheat and barley "require no further care after the seeds are put into the ground." Indian corn, by contrast, "requires a laborious and constant tillage from the time of planting until the crop is nearly made."[57]

While corn was less consistently demanding of slaves over the calendar year than tobacco and therefore less suitable to slavery, it was certainly better suited for profitably using slave labor than such bread grains as wheat, rye, and barley. Because no master benefited when his slaves were idle for extended periods of time, the bread grain producers soon realized that hiring free labor for the few weeks of planting and harvesting was less costly and therefore more economical than owning slaves who had to be maintained in food, clothing, and shelter throughout the entire year.

As with tobacco, working in the corn fields demanded considerable strength. The grubbing hoe, used by slaves to break the ground, taxed the physical resources of even a powerful man. However, it lost its preeminence by the mideighteenth century when plow-pulling oxen became more common throughout Delaware. Oxen were far more numerous than horses on eighteenth-century farms because they were better at pulling the era's relatively primitive, iron-tipped wooden plows through virgin sod. Moreover, they did not seem to need grain in their diet, and, "after serving at the plow and cart to a good age, they could be fatted for the table."[58]

Helping with plowing was one way that African-American children were introduced to the work world. Generally one slave, usually a male, held the plow's handles while a second put his weight on its beam to keep the point in the soil. A third slave drove the four to six oxen while an enslaved boy or girl cleared the plow of debris.[59] If fewer African-Americans were available, they simply doubled up on the plowing tasks or shared them with the master, who, if he owned only a few slaves, generally worked with them in the fields. As elsewhere in early America, the actual steering and handling of the plow was a predominantly male responsibility.

~

Ann Hazzard's farm, located in northeastern Sussex, offers us a glimpse of slaves at work during the mid-1780s. On a spring day two yokes of oxen are pulling a wooden plow through a recently cleared field. Walking beside them with whip in hand is fifty-five-year-old Paris, who gets the attention of the oxen by calling out their names and then commands them with the standard cries of "geeup," "gee," "whoa," and "back." At the plow handles is eighteen-year-old Paris, Jr., who directs his fourteen-year-old sister Betty as she darts in front of the moving plow to clear it of weeds, sticks, and clods of dirt.[60]

After the soil is turned over, the field is crossplowed and harrowed. Then Paris and his son bring out the weeding hoes—the inventory of the Hazzard farm does not list hilling hoes—to break up any large clods that are left and to hill up the field. The corn hills are spaced four to six feet apart in a grid pattern that dates back to before the plow took the place of the grubbing hoe in breaking the soil. Seed kernels are planted by hand, as they would be until at least the midnineteenth century. Throughout the late spring and early summer the weeding hoe is used by the three slaves as well as by Paris's fifty-year-old wife Hannah to keep the area around the planted corn hills free of unwanted growth. Also joining her family in the fields to do some of the lighter work is Betty's twelve-year-old sister Cotto.

While working, Paris and his family swing their hoes to the cadence of some of the same songs sung by African-Americans elsewhere in Delaware. (In central Sussex in the early nineteenth century, field slaves were described by whites as "droning monotonous repetitions of crude songs" as they labored "in the hot sunshine." Even after being freed, some blacks continued to sing as they worked in the fields. This pattern of cultivation to song was probably rooted in West Africa and then altered to meet the needs of enslaved blacks on the farms of the New World.[61])

Once the corn reaches its full height in late summer, sickles are used to top the cornstalks and to cut off the blades, which then are stacked to be used as winter fodder for the livestock. (The inventory of the Hazzard farm in 1785 listed nine stacks "of blades and top fodder." Not until the nineteenth century would most corn be "cut close to the ground and shocked."[62]) The ears of corn are left to ripen on the rooted stalks and will be picked at leisure in the fall or early winter, since it was thought that this process would improve the corn and make the fodder easier to handle.

After picking the ears in early October, Paris hauls the harvest to a corncrib in a two-wheeled oxcart. (The common means of transport on most eighteenth-century Delaware farms, it continued to be very common well into the nineteenth century. The four-wheeled farm wagon, pulled by horses, was not widely used until the late eighteenth and early nineteenth centuries.) During the winter months some of the corn is fed to livestock while the remainder is first husked and then shelled by Paris and his family, perhaps with flailing sticks. If there is a great deal of corn to be shelled, the ears are spread on a hard surface and the oxen are driven over them to tramp off the kernels. Some of the loose kernels are then sent to a nearby mill to be ground into cornmeal to feed everyone on the Hazzard farm. Surplus corn is shipped to market. (Four years earlier and about thirty miles to the north, an account book for the Dickinson plantation recorded that bondsmen Liverpool and Isaac had "threshed and cleared" three hundred bushels of corn that were then sent by shallop to Philadelphia.[63])

Before deciding on what to plant, Mistress Hazzard probably turns to Paris for advice. If wheat is the crop of choice, then he and his family pick the corn in August and begin to clear the field of stalks. In September or early October the field is plowed again and winter wheat is sown by Paris, Hannah, and Paris, Jr. After harrowing the sown field, the slaves turn to other chores because the wheat prior to harvest makes few demands on their time except for the need to weed along the edges of the field and to keep out hungry, free-roaming livestock. The intense heat and dryness of July and August force most Delaware farmers and their slaves to plant wheat in the fall. Even in Sussex, where corn is dominant, most farms and plantations grow at least some wheat. Sometimes, however, some of Mistress Hazzard's fields are not planted in wheat after the corn harvest but instead are allowed to lie dormant for two out of three years in the hope of restoring fertility. Despite the precaution of letting the land lie fallow, on the Hazzard farm, as well on most other Delaware farms, the crops of corn and wheat grow "less and less as the unfertilized fields [become] more and more sterile."[64]

Although less soil-depleting than corn, wheat required that the land be plowed before planting could take place. The increased presence of plow-pulling oxen in the lives of Delaware's slaves by the mideighteenth century was largely dictated by the response of its planters to Philadelphia's growing demand for wheat. Plowing subsequently became so common in the state that one observer declared in 1788 that the plow "is the only instrument used for breaking up our farmland."[65] At harvest time, which varied slightly from Sussex to New Castle but generally lasted from June through early July, slaves used sickles to cut down the wheat at the daily rate of one acre or less per man. The introduction of the scythe and cradle on the Hazzard farm and others during the late eighteenth century increased daily wheat-harvesting capabilities to at least two acres per adult male slave, but using a sickle or scythe could be dangerous work.[66]

On the Hazzard farm and across Delaware, slaves gathered up the scythed wheat, shocked it, and left it in the field until fall or winter when it was spread on a hard, earthen treading floor. Then oxen or horses were driven over it again and again in a circular pattern, their hooves tramping on the wheat and separating the kernels from the straw. One boy might ride the "nigh" horse or ox to give direction, while older blacks would turn the wheat straw with wooden forks. A four-horse team could tramp out about thirty bushels of wheat in "a good day's work." The wheat then might be shipped to a nearby mill, or up the Delaware Bay and River to flour mills along the Brandywine River or in the Philadelphia area. Unlike Delaware tobacco, the state's wheat had a very good reputation in the national and international marketplace. Ironically, however, the slaves who planted and harvested much of the wheat had to make do with meals of corn bread and hominy.[67]

~

In addition to knowing how to work the soil, many blacks brought with them to the New World considerable experience in raising cattle in an environment that featured a warm climate and considerable open grazing land. In Africa it was not necessary to build barns or store fodder to protect cattle from cold weather or to fence in pastureland. By contrast, raising cattle in northern Europe's colder climate and more populated landscape required the building of barns, the storing of fodder, and the fencing in of fields. Because it was expensive to keep livestock throughout the entire year, most European cattle were slaughtered before reaching maturity. But in Africa, keeping cattle for more than one year was relatively inexpensive, and most herds were allowed to graze on open land until they reached maturity and beyond.[68]

The demand for red meat by Philadelphia's growing population in the early eighteenth century stimulated the development of the cattle industry in Delaware. But what developed, because of the colony's relatively short winter and considerable open land, was a cattle culture that more closely followed West African than northern European practices. The coastal region from northern New Castle County to Fenwick Island in the south was particularly well suited for cattle raising because of the extensive marshlands that provided "salt hay," for grazing or for mowing as winter fodder. Because they were fairly inexpensive to keep, cattle were allowed to reach three or four years of age before being driven north to fatten on the lush meadows of New Castle County and then on to the slaughterhouses in Wilmington and Philadelphia.[69]

Although some slaves undoubtedly worked as drovers, their most significant contribution to the cattle industry was in serving as herdsmen who nurtured and guided the cattle to maturity before they were driven north to their destiny. Delaware herds numbered as many as two hundred head.[70] Because most whites with large herds depended heavily on slave labor, they probably recognized that many Africans and their offspring were particularly skilled in bovine husbandry. On William Thompson's plantation in Lewes-Rehoboth Hundred in 1801, for example, four adult slaves and six children looked after one hundred cattle. Many very young and very old slaves who were not physically up to strenuous work in the corn and wheat fields or in clearing new land tended livestock, which was less demanding. In 1776, for example, Caesar Rodney's cattle in eastern Kent County were "constantly" tended by "old Charles and one of the boys." It is even possible that a ninety-nine-year-old slave on the farm of Thomas Marsh of Lewes-Rehoboth Hundred was helping a little with his master's forty-five cattle in 1801. By following practices used in West Africa and by depending on the use of black herdsmen, Delaware's colonial cattle industry was following patterns already in place in South Carolina.[71]

By contrast with coastal Delaware, landowners in the southwestern part of the state seemed little interested in raising large herds of cattle, but they did own far more oxen. The presence of so many oxen reflected a commitment by this region to timbering as well as to soil cultivation. A few miles to the east of Laurel, along the Sussex-Maryland border, lay the relatively untapped forests of Cypress Swamp, which provided highly valued shingles as well as lumber. Sawmills were set up on the streams that drained westward from Cypress Swamp to Broad Creek and then on into the Nanticoke. Slaves cut down trees; drove yokes of oxen, which dragged the logs to the mills; and then did much of the hard work of turning the logs into lumber and shingles—in short, whatever was needed the slaves were called on to do. In the early nineteenth century, Suthy went so far in protecting his master's logging interests in Cypress Swamp as to exchange gunfire with a white man, and was wounded.[72]

Delaware's African-Americans also tended sheep, which were raised more for their wool than for their meat because mutton neither kept well nor tasted very good when smoked or salted. Although major predators were no longer present in most of the region at the beginning of the nineteenth century, slaves were constantly on the lookout for the wily fox that continued to be a threat to the defenseless lambs. But pork was what most Delawareans preferred to eat, and most slave owners raised large numbers of pigs.[73] After their ears were cropped to show ownership, swine were turned loose to roam nearby fields and woods, surviving on roots, acorns, and some unlucky neighbor's corn. In the late fall, a few weeks before slaughter, slaves rounded up the swine and herded them to the home farm, where some were driven into a fenced-in orchard to fatten on fallen apples and peaches while others were driven into a pen to fatten on corn. Among the unfree African-Americans who spent some of their time tending pigs as well as other livestock were Caleb, Ireland, Solomon, Hannah, and Lidia, who lived on the holdings of Woolsey Burton in eastern Sussex in 1804. In addition to field work and probably some timbering, their responsibilities included looking after sixty-nine sheep, fifty-seven cattle, and thirteen pigs, all scattered on five different parcels of land.[74]

Complaints about destruction by free-roaming pigs first surfaced in 1656 in New Amstel and reached extraordinary intensity throughout the state by the early nineteenth century. Pigs were a particular threat to cash crops, and appeals for help in limiting their depredations were often sent to the legislature. As a petition from Milford, on the Kent-Sussex border, pointed out, large numbers of pigs "constantly unrestrained, every year ravage the corn fields, and trespass upon the pasture-grounds in this district in a manner as vexatious as destructive." One obvious solution was for farmers to protect their fields with fences.[75] Slaves, not surprisingly, helped to erect them. They cut up logs, preferably of red cedar, into lengths of ten to twelve feet and split them by first inserting an iron or wooden wedge that was driven deep into the log with a maul. These split rails were used for building worm fences that crept along the terrain in a zigzag pattern. Toward the end of the eighteenth century, as timber became scarce, slaves found themselves constructing wood-conserving post-and-rail fences. Later, digging ditches became the prelude to planting even more wood-conserving hedgerows. The ideal fence, as one Delawarean observed, was "cow and hog proof."[76]

Some male African-Americans who lived along the estuaries and seacoast worked on their masters' boats, while others worked the bays with clam rakes and oyster tongs. But the latter jobs were not always safe. In 1818, Peter and Solomon drowned while clamming in the Indian River. After freedom, a significant number of black Delawareans became sailors and watermen because of their maritime experiences under slavery.[77]

To gain some sense of the variety of demands made of enslaved blacks in the mideighteenth century, a look at the plantation of Nehemiah Draper of Cedar Creek Hundred in northeastern Sussex County is helpful. In addition to clearing, plowing, planting, cultivating, and harvesting corn and wheat, his thirty slaves looked after 105 cattle, 76 sheep, 54 pigs, 20 oxen, 8 horses, and 55 geese. Draper, like many of the era's gentry, was a rural merchant, and his slaves helped in his store and sailed his shallop up and down inland waterways and the Delaware Bay. In addition, several of his slaves played essential roles in his extensive timbering activities.[78]

One or two of Draper's slaves were probably skilled or semiskilled craftsmen. In a time when towns and villages were few and far between, plantations and large farm units had to house at least a few craftsmen and artisans in order to develop the level of self-sufficiency necessary for economic survival. As Gerald Mullin has pointed out about early Virginia, artisans were particularly "dear for want of towns, markets and money."[79] During much of the colonial period, Delaware's rural artisans were primarily white indentured servants, but, as we know, that source dried up with the Revolution. Moreover, many of those whites who had been skilled servants during the colonial period left the state at the end of their indentures. Thus, by the late eighteenth century, planters were forced to turn to their unfree blacks for carpenters, tanners, blacksmiths, spinners, and weavers.

Some male slaves, brought directly from West Africa via Annapolis or Philadelphia, had worked with iron in their homeland and moved comfortably into blacksmithing. Subsequently, they probably passed on much of what they knew to their male offspring. In 1772 the owners of Unity Forge in western Sussex spoke of the skills of their black slaves in manufacturing iron. An example of an iron-working slave in eastern Sussex was Phillip, who was "by trade a blacksmith." His owner, Sussex Tory Thomas Robinson, had fled to Nova Scotia during the Revolution. Phillip, however, remained behind in the service of his master's brother, Peter Robinson, who was given title to him in 1786. Six years later, also in Sussex, "Isaac, a blacksmith," was left by William Bell to his son, while in Kent County, Charles, "by trade a blacksmith," was rented out for four years to a new master. In southern New Castle County in 1762 a twenty-one-year-old male slave was advertised as "always accustomed to work at the blacksmith trade, particularly shipwork."[80]

Other Africans brought woodworking skills with them and became carpenters. They and their offspring, once freed, sometimes became coopers, such as Solomon Bayley of Kent County, or shipbuilders, such as Gabriel Jackson of Wilmington. Tanners and curriers were also numbered among Delaware slaves. One African-American in the Newark area in 1761 was described as a "Negro man, that understands the tanning and currying trades well." Ben Valentine, a sixteen-year-old in Wilmington, worked in a printing business for a year and was thought accomplished enough to get a job as "a print-man" in 1763.[81]

Some male slaves were skilled at preparing food and at cooking. Julius of Newport, in New Castle County, was described in 1764 as "bred to the biscuit business," while Dick, a slave of Vincent Loockerman of Dover in 1752, was "by trade a chocolate grinder." Simon, an experienced farm worker in southern New Castle County, was described in 1785 as "an excellent cook" who could also wash, spin, sew, and knit. At least as versatile as Simon was Harry of Sussex County, who in 1767 was described as "bred a miller, and understands very well how to manufacture flour, can invoice the same; . . . understands the carpenter's and millwright's business middling well." In putting up for rent part of the Dickinson holdings southeast of Dover in 1764, Philemon Dickinson, brother to John, advertised that "there will be let with the plantation, as many Negroes of either sex, and of any age if the person taking it shall desire; among them are tailors, shoemakers, tanners and carpenters, who can do rough common work, besides being acquainted with farming and planting."[82] Although slaves with special skills were most common on the largest plantations, such as that of the Dickinson family, even on small farms with only a few slaves they exhibited at least some acquaintance with a variety of talents beyond those needed in the fields.

In turning from tobacco to corn, wheat, and other grains, Delaware owners created a significant problem for themselves by making it more difficult to employ their slave labor profitably. Because corn and, particularly, wheat created more slack time in the agricultural calendar than tobacco, there was little for their slaves to do for weeks on end. Females were a special problem because their constant attention to tobacco plants was made unnecessary by the switch to new cash crops. While corn demanded some hoeing, the cultivation of wheat, rye, and barley made the hoe almost obsolete. Male slaves could occupy their time by clearing new land, draining swamps, building fences, turning timber into lumber, or serving as craftsmen, but black women were not assigned these tasks because of gender stereotyping or because masters considered them less accomplished in this type of work. The domestic production of textiles for home and market consumption, however, offered a profitable way to employ African-American women during slack times in field work.

To supply one of the raw materials for a domestic textile industry, masters had their slaves grow flax, which was made into linen. By the mideighteenth century, flax had become a common crop on most Delaware farms. At about the same time, slaveholders and their slaves began raising increasing numbers of sheep to provide the raw material for woolen cloth and for the combined fabric of linen and wool called linsey-woolsey. In addition, some masters and their slaves raised a small amount of cotton for personal use. As a result, until the 1830s and 1840s many plantations and farms wove their own cloth, which was then made into clothing, sometimes for the master's family but more often for his slaves. Many slave households, particularly in Sussex, produced a surplus of textiles that was sent to local markets and beyond.[83] However, domestic textile manufacturing in Delaware declined dramatically in the third and fourth decades of the nineteenth century because of the increasing availability of cheap factory-made cloth. But while it lasted, this sometime cottage industry depended largely on the skills of female slaves. Indeed, many black females were "brought up to housework, principally spinning"; and one resident of Sussex observed that "where slaves were owned, the clever negro woman did the weaving and sewing."[84]

An example of a slave master who turned to textile production was Nehemiah Davis of Cedar Creek Hundred, Sussex County, whose estate was inventoried in 1789. Many of his eleven slaves were constantly busy at raising and processing flax, herding sheep, or sitting at his four spinning wheels and three looms. Davis's inventory listed sixty-five yards of home-manufactured cloth along with considerable amounts of thread and lesser amounts of yarn.[85] In fact, by the mideighteenth century, most masters had spinning wheels in their homes or in outbuildings, and some also had looms. Some planters even could point to vertical integration from the production of the flax, wool, and a little cotton through the spinning and weaving process to the cutting and sewing of cloth into articles of clothing. But in an economy that depended a great deal on the local exchange of products, others farmed out part of the process. At John Dickinson's plantation, both patterns were followed. In 1782 forty-seven pounds of wool were placed under Pompey's care which he, in turn, delivered to Dinah and Priscilla for spinning. About the same time, Betty and Dinah were to spin, respectively, eighteen and fifteen pounds of "hackled" flax and were also to spin the yarn and thread "for the shirts, the jackets and overalls which Jenny is to make." But a year earlier, Dickinson temporarily abandoned vertical integration when he sent the end product of Dinah's spinning to a local weaver to be made into cloth.[86]

In addition to spinning, weaving, and sewing, African-American women served as cooks and maids and helped raise their masters' children. One example was Serena, slave of the Ridgelys of Eden Hill west of Dover in the late 1820s, who, in addition to other domestic duties, cared for her mistress's young daughter. In New Castle County in 1796 a slaveholder drew up a will to protect Grace from sale so that she could continue to take care of his children. Typical of these domestics were two unnamed black females, advertised for sale on the same day in 1811: the first was "an excellent cook," while the second was "perfectly well acquainted with all kinds of housework."[87] Obviously, just as African men brought previously learned skills to Delaware, female Africans also brought prior experience in such tasks as field work, textile production, child raising, cooking, and housekeeping.

In some cases, black women were assigned domestic responsibilities because injury, illness, or old age limited their ability to work in the fields. But many of those chosen to spend at least some of their time and energies on such tasks in their masters' homes were seen by their owners as the most highly skilled, intelligent, and dependable slave women. One example was Maria of Kent County, who, during the late eighteenth century, "had been a faithful servant and very tender of her [mistress]" and had helped to raise the children. Conversely, those African-American women assigned to work full time in the fields were often perceived to be less skilled and less intelligent than their sisters in the big house. Another Grace, who lived in western Sussex during the early nineteenth century, was thought by her master to be "not very intelligent" and thus was "accustomed entirely to work in the field."[88]

Few Delaware slaves of either sex spent most of their working days as carpenters, blacksmiths, tanners, spinners, weavers, housekeepers, or cooks. While the very large plantations of the Deep South with their enormous numbers of slaves could afford this kind of full-time specialization for a select few bondsmen and bondswomen, this

option was out of the question for the small slave units that characterized Delaware. Even such enslaved artisans as blacksmiths had to devote much of their time to the more mundane tasks regularly assigned
to field hands.

"Jints," owned by James Anderson whose farm was located a few miles southeast of
Georgetown, holding her master's granddaughter Hanna Stockley, ca. 1860–61. *Courtesy
of the Delaware State Archives, Dover.*

A brief examination indicates just how small these units were. Samuel Chew of central Kent County with sixty-three slaves in the early 1740s; Nehemiah Draper of Cedar Creek Hundred with thirty slaves in the 1760s; John Dickinson of Jones Neck with somewhere between thirty-seven and sixty slaves in the 1770s; and Joseph Porter of Duck Creek Hundred, who had forty-six slaves in 1800, were among the largest slaveholders in the state's history. Compared to other Delaware masters, the numbers of slaves owned are impressive; but when compared to wealthy planters of their era beyond Delaware, the holdings of all four were relatively insignificant. Thomas Jefferson, for example, had more than 200 slaves in the 1770s, and George Washington had 277 in 1799. Closer to home, Edward Lloyd IV of Talbot County, on Maryland's Eastern Shore, had accumulated more than 300 slaves by his death in 1796.[89]

Sometimes masters realized that, rather than assigning their bondspeople to field work, they could obtain better financial returns by hiring them out. Indeed, hiring out slaves was as common in Delaware as in many other parts of the South and was often practiced by such important slaveholders as John Dickinson.[90] Hiring out began prior to the mideighteenth century and continued throughout the slave era. As with the domestic production of cloth, hiring out was a way for masters to make profitable use of some of their slaves after the switch from tobacco to new cash crops made superfluous the labor of many African-Americans on the home farm.

One of the first hired-out slaves of record was the same Pompey of Kent County, who in the early 1740s was rented to a third party by the executors of the estate of his deceased master, to pay for the education of the latter's son. Hiring out slaves who were part of a recently probated estate was a common practice by the executors because it provided for the support and education of young heirs while simultaneously removing from those executors the burden of slave supervision. Typical was the case of Sambo and Isaac of Sussex County, who, upon their master's death in 1781, were "hired out annually for the best price that can be gotten" by the executors to pay "towards raising, educating and maintaining" their late master's young son and daughter.[91]

Field hands like Grace of western Sussex, who was perceived in 1818 as "not very intelligent," and talented blacksmiths like James and Isaac of near Dover in 1790 represented the wide variety of unfree African-Americans hired out to provide additional income for planter families. Perhaps typical in the disposition of his slaves was John Wilson of Sussex, who in 1825 owned at least sixteen slaves, four of whom were hired out.[92] Representative of the income generated by hiring out slaves was the £15 per year for Abraham and twenty silver dollars per year for Pompey received by John Dickinson in 1785. (£15 would purchase four oxen.[93])

Whether hired out or kept on the home farm or plantation, the broad backs and skilled hands of unfree African-Americans did much to shape the remarkable ecological changes and economic development that characterized the first two centuries of Delaware's history. Forests were turned into cultivated fields, and marshes into meadows, as black slaves joined with free and unfree whites in transforming a wilderness landscape into a rough but semicultivated countryside that produced first tobacco and then corn, wheat, lumber, and livestock. Although planters wanted to recreate a rural England, the skin color and the particularly oppressive servile condition of their dependent labor force were reminders that New Castle, Kent, and Sussex on the Delaware were not, and never would be, exactly like Kent and Sussex in the south of England.

Notes

*Box 6, folder 9, Caesar Rodney signer, Rodney Collection, Historical Society of Delaware (hereafter HSD), Wilmington, Delaware.

1. Logan Papers, 9:65, Historical Society of Pennsylvania (hereafter HSP), Philadelphia, Pennsylvania.

2. Lewis Prettyman (1827), Kent County Depositions, Slavery Material, 1764–1866, DSA.

3. Joseph Jones, June 22, 1764, Kent County Will Book A, microfilm, DSA.

4. George T. Welch, ed., *Memoirs of Mary Parker Welch (1812–1912)* (Brooklyn, NY, 1947), 147.

5. Edgar T. Wherry, "Notes on the Vegetation of Delaware," in Reed, ed., *Delaware*, 1:17–20.

6. Hendrick Hendrickson (1759), Kent County Will Book K, 215; Jonathan Caldwell (1781), Kent County Will Book L, 238; Elijah Houston (1788), Kent County Will Book M, 193, all in KCCH; December 2, 1803, indenture, John Dickinson folder, 1800–1810, Box 80, Laudon Papers, HSP; G. E. Gifford, Jr., ed., *Cecil County, Maryland, 1608–1850, As Seen by Some Visitors, and Several Essays on Local History* (Rising Sun, MD, 1974), 12; Stevenson W. Fletcher, *Pennsylvania Agriculture and Country Life, 1640–1840* (Harrisburg, PA, 1950), 86–87; Bernard L. Herman, *The Stolen House* (Charlottesville, VA, 1992), 145–51; Bernard L. Herman, "Fences," in J. Ritchie Garrison et al., eds., *After Ratification: Material Life in Delaware, 1789–1820* (Newark, DE, 1988), 9, 11, 14, 18–19.

7. Lois Green Carr, Russell R. Menard, and Lorena S. Walsh, *Robert Cole's World* (Chapel Hill, NC, 1991), 68.

8. William H. Williams, *The First State: An Illustrated History of Delaware* (Northridge, CA, 1985), 25. Judith Quinn, "Traversing the Landscape," *Delaware History* 33 (Spring–Summer 1988): 51, fails to list beaver among the wildlife of Cypress Swamp, the largest undeveloped region in the state in the early nineteenth century.

9. *Laws of the State of Delaware*, 1: passim.

10. For elk see Reed, ed., *Delaware*, 1:2–3; for buffalo see Benson, ed., *Peter Kalm's Travels in North America*, 1:110, 150. In Scharf, *History of Delaware*, 2:1169n, Drummer Gray, a Kent County slave, is reported to have seen the last wild buffalo in the state in the late eighteenth century when he spotted a small herd at Murderkill Neck, southeast of Dover. For the use of buffalo as domestic animals by Delaware farmers throughout most of the antebellum years see inventories for Kent and Sussex Counties, DSA, passim. The last large herd in the Pennsylvania, Delaware, and Maryland area was recorded to have appeared along the west bank of the Susquehanna River in 1773 and to have contained over twelve thousand buffalo. See Fletcher, *Pennsylvania Agriculture*, 69.

11. For bears see Quinn, "Traversing the Landscape," 49–52; and Jane Scott, *Between Ocean and Bay: A Natural History of Delmarva* (Centreville, MD, 1991), 70. For deer see *Laws of the State of Delaware*, 9:432 passim. Deer were extinct in Delaware by the Civil War. It was not until the 1940s that they were seen again in the state.

12. Williams, *The First State*, 18; C. H. B. Turner, ed., *Some Records of Sussex County*, 198, 199; John A. Munroe, *Federalist Delaware* (New Brunswick, NJ, 1954), 118. For a sense of the dependence on Delaware's abundant supply of fish see probate inventories for all three counties in DSA.

13. Richard L. Bushman, "Opening the American Countryside," typed paper, 1–11, in author's possession; Clemens, *The Atlantic Economy*, 196; Lois Green Carr and Lorena S. Walsh, "Economic Diversification and Labor Organization in the Chesapeake, 1650–1820," in Stephen Innes, ed., *Work and Labor in Early America* (Chapel Hill, NC, 1988), 151; R. O. Bausman and J. A. Munroe, eds., "James Tilton's Notes on the Agriculture of Delaware in 1788," *Agricultural History* 20 (July 1946): 176–87; Benson, ed., *Peter Kalm's Travels in North America*, 1:97-98; Fletcher, *Pennsylvania Agriculture*, 125.

14. Benson, ed., *Peter Kalm's Travels in North America*, 1:141; Reed, ed., *Delaware*, 1:3n–4n. For examples of trousers as well as breeches worn by slaves and indentured servants in the late colonial period see *Pennsylvania Gazette*, 7/18/1765, 9/5/65, 8/1/65, 8/29/65.

15. Simon Hart, "The City Colony of New Amstel on the Delaware: I," *Halve Maen* 39 (October 1964): 13; Reed, ed., *Delaware*, 1:4n.

16. Reed, ed., *Delaware*, 1:4n; William H. Williams, *The Garden of American Methodism: The Delmarva Peninsula, 1769–1820* (Wilmington, DE, 1984), 131–32; C. H. B. Turner, ed., *Some Records of Sussex County*, 240; Hart, "The City Colony of New Amstel," 13; Todd L. Savitt, *Medicine and Slavery: The Diseases and Health Care of Blacks in Antebellum Virginia* (Chicago, 1978), 20.

17. Peter J. Parish, *Slavery: History and Historians* (New York, 1989), 65; Wood, *Black Majority*, 91, 86–87, 90; Todd K. Savitt, "Black Health on the Plantation: Masters, Slaves, and Physicians," in Ronald L. Numbers and Todd K. Savitt, eds., *Science and Medicine in the Old South* (Baton Rouge, LA, 1989), 330–33; Savitt, *Medicine and Slavery*, 31, 19, 27–32; Darrett B. Rutman and Anita H. Rutman, "Of Agues and Fevers: Malaria in the Early Chesapeake," *William and Mary Quarterly* 33 (January 1976): 34, 40–42. Delaware's most famous slave, Richard Allen, seems to have been susceptible to malaria; see Richard Allen, *The Life Experience and Gospel Labors of the Right Reverend Richard Allen* (New York, 1960), 19.

18. Darold D. Wax, "Quaker Merchants and the Slave Trade in Colonial Pennsylvania," *Pennsylvania Magazine of History and Biography* 86 (April 1962): 153; Russell R. Menard, "The Maryland Slave Population, 1658–1730: A Demographic Profile of Blacks in Four Counties," in Stanley Katz and John Murrin,

eds., *Colonial America: Essays in Politics and Social Development* (New York, 1983), 306; Bausman and Munroe, eds., "James Tilton's Notes," 179.

19. Kulikoff, *Tobacco and Slaves*, 326; Kulikoff, "The Origins of African-American Society in Tidewater Maryland and Virginia, 1700–1790," *William and Mary Quarterly* 35, 3d series (1978): 236–37.

20. Bushman, "Gentrification of Kent County," 1–47.

21. Ibid.; Bushman, *The Refinement of America*, 16; Philemon Dickinson to Caesar Rodney, no date, Manuscripts Biography, Dickinson, Philemon and Family, DSA; Munroe, *Federalist Delaware*, 213. Keeping tame deer was not restricted to Kent County; see, for example, Ebenezer Hearn, April 21, 1785, Sussex County Estate Inventories, DSA.

22. See Clemens, *The Atlantic Economy*, 217, for the status that slaveholding on Maryland's Eastern Shore gave to white families. It was "the most important symbol of having become an established planter." Here I perceive Delaware's gentry in much the same way that Jack P. Greene, in *Pursuits of Happiness: The Social Development of Early Modern British Colonies and the Formation of American Culture* (Chapel Hill, NC, 1988), 198, sees the gentry throughout colonial Anglo-America.

23. Jack P. Greene, "Independence, Improvement, and Authority: Toward a Framework for Understanding the Histories of the Southern Backcountry during the Era of the American Revolution," in Ronald Hoffman, Thad W. Tate, and Peter J. Albert, eds., *An Uncivil War: The Southern Backcountry during the American Revolution* (Charlottesville, VA, 1985), 3–36; William H. Williams, "Delaware and Ratification: A Paradox Examined," *Delaware Lawyer* (Fall 1987): 9–10.

24. Justice, *Life and Ancestry of Warner Mifflin*, 81.

25. Percentages of Delaware families owning slaves are based on statistics culled from Will Books for New Castle, Kent, and Sussex, passim; Bushman and Hawley, eds., "A Random Sample," passim; Ronald V. Jackson, ed., *Delaware Census Index for 1800* (N.p., n.d.), passim; Harold B. Hancock, ed., "William Yates Letter of 1837: Slavery and Colored People in Delaware," *Delaware History* 14 (April 1971): 207. The percentage of families south of Pennsylvania holding slaves in 1830 is from Kolchin, *American Slavery*, 180.

26. *Weekly Union* (Georgetown, DE), 1/29/1864.

27. Gehring, ed., *New York Historical Manuscripts, Dutch Delaware Papers*, 309–10.

28. Munroe, *Colonial Delaware*, 196. For a detailed view of indentured servitude in nearby Pennsylvania see Sharon V. Salinger, *To Serve Well and Faithfully: Labor and Indentured Servants in Pennsylvania, 1682–1800* (New York, 1987).

29. Generalizations on the ethnic nature of the second wave of indentured servants is based on the reading of advertisements for Delaware runaways in the *Pennsylvania Gazette*, 1730–1775; and also in F. Edward Wright, ed., *Delaware Newspaper Abstracts, 1786–1795* (Silver Spring, MD, 1984). On the nature of servitude see Salinger, *To Serve Well and Faithfully*, 53; and Fletcher, *Pennsylvania Agriculture*, 112–13. For mortality rates of Africans aboard slave ships in the colonial era see Kolchin, *American Slavery*, 18.

30. Fletcher, *Pennsylvania Agriculture*, 113. The story of Carl Springer and one of his descendants lends a touch of irony to the servant-master relationship that characterized early Delaware. Carl, a native of Sweden studying in London, was abducted in the late 1670s and shipped to Virginia, where he was "sold off like a farm animal that is driven to market." He hated indentured servitude because of the "unspeakable" work, the climate, and his "very hard master." After

gaining his freedom in 1683, he headed north and settled in New Castle County, where he eventually purchased farmland. A century later, Carl's direct descendant, Thomas Springer, continued to farm in New Castle County and was the owner of four black slaves. For the story of the Springer family see Barbara C. Smith, *After the Revolution: The Smithsonian History of Everyday Life in the Eighteenth Century* (New York, 1985), 45–86.

31. Salinger, *To Serve Well and Faithfully*, 2–3.

32. For a few examples of the accents of indentured servants in Delaware see *Pennsylvania Gazette*, 11/12/1741, 5/18/43, 3/16/47, 2/14/49, 5/4/49, 7/25/51, 9/6/53, 3/4/65, 10/3/65.

33. Munroe, *Colonial Delaware*, 162–64; Williams, "Delaware and Ratification," 11.

34. *Pennsylvania Gazette*, 1730–1775 passim. The more oppressive nature of indentured servitude experienced by non–English servants in the eighteenth century can be seen in Pennsylvania in Salinger, *To Serve Well and Faithfully*, 3–4.

35. King vs. Charity Brinckloe (1737), manuscripts, Court Papers 1736–1795, Kent County Court of Oyer and Terminer, DSA.

36. *Pennsylvania Gazette*, 10/24/1754, 10/31/54, 5/9/63, 10/10/65, 10/31/65.

37. Ibid., 6/30/1750, 11/9/49, 6/6/51.

38. Ibid., 8/6/1752, 1/3/49, 10/1/41, 12/1/37.

39. Ibid., 10/13/1743, 8/20/47.

40. *Delaware Gazette*, 7/25/1789, 8/15/89, 10/2/90, 10/13/92; *Delaware and Eastern Shore Advertiser*, 1/14/95. During that same period, fifty-two slaves escaped from their masters according to individual citations in Wright, ed., *Delaware Newspaper Abstracts, 1786–1795*, passim.

41. Albert Vansandt, St. George's Hundred, New Castle County Will Book N, 1:141, DSA.

42. Kolchin, *American Slavery*, 38–40.

43. This assumption about the part of the slave population that was African-born is based on the fact that most slave imports into Anglo-America after 1680 came directly from Africa. Except for the 1660s, when some imported slaves may have been born in the West Indies, most of those brought into Delaware arrived after 1713 and therefore were born primarily in Africa. In addition, it was not until 1720 or so that the reproduction rate among slaves in Anglo-America was high enough to produce a natural population increase. In Delaware, because the large slave influx came later there than in the Chesapeake region, it may have been a decade or two after 1720 before slaves were producing such an increase. Kolchin, *Unfree Labor*, 34; Bushman and Hawley, eds., "A Random Sample," 66. For estimates of the African-born in the Chesapeake see Kolchin, *American Slavery*, 38.

44. *Pennsylvania Gazette*, 9/18/1740, 7/24/46, 10/12/52; Eugene Genovese, *Roll, Jordan, Roll* (New York, 1976), 432; Gerald W. Mullin, *Flight and Rebellion: Slave Resistance in Eighteenth-Century Virginia* (New York, 1974), 46. John W. Blassingame in *The Slave Community: Plantation Life in the Antebellum South* (New York, 1979), 26, points out that "eighteenth-century travelers and clergymen frequently observed that African-born slaves throughout the American colonies did not understand English."

45. *Pennsylvania Gazette*, 8/16/1764; Harold B. Hancock, "Descriptions and Travel Accounts of Delaware," in Carol E. Hoffecker, ed., *Readings in Delaware History* (Newark, DE, 1973), 39.

46. Hancock, "Descriptions and Travel Accounts of Delaware," 39; *Pennsylvania Gazette*, 11/29/1764, 7/9/47, 6/22/69; *Delaware and Eastern Shore Advertiser*, 2/7/1795.

47. August Meir and Elliott Rudwick, *From Plantation to Ghetto* (New York, 1976), 13; John T. Schlebecker, *Whereby We Thrive: A History of American Farming* (Ames, IA, 1975), 27; Rutman and Rutman, *A Place in Time*, 40–44; John Hope Franklin and Alfred A. Moss, Jr., *From Slavery to Freedom: A History of American Negroes* (New York, 1988), 14–15. For the cultivation of corn (maize) in West Africa by the second half of the sixteenth century and its subsequent spread throughout the region see Alfred W. Crosby, *The Columbian Exchange: Biological and Cultural Consequences of 1492* (Westport, CT, 1972), 186–87.

48. Kolchin, in *Unfree Labor*, 32, points out that by 1705 in Virginia white women were no longer assigned fieldwork; and in *American Slavery*, 17, he notes that virtually no women in the southern colonies engaged in agricultural labor in the eighteenth century. Fletcher, *Pennsylvania Agriculture*, 107, maintains that during the eighteenth century, farmers' wives worked in the fields when necessary, certainly at harvesttime. However, Fletcher finds even this limited duty less common among the English and Scots-Irish than among the Germans. (Delaware had few Germans but many English and Scots-Irish.) For a more equivocal view of indentured white women and free white women working in the fields, particularly in seventeenth-century Maryland, see Lois G. Carr and Lorena S. Walsh, "The Planter's Wife: The Experiences of White Women in Seventeenth-Century Maryland," in Katz and Murrin, eds., *Colonial America*, 99, 112–13. Even after freedom, in the 1860s, in the Milton area of Sussex County a number of black women continued to do fieldwork. Harold B. Hancock and Russell McCabe, *Milton's First Century, 1807–1907* (Milton, DE, 1982), 299.

49. Welch, ed., Me*moirs of Mary Parker Welch*, 147.

50. Rhys Isaac, *The Transformation of Virginia, 1740–1790* (Chapel Hill, NC, 1982), 24–27; Rutman, *A Place in Time*, 40–44; Carr and Walsh, "Economic Diversification," 150; Sussex, Kent, and New Castle County probate inventories, passim, DSA. For a detailed look at growing tobacco and corn on Maryland's lower Western Shore see Carr, Menard, and Walsh, *Robert Cole's World*, 56–66.

51. David Freeman Hawke, *Everyday Life in Early America* (New York, 1989), 44. Auyuba ("Job") Suleiman's quote is taken from Kulikoff, *Tobacco and Slaves*, 326.

52. Rutman, *A Place in Time*, 42–44; Clemens, *The Atlantic Economy*, 184. The omission of oxen, horses, and plows and the frequent mention of the grubbing hoe—traditionally used for breaking unplowed ground—in the inventories of Delaware farmers indicate that before the mideighteenth century, only a small minority annually plowed their fields. See New Castle, Kent, and Sussex County probate inventories, passim, DSA.

53. Hazard, *Annals of Pennsylvania*, 468; Edward Booth (1682), Sussex County Will Book No. 1, SCCH; Munroe, *Colonial Delaware*, 94; Bushman and Hawley, eds., "A Random Sample," 66; *Pennsylvania Gazette*, 5/9/1754.

54. Fletcher, *Pennsylvania Agriculture*, 165. Evidently, even in the Chesapeake colonies, there was a pecking order concerning quality. Virginia tobacco was considered superior to Maryland tobacco.

55. Bushman and Hawley, eds., "A Random Sample," 65; John Johnson (1746), Kent Co. Will Book No. 1, 165, DSA; Ebenezer Hearn, April 21, 1785, Sussex County Probate Inventories, DSA; Bausman and Munroe, eds., "James Tilton's Notes," 178. For one of the last records of tobacco grown for personal use see Stephen Hill, April 8, 1837, Sussex County Probate Inventories, DSA.

According to Schlebecker, *Whereby We Thrive*, 31, a good crop of tobacco yielded one thousand pounds per acre.

56. Kolchin, *American Slavery*, 24–25.

57. Bausman and Munroe, eds., "James Tilton's Notes," 181.

58. Fletcher, *Pennsylvania Agriculture*, 271; Elizabeth B. Pryor, *Agricultural Implements used by Middle-Class Farmers in the Colonial Chesapeake* (Accokeek, MD, 1984), 36–39; Welch, ed., *Memoirs of Mary Parker Welch*, 102. For the decline in the importance of the grubbing hoe and the increase in the number of oxen see Bausman and Munroe, eds., "James Tilton's Notes," 184; and estate inventories, DSA. Benjamin Franklin pointed out in 1769 that horses required twice as much food as oxen and "are not good to eat, at least we do not think so." A. H. Smyth, ed., *Writings of Benjamin Franklin* (New York, 1905–07), 5:194–95.

59. Fletcher, *Pennsylvania Agriculture*, 92; Bausman and Munroe, eds., "James Tilton's Notes," 184.

60. Ann Hazzard, December 2, 1785, Sussex County Probate Inventories, DSA; Hancock and McCabe, *Milton's First Century*, 298.

61. Welch, ed., *Memoirs of Mary Parker Welch*, 1; Hancock and McCabe, *Milton's First Century*, 299; Wood, *Black Majority*, 61.

62. Ann Hazzard, December 2, 1785, and John Cannon, 1788, Sussex County Estate Inventories, DSA; Fletcher, *Pennsylvania Agriculture*, 150–51; Hancock and McCabe, *Milton's First Century*, 299. The number of corn hills depended on the size of the labor force, the number of beasts of burden, and the availability of farm implements. One of the largest numbers that I have encountered was the 182,000 corn hills in 1823 on the farm of John Dashiell of Sussex, who had six slaves; John Dashiell (1823), Sussex County Probate Inventories, DSA. For an example of cornstalks and ears left in the field while fodder is stacked see Ezekiel Hitchins, November 6, 1783, Sussex County Estate Inventories, DSA.

63. Fletcher, *Pennsylvania Agriculture*, 102, 226; Hancock and McCabe, *Milton's First Century*, 299; May 10, 1781, Land and Business Records, 1779–1795, Box 9, Folder 5, Dickinson Papers, HSP. The first wagon listed in an inventory of a slaveholder that I have encountered was in 1790. However, in Bausman and Munroe, eds., "James Tilton's Notes," 285, Tilton himself mentions the use of wagons. Israel Holland, August 19, 1790, Sussex County Estate Inventories, DSA.

64. Book D, 1784, 66, and Book C, 1774, 270, Kent County Orphans Court Records, KCCH; Daniel Burton, November 14, 1803, Sussex County Orphans Court Records, Microfilm reel 760, DSA; Welch, ed., *Memoirs of Mary Parker Welch*, 101. As early as 1713 some Sussex farmers had turned from tobacco to a combination of corn and wheat; see Adam Johnson, Sussex County Will Book No. 1, 78, SCCH, as one example. For the case of a late eighteenth-century farm leaving much of its acreage fallow while planting corn and wheat in the remaining acreage see Book D, 66, Kent County Orphans Court Records, KCCH.

65. Schlebecker, *Whereby We Thrive*, 26; Bausman and Munroe, eds., "James Tilton's Notes," 180, 181.

66. Bausman and Munroe, eds., "James Tilton's Notes," 184; Fletcher, *Pennsylvania Agriculture*, 98. For the movement to scythe and cradle by slave owners and nonowners see Nehemiah Davis, April 1789; Thomas Davis, June 14, 1811; Jesse Deputy, March 3, 1797; Charles Downs, December 20, 1796; Avery Draper, March 12, 1792; John Draper, April 5, 1784; John Heavelo, August 30, 1783, all in Sussex County Estate Inventories, DSA. For examples of what were probably sickle and scythe wounds see *Pennsylvania Gazette*, 8/7/1755; 8/16/64.

67. Manlove Hayes, *Reminiscences* (N.p. or p.d.), 44; Bausman and Munroe, eds., "James Tilton's Notes," 183, 184.

68. Wood, *Black Majority*, 29–30.

69. Schlebecker, *Whereby We Thrive*, 46; Fletcher, *Pennsylvania Agriculture*, 180; Bausman and Munroe, eds., "James Tilton's Notes," 185; Thomas Rodney to Caesar Rodney, April 26, 1776, box 6, folder 9, Caesar Rodney signer, Rodney Collection, HSD.

70. *Pennsylvania Gazette,* 8/16/1764.

71. Thomas Rodney to Caesar Rodney, April 26, 1776, box 6, folder 9, Caesar Rodney signer, Rodney Collection, HSD; William Thompson, Thomas Marsh, Sussex County Tax Assessment, Lewes-Rehoboth Hundred, 1801, DSA; Wood, *Black Majority*, 29–31.

72. Sussex County Tax Assessment Records, Little Creek Hundred, 1801, DSA; Herman, *The Stolen House*, 80. General John Dagworthy of Dagsboro Hundred, Sussex, in 1788 left an estate that included 14 slaves and 300,000 shingles in Cypress Swamp. Clearly some of his slaves had produced those shingles. General John Dagworthy, May 26, 1787, Sussex County Estate Inventories, DSA.

73. Fletcher, *Pennsylvania Agriculture*, 191–92; Hancock and McCabe, *Milton's First Century*, 97. Estate inventories in DSA indicate that little mutton but considerable pork was consumed in the eighteenth and early nineteenth centuries in Delaware. Moreover, the widespread ownership of pigs can be seen in inventories of the period.

74. Gehring, ed., *New York Historical Manuscripts, Dutch Delaware Papers*, 61; Fletcher, *Pennsylvania Agriculture*, 207, 189; Herman, *The Stolen House*, 119, 153; Woolsey Burton, 1804, and Thomas Hearn, April 8, 1833, Sussex County Estate Inventories, DSA.

75. Herman, "Fences," 11, 14–15.

76. Hancock and McCabe, *Milton's First Century*, 299.

77. For examples of the number of coastal slaveholders with interests in shipping, oystering, and clamming see Estate inventories, DSA. For some indication of the number of free black Delawareans who became sailors or watermen see Ira Dye, "Early American Merchant Seafarers," *Proceedings of the American Philosophical Society* (1976): 350–51; *Wilmington, Delaware Directory of 1814* (Silver Spring, MD, reprint), 18–19; Hancock and McCabe, *Milton's First Century*, 115–23; *Delaware Gazette*, 1/20/1826.

78. Nehemiah Draper, Esq., July 1, 1767, Sussex County Probate Inventories, DSA.

79. Mullin, *Flight and Rebellion*, 7.

80. Charles Joyner, *Down by the Riverside: A South Carolina Slave Community* (Urbana, IL, 1984), 238; Harold B. Hancock, *Delaware Two Hundred Years Ago: 1780–1800* (Wilmington, DE, 1987), 14; Thomas Robinson (1786), Sussex County Will Book No. 6, 83, SCCH; William Bell (1792), Sussex County Will Book D-4, 381, ibid.; *Pennsylvania Gazette*, 10/21/1762.

81. Solomon Bayley, *A Narrative of Some Remarkable Incidents in the Life of Solomon Bayley, Formerly a Slave in the State of Delaware* (London, 1825), iv; Scharf, *History of Delaware*, 1226; Hancock and McCabe, *Milton's First Century*, 115–23; *Pennsylvania Gazette*, 7/9/1761; 9/28/63; 6/21/64; 6/2/84.

82. *Pennsylvania Gazette*, 6/21/1764; 4/2/52; 1/22/85; 10/1/67; 1/5/64.

83. An examination of estate inventories, DSA, for all three counties supports this generalization. The concentration of home commercial textile production in Sussex can be seen in Herman, *The Stolen House*, 206. According to

Bausman and Munroe, eds., "James Tilton's Notes," 185, flax was "spun in almost every private family."

84. *Delaware Gazette*, 2/16/1796; Welch, ed., *Memoirs of Mary Parker Welch*, 107.

85. Nehemiah Davis (1789), Note Book B, Sussex County Estate Inventories, DSA.

86. June 25, 1782, May 10, 1781, Box 9, folder 5, Land and Business Records, 1779–1795, Dickinson Papers, HSP.

87. Leon de Valinger, ed., *A Calendar of Ridgely Family Letters, 1742–1899* (Dover, DE, 1948), 1:237; *American Watchman and Advertiser* (Wilmington), 6/9/1811; Benjamin Bunker, St. George's Hundred, New Castle County Will Book O, 1:142, DSA.

88. Ann Walker (1786), Kent County Will Book M, 105–7, KCCH; *American Watchman and Advertiser* (Wilmington), 9/23/1818.

89. U.S. Bureau of the Census, manuscript returns for 1800, Delaware, No. 4 microfilm; Dumas Malone, *Jefferson the Virginian* (Boston, 1948), 391; John R. Alden, *George Washington: A Biography* (Baton Rouge, LA, 1984), 302; Papenfuse et al., eds., *A Biographical Dictionary of the Maryland Legislature*, 2:539; Jean B. Russo, "A Model Planter: Edward Lloyd IV of Maryland, 1770–1796," *William and Mary Quarterly* 49 (January 1992): 78–79.

90. Logan Papers, 23:79A, 33:23, 36:30, HSP, in Dickinson File, passim, Rose Cottage, Bureau of Museums, Dover, Delaware. For the practice elsewhere see, for example, Randolph B. Campbell, "Slave Hiring in Texas," *American Historical Review* 93 (February 1988): 107–14.

91. Kent County Will Book I, 53, KCCH; Isaac Smith, 1781, Sussex County Will Book No. 3, 260, SCCH.

92. *American Watchman and Advertiser* (Wilmington), 9/23/1818; Richard Smith, Esq., Kent County Will Book M, 224–25, KCCH; John Wilson (1825), Sussex County Will Book No. 7, 408–9, SCCH.

93. Logan Papers, 33:23, 36:30, HSP, in Dickinson File, Bureau of Museums. For the buying power of pounds currency see Sussex and Kent estate inventories, DSA, for the mid- and late 1780s.

III

Images, Perceptions, and
the Exercise of Control

From infancy they have been trained to receive, without a murmur, the white man's scourge and to move with obedience to the white man's command.
—*Weekly Union* (Georgetown), February 12, 1864

Because their role was central to the institution of slavery, the physical and spiritual dimensions of the world of Delaware's slaveholders deserve further examination. The masters' homes, furnishings, food, clothing, education, amusements, and religion not only emitted visible and cultural messages that were hard to ignore, but they also established standards of comparison against which some aspects of the lives of their slaves can be measured.

With the possible exception of some parts of Sussex County, where the Chesapeake tradition of frame houses was strong, log structures comprised the homes of a large percentage of slave masters as well as a majority of other whites until the end of the eighteenth century. This style was particularly true of Kent County, where Mispillion and Dover Hundreds led the way in 1797 with 87 percent of their homes either crude log cabins or houses of hewn logs.[1] During the eighteenth century, the least successful slave masters joined with the majority of other white Delawareans in living in one-and one-half-story log structures that usually measured 16' by 20', with one dirt-floored, multipurpose room downstairs and a sleeping loft above. The more prosperous owners, however, could afford a wood-framed or brick structure with wooden floors, several rooms, and considerably more square footage. One example during the mideighteenth century was William Barns, a wheat farmer from Little Creek Hundred, Kent

County, who owned ten slaves and lived in a house with four rooms downstairs and three bedrooms upstairs.[2]

Although the two-and-one-half-story brick structures built by the Delaware gentry seemed imposing to their less affluent contemporaries, they were only diminutive imitations of the great country houses that graced the English landscape and were significantly smaller than the homes erected by some of the wealthy tobacco planters of the Chesapeake. An example was the home of Kent County's Samuel Dickinson, one of the state's wealthiest slaveholders, who lived in a rather modest two-and-one-half-story brick house that measured only 25' by 45'. Even smaller was the more typical home of Thomas Springer, a slave owner who lived near Stanton, in New Castle County, in the late eighteenth century. When Springer's four slaves—Ace, Will, Sara, and Amelia—entered their master's house, they found themselves in a 19'-by-23' two-story, planked log structure with wooden floors, with one large room down and one up. In some sections of Delaware, such as the region around the Cypress Swamp, some slaveholders continued to live in 18'-by-20' houses into the early nineteenth century.[3]

During the colonial period, most of these slave owners' homes were rather bare of furnishings because only the wealthiest could afford more than a few trunks, a couple of spindle-back chairs, and a wooden table. Generally, there were no rugs on the floor or stoves for cooking. The fireplace was the focus for meal preparation and a magnet for family members on cold evenings. Only a few households could afford the decorative symbols of high fashion. While some of the wealthiest gentry increased the number and sophistication of their furniture and cooking utensils after the mideighteenth century, it was not until the early nineteenth century that dramatic changes took place in the interiors of the homes of most Delaware slaveholders. George Hazzard of Seaford, for example, was a man of modest means who owned only four slaves. By 1830, however, he used a stove rather than an open fireplace for cooking and heating. In contrast to the colonial practice of usually leaving wooden floors bare, he covered his floors and stairway with carpets. Moreover, Hazzard owned two mahogany side tables, one dining table, twelve rush-bottom chairs, and seven expensive beds with attached curtains.[4]

The gentry were particularly sensitive to visual images. The wealthiest slaveholders built their brick Georgian homes to impose some order on an otherwise unruly landscape. They preferred being seen by the rest of the community while mounted on a horse or riding in a carriage, because either image symbolized to the horseless and carriageless "middling and lesser sorts" (and to their own slaves) that eighteenth-century Delaware was a deferential society, dependent on its virile gentry class for leadership. Moreover, owning a large number of slaves was perceived as further proof of the gentry's command experience and its leadership potential in the public arena.[5]

Clothes also played an important role in visually affirming dominance. A case in point was the wardrobe of Joseph Forman of Sussex, who owned sixteen slaves. His estate inventory of 1778 included "7 linen caps, 9 summer vests, 4 cloth jackets, 1 blue taffeta jacket, 1 flannel jacket, 1 shirt, 6 coats, 7 pairs of britches, 2 pairs of trousers, 4 pairs of thread stockings, 3 pairs of worsted stockings, 2 pairs of fur and cotton stockings, 1 pair of raw silk stockings, 11 pairs of socks, 3 pairs of shoes and 1 wig box."[6] Certainly, neither Forman nor any other eighteenth-century Delawarean came close to matching the sartorial splendor of the Carters and other great planter families of Virginia, but a wardrobe such as his made a strong statement.

As for diet, slave owners, like other whites, generally ate meat at least twice daily. In 1788, James Tilton observed that "the inhabitants of Delaware use a great proportion of animal food. Few men breakfast without a portion of meat and it is a universal practice to dine in the middle of the day on a full meal of meat with bread and vegetables." Even supper, the "lightest meal," may have included meat. White residents of the state consumed far more pork than beef, mutton, or poultry because they liked the taste of pork, they believed it nutritious, and they found it easy to preserve. By contrast, the flesh of other domestic animals did not taste very good after being salted. While large quantities of salted pork and bacon were consumed, some fresh-killed beef, mutton, fish, poultry, and wild game were enjoyed in season, particularly in the fall and winter. In New Castle County, where patterns followed in Pennsylvania had considerable impact, less pork and more beef and mutton were eaten than in Kent and Sussex.[7]

Milk and butter were part of most breakfasts of both the gentry and the "lesser sort," but milk consumption was considerably less than it would be in the twentieth century. Cheeses were more commonly eaten after the American Revolution, especially in New Castle County. During most of the eighteenth century, only among the gentry were vegetables served on a plate in individual portions. The rest of white Delaware ate their onions, cabbages, beans, peas, corn, and white and sweet potatoes primarily in stews and sauces. Initially, English colonists did not care for sweet potatoes, and it was only after the Revolution that they became popular. The white or Irish potato was first introduced into Delaware by Scots-Irish immigrants in the early eighteenth century, while cabbage probably had been introduced in the previous century by the Dutch. Corn was often consumed on the cob or made into succotash, corn mush (hominy) with milk, or corn bread, but wheat bread rather than the latter was usually found on the tables of the gentry. Imported sugar and molasses vied with home-grown honey as sweeteners. In all, most slaveholders and other whites ate meals that were filling but, by our standards, overcooked and taste-less. Often their food was washed down with imported wine along with cider, brandy, and other alcoholic drinks made at home from orchard-grown fruit and grain. Coffee and tea were also favored, par-ticularly at breakfast. In the afternoon, the gentry favored "the parade of tea" in the English manner.[8]

Although they may have been well fed, few Delaware slaveholders were well educated. John Dickinson of Kent County enjoyed a fine formal education that took him to Philadelphia and London, but that level of attainment was unusual. Most masters exhibited little interest in books, and many were even illiterate. In Sussex County during the eighteenth century, a majority of female and a sizable minority of male slaveholders signed their wills with an "X". In the same period in the other two counties, slaveholders tended to be more literate but were not, if the size of their private book collections is any indication, in-terested in literature, history, or the sciences. Rather, their educational priorities were shaped and molded by the pragmatic demands of eco-nomic survival on the agrarian landscape of eighteenth- and early nineteenth-century Delaware.[9] The limited education of slaveholders did not mean that the needs of their sons and daughters were ignored, but without a public school system it was both awkward and expen-sive to educate children. Generally, parents hired tutors or sent their children off to local or distant private schools. And, as previously mentioned, some masters provided in their wills that certain slaves be hired out for a period of years to pay for a son's or daughter's education.[10]

~

The mimetic nature of the rest of the population made the slave-holding gentry the arbiters of early Delaware's tastes and values. Al-though the "middling and lesser sorts" were financially incapable of replicating the brick or frame houses of their betters, they were eager to emulate some of the leisure-time activities of the upper class. As a result, the same dancing, drinking, card playing, horse racing, cock fighting, and general revelry that often marked the gentry's free mo-ments also occupied many of those further down the social scale. The latter showed their approval of another aspect of the gentry's value system by dreaming of the day when they, too, would be masters of black slaves.[11]

There were certain white Delawareans, however, who were in-creasingly uncomfortable with the dominant culture and its underly-ing values. Among the first were the Quakers, or Friends, and their religious cousins the Nicholites, who were followers of the Dover-area evangelist and preacher John Nichols. The Quakers were vocal and judgmental but never numerous enough in the state to raise unaided a serious challenge to the ways of the slaveholding gentry. The Nicholites, although briefly active in Kent County during the late colonial period, were no longer a significant force by the last two decades of the eighteenth century.[12]

The third faith to challenge the values and life-styles of the slaveholders was Methodism. Unlike the Society of Friends, Methodism drew large numbers of adherents, and, unlike the Nicholites, possessed long-term staying power. Methodism first appeared in Delaware a few years before the Revolution and proved particularly attractive to the heavily Anglo-Saxon populations of Kent and Sussex. By 1784 more Delawareans were attending Methodist services than those of all the other faiths combined. The Methodists' religious dominance downstate was reinforced by a surge of conversions in the first decade of the nineteenth century.[13]

Along with the fast-fading Nicholites, whose founder had died in 1770, and the influential but never numerous Quakers, Methodists found much to condemn in the prevailing customs and underlying social values of eighteenth-century Delaware. They judged as unattractive a life-style that emphasized exploitation, competition, brutality, frivolity, and deference to higher social rank, and their remedy called for a revolution in values. To move from the sinful habits of the slaveholding gentry and the mimetic "lesser sort" to the ways of God, Methodism demanded the substitution of fairness for exploitation, cooperation for competition, compassion for brutality, seriousness for frivolity, and egalitarianism for deference.[14] This call for a revolution in values combined with the antislavery sentiments of their English founder, John Wesley, to make early Methodists strong enemies of slavery. In Delaware, Methodist preachers attacked the "peculiar institution" vigorously and continued to flail away at it into the first decade of the nineteenth century.[15]

Surprisingly, some members of the very class whose life-style and values were excoriated by Wesleyan preachers became Methodists. Evidently, a number of the gentry had serious reservations about their own class's behavior and moral standards and were willing to adopt a serious, pious air and abandon revelry, gambling, sports, frivolity, and even slavery. Moreover, during the late eighteenth century, a cooperative working relationship between Methodist preachers and Anglican clerics in Delaware made it easy for some of the elite to move from the collapsing Anglican/Episcopal Church to Methodist congregations. Revolutionary War hero Allen McLane, future governor and U.S. senator Richard Bassett, Kent County sheriff Phillip Barratt and his three sons, and Judge Thomas White of Kent County were only a few

examples of those gentry who became Methodists. In addition to freeing their own slaves, many of these men joined with Quakers to push
for the end of slavery.[16] However, an overwhelming majority of the
state's wealthy landowners, and therefore its slaveholders, remained
Anglican/Episcopalian or were simply unchurched. They were the ones
who in spite of pressure from Friends and the followers of Wesley
kept slavery alive in Delaware.

~

During the colonial period, Delawareans and other Anglo-
Americans rarely questioned the institution of slavery. After all, it was
only one of the many forms of unfree labor experienced throughout
history by a majority of men and women. As Englishman Arthur Young
pointed out in 1772, only about 5 percent of the world's laboring population could rightly claim to be free.[17] To deny another's freedom in
order to exploit his or her labor was simply to act as powerful men and
women had always acted since time out of mind. But what distinguished
slavery in Delaware and in the rest of the New World from unfree
labor practices in most other places was its overwhelmingly racial
nature: the masters were white, and the slaves were black.

From Delaware's seventeenth-century colonial beginnings, whites
generally perceived Africans as different because they were "black,
uncivilized and heathen."[18] To white colonists, this distinctiveness
vaguely justified African enslavement. But precise justification of racial slavery would await a later date. During the eighteenth century,
most Anglo-Saxon Delawareans saw the Scots-Irish and Irish as also
distinctive and therefore well suited for indentured servitude. Throughout the colonial period, Delawareans and other Anglo-Americans simply accepted black slavery and white servitude as such an integral part
of the natural order that they needed no formal justification.

The rhetoric of freedom and liberty sparked by the Enlightenment,
the American Revolution, and the simultaneous quickening of Quaker
and Methodist opposition to slavery caused many Delawareans to
seriously examine their own system of unfree labor for the first time.
They discovered that white indentured servants had almost disappeared
from the local scene by the end of the Revolution, thus making unfree
labor a fate reserved only for African-Americans. Clearly, race rather
than class or ethnic affiliation now solely dictated who would make
up the unfree labor force.

When slaveholding in Delaware first came under serious attack
during the late eighteenth century, its supporters recognized the need
to justify racial slavery in more specific terms. (This need was also
true in much of the rest of the South.) Leading the proslavery defense

was Thomas Rodney of Kent County, who insisted that he was not alone in believing that "nature found Negroes for slavery." Not only were African-Americans intended to be "hughers [hewers] of wood and drawers of water," but they also were so fulfilled by the physical demands of slavery that "they are never happy but when at it."[19] The subsequent depiction of blacks by the proslavery faction, however, went far beyond portraying African-Americans as a simple people incapable of constructive work and real happiness beyond the confines of bondage. Simultaneously playing on and contributing to a rising racism, slavery's apologists argued that the inherent nature of the African-American made it imperative to keep him in bondage so that the property and physical well-being of white Delawareans might be protected. But what was that nature? In 1817, nineteen Kent County petitioners claimed to be "by no means hostile in any way to negroes."[20] The record shows, nevertheless, that by 1817 whites had grown increasingly hostile to blacks. This hostility was partially based on growing white perceptions that blacks were naturally lazy, prone to steal, violent, and sexually promiscuous. But throughout history, whatever the color, slaves often had been portrayed by their masters as possessing these undesirable traits.[21] What was new in Delaware and in the rest of Anglo-America was that, in the minds of whites, black skin now replaced slave status as the explanation for the presence of these socially threatening characteristics.

Although racism existed in Delaware in the late seventeenth century, by the standards of a later day it was a relatively mild variety. It led to African-Americans being enslaved, but not necessarily for life; to interracial marriages being frowned on, but not banned by law. At this early date, blacks represented only a small fraction of the colony's total population, and their alien ways were not seen as a major threat to social stability. During the great influx of black slaves into Delaware in the early and mideighteenth century, harsher racial stereotypes began to appear, but they were softened by the simultaneous influx of the troublesome Celtic indentured servants. With many Celts moving west at the end of their servitude and with most of those remaining being absorbed into the dominant Anglo-Saxon culture, by the end of the eighteenth century African-Americans increasingly stood out in the eyes of many as the only really alien people in the state. And their perceived nature marked them as a people needing enslavement.

In 1789 one Delawarean wrote that the manumitters of slaves were doing "essential injury" to their neighborhoods because it is "well known that Negroes have a rooted aversion to work," and therefore "they must steal and rob in order to get a subsistence." This charge of natural laziness was first used by the colonial legislature in 1740 and repeated in 1767 to justify bills that impeded masters from freeing their slaves. According to both laws, "It is found by experience that free Negroes and mulattoes are idle and slothful . . . and are an evil example to slaves." The legislators went on to imply that the idle and slothful character of newly freed blacks made many of them unable "to maintain or support" their children. As for those slaves who ran away from their masters, a downstate newspaper pointed out in 1859 that their destination was probably "some land of the free where it is supposed that hog and hominy may be had without the hateful pre-liminary: work." Manumitting slaves or allowing them to escape from their masters was upsetting to many whites because they saw those released as nothing more than "a parcel of lazy, worthless negroes."[22]

Not only did many whites justify slavery on the grounds that it forced at least some work from otherwise indolent blacks, but they also saw in it an institution that exercised some positive control over a people whom they perceived to be naturally prone to "stealing." (Con-veniently ignored was the fact that whites defined "stealing" in a way that excused masters from stealing the freedom of black men and women.) Incidents such as the one that took place at the John Dickinson plantation on Jones Neck in 1793 persuaded many whites that there were serious problems ahead if many African-Americans were manumitted. A white tenant farmer's wife complained that a group of black-inhabited houses clustered near the peach orchard was a "den of thieves" and then accused the free blacks who lived there of pilfering two-thirds of the wool sheared on the farm since last fall. Lacking long-term prisons, many white communities believed that placing free blacks judged guilty of stealing back into controlled bondage was one way to limit future larcenies. In 1822, for example, Kent County whites requested that free blacks Alexander Clarkson and Martin Doherty, who had gained remarkable reputations as thieves in southern Dela-ware, be sold back into slavery.[23]

There was little doubt in the minds of most whites that even under the controls of slavery, some blacks, if given the opportunity, would emulate their free brothers and sisters in stealing anything not bolted down or locked up. Warner Mifflin of Kent County, who was usually an apologist for the actions of slaves, admitted that among unfree African-Americans there was a "disposition to pilfering" and felt com-pelled to speak to enslaved blacks on the necessity "of departing from these practices."[24] Particularly alarming to whites was the fact that some slaves did not restrict larceny to their master's holdings. In 1793, for example, Anthony of Kent County, who "hath given much evi-dence of the depravity of his heart and of his irreclaimable hardiness and perseverance in vice," went on to steal "goods out of the store of James Whiteacre" and was suspected of a number of other crimes "of like nature." In 1836, Andrew of New Castle County, after stealing all of his master's hams, a quantity of lead, ten to twenty dollars, and a pair of pantaloons, then robbed a Wilmington storekeeper. As deeply involved in stealing as some slaves may have been, it continued to be the prevailing opinion among slaveholders that even more intense thievery would follow if enslaved blacks were freed. If there were any doubts, one had only to look to the neighboring state of Pennsylvania, where by 1826 free African-Americans made up one-thirty-fourth of the total population but represented one-third of the prison inmates.[25] To a large number of white Delawareans, slavery had become an institution necessary for the social control of blacks.

White masters were frustrated by the reluctance of some of their slaves to work hard and by their apparent inclination to steal. But even more upsetting was the white-held perception that blacks, if given the opportunity, would become violent. Although no organized slave or free black revolt took place in Delaware, the white community in general and slave owners in particular were constantly on guard throughout the eighteenth and the first half of the nineteenth centuries because uprisings in other parts of Anglo-America or in the West Indies were unsettling reminders of what could happen. In 1712 an attempt by slaves to burn New York City, kill its white residents, and gain freedom led to the destruction of several buildings and the death of at least nine whites before the revolt was suppressed. But in 1712 white Delawareans were not particularly concerned because their own slave population was still relatively small.

The large influx of slaves after 1713, however, dramatically altered the racial makeup of the colony. By 1740, with unfree African-Americans representing perhaps 15 to 20 percent of Delaware's total population, the possibility of a slave insurrection had to be taken much more seriously. The news from outside was not reassuring. In 1739 an armed group of runaway slaves forced the British governor of Jamaica to negotiate a military truce. That same year the Stono Rebellion broke out in South Carolina, and more than twenty whites lost their lives before it was suppressed. In 1740 slaves were suspected of setting ablaze Charleston, South Carolina, and a revolt aimed at uniting both the Eastern and Western Shores of Maryland under the control of rebellious slaves was headed off, it was said, only by the timely arrest and execution of the ringleader. In 1741 a slave conspiracy was perceived in New York City, while in Hackensack, New Jersey, slaves were accused of barn burnings.[26]

Adding to the general unease in Delaware was the ongoing war between Spain and Great Britain, begun in 1739, which was bound to drag in France on the Spanish side. It was easy for the colony's slaveholders to envision Spanish and French landing parties plundering unprotected plantations along the Delaware Bay and River and encouraging slave insurrections. Summarizing the concerns of most whites was a letter sent by colonial legislators to Lieutenant Governor George Thomas in 1741, in which they pledged to consider some means of defense "for securing ourselves at least in some measure against a foreign enemy as well as against any Domestic Insurrections from our slaves who of late have given us too much reason to fear, that they will become troublesome to us in like manner as Negroes have been in some of our neighboring governments."[27] Although nothing came of these fears, Delaware's slaveholders continued to be concerned about insurrections. The successful rebellion of slaves in Haiti in the 1790s; Gabriel Prosser's aborted rebellion in Virginia in 1800; Denmark Vesey's insurrection in South Carolina in 1822; and, most important, Nat Turner's revolt in which at least sixty whites were killed in Southampton County, Virginia, in 1831 would periodically remind masters that their own unfree blacks had the potential for staging a bloody uprising. Indeed, so paranoid were Delaware whites that many of them fell victim to an elaborate hoax.

Soon after news of Turner's insurrection had spread beyond Virginia, rumors began to circulate in Delaware of plots and conspiracies by enslaved and free blacks. One report predicted that on election day in October 1831 blacks would stage a violent rebellion. While most people were in a "feverish state of excitement," a group of "mischievous" young whites, "in cruel sport, laid a plan" to further excite imaginations. On election day they gathered along the south bank of the Nanticoke River, directly across from Seaford, and divided themselves into two groups, with one group covering its faces with black handkerchiefs. Within full view of the residents of Seaford, those pretending to be black insurrectionists opened fire on those who were clearly white, and some of the latter feigned being hit and fell to the ground. Others crossed the Nanticoke and ran into town to report that blacks had landed just below Seaford, had killed several white men, and were planning "a destructive march through the countryside."[28]

Pandemonium reigned in Seaford as some residents hid themselves in the woods while others flew to arms. Messengers were dispatched to other communities to spread the alarm, "which lost nothing by carrying." A messenger sent to Kent County stopped at the first polling place that he encountered and reported to the assembled crowd "that 1,500 Negroes had landed on the Nanticoke from Maryland, and were in full march up the country." One of the clerks present was so frightened that he ran off with the ballot box and could not be found until the alarm had partially subsided the next day. In the days that followed, emergency meetings were called, and for several weeks squads of armed white men patrolled every town and village in southern Delaware. Indeed, war preparations were more extensive than if it were "a certainty, that a foreign enemy had landed an army in Lewes." During the panic and frantic preparations for battle, Delaware's African-Americans "looked on with wonder and amazement, and no doubt with considerable pride, to find that they suddenly had grown to such consequence in the eyes of white people."[29] Although it soon became apparent that all the consternation had been the result of a hoax, the paranoia over a black uprising did not completely subside. Indeed, Kent and Sussex Countians continued to act as if the wild rumors were fact.[30]

Paranoia about collective uprisings was far less justified by subsequent events than was the fear of acts by individual slaves against masters and their property. In a number of cases, lone slaves became so prone to violence that not even the strict regulations that characterized slavery were enough to control them. All of this came as a surprise to many masters who claimed that their "problem" slaves had always received "kind and benevolent treatment," and they were "at a loss" to explain these violent actions. One New Castle County slaveholder, for example, maintained that he had always treated his "problem" slave Andrew "with kindness and humility which his conduct never warranted."[31]

In some cases, slave conduct justified concern. The earliest recorded physical attack occurred in 1690, when William Futcher of eastern Sussex was killed by his slave. A much later example involved Luke, owned by James Whitaker of Mispillion Hundred in southern Kent County. One morning, in 1821, Luke simply refused to get out of bed. His master's son, James, Jr., struck him, only to have the slave respond in kind. James, Sr., came to his son's defense but was "choked" and cut across one of his hands by the knife-wielding Luke. After running away to Philadelphia, Luke was captured and returned to his master. Subsequently, he was accused of setting fire to the Whitakers' barn, which contained four hundred bushels of corn together with fodder and other crops; of trying to kill other slaves; of stealing corn and wool; of throwing Whitaker's daughter to the kitchen floor and pushing her female cousin into the cooking fire; and stealing his master's gun. Understandably, the Whitakers were "really afraid of Luke" when he was at home.[32]

Other slaves who attacked or threatened their masters included Absalom Morris of Sussex, who armed himself with pistols and a knife and "declared himself resolved to take his master's life in 1807." In 1827 in Kent County, Francis Register's slave, Jacob Fisher, refused to work, stole from his master, and carried with him a large knife for the avowed purpose of murdering Register "if he attempted to correct him." Not surprisingly, Register maintained that Fisher acted in a manner "to endanger the safety" of his family. In 1833, New Castle

County slave George Robinson was described as so dangerous that no one would buy him or rent him from his master for fear "of some violence to their persons or property." The twenty-two-year-old Robinson at the time was in jail where he "swears that he will be revenged if he ever gets out." Peter Bostic of eastern New Castle County not only defied his mistress's authority but also, in 1838, "struck with an ax and wounded" a male member of her family while "swearing at the same time that he would kill him."[33]

Slave owners found that black women could be as dangerous as their male counterparts, especially when they turned to arson. In 1836, Grace Nathan of Red Lion Hundred, in southern New Castle County, not only stole from her master but also twice tried to burn down his house and then threatened his wife. Phyllis, a slave in central Kent County, set her owner's home ablaze in 1783 and then, when confronted by authorities, insisted that "the Devil tempted her to burn the house." In 1848, twenty-one-year-old Maria Williams from Appoquinimink Hundred, New Castle County, burned to the ground her master's barn, stable, and corn sheds and in the process destroyed two thousand bushels of corn, considerable stores of oats and fodder, and farming implements. Leah from Northwest Fork, Sussex County, set her master's home on fire in 1822 and afterward confessed.[34] Arson was a particularly difficult form of terrorism for slave owners to control because it was hard to gather enough evidence for a conviction. Cassandra Holland of near the town of New Castle, for example, was perceived by her owner as impudent and troublesome despite his kindly treatment of her. On December 18, 1848, while he was away, she was suspected of burning his house to the ground. The evidence, however, was not sufficient to convict her.[35]

Equally alarming throughout Delaware and the rest of the South was the perception that female slaves were particularly prone to poisoning their owners. In 1837, Abraham Eves, a farmer living near New Castle, reported that his two female slaves tried to poison his entire family. It seems that twenty-two-year-old Phillis and thirteen-year-old Betsey routinely served their master and mistress by "doing kitchen work and cooking." On February 12, as usual, the two slaves prepared breakfast. On drinking their coffee, several members of the Eves family remarked "that the coffee had a peculiar taste, different from what it usually had." Abraham became dizzy, developed a headache, and staggered when he walked; the others had the same symptoms. A physician was called in and discovered that they had been poisoned by jimsonweed added to the coffee. (This method of poisoning was common in Africa.) Although Phillis and Betsey were arrested and placed in jail, we do not know the outcome of their trial. More often than not, however, the poison of choice was not jimpsonweed but arsenic, as used by Sarah Ann Thomas of Little Creek Hundred, Kent County, in an unsuccessful attempt to kill her master in 1844.[36]

Occasionally, poisoning could be a clumsy affair, easily detected by the owner. In 1840, Hannah Hall, also of near New Castle, was declared by her master, David Booth, as "unsafe and dangerous to keep" after she had mixed "tobacco, lamp oil, grease, or other nauseous substances into the coffee and victuals of the family, to the alarm and uneasiness" of his wife and children. Sometimes, after the purchase, the new master discovered that his slaves had a history of attempting to poison their previous owner, but poisoning was not restricted to female slaves. In 1792 an owner in southern Kent County was convinced that he was in danger of being poisoned by his slave Simon. In 1811, Michael, a slave in southern New Castle County, was accused of providing his niece Judith with the poison to kill her master. Two decades later, George Russell of Kent County made three different attempts to poison his owner's family. The potential victims were not always restricted to the master and his family. Indeed, in 1840, Peter Wilson threatened to poison every one of his fellow slaves if he were sold.[37]

The scarcity of extant records makes it impossible to generalize about how often Delaware slaves engaged in physical attacks, poisoning, and arson against their owners, or to trace trends in these types of violence over time. But there is evidence that these sometimes hard-to-detect crimes created a climate of distrust and unease among masters as they contemplated possible actions by their slaves. Also contributing to this unease among slaveholders and other whites was their perception that male African-American slaves were dangerous because they lusted after white women. The earliest record of the possible rape of a white woman by a black slave appeared in New Castle County in 1731.[38] For rapes of this nature, death was the usual punishment. For attempted rape a convicted slave faced the same punishment inflicted in 1770 on Joe of Kent County, who was forced to stand "with both ears nailed to the pillory" for four hours, after which they were to be "cut off low to his head." Ten years later in Sussex, Prince was found guilty of the attempted rape of a white girl and also was sentenced to have his ears nailed to the pillory and then cut off. Due to the intercession of his master, who doubtless feared the permanent scarring of a valuable slave, Prince was pardoned by President (that is, Governor) Caesar Rodney.[39]

In 1789, Delaware's special negro courts were abolished only to be resurrected in 1797, but now their jurisdiction was restricted to rape charges brought by white women against male slaves. In 1827, probably due to the declining numbers of enslaved blacks, the special courts were finally abolished and the responsibility for trying slaves charged with raping white women was transferred to the Courts of General Quarter Sessions. Although violation of white women by slaves was not common according to the meager evidence available, the resurrection of the special courts for the sole purpose of trying rape cases testifies to continued unease in white Delaware over the possibility of such sexual assaults.[40]

Particularly unsettling to whites was the possibility of sexual attacks in isolated settings. Those fears were realized on the Sussex farm of John Jones, not far from Milton, in 1800. The farm included a cow pen, located about one-half mile from the house where Jones's wife, Sarah, went every morning to milk the family's cows. George, owned by Susan Heavelow but probably hired out to Jones, had been with the family for almost five months. On August 22, while Jones was at work in his shop near the house, George surprised the unsuspecting Sarah at the cow pen and, in her words, "threw me down, choked me and smothered me, and proceeded to commit a rape." After warning her not to say anything to anyone, George fled the scene. Sarah, her nose and mouth bleeding and her body bruised, told her husband what had happened, and he took down his gun to shoot George but the slave had already gone. When he was finally apprehended a few days later, George admitted to grabbing Sarah but not to raping her. After hearing other testimony, however, the court found him guilty, and he was executed in Georgetown. As was customary, the court also determined two-thirds of the dead slave's value which then was given by the county as compensation to his owner, Mistress Heavelow.[41]

Slaveholders' daughters, apprenticed white girls, and neighbors also were perceived to be sexual targets. In 1841, for example, Jeremiah of Pencader Hundred, New Castle County, was accused of attempting "by force to have carnal knowledge" of his master's seven-year-old daughter. That same year, in nearby Red Lion Hundred, twenty-two-year-old Israel broke into his master's home and forced his way into the bed of a thirteen-year-old bound white servant "with the intention of having carnal intercourse with said girl against her will." And finally, a neighbor was assaulted by Manuel of Little Creek Hundred, Kent County, in 1826. Evidently this was not the first time that Manuel was accused of attempted rape.[42]

~

Many masters, however, found virtue and other admirable traits in certain slaves and learned to trust and appreciate them. John Dickinson expressed his confidence in Cato and Mingo by sending them on long journeys to deliver important messages during the Revolution. A decade later, Thomas Lewis of Kent County referred to

Belinda as "my trusty negro woman."[43] Riley Ake of Sussex called George "an obedient servant" in 1798, while the previously mentioned Maria of Kent County, who had helped to raise her mistress's children, was described in 1786 as "a faithful servant." In the same year in Kent County, Adam, Rebecca, and their daughter Mintee were given their immediate freedom "for and in consideration of their good services." In the town of New Castle in 1785, Caesar was praised for his "long and faithful service in our family." In the same county two years later, bondswoman Grace Bailey was described by her master as having "behaved herself honestly, soberly and industriously." On rare occasions, the gentry might even recognize certain exceptional talents in their slaves. Cuffe, owned by Abraham Pryor of Sussex County, used such "a pure and elegant" language in prayer that it clearly testified to the presence of "the natural force of genius and inspiration."[44]

Slaveholders were often sensitive to at least some of the concerns of their blacks. Many masters were aware of their slaves' fears of being sold or bequeathed to new owners, and they understood that their bondsmen and bondswomen were most concerned with being sold, either legally or illegally, out of state. They also understood that no event was more unsettling than the death of the master or mistress because of the subsequent division of the estate. To relieve these concerns, many owners added specific clauses to their wills to protect and reassure certain favored blacks.

Caesar Rodney, with holdings southeast of Dover, directed in his will in 1784 that those slaves not freed outright were to be manumitted upon reaching the age of twenty-five; and, while waiting for manumission, they were not to be sold out of state. In 1799 an illiterate master from Sussex directed his executor to take care that Isaac, George, and Dinah "not be sold or sent out of state." Simon Kollock's will, written in 1816 in Dagsboro Hundred, Sussex, required that slaves Harry, Cyrus, Juba, and Sabra not be sold by his heirs to anyone who might take them to the Carolinas. In 1812, Robert Marvel of Sussex willed that his three slaves not be moved out of state; and, in the same county in 1820, a mistress specifically directed the same in her will for Rose and her son William.[45]

To ease some of these apprehensions, a small number of slaveholders simply banned all in-state as well as out-of-state sales by heirs of their favorite slaves. In 1721, Joseph Wood of New Castle County provided in his will that his wife could not sell Grace or even hire her out "to any other person whatsoever." In the southern part of the same county in 1789, John Taylor stated in his will that "old negro man Seaser" be allowed to live with Taylor's son and "not to be sold ever." In Kent County in 1733, another slaveholder's will dictated that his slaves were "to be kept on the same land, not to be removed." In

Sussex in 1800, Joshua James left Nathan to his son Elias James, with the proviso that the slave be taken from Elias if the latter attempted to sell him in or out of the county.[46]

In 1785 a southern New Castle County resident expressed the sentiments of a number of owners when he provided that his enslaved blacks "be permitted to choose their own masters" upon his death. Likewise, in 1763, Susannah of Kent County was allowed by her mistress's will "to choose the [future] master." In Sussex in 1766, Peter also was allowed "the liberty of choosing a master" for himself provided that his new owner "pay £50 for him"; three decades later, Daniel, after the death of his owner's wife, was also "to choose his master." In the same county, in 1798, Amy was left to her owner's daughter, but only "if she will go willingly." For Flora, who lived in New Castle County in the 1780s, the right to choose her master also included the right to choose the new owners of her four children. One master did not wait for his own death to give his slave a choice. In 1766 a well-regarded "healthy negro man, aged twenty-one," from Mill Creek Hundred, New Castle County, was given the option of moving to the frontier with his owner or remaining in Delaware to be sold; he chose to stay.[47]

Slaveholders' wills often provided favorite blacks with a small inheritance. In 1743 in Sussex, James Martin left Timothy "an old jacket and old breeches and four of the worst" of his shirts. In 1769, also in Sussex, Comfort Jenkins left her three slaves "their beds and furniture," which they evidently took with them to the homes of their new owners. Five years later in Sussex, Sarah Black, who signed her will with an "X", left "one of my worst gowns and petticoats" to her slave Hara and an old gown to Ummi, while Adam received some of his mistress's dead husband's "worst clothes." About the same time, a Kent County mistress favored Ruth with some of her own wearing apparel. In northern New Castle County, a will written in 1789 provided Deray with £10.[48]

Clearly, a slaveholder could register appreciation of and fondness for an individual black through manumission. There were so many other motives behind manumissions, however, that the act alone cannot be regarded as proof of a master's high regard for his slave. (Manumissions will be dealt with further in Chapter V.) If, however, a manumission was accompanied by a significant bequest from the master's estate, then this act indicated considerable affection. Among the earliest examples was the 1720 will of Evan Jones of Kent County, which manumitted Coffey and Sue and provided that they be "well clothed." Coffey even inherited Jones's farm and fifty additional acres. Jones also left to his two slaves a ewe, cow, horse, and his gun. In

1784, Charles and Rachel of Kent were left a cow and calf and up to an acre of land along with manumission.[49]

In Sussex in 1790, Abner and his wife Hannah received their freedom and a horse, cow, calf, ewe, lamb, several pigs, a loom, and £10 in specie. In Lewes, four years earlier, Penelope Holt Jones left Charles, "whom I have lately manumitted," £20 when he reached the age of twenty-one. In his mistress's will of 1820, George of Sussex County received twelve dollars along with his freedom. Just to the north, near the St. Jones River in Kent in 1790, James, a blacksmith, was given delayed manumission by his master's will along with a set of blacksmith tools "as a further reward for his labor." In the town of New Castle at about the same time, Cesar was guaranteed £10 per year along with his freedom on the death of his master.

Among the more generous owners was Elizabeth Dushane of the town of St. George's in southern New Castle County. Her will, written in 1790, granted freedom to Catherine, Phebe, and Plato along with the use of thirteen acres of land and a newly built log house with a brick chimney, oven, and pine floors "above and below." In addition, the three slaves were to receive most of the furniture, kitchen utensils, and domestic implements such as two spinning wheels, two hackles, and some soap tubs together with blankets, a bed quilt, farming tools, two cows, four sheep, a pig, five bushels of corn, five bushels of rye, and three bushels of wheat. In the early nineteenth century in Broad Creek Hundred, in southwestern Sussex, Samuel Tilden's will freed Cuff and left him "my cart and oxen." In 1833 in Little Creek Hundred, Sussex, Hessy's master's will freed her when she reached thirty-five and left her twenty-five dollars.[50]

In their bequests to newly freed African-Americans, a few Delaware slave masters explicitly adopted the concept of freedom dues, which were given to white indentured servants at the end of their period of servitude. One example was an owner from the town of New Castle, whose will, written in 1789, gave Nel Jacobs her freedom when she reached twenty-three as well as "freedom dues according to the custom of the country in the cases of apprentices and servants." Freedom dues traditionally included new clothes and artisans' or farmers' tools. The 1817 will of an illiterate master from western Sussex provided each of his female slaves with freedom and a new suit of clothes, and the 1805 manumitting will of an owner from Sussex gave each of her enslaved women a spinning wheel and her male slave an ax.[51]

One of the most varied bequests accompanying manumission was that left by an illiterate mistress from Broad Creek Hundred, in eastern Sussex, to her five freed slaves in 1818. Daniel was given a horse and lamb; Rachel, a horse, lamb, ewe, pewter basin, and six cups and saucers; Isaac, a colt, ewe, and lamb; and Abraham, two sheep, one yoke of oxen, one of the "worse beds," one sheet, and three blankets. Benjamin received no material goods but was left forty dollars. Numerous bequests by other masters left items ranging from money, land, and freedom suits to plow horses, oxen, farm equipment, and harvested crops. In 1819 the will of Mitchell Kershaw of southwestern Sussex immediately freed two adult slaves and promised freedom to eleven others when they reached twenty-one. In addition, he left two-thirds of his estate to be equally divided among his young slaves when they became free. The remaining third was also to go to the young blacks after Kershaw's wife died. One slave master in Kent summarized the feelings behind these manumissions and bequests when he wrote in his will in 1773 that Sabena was to "be set at liberty in recompense of her past good services," and that his heirs must take care of her if bodily infirmities or sickness made her "incapable of maintaining herself."[52]

The desire to look after his slave in her old age was not unique to Sabena's master. While many owners cynically freed older blacks when they were no longer capable of productive work,[53] still others were genuinely committed to those slaves who had toiled hard for them through the years. An honest concern is reflected in the wills of some slaveholders as they attempted to establish rather crude and certainly meager old-age provisions for their favorites, whether they were now free or remained in bondage. This spirit is captured in the 1765 words of Nicholas Loockerman of near Dover. After leaving at least thirteen slaves to various heirs, Loockerman's will made a special case of old Hagar, whom "I desire may not be put to hard labor" so that she may spend "the remainder of her days in quiet."[54]

In general, old-age maintenance of both enslaved and newly freed blacks became the responsibility of the master's executors and heirs. In 1753 a Kent County slaveholder stipulated that if old Judah "should grow invalid," his executors "shall maintain her." In 1774 in New Castle County, a "yeoman" depended on his heirs for the maintenance of his female slave in old age, while in the same county ten years later another master required his son Isaac to support Peg in her declining years. In 1762 in Sussex, a slaveholder left to her grandson "the maintenance of . . . Mirea if she should necessarily want." Eight years later, also in Sussex, a master provided that if "anything befall" any of the three slaves he had freed "so that they can not maintain themselves," then "my children shall maintain them."[55] In 1794, Betheul Wattson of Cedar Creek Hundred, Sussex, directed in his will that "whereas my Negro woman Nancy may live to become a charge, my desire is that she be supported by all my heirs in general." And in 1822 another

Sussex slaveholder left his "two old black people, Abner and Comfort, for my said son Isaac to take care of."[56]

To help heirs support favored slaves in their old age, masters sometimes left livestock, land, tools, a guaranteed place to stay, or part of the estate. In Kent County in 1789, for example, Thomas Lewis left to his son Thomas "a cow and a calf in order to help support my trusty Negro woman Belinda." In 1803 in Broad Creek Hundred, Sussex, Joseph Johnson willed that Sarah could be free if she desired; and, if so, she was to be given two acres by his son on which to build a house and garden "to cultivate as she may choose" during the remaining years of her life. On Sarah's death, her daughter was to inherit the property. In Broadkill Hundred, Sussex, in 1797, Rispah's master's will granted her freedom at the death of his wife, along with a spinning wheel and "the privilege of a home upon my plantation during her life." In 1833, just to the north in Cedar Creek Hundred, David Smith freed four slaves through delayed manumission and simultaneously willed that "old George and Rachel be well taken care of when they become infirm, out of my estate." More specific was the £30 left by John Way to provide for the old age of his female slave living in Mill Creek Hundred, New Castle, in 1774.[57]

Other types of support for older slaves were spelled out in masters' wills. In 1795, Ann Waller of Cedar Creek Hundred directed that Sam be rented out, "his hire to be applied to support my Negro woman called Sarah." Sam was to continue to work in that capacity until Sarah died. Also in Sussex in the same year, a will required Isaac, who would be freed when he reached twenty-eight, subsequently to support his mother at the rate of £6 per year. In a third example in Sussex fifteen years later, a master offered freedom to Draper provided that the latter "maintain" his own grandmother Rose until she died. Some planters expressed concern for the welfare of their blacks in other ways. John Dickinson, for example, had Quaker physician Nathaniel Luff look in on some of his former slaves, "part of whom have the marks of extreme old age and its concomitant consequences, infirmity." Stokeley Sturgis, also of Kent, told his former slaves to make his house their home if they were sick or without a place to stay.[58]

~

Perhaps even more than elsewhere in early America, Delaware slaveholders felt responsible for the welfare of their black bondsmen, in some cases even after manumission. The master's paternalism may have reflected appreciation for certain slaves or it may have been encouraged by the spread of the principles of justice and equality

espoused by the Society of Friends, the Methodists, and the supporters of the ideals of the Revolution. But the roots of this paternalism
may also be found in the remnants of some Old World traditions that
were preserved in conservative Delaware. In premodern England,
seignorial rights had been accompanied by seignorial obligations and
duties. While the lord of the manor had the right to exploit the labor of
his peasants, he was also expected to provide for their security. This
unwritten law of reciprocal obligation gave Englishmen of the period
a sense of community.

Although the Anglo-Saxon gentry in Delaware and elsewhere in
the colonial South exhibited strong individualistic traits from the very
beginning, they neither totally rejected their ancestral traditions nor
turned their backs on custom. In their rush to emulate the English gentry during the mideighteenth century, Delaware planters reinforced
latent traditions brought over from England decades earlier. One of
those traditions, in theory at least, held that those possessing landed
wealth were responsible for the welfare of dependent laborers. Serfs
and, later, a semi-free peasantry fit that category in the Old World;
and in the New World, it was black slaves.

Strengthening this sense of personal responsibility was the changing nature of the slave population. By the late colonial period, slaveholders were dealing with blacks who were increasingly American-born
rather than African-born. Thus, on the eve of the Revolution, Delaware masters now knew most, if not all, of their bondspeople from
birth and were developing personal attachments that often lasted a
lifetime. And because these slaves had been born into servitude, owners spent less time in training them and thus had more time to observe
their changing culture as the alien ways of the African-born gave way
to less "outlandish" patterns of behavior by their American-born children and grandchildren. Therefore, it was easier for a slaveholder to
view his blacks as "my people."[59]

All of these factors contributed to the development of a relatively
strong paternalistic tradition among many Delaware slave owners by
the late eighteenth century. Although paternalism in the Chesapeake
followed a similar developmental time frame, it did not become really
widespread in the Deep South until well into the nineteenth century.
There, the time lag may have been due partly to the continuing flow
during the late eighteenth century of "outlandish" Africans into the
ports of Charleston and Savannah long after slave imports into Delaware and the Chesapeake had ceased.[60]

The increasing sense of personal responsibility, however, was only
one part of the paternalism that marked the relationship of many Delaware masters to their slaves after the mideighteenth century. Even more
central to that paternalism was the exercise of control. Indeed, some

might argue that taking responsibility for slaves in their old age was merely one more example of the master keeping control over the lives of his African-Americans. An owner's dominance was established through physical and psychological techniques that were aimed at making his slaves both fearful and servile. Unfree blacks were constantly reminded by forms of reward and punishment just how dependent they were on the master's goodwill.

Success in controlling the lives of blacks was aided by the small size of the state's slave units. In the late colonial period the average number of slaves per master may have reached seven, but by the nineteenth century it had dropped to three. Thus, most masters had no choice but to labor in the fields alongside their black bondsmen and bondswomen on a daily basis, often from nine to fourteen hours per day. But even when they returned from the fields at night, slaves found little relief from contact with the master and his family. Unlike other areas of the South where, by the nineteenth century, large numbers of unfree African-Americans found some privacy in their own quarters some distance from the big house, Delaware slaves continued to live in the attic, storeroom, cellar, or kitchen of their master's house, or in nearby cabins or other outbuildings. For the entire slave era, the vast majority of them spent the whole day in close proximity to the master and his family.[61]

Just how intimate the relationships were between these masters and their slaves is indicated by statistics on slave unit size. In 1800, the first year for which detailed census figures are available for Delaware, 1,816, or 22 percent, of its households owned slaves. But only nine families, which represented considerably less than 1 percent of the state's slaveholders, owned more than twenty slaves. Only two— Joseph Porter of Duck Creek Hundred in northern Kent County with forty-six slaves and Cantwell Jones of Appoquinimink Hundred in lower New Castle County with thirty-two slaves—owned more than thirty.[62] Even the two largest slave units in 1800 were small enough so that the masters were intimately acquainted with all of their unfree blacks. Under these conditions, very little that happened went unnoticed. And this knowledge, in turn, was helpful to slaveholders as they sought to control almost every aspect of their bondspeople's lives.

Control was exercised from cradle to grave by the denial of certain basic human rights. In Delaware, African-American slaves were not allowed to testify in court against a white person for most of the era; moreover, they were sometimes denied a jury trial, and they always were denied a trial in which the jury included blacks. In addition, enslaved blacks generally could not congregate in large groups or travel very far without a pass. Perhaps most important, Delaware joined other southern states in denying any official recognition of slave

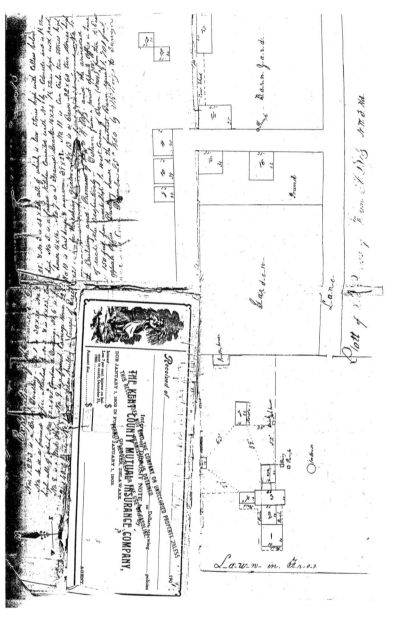

Plat of Ross Mansion and slave cabin near Seaford, 1861. *Courtesy of Claudia Melson and the Delaware State Archives, Dover.*

marriages and therefore of the integrity of the slave family. Denying the official existence of family ties allowed masters in good conscience to sell some husbands or wives or children while keeping others. A master's denial of black family ties also may have been driven by the desire to weaken biological kinship and thus force his slaves to become even more dependent on him for both physical and psychic sustenance.

Slaveholders further diminished black families by denying them surnames. Only in the nineteenth century would even a sizable minority of Delaware slaves, such as Rachel and Maciah Bell, Ann Griffith, William Stone, and Elizabeth Hambleton, have last names attached to given names.[63] Although most inhabitants of premodern rural societies lacked surnames, to live in Delaware or in any other part of the South where everyone but the enslaved had them must have been demeaning.

To further demonstrate their inferiority, slaves were usually interred in ground separate from the burial plot used by the master's family. Moreover, although the dinner table was sometimes more difficult to segregate than the burying ground, Delaware slaves usually took their meals separate from the master's family. Mary Parker Welch confirmed this pattern of segregation when she reported that former slaves visiting her family in Milton, Sussex County, were asked to stay and take a meal with the cook or with the house servants but never with the Welch family.[64]

To better control their slaves and encourage hard work, masters created a system of rewards. If, as has already been noted, a slave performed well over a number of years, the reward could be freedom or a simple form of old-age maintenance. In some cases, the promise of manumission at some future date depended on continued good behavior. In Sussex in 1795, James was to have his freedom in four years if he "behaves himself . . . as he ought to do"; but if he "misbehaves himself," he was to be sold. In northern New Castle County in 1783, Ben and Dinah were promised freedom when they reached the age of twenty-one provided that they "do and faithfully obey the commands of my said wife."[65]

Slaves were also rewarded for good behavior with vacations, passes, and provisions. Except during harvesttime, masters may have given their slaves some Saturday afternoons and certainly all day Sunday off as well as an extended Christmas-New Year's holiday. These holidays and other liberties could be contracted or expanded for certain favored slaves. Travel passes and provisions of food might be altered in response to behavior, and sometimes favorites were rewarded with gifts. Sally Ridgely of Dover, about to return from Washington in

1813, promised handsome presents for her slave Serena as well as for all of the Ridgely children.[66]

Punishments and threats of punishments were constantly used to keep slaves in line. If black bondspeople did not obey their masters in Delaware or elsewhere in the Upper South, their owners threatened to sell them to a state where they would be treated very harshly. In the eighteenth century, the most feared destinations were Georgia and the Carolinas; while in the nineteenth century, Alabama, Mississippi, Louisiana, Texas, Arkansas, and Florida were added to the list. Indeed, Delaware's slaveholders made it clear that "a negro that showed any spirit was looked upon as one would upon a vicious horse, and would suddenly disappear, being sold to the traders for the far southern market." Mulatto Amy of Kent County admitted in 1794 that she was afraid "of being transported [as] a slave into the most Algerian parts of this continent." Levin Holden of near Laurel in the 1850s also "had a perfect horror of a more southern latitude." (For obvious reasons, Delaware slave masters encouraged that "horror.") Particularly upsetting to enslaved African-Americans was the prospect of their children being sold to the Deep South. Grace Hayes of New Castle County reflected this concern when she became "apprehensive" in 1803 that her daughter Rachel would be "sold to Georgia." Even some slaveholders expressed the same concern. Simon Kollock of southern Sussex, upset over the possibility of that fate for his slaves after his own death, wrote in 1816, "I detest the trade." Especially upsetting to Kollock and to many other whites was the fact that this interstate trade in bondspeople was illegal.[67]

Throughout most of the eighteenth century, slavery in Delaware was profitable because, in addition to providing cheap labor, it produced a human commodity for sale. Prior to 1787 the value of a Delaware slave was comparable to one in the nearby Chesapeake region. In the post-1787 period, however, the price of Chesapeake slaves increased remarkably, with a prime Virginia field hand selling for $350 in 1800, $900 in 1837, and $1,300 in 1856.[68] Driving up the value of Chesapeake slaves was the almost insatiable demand for more African-Americans by the rapidly developing cotton-producing states of the Deep South, but Delaware's slaveholders were not the beneficiaries of this bull market in unfree African-Americans. In 1787 the General Assembly banned further exportation of slaves to the Carolinas, Georgia, and the West Indies; and in 1789, Maryland and Virginia were added to the list of states to which Delaware slaves could not be sold. In practical terms, the legislation of 1787 and 1789 outlawed the sale of these slaves beyond the state's boundaries. But to remove any lingering doubts, in 1797 the General Assembly declared any slave sold out of state to be automatically free.[69]

The legal banning of interstate sales led to a pronounced decline in the market value of Delaware slaves when compared to those in other southern states. After 1789 the only legitimate market for these unfree blacks was intrastate, and Delawareans were far less inclined to pay premium prices for black bondspeople than were the hard-driving cotton planters of the lower Mississippi Valley. By 1806 the value of a prime Delaware field hand had fallen to about 36 percent of the value of a comparable slave in Virginia. Over the next five decades, the disparity widened slightly so that by 1853 a prime Delaware field hand was worth only about 28 percent of the value of his Virginia peer.[70]

The ban on slave exports and the resulting dramatic drop in the comparative market value of its slaves played a crucial role in the early decline of slavery in Delaware. Because it was the only southern state to outlaw the exportation of slaves, bondage in Delaware diverged significantly from the Chesapeake pattern during the antebellum era.[71] Not surprisingly, however, despite the halt in legal interstate trafficking, a few masters found ways to sell their bondspeople illegally to slave markets in the Deep South.[72] Some of these men, such as Jacob Griffin of Kent County, were caught and indicted. A few, such as Enoch Gabb of Kent County, were found guilty and heavily fined for selling slaves to "Carolina" or other destinations, but most indicted defendants were not convicted.

Oftentimes, the slaveholder used deception to avoid the law and to lull his slaves into complacency during the first stage of an illegal out-of-state sale. In 1835 in Lewes, for example, Robert Hall told his four slaves that he was moving them to Concord in western Sussex when their real destination was Alabama.[73] Among the most devious masters was Robert Dawson of western Kent, who in 1822 wanted to sell his slave, Louisa Bayard, to an out-of-state buyer. To circumvent the law, he arranged to have Bayard's disappearance look like a kidnapping in the presence of a white witness. Samuel Rich, an unsuspecting white hired hand, was told by Dawson to drive a wagon with the slave aboard toward the Maryland border. As planned by Dawson, a stranger overtook them in a gig and asked for directions to Denton, Maryland. He then pretended not to understand Rich's answer and offered to pay both Rich and Bayard if they would accompany him on the road to Denton. Rich untied the horse from his wagon and followed on horseback while the stranger and the slave rode together in the gig.[74]

As darkness approached, the slave trader suddenly turned on Bayard and attempted to tie her hands and feet, but the now-frightened slave fought back. Despite several blows to the head, she broke away and hid in nearby bushes. The frustrated trader, unable to find her, rode on toward Denton while a puzzled Rich rode back in the direction of Dawson's farm to pick up the wagon. On the way he met Bayard, who climbed up behind him on the horse. The two then returned to the farm. The next year, in court, Rich testified to Dawson's deviousness.[75]

Delaware slaves were well aware that some interstate sales would continue despite being banned. This fear of being illegally sold to "Algerian" parts of America was used by masters to intimidate their bondspeople right up until the Civil War. Even being sold to another master in Delaware was upsetting. Owners knew this and used this threat to make examples of wayward slaves. In 1812, for instance, Elizabeth McKee of Wilmington advertised two male slaves for sale as their punishment for stealing.[76]

The master's whip created fear of another sort. When other forms of physical and psychic rewards and punishments were exhausted, slave owners generally turned to the lash. Indeed, a Sussex County newspaper pointed out in 1864 that the Union side hoped to convince Delaware's slaves to enlist because Uncle Sam would pay "in greenbacks, instead of lashed backs."[77] Brutal punishment such as flogging and mutilation was taken for granted in colonial Delaware and was administered to both blacks and whites. Although public mutilations were less common by the late eighteenth century, the whipping post continued to be part of the state's criminal justice system until the midtwentieth century.[78]

Traditionally, the whip was used as a corrective punishment for disobedient children as well as for criminals and slaves. Joseph A. Conwell, who was raised on a Sussex farm near Milton during the midnineteenth century, remembered "a good sized white girl" being whipped in school "until her back was a mass of welts." But more than any other group, enslaved African-Americans felt the sting of cowhide. As Conwell also observed, "The lash was applied to the backs of slaves because the belief prevailed that corporal punishment was both necessary and wholesome."[79]

How often did Delaware slaveholders use the whip? Probably as much as in the rest of the South, where "it was the rare slave who totally escaped the lash." The runaway slave notices that appeared in eighteenth-century newspapers went into considerable detail about scars on the bodies of certain black fugitives, although, of some ninety-eight notices for Delaware runaways, not one listed a whipping scar.[80] But there were other indications that some masters routinely used the whip and other kinds of corporal punishment. In 1787 the General Assembly received a petition from abolitionists which urged that until slavery could be abolished in the state, it was hoped that the legislature "would adopt some measures . . . to restrain the punishment of slaves at the mere will and pleasure of their masters, which is often very tyrannically and cruelly exercised, and which may legally extend to everything but murder."

Punishment "tyranically and cruelly exercised" usually meant the whip. This and two other petitions of the same year had a total of 170 signatures, and many of the signatories were prominent Quakers and Methodists. In the following year a number of similar petitions appeared, but evidently no action was taken that restricted slaveholders from physically abusing their bondspeople.[81] Thomas Rodney of Kent County may have been typical. In 1790 he sent a slave to his son with the admonition not to threaten or abuse him but to treat him in a gentle manner. However, four years later, when his slave Jim neglected his duties, Rodney gave him "a little of the cow skin." In the 1850s, Robert, a slave from Seaford, Sussex County, reported that in his neighborhood flogging was an "everyday occurrence."[82]

In the hands of a few particularly brutal whites, unrestricted use of the whip led to death. In 1781, near Christiana Bridge in New Castle County, Sabrina was tied up and whipped so severely that she died from the effects of the beating. Although the white man who whipped her was indicted for manslaughter, the charges were subsequently dropped. In northeast Sussex in 1805, Adam Black accused Solomon of stealing and then bragged that five hundred lashes would cause him to mend his ways. Later, a coroner's inquest charged Black with beating Solomon to death with a "cowskin whip." Prettyman Cannon of Broad Creek Hundred, in southwestern Sussex, severely flogged his hired slave woman Ador in 1827 for refusing to follow instructions and for attempting to damage a loom. Cannon, too, bragged that he gave Ador "the worst beating he had ever gave a Negro in his life." The lash wounds on her back and buttocks became infected, and she died twenty-six days after his whip cut into her body. An inquest was held, but the results are not known.[83]

The most chilling account of death by flogging concerned Michael, originally owned by William Corbit of St. George's Hundred in southern New Castle County. In 1811 he gave poison to his niece Judith, the slave of Benjamin Walmsley who lived near Corbit, and told her to put it in her master's tea because it would make him "a sound man." But Judith had second thoughts and removed the poison with a spoon and "throwed it in the mud." Somehow, Walmsley found out and, after questioning Judith, met Corbit in a room in a nearby tavern where he demanded that Michael be either sold to him or shipped out of state. Corbit responded by selling him to Walmsley on the spot and then called an obviously shaken Michael into the room to meet his new master. After plying his new slave with a drink, Walmsley ordered him to cross his wrists so that he could be tied up. Michael's reluctance to obey abruptly ended when Walmsley drew a pistol and threatened "to blow [his] brains out." Michael then was dumped into a cart. All the way to Walmsley's farm he muttered that he would "be a dead man by tomorrow morning."

Michael was no sooner out of the cart and into Walmsley's house when his new master demanded to know how he had gotten the poison, but he "would be damned if he would tell him." An angry Walmsley shot back that if Michael did not tell, he "would receive a hell of a beating." Michael was then taken into another room and stripped; his hands were tied over his head to a horizontal pole set up to hang pig carcasses. Walmsley flogged him for about an hour with a cart whip, but Michael refused to disclose his source. Afterward, two slaves cut him down and led him into a room where his new master and mistress were sitting.

Michael was placed in chains next to the fireplace. Twice the now disoriented and very ill slave fell against the fireplace, cutting his head. For a while he lay on the floor but then attempted to thrust various parts of his body into the flames. When he calmed down, he was left, tied hand and foot, on the floor while Walmsley and his wife retired to another room for the night. At daybreak, Michael was found dead. Walmsley was subsequently indicted for murder but was found not guilty by the Court of Oyer and Terminer in 1814.[84]

To break the spirit of resistance and independence in their enslaved African-Americans and turn them into dependent and loyal servants was the goal of Delaware's slaveholders. A Kent County master aimed at this objective in 1822 when he spoke about his slave, Jane Willis, whom he "thought he could brake [*sic*] . . . by working her in the cornfields."[85] Some slaveholders were convinced that their system of rewards and punishments produced submissive and obedient servants. In the 1830s some freedmen visited their former master's family in Milton, first "knocking humbly on the kitchen door" and then lingering "with reminiscences of the good old days." Obviously, although no longer slaves, these erstwhile bondsmen and bondswomen continued to exhibit traits that slaveholders expected their paternalistic system of bondage to produce. Indeed, in the minds of some whites, Delaware's slaves were loyal, dependent, and docile. A downstate newspaper in 1864 noted that from infancy slaves "have been trained to receive, without a murmur, the white man's scourge and to move with implicit obedience to the white man's command."[86]

Other whites in the state, however, believed that their slaves did not necessarily fit this idealized image. Not only did the many physical confrontations and attempts at arson and poisoning challenge this submissive stereotype, but also there was a sense that even seemingly docile African-Americans were deeply resentful of their bondage and would express this resentment and hostility if given a chance. John Dickinson was only one of many who recognized this threat when he wrote from Wilmington in 1804 that slaves are "internal enemies to be watched and guarded against." The reason was self-evident. In a court case in Georgetown in 1793, defense attorneys argued convincingly that African-Americans "can not love those who depress and enslave them." To the contrary, "their sentiments growing up from infancy, their prejudices, their wishes must all be hostile to those parts of the community who look down on them with contempt."[87]

These, then, were some of the perceptions held by slaveholders and other whites of slaves and the "peculiar institution" in Delaware. But what were the perceptions of the slaves themselves? Moreover, how did they live and survive physically, mentally, and spiritually under a system that attempted to eviscerate the spirit in order to subjugate the body?

Notes

1. Laura Gehringer, "Analytical Summaries of 1797 Tax Assessments of Kent County Hundreds," Bureau of Museums and Historic Sites, Dover, Delaware.

2. Orphans Court Records, Sussex, Kent, and New Castle counties (Kent records are in KCCH, Sussex and New Castle records are in DSA); Bushman and Hawley, eds., "A Random Sample," 112–15.

3. Smith, *After the Revolution*, 50–53; Herman, *The Stolen House*, 183.

4. George Hazzard (1830), Sussex County Estate Inventories, DSA. The generalizations about eighteenth- and nineteenth-century slaveholders are based on estate inventories from all three counties.

5. Jonathan Prude, "To Look Upon the Lower Sort," *Journal of American History* (June 1991): 127, 158; Isaac, *The Transformation of Virginia*, 39, 99; Mullin, *Flight and Rebellion*, 19.

6. Joseph Forman, September 2, 1778, Sussex County Estate Inventories, DSA.

7. Bausman and Munroe, eds., "James Tilton's Notes," 186.

8. Ibid.; New Castle, Kent, and Sussex estate inventories, passim, DSA; Hawke, *Everyday Life in Early America*, 74–78; Jack Larkin, *The Reshaping of Everyday Life, 1790–1840* (New York, 1988), 169–77.

9. Sussex, Kent, and New Castle County will books, passim, DSA and KCCH; Sussex, Kent, and New Castle County estate inventories, passim, DSA. Gloria L. Main in "Probate Records as a Source for Early American History," *William and Mary Quarterly* 32 (January 1975): 93, points out that few estate inventories of colonists south of Pennsylvania "included books of any kind."

10. Thomas Procter (1788), Kent County Will Book M, 184–85, and Elizabeth Goldsmith (1789), Kent County Will Book M, 220, KCCH; John B. Frame (1811), Sussex County Will Book No. 6, 461–62, SCCH.

11. Williams, *The Garden of American Methodism*, 98.

12. Ibid., 7–11, 96–97.

13. Ibid., passim.

14. Ibid., 97–98.

15. Ibid., 112–13.

16. Ibid., 99–102, 164–65.

17. Seymour Drescher, "British Way, French Way: Opinion Building and Revolution in the Second French Slave Emancipation," *American Historical Review* 96 (June 1991): 709.

18. For a brief summary of this Anglo-American perception see Kolchin, *American Slavery*, 14–15.

19. Ibid., 90; Thomas Rodney, undated, box 23, file 24, and Thomas Rodney, Origin of Subordination and Servitude, 1787, box 22, file 5, H. F. Brown Collection, HSD.

20. Case of Francis, Kent County, 1817, Slavery Material No. 2, 1764–1866, DSA.

21. David Brion Davis, *The Problem of Slavery in the Age of Revolution, 1770–1823* (Ithaca, NY, 1975), 41.

22. *Delaware Gazette*, 10/24/1789; *Laws of the State of Delaware*, 1:214; *The Messenger* (Georgetown, DE), 12/22/1859; *Delaware Gazette*, 8/24/1789; Justice, *Life and Ancestry of Warner Mifflin*, 85.

23. Deborah White to John Dickinson, June 3, 1793, John Dickinson Mansion Tenants' Correspondence, DSA; Cases of Alexander Clarkson and Martin Doherty, 1822, Kent County, Slavery Material, 1764–1866, Miscellaneous, DSA.

24. Justice, *Life and Ancestry of Warner Mifflin*, 97–98.

25. William Hughletts, 1793, Kent County, Slavery Material, 1764–1866, Miscellaneous, DSA; *Delaware Gazette*, 12/8/1792; John Gordon, 1836, Licenses to import and export slaves, Slavery Material, DSA; Justice, *Life and Ancestry of Warner Mifflin*, 79; Leon F. Litwack, *North of Slavery: The Negro in the Free States* (Chicago, 1961), 95.

26. Wood, *Black Majority*, 308–26; Thomas J. Davis, *A Rumor of Revolt: The "Great Negro Plot" in Colonial New York* (New York, 1985), 1–263; Kulikoff, "The Origins of Afro-American Society," 239–40.

27. *Minutes of the House of Assembly of the Three Counties upon Delaware, 1740–42* (N.p., 1929), 46–47.

28. *The Delaware Register*, I (1838), as printed in Harold B. Hancock and Madeline Dunn Hite, *Slavery, Steamboats, and Railroads: The History of 19th Century Seaford* (Seaford, DE, 1981), 71.

29. Ibid., 71–72.

30. Ibid.

31. John Ham, 1795, and Daniel George, 1825, Kent County, Slavery Material, 1764–1866, Miscellaneous, DSA; John Gordon, 1836, Elizabeth Clelands, 1838, and John McCone, 1848, New Castle Hundred, Licenses to import and export slaves, Slavery Material, DSA.

32. Horle, ed., *Records of the Courts of Sussex County, Delaware, 1677–1710*, 691, 693; James Whitaker, 1823, Kent County Depositions, Slavery Material, 1764–1866, Miscellaneous, DSA.

33. Boorstin, ed., *Delaware Cases*, 2:23–24; Francis Register, 1827, Kent County Depositions, Slavery Material, 1764–1866, Miscellaneous, DSA; Henry Whiteley, 1833, and Elizabeth Clelands, 1838, New Castle Hundred, Licenses to import and export slaves, Slavery Material, DSA.

34. John L. Deputy, 1836, New Castle Hundred, Licenses to import and export slaves, Slavery Material, DSA; Folder No. 3425, Examinations of Confessions, Slavery Material, ibid.; Elias S. Naudain, 1848, Appoquinimink Hundred, Licenses to import and export slaves, Slavery Material, ibid.; Harold B. Hancock,

Bridgeville: A Community History of the Nineteenth Century (Bridgeville, DE, 1985), 77.

35. John McCrone, 1848, New Castle Hundred, Licenses to import and export slaves, Slavery Material, DSA.

36. Abraham Eves, 1837, New Castle Hundred, Licenses to import and export slaves, Slavery Material, DSA; Sarah Ann Thomas (1844), Indictments, Kent County Court of General Sessions, ibid.

37. William Booth, 1840, and John Sutton, Jr., 1840, New Castle Hundred, Licenses to import and export slaves, Slavery Material, DSA; Lewis Prettyman, 1827, Kent County, Slavery Material, 1764–1866, ibid.; Joshua Clark, 1792, Petition, Read Petitions [1781–1793], R.G. 3200, ibid.; State vs. Benjamin Walmsley (1811), New Castle County Court of Oyer and Terminer, ibid.; John M. Layton to Jacob Stout, January 21, 1830, Jacob Stout, box 25, folder 12, H. F. Brown Collection, HSD.

38. *Pennsylvania Gazette*, 6/24–7/1/1731; 7/15–7/22/31.

39. Negro Joe, 1770, and Negro Charles, 1770, Court Trials, A Docket of the Trials of Negroes, Slavery Materials, DSA; Prince, 1780, Special Court for Negroes, Sussex County Court of Oyer and Terminer, ibid.

40. Delaware Agency Histories, Court for Trial of Negroes, reel 810, ibid. There is some indication that some slaves accused of rape were tried, after 1797, in other courts in addition to the slave courts. See, for example, Boorstin, ed., *Delaware Cases*, 1:137–39.

41. State vs. Negro George, November 21, 1800, in Boorstin, ed., *Delaware Cases*, 1:137–39.

42. Peter Springer, 1841, and Philip Reybold, 1841, Licenses to import and export slaves, Slavery Materials, DSA; Joseph Buckminster, 1826, petition, Slavery Material, 1764–1866, Miscellaneous, ibid.

43. Nash, *Forging Freedom: The Formation of Philadelphia's Black Community, 1720–1840* (Cambridge, MA, 1988), 50; Thomas Lewis (1789), Kent County Will Book M, 199, KCCH.

44. Riley Ake (1798), Sussex County Will Book D-5, 55, SCCH; Ann Walker (1786), 105–7, and Richard Lockwood (1786), 108, Kent County Will Book M, KCCH; Richard Williams, Esq. (1785), New Castle County Will Book M, 199–200, DSA; James Latimer, February 3, 1787, Slavery Folder 2, HSD; Thomas Rodney to Dr. Abraham Pryor, November 6, 1791, box 10, folder 8, Rodney Collection, HSD.

45. Caesar Rodney, Esq. (1784), Kent County Will Book L, 238, KCCH; Thomas Carlisle (1799), Sussex County Will Book D-5, 247, SCCH; Simon Kollock, Esq. (1816), 105–6, Robert Marvel (1817), 317, and Elzey Spicer (1820), 199, Sussex County Will Book No. 6, ibid.

46. Joseph Wood (1721), New Castle County Will Book C, 363–64, and John Taylor (1789), New Castle County Will Book N, vol. 1, DSA; Jonathan Stanton (1733), Kent County Will Book D, 60, KCCH; Joshua James (1800), Sussex County Will Book No. 6, 196, SCCH; Susannah Lewis (1763), Kent County Will Book K, 312, KCCH; Hannah Jacobs (1766), Sussex County Will Book No. 2, 316, SCCH; John Evans (1791), Sussex County Will Book D-5, 49, ibid; *Pennsylvania Gazette*, 12/4/1766.

47. John Meriss (1785), New Castle County Will Book M, 215, DSA; Susannah Lewis (1763), Kent County Will Book K, 312, KCCH; Hannah Jacobs (1766), Sussex County Will Book No. 2, 315, SCCH; John Evans (1791), 49, and Sarah Phillips (1798), 186, Sussex County Will Book D-5, ibid.; Sarah Noxon

(1780), New Castle County Will Book L, 186, DSA; *Pennsylvania Gazette*, 12/4/1766.

48. James Martin (circa 1743), 388, Comfort Jenkins (1769), 427, and Sarah Black (circa 1774), 536–37, Sussex County Will Book No. 1, SCCH; Elizabeth Fults (1772), Kent County Will Book L, 119, KCCH; Elizabeth Baldwin (1789), New Castle County Will Book N, 100, DSA.

49. Evan Jones (1720), Kent County Will Book D, 50, KCCH; Thomas Irons (1784), Kent County Will Book M, 44, ibid.

50. John Laws (1790), 264, and Penelope Holt Jones (1786), 308, Sussex County Will Book D-4, SCCH; Mary Lockwood (1820), Sussex County Will Book No. 7, 323, ibid.; Richard Smith (1790), Kent County Will Book M, 224–25, KCCH; Richard Williams (1785), New Castle County Will Book M, 199–200, DSA; Elizabeth Dushane (1790), New Castle County Will Book N, 234–36, ibid.

51. Ann Clay (1789), New Castle County Will Book N, 42–45, DSA; John Short (1817), Sussex County Will Book No. 7, 126–27, SCCH; Elizabeth Jackson (1805), Sussex County Will Book No. 6, 213, ibid.

52. Rhoda Mitchell (1818), Sussex County Will Book No. 6, 110–11, SCCH; John Martin (1773), Kent County Will Book L, 129, KCCH. A few other examples of bequests include Thomas Blackshare (1790), Kent County Will Book M, 235–36, KCCH; Covey Emerson (1773), Kent County Will Book L, 133–34, ibid.; John Short (1817), Sussex County Will Book No. 8, 126–27, SCCH; Samuel Tindal, Sr., Sussex County Will Book No. 6, 82, ibid.; Ann Hazzard (1801), Sussex County Will Book D-5, 286, ibid.; Mitchell Kershaw (1815), Sussex County Will Book No. 7, 127, ibid. Kershaw's will was not executed until four years after his death because the original executor found the will "unacceptable" and a second executor had to be found.

53. For indications that some masters simply dumped some old and crippled slaves on society by manumitting them see provisions in *Laws of the State of Delaware*, 1:214, 4:399. In general, however, there are few indications that in Delaware, as well as elsewhere in the United States, the widespread practice found in Brazil of freeing old, sick, and crippled slaves was common. See Carl Degler, *Neither Black nor White: Slavery and Race Relations in Brazil and the U.S.* (Madison, WI, 1986), 71.

54. Nicholas Loockerman (1765), Kent County Will Book L, 93, KCCH.

55. John Sipply (1753), Kent County Will Book K, 82, ibid.; John Way (1774), New Castle County Will Book K, 111, DSA; Isaac Alexander (1784), New Castle County Will Book M, 174, ibid.; Mary Humphrey (1762), 340, and Levi Spencer (1770), 395, Sussex County Will Book No. 2, SCCH.

56. Betheul Wattson, Sr. (1794), Sussex County Will Book D-4, 133, SCCH; Elihu Bredel (1822), Sussex County Will Book No. 6, 276, ibid.

57. Thomas Lewis (1789), Kent County Will Book M, 199, KCCH; Joseph Johnson (1803), Sussex County Will Book No. 6, 92, SCCH; Robert Jones (1797), Sussex County Will Book D-5, 136, ibid.; David Smith (1833), Sussex County Will Book No. 8, 132, ibid.; John Way (1774), New Castle County Will Book K, 111, DSA.

58. Ann Waller (1795), 141, and David Tubbs (1795), 90, Sussex County Will Book D-5, SCCH; John Williams, Sussex County Will Book No. 6, 430, ibid.; Logan Papers, 27:100, HSP; Allen, *The Life Experience*, 18.

59. The assumption that paternalism among Delaware masters increased after the mideighteenth century is based in part on what happened elsewhere in the

South (Kolchin, *American Slavery*, 59–60) and on the projection that after 1755 the majority of their slaves were American-born (see Chapter I). But it is also reflected in the increased mention of slaves in wills and personal records, which indicate that Delaware slaveholders were now developing a more personal interest in their blacks because the master had known them for his entire life (Wills and journals, passim, DSA). John M. Clayton reminisced about his great concern for his own slaves, which grew out of the fact that they were "companions in my childhood." John M. Clayton to Josiah Randall, New Castle, February 26, 1844, John M. Clayton Correspondence, HSD.

60. Kolchin, *American Slavery*, 111–13, 79; *Laws of the State of Delaware*, 2:886. Delaware outlawed the importation of slaves in 1787, as had Virginia in 1778. The U.S. Congress banned the importation of slaves anywhere in the country in 1808, which put an end to the international slave traffic in Charleston and Savannah.

61. Material supporting this generalization can be found in assorted will books, probate inventories, and in numerous other local sources. Cheryl Hayes, in "Cultural Space and Family Living: Patterns in Domestic Architecture, Queen Anne's County, Maryland, 1750–1776" (M.A. thesis, Georgetown University, 1974), 526, finds that slaves in this nearby Eastern Shore county lived in close proximity to their masters during the eighteenth century. By contrast, farther south, the villages of slave cabins that became increasingly common in the late eighteenth and early nineteenth centuries were usually set a considerable distance from the big house and the master's constant presence. Kolchin, *American Slavery*, 149.

62. Calculations made from figures compiled from Jackson, ed., *Delaware Census Index for 1800*, passim.

63. John Short (1817), Sussex County Will Book No. 8, 126–27, SCCH; Sussex, Kent, and New Castle County will books, passim, DSA.

64. For an example of a separate burial ground see "John Dickinson's Negroes," material collected and Xeroxed by James Stewart and Madeline Thomas from Logan Papers, 9:65 (microfilm reel, no. 1), HSP, stored in Bureau of Museums; Welch, ed., *Memoirs of Mary Parker Welch*, 140.

65. William Hall (circa 1799), Sussex County Will Book D-5, 208, SCCH; Evan Rice, Esq. (1783), New Castle County Will Book L, 408, DSA.

66. Blassingame, *The Slave Community*, 106; Kolchin, *Unfree Labor*, 107; de Valinger, ed., *A Calendar of Ridgely Family Letters*, 1:239.

67. Kulikoff, *Tobacco and Slaves*, 430; Welch, ed., *Memoirs of Mary Parker Welch*, 147; Warner Mifflin on behalf of Mulatto Amy, 1794, Petitions for Freedom, Slavery Material, 1764–1866, Miscellaneous, DSA; William Still, *The Underground Rail Road* (Chicago, 1970), 513; January 27, 1803, Abolition Society of Delaware Minutes, 1802–1807, HSD; Simon Kollock (1816), Sussex County Will Book No. 7, 106, SCCH.

68. Degler, *Neither Black nor White*, 62; Franklin and Moss, *From Slavery to Freedom*, 108.

69. *Laws of the State of Delaware*, 2:884–85, 942–43, 1321–25.

70. Munroe, *Federalist Delaware*, 158, 159n. Figures for Delaware are drawn from estate inventory records of all three counties. Specific sources include William Bradley (1806), and William Brown (1853), Sussex County Estate Inventories, DSA. Virginia figures are drawn from Franklin and Moss, *From Slavery to Freedom*, 108.

71. Kolchin, *American Slavery*, 129.

72. *Laws of the State of Delaware*, 2:667, 943, 1093; 4:339; 6:717; 7:126.

73. Jacob Griffin, 1837, Indictments, Manuscripts of Kent County Court of General Sessions, DSA; Boorstin, ed., *Delaware Cases*, 2:231; Negro Spicer, 1835, Petitions for Freedom, Slavery Material, 1805–1865, DSA.

74. Louisa Bayard, 1823, Petitions for Freedom, Slavery Material, 1805–1865, DSA.

75. Ibid.

76. de Valinger, ed., *A Calendar of Ridgely Family Letters*, 1:150.

77. *Weekly Union* (Georgetown, DE), 2/12/1864.

78. Two of the last examples of Delaware laws that prescribed public mutilation were enacted in 1793 and 1797. The 1793 law provided that for kidnapping free blacks, in addition to thirty-nine lashes, the guilty party was to have the soft part of his ears cut off. The 1797 law decreed that if a slave raped a white woman, in addition to thirty-nine lashes, both ears were to be nailed to a pillory for one hour and then the soft part of the ears was to be cut off. *Laws of the State of Delaware*, 2:1094, 1324. The last public whipping in the state took place in 1952, and the whipping post was officially abolished in 1972. For a study of the whipping post in Delaware see Robert Graham Caldwell, *Red Hannah, Delaware's Whipping Post* (London, 1947).

79. Hancock and McCabe, *Milton's First Century*, 301.

80. Kolchin, *American Slavery*, 121. The notices examined by the author appeared in eighteenth-century editions of the *Pennsylvania Gazette, Delaware and Eastern Shore Advertiser*, and *Delaware Gazette*. Some slaveholders may not have wanted to admit publicly that they whipped their slaves and so intentionally omitted mention of any whipping scars in their descriptions of fugitives. Gerald Mullin, *Flight and Rebellion*, 105, found only a few runaway slave notices that mentioned whip marks.

81. Petition of the Delaware Society for Promoting the Abolition of Slavery, 1787, No. 051 (Microfilm No. 10), Petitions: Negroes and Slavery, Legislative Papers, DSA; Claudia L. Bushman, Harold B. Hancock, and Elizabeth M. Homsey, eds., *Proceedings of the House of Assembly of the Delaware State, 1781–1792* (Cranbury, NJ, 1988), 539.

82. Thomas Rodney to Caesar A. Rodney, Poplar Grove, September 3, 1790, Rodney Collection, HSD; Thomas Rodney, Journal, June 6, 1794, H. F. Brown Collection, ibid.; Still, *The Underground Rail Road*, 534.

83. State vs. Andrew Read (1781), New Castle County Court of Oyer and Terminer, 1726–1799, DSA; Solomon (1805), Negro, and Ador (1827), Negro, Sussex County Coroner's Inquest, DSA.

84. State vs. Benjamin Walmsley (1811), and April 1814 Session Docket, 1751–1939, New Castle County Court of Oyer and Terminer, DSA.

85. Jane Willis, 1822, Petitions for Freedom, Kent County, Slavery Materials, 1805–1865, DSA.

86. Welch, ed., *Memoirs of Mary Parker Welch*, 139–40; *Weekly Union*, 1/12/1864.

87. John Dickinson Research File, 64/2, Delaware State Museum, Dover; Boorstin, ed., *Delaware Cases*, 1:655.

IV

Making a Life Despite Slavery

I did not believe in working my life out just to support some body else.
— James Alligood, Sussex County, 1858*

In 1860, with the issue of slavery about to split the Union, Delaware remained, but only barely, a slave state. Its dwindling slave population was down to only 1,798 African-Americans, with the overwhelming majority living and laboring in Sussex County.[1] Because of this concentration in Sussex, most Delawareans of the 1860s were probably convinced that slavery had always been primarily a downstate institution. During the late colonial era, however, all three counties were heavily dependent on the labor of a resident population of unfree blacks. It was not until the large number of manumissions that characterized the years during and after the American Revolution that the state's declining slave population became increasingly concentrated in Sussex.

Nearly one out of four Delawareans was a slave in the late colonial period. If we accept the 1790 federal census of both free and unfree African-Americans as a rough indicator of the demographic concentration of enslaved people in the colony in 1775, on the eve of the Revolution about 25 percent lived in New Castle County, 38 percent in Kent County, and 37 percent in Sussex. In subsequent years, with the number of slaves declining, the latter's share of the unfree black population increased dramatically. By 1810, when one out of twenty Delawareans was enslaved, 58 percent lived in Sussex; in 1840, when only one in every thirty-three was enslaved, 63 percent lived in Sussex; and by 1860, when only one in every fifty was enslaved, 75 percent were in Sussex.[2] Although the typical slave of the eighteenth century might be found in any one of the three counties, in the nineteenth century he or she was increasingly a Sussex Countian.

In eighteenth-century Delaware, slavery was overwhelmingly concentrated in the countryside. Even after some towns and villages began to grow in the late eighteenth and early nineteenth centuries, they included few slaves. In 1800, for example, unfree blacks made up less than 6 percent of the total population of the seven largest communities, compared to 10 percent for the entire state. Wilmington, which was probably five times larger than any other community, counted slaves as only 4 percent of its population. A similar pattern of demographics characterized Delaware throughout the antebellum era and reflected the pattern found in most of the South where, as Peter Kolchin has pointed out, "in general, slavery and urban life made a poor mix." Summarizing this attitude, a master moved from rural Sussex to Milton in 1834. Realizing that taking his slaves "to town was utterly out of the question," he sold them to friends and relatives.[3]

Slave concentrations were considerably higher in flat Delaware than in the Piedmont region. In the rolling hills of northern New Castle County, slaves were only 3 percent of the population in 1800. But in the hundreds (political subdivisions of counties) of southern New Castle County, slaves amounted to the same 11 percent of the total population as in the rest of flat Delaware.[4]

By 1800, according to Patience Essah, the average size of a slave unit in the state had dropped from the 5 to 7 blacks of the late colonial era to 3.3. In 1810 this figure further declined to 2.8 and then remained at about 3 slaves per unit over the next fifty years. Elsewhere in the South, the units were considerably larger, averaging ten unfree blacks in 1860.[5] In attempting to reconstruct a typical slave's experience, however, the average size of a unit can be misleading. If, for example, one master owned ninety-two African-Americans while four other owners held only two each, then the average of the five units would be twenty slaves. But more meaningful in this hypothetical case is the fact that 92 percent of the unfree African-Americans lived and worked on a single unit containing more than ninety other slaves. Clearly, in Delaware the size of the units experienced by a typical slave was larger than the average size of units owned by a typical master.

The disappearance of the 1790 U.S. Census manuscripts for Delaware, lost probably in the burning of Washington by the British during the War of 1812, and the lack of earlier census statistics make it impossible to speak precisely of the size of units lived in by a typical slave during the eighteenth century. However, a random sample of 16 percent of Kent County inventories from 1727 to 1775, an analysis of the slaveholdings of the members of the colonial legislature, and some random inventories from Sussex and New Castle suggest that in the late colonial period 60 percent of bondspeople lived in units of more than seven slaves, but only 35 percent lived in units of more

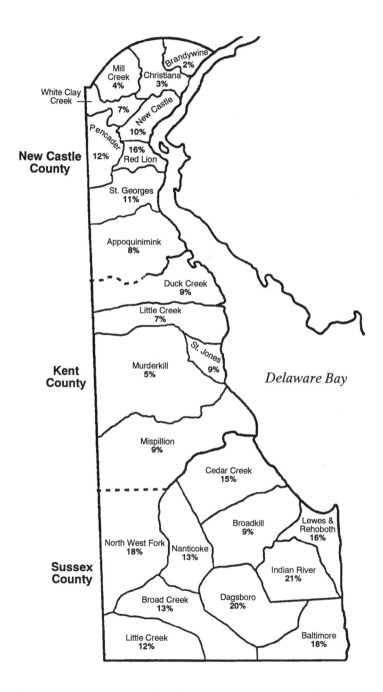

Percentages of Delawareans enslaved, by hundreds, based on U.S. Census Bureau, Manuscripts, 1800, Delaware.

than ten.[6] Because of the subsequent decline in size, by 1800 more than one-half of the state's slaves lived in units of five or less, while only about 29 percent resided and worked in units of more than seven. Over the next sixty years, according to Essah, approximately 60 percent of enslaved Delawareans lived in units of five or fewer.[7]

While Delaware blacks were living in smaller and smaller slave units, the opposite trend characterized Tidewater Virginia and Maryland. During much of the late colonial era, slave units in the Chesapeake were relatively small, with only about 50 percent of unfree blacks living in units of eleven or more. By the end of the Revolution, however, that figure had grown to 70 percent. By the 1780s not only was an overwhelming majority of Chesapeake slaves living in units of eleven or more, 44 percent were living in units of twenty-one or more.[8] In short, prior to the Revolution, a typical Delaware slave lived and worked in a unit only slightly smaller than that experienced by his Chesapeake counterpart. By the late eighteenth century, however, enslaved Delawareans were living and working in units far smaller than those found in Tidewater Virginia and Maryland.

During the nineteenth century, the size of slave units continued to increase throughout the Chesapeake and in most of the rest of the South. By 1850 a slight majority of southern slaves lived in units that included more than twenty blacks,[9] which were at least four times the size of those experienced by typical slaves in Delaware at the same time. The implications of this size disparity are considerable and will be explored later in this chapter.

~

As previously mentioned, whether in Delaware or in the rest of the South, most slaves lived in makeshift quarters in their master's houses or barns during the colonial years. The increasing size of slave units and the balancing of sex ratios during the mid- and late eighteenth century led to the construction of ordered rows of cabins on many southern plantations.[10] In Delaware, however, the decreasing size of slave units made rows of slave cabins unnecessary. Even the state's greatest landholders had little reason to construct more than a handful of cabins. Samuel Chew, probably the largest slaveholder with sixty-three blacks in Kent County in the early 1740s, did not build an extensive slave village because his labor force was divided into three groups, with each one working and living some distance from the other two. John Dickinson constructed some slave cabins, but the only specific mention is of "three log houses inhabited by black servants" in 1784.[11] Plantations with slave quarters were occasionally listed for sale during the late colonial era, but the number of cabins was not given. In the early nineteenth century, the slaves of James Johnson of Indian River Hundred, Sussex County, were said to live in "a diminutive village" where "their cabins bordered on the manor ground." But despite the example of Johnson's place and perhaps a few others, more than two or three cabins to a farm was an unusual sight in the state during the entire slave era.[12]

Delaware's slave cabins, like those elsewhere in early America, were typically one-and-one-half stories high, built of logs, and measured 16' by 18' or 20'. The first story was one large, usually dirt-floored room with a loft above, where children often slept. A fireplace, occasionally made of brick but usually of clay and wood, was essential to both heating and cooking. Predictably, chimney fires were a constant hazard and often spread to the entire structure. As with other agricultural outbuildings of the era, slave cabins were poorly maintained; and in their shape, dimensions, and general floor plan they were similar to the homes of poor whites that were scattered across the rural landscape.[13] Throughout most of the South in the antebellum period, five or six blacks, often an entire family composed of father, mother, and children, lived in each cabin.[14] In Delaware the number of occupants may have been about the same, but the presence of a complete family was uncommon. A mother and three to five children might live in a cabin owned by one master while the enslaved father resided with a second master some distance away.[15]

Despite the fact that elsewhere in the South, by the antebellum period, most slaves were living in cabins and some farms and plantations in Delaware had a few cabins, still many, if not most, of the state's slaves continued to sleep in the same makeshift quarters that had served them in the colonial period—in attics and lean-tos or, like Cloe and Jim, in a cellar or, like George, sleeping next to a cow pen or, like Charles and Peter, in a run-down cookhouse in their master's backyard.[16] If the master's house was large enough, its kitchen was often the congregating place for unfree blacks. During the 1770s, for example, a few miles northeast of Dover, the prayer meetings of the slaves of Stokeley Sturgis were carried on in the kitchen, but after he and his wife got religion, the slaves were invited into the parlor to join the master and mistress in prayer.[17]

After gathering in the kitchen or in the parlor, slaves still returned to sleeping quarters that were minimally appointed. What little furniture they had to sit in, to eat from, or to sleep on, they usually made or scavenged. In some cases, corn stalks, straw, a blanket, or rags, sometimes placed on a board or not, were all that separated sleeping African-Americans from the dirt floor. Crude wooden beds, worth perhaps one-third to one-fourth of the value of those used by adult members of the master's family, were specifically constructed for the slaves

The alleged home of Stokeley Sturgis (located a few miles northeast of Dover), where Richard Allen prayed with his master in the parlor. *Courtesy of Dr. Charles Kopay.*

and indentured servants who slept in his house. Stools, boxes, crates, and barrels substituted for chairs and tables everywhere that slaves lived.[18] In a few cases, slaves with access to a craftsman's tools fashioned a few pieces of more sophisticated furniture.

Like unfree blacks elsewhere in the United States, enslaved Delawareans were given periodic allotments of clothing and shoes. During the eighteenth century, much of their clothing was cut from osnaburg, a crude and durable textile made from flax. So tough was osnaburg that it was also used to make bags and sacks for storing and shipping grain.[19] Other cloth for slave wear was woven from the broken fibers of flax called tow, from wool, and from cotton.[20] Leather for breeches and wool and felt for hats were also used.[21]

Some sense of the master's distribution of clothing can be gained from an agreement by John and Philemon Dickinson to rent out land, along with three male and two female slaves, for seven years to William Howell of Kent County in 1767. The original contract called for Howell to "properly" clothe the five slaves with attire that was to be entirely "new and good." For each of the three men, this meant "a jacket and a pair of ozenbrigs [*sic*] trousers, two pair of yarn stockings and one pair of strong shoes"; and for each of the two women, "one jacket of milled cloth, one good lincey [coarse linen] petticoat, two ozenbrigs shifts, two caps, two aprons, two handkerchiefs, two pairs of yarn stockings and one pair of strong shoes."[22] Although all of the clothing requirements except to "properly" dress the five slaves were subsequently deleted from the contract, probably at Howell's request, to the Dickinson brothers those specifics represented a slave owner's responsibilities.

As pointed out in Chapter II, the spinning and weaving of cloth to be made into this wearing apparel was often done by the slaves themselves, particularly downstate, from the mideighteenth to the early nineteenth century. On the Dickinson plantation or on small farms with only a few bondspeople, slaves grew and processed flax and a limited amount of cotton, sheared sheep, skinned cattle, and then spun, wove, tanned, cut, or sewed the raw material into much of what they wore. Supplementing homemade clothing were the articles distributed by the master who probably followed the pattern of nearby Talbot County, Maryland, where slaves were annually given new shoes, stockings, shirts, shifts, trousers, and breeches. Over more extended periods, other items such as hats, coats, and blankets were distributed.[23] In Delaware, as elsewhere in the South, these practices varied from master to master.

Shoes for adult slaves usually were purchased by masters rather than produced on the home farm. Even planters with large holdings, such as John Dickinson, often bought shoes. In the case of Kent County slaveholder William Barns in 1753, the master provided for each of his ten slaves two pairs of shoes, but they were probably stiff brogans, which were so uncomfortable that adults went barefoot for as much of the year as possible. Slave footwear was clearly inferior to the shoes worn by "middling" and upper-class whites and was simply referred to as "negro shoes."[24] Indeed, the quality of all slave clothing was considered less good than that worn by many whites. A coat made of a coarse and cheap ribbed woolen cloth called kersey was "fit for negroes to wear," while cheap cotton cloth and buttons used for slave garments were known as "negro cloth" and "negro buttons."[25] Black children probably wore the same sack-like garments that covered them in other slave states, and they rarely wore shoes.

An analysis of the clothes worn by nearly one hundred of Delaware's fugitive slaves during the eighteenth century indicates, even after taking into consideration some stealing from the master's wardrobe, that the majority were simply but sufficiently attired to face all but the most extreme weather conditions. Typical was Clem of Jones Neck in Kent County, who was wearing "a home-made, dark gray cloth great coat, a jacket of the same cloth," a pair of linsey-woolsey trousers, a black wool hat half worn, "and a pair of shoes almost new" in late February 1790.[26]

By modern standards, the diet of unfree Delawareans was extraordinarily monotonous and in at least a few cases very skimpy. In 1864 a Sussex County newspaper accused local masters of having provided their slaves with only "hog and hominy" to eat. Years earlier, James Handy, a fugitive from Seaford, reported that his former owner "ill-treated his slaves, especially with regard to diet, which was poor," and a number of other fugitive slaves lodged the same complaint.[27] There is considerable evidence, however, that supports a different view and argues that for at least part of the year Delaware slaves were able to relieve the monotony of pork and corn meal with fresh meats, fish, and vegetables as well as fruit from the master's orchards.[28] Moreover, there is good reason to believe, with a few exceptions cited later in this chapter, that most unfree blacks were not any more malnourished than were most of Delaware's poor and even some "middling" whites.

Because many slaves lived in the master's house, they were fed in the master's kitchen. Although they may have eaten at a different time or at a separate table, their meals were prepared from the same general provisions that the white family ate. Indeed, while the cuts of meat may have been less desirable, a slave who lived in the big house probably was nourished by most of the same basic foods that were central to his master's diet. Those blacks residing in outbuildings were supplied with pork and corn meal to be broiled, boiled, or baked in the crude fireplaces of the slave cabins. By the mideighteenth century, slaves were significantly supplementing their food rations by growing their own vegetables and raising their own chickens. In 1748, for example, slaves in Appoquinimink Hundred in southern New Castle County, when "pinched in food," employed themselves "on Sundays in raising potatoes, peas, melons, etc., for their own use." As was common in other slave states, masters routinely allotted a plot of ground to individual blacks for a chicken yard and vegetable garden. Richard Allen remembered that at the time of the Revolution, Kent County slaves "would toil in their little patches many a night until midnight to raise their little truck." A decade earlier, the slaves of John Dickinson had their own henhouses, and small plots had been assigned to them so that they could grow their own "peas, beans, potatoes, cabbages and any kind of roots." In Sussex in 1818, Obed was guaranteed a quarter-acre of land and one day per week to work it as long as he remained a slave.[29]

A number of these slaves raised enough poultry and vegetables to sell excess amounts to free blacks and whites living in the neighborhood, to other slaves, and even to their own masters. Among the poultry was the guinea fowl which, like the blacks themselves, had been imported from Africa during the colonial period. Thus, a slave-run economy was operating in Delaware that provided at least some unfree African-Americans with money to purchase additional food, drink, clothes, and other necessities. One Kent County slave even earned enough money to make loans at interest to whites.[30]

Whether purchased in the slave-run economy, provided by the master, or caught by the slave, fish, oysters, venison, rabbit, opossum, and other wild denizens of water and land were added to the slaves' diet. The dramatic decline in the number of deer, however, caused venison to appear less often on the table by the late eighteenth century. Because cows' milk caused severe diarrhea among many African-Americans, it was even less central to the diet of Delaware's slaves than to that of the white population.[31]

Across the South, male slaves averaged 5'7", or an inch shorter than southern white males during the early nineteenth century. But when compared to European laborers and peasants of the same era, American slaves were a full inch taller. Indeed, evidence suggests that they were two or three inches taller than most West Africans. This height edge may reflect a superior level in the bulk and variety of foods consumed by American blacks as compared to the diet of most of the rest of the world's population. But because southern slaves were shorter in stature than southern whites, they probably enjoyed a less nutritious diet.[32]

In Delaware, the average height of thirty black males who fled slavery during the late colonial period as well as forty-two others who ran away during the years from 1786 to 1795 was nearly 5'8", or almost an inch taller than the average enslaved male in the South in the early nineteenth century and matching the average height of white southern males for the same period.[33] Statistics on the height of the seventy-two black Delawareans together with evidence of a relatively wide variety of meats, fruits, and vegetables available to them at certain times of the year suggest that the state's unfree African-Americans were as well nourished as slaves elsewhere in the South and, in many cases, may have enjoyed a more balanced diet than that found on the majority of southern plantations. Indeed, Delaware's slaves were probably better fed than most working-class people in Europe, Asia, Africa, and Latin America.

In summary, when the key elements of material existence such as clothing and shelter are combined with nutrition, Delaware slaves lived comparatively well. There were, of course, a number of exceptions. The "dwarf slaves" seen in Sussex County in the early nineteenth century likely suffered as much from malnutrition as from "grinding labor." But if we ignore these exceptions and focus on only the material well-being of the typical Delaware slave, then there are grounds for believing that he or she, along with slaves from other southern states, enjoyed a standard of living that compared favorably with that of most of the world's population.[34] This relatively high standard of living reflected America's abundant material resources as well as the concerns of most of the state's slaveholders.

~

During the slave era, the disease environment in Delaware can best be compared to one found in a Third World nation of today. Poor sanitary conditions and primitive medical care led to a very high incidence of sickness and death for both blacks and whites. Except for malaria, respiratory infections, and sickle cell anemia, blacks and whites were almost equally vulnerable to most other diseases of early Delaware, such as smallpox. Because of smallpox's high mortality rate and the conditioned immunity gained by its survivors, enslaved blacks who lived through the disease immediately became more valuable. Predictably, slave sale notices called attention to unfree African-Americans who had survived smallpox and other contagious diseases. In 1763 one master advertised "a negro man" who "has had the smallpox and measles," while a second slave owner called attention to a "healthy negro girl" who "has had smallpox." That many Delaware blacks contracted smallpox is verified by the number of fugitive slave notices that called attention to facial scars. Sharper was described as "pitted with the small pox"; Beck, "pock broken"; Sip, "pretty much pocked marked"; and Francis, "pretty much pock broken."[35] Some owners, in a prudent step to protect their investment and perhaps to test the treatment, had their slaves inoculated, but the procedure did not always work. In the 1760s the previously mentioned Congamochu of the town of New Castle was "inoculated for the small pox in the left arm, but took no infection."[36] By the early nineteenth century, masters were probably turning to the less dangerous vaccination to protect their slaves.

Due to living and sleeping quarters that were close and confining, smallpox and infectious respiratory diseases spread quickly. Another factor in the spread of disease was the contamination of both water and soil near slave quarters. In Delaware, as in much of the South, outdoor privies or outhouses did not exist for most of the rural population until after the Civil War. Although the gentry might use chamber pots indoors and then have the contents dumped at a considerable distance from their homes, most rural whites and blacks simply used the nearest bush, tree, or log for privacy and convenience as they carelessly scattered human waste across the landscape. At the time, no one really understood the relationship of human excrement to the spread of disease-causing pathogens.[37]

While pathogens found in human urine and feces leached into the soil to make water from shallow wells a significant carrier of disease, flies shuttled other germs from nearby deposits of human waste through unscreened windows to the crude tables of the slave cabins and to the more elaborate facilities of the master's kitchen. Cholera, contracted through drinking contaminated water, and certain varieties of parasitic worms, picked up from walking barefoot on soil often laden with human waste, must have been constant threats to the health of Delaware's slaves as well as to the well-being of free blacks and many whites. Both illnesses were probably as serious a problem in Delaware as in Virginia, where at least one-half of the slaves harbored parasitic worms "during their lifetimes."[38] Furthermore, during the winter, when fresh fruits and vegetables were scarce, a constant diet of corn and salt pork without milk often led to pellagra. Because milk was usually excluded from slave diets, some blacks must have suffered from skin eruptions along with the digestive and nervous disorders that are symptoms of the disease. Perhaps it was pellagra that plagued a young slave in Sussex in January 1826 who was described as "erupted badly."[39]

In giving birth, Delaware slave mothers faced the same threat from serious infection that confronted both free and unfree mothers across early America. In general, concern for cleanliness and asepsis during childbirth was a development of the late nineteenth century and therefore many decades away. After giving birth, usually with the aid of black midwives, most slave mothers throughout the South were allowed from two weeks to a month to rest and take care of their newborn infants. In Delaware that practice also was probable. In at least one case, however, a brutal master simply ignored convention and even common sense and forced a new mother to resume work a few days after giving birth, which led to her death.[40]

Although a slaveholder's net worth increased with every child born to his bondswomen, most historians now are in agreement that the deliberate breeding of slaves to produce large numbers of offspring for eventual sale was not practiced regularly in early America. Certainly, with the relative decline in the value of Delaware slaves after 1787, there was considerably less financial incentive to encourage propagation in the slave quarter or wherever else unfree African-Americans lived. Nevertheless, a few eighteenth-century Delawareans viewed their slaves in much the same manner as their breeding stock. As late as 1796, John West of southeastern Sussex referred to Judah and Florah as his "breeding women."[41]

Far more significant than deliberate breeding in contributing to the natural increase in Delaware's unfree black population was a change in the breast-feeding practices of many of the women. Evidently, during the months that mothers breast-feed their children, they have some difficulty in conceiving. Moreover, in some West African communities, tradition dictated a taboo against sexual intercourse with a nursing mother. In West Africa the typical period of breast-feeding lasted more than two years, thus causing children to be widely spaced, perhaps three or four years apart. After Africans arrived in the West Indies, Brazil, or in some parts of America's Deep South, where they formed a very large percentage of the population, indications are that they continued the lactation traditions of their homeland.[42]

In Delaware, where whites outnumbered blacks by at least four to one, African cultural traditions had greater difficulty in surviving. In place of the African breast-feeding period of two or three years, some evidence suggests that many slave mothers were forced by their masters to comply with the Anglo-Saxon lactation tradition of only one year. An example was the treatment of Miriam of Kent County in 1741, whose new-born baby was allowed to "sucketh" for only one year before being taken from her. In 1750 in New Castle County, Dinah was separated from her new-born child and thus forced to halt breast-feeding after only thirteen months. The period might be allowed to stretch a bit longer, as in the eighteenth-century cases of Jenny and Hagger of Sussex, who were permitted to nurse their children for eighteen months and two years, respectively. However, Phillis of Sussex was allowed only eight months for each of her four children before turning them over to new owners in the 1770s. Two decades later, Nell of Sussex was allowed to feed her firstborn for only a year. Former slave Frederick Douglass found that this shortened lactation period was also common among slave mothers on Maryland's Eastern Shore: "Frequently, before the child has reached its twelfth month, its mother is taken from it." What a contrast with practices on a large nineteenth-century plantation in Florida, where it was a "common occurrence to see a child of two or three still nursing at his mother's breast"![43] The shortened lactation period forced on at least some of these enslaved mothers dramatically increased their child-bearing potential over a lifetime, but its enforcement was usually dictated by the master's Anglo-Saxon perspective rather than by a conscious effort to turn slaves into a more prolific breeding stock.

For some of Delaware's slave children, the shorter period of breast-feeding was balanced by many years of psychological nurturing and support provided by their often fractured but still viable families. With the end of the Revolution, some masters seemed more willing to recognize and accept long-standing relationships between male and female slaves as marriage, even though they still were not recognized as such by the state.[44] The practice of selling off part of a family, however, forced an undetermined number of Delaware slave children to grow up without the presence of either parent. The breaking up of families through slave sales meant in many cases that children completely lost touch with their brothers and sisters as well as with both parents. In his autobiography, former Kent County slave Richard Allen indicates that he never again made contact with his mother, father, or his younger siblings after they were sold by Stokeley Sturgis.[45] In addition, the practice of separating many mothers from their new-born infants only twelve months or so after birth (the mother or the child might be sent to another farm and an elderly female slave would raise the child) often made it difficult for these children to really know their mothers. On the Eastern Shore, Douglass also noted this practice and then pointed out that this early separation hindered "the development of the child's affection toward its mother" and blunted and destroyed "the natural affection of the mother for the child."[46]

The small size of the state's slave units raised a second barrier to family unity. As noted earlier, from 1639 to 1865 most unfree Delawareans lived in units that contained fewer than ten people. As Allan Kulikoff has written, "On quarters of fewer than ten slaves, complete families of husbands, wives, and children were uncommon."[47] Although some of the state's largest plantations contained a few nuclear families, far more representative was the slave unit owned by Catherine Gordon of Sussex County, which in 1776 consisted of one "old" female and five children. In 1801, William Gray of Baltimore Hundred, Sussex, owned thirty-four-year-old Easter and twenty-year-old Creesha, along with two boys and two girls aged two to thirteen. Obviously, the bondsmen who sired the children on the Gordon and Gray farms lived elsewhere.[48] A baptism held in 1786 at St. George's Episcopal Church in eastern Sussex further demonstrates the common separation of husband and wife. Christened were Caesar, Rachel, and Moses, the children of Fisher, owned by John Morris; and Dinah, the property of loyalist exile Thomas Robinson.[49]

There is no doubt that in Delaware only a small percentage of male slaves lived with and therefore had daily contact with their wives and children. The estimate that on small slave units in the Chesapeake region only one-fifth of fathers resided with their children may be, according to evidence from probate records, too high for Delaware.[50] In other parts of the South, most male slaves who lived apart from their families were within easy walking distance of their wives and children. But in Delaware, where the slave population was generally smaller and more thinly scattered across the landscape, most bondsmen did not have an easy commute and could make only periodic visits.[51] Even those lucky enough to live only a few miles from spouses and offspring found that long hours of exhausting labor, poor roads, and inclement weather restricted most of their visits to the weekends.

Because so many males were absent most of the time, it was difficult for the majority of slave children to really know their fathers. To author George Alfred Townsend, who was born and raised in pre-Civil War Delaware and Maryland's Eastern Shore, this fact of life was recognized by both blacks and whites. In his *The Entailed Hat*, a novel set in Delaware and the Eastern Shore during the early nineteenth century, slaves Mary and Virgie lament the absence of a father from their lives. In consoling Virgie, Mary asks her "to remember we are black! We hardly ever have fathers: they is for white people."[52] As a result, more than in any other state south of the Mason-Dixon Line, Delaware's slave children grew up in households dominated by women.

A third threat to the unity of the slave family was the sexual liberty taken with unfree African-American women by masters and other white males. However, specific evidence of white men forcing themselves on almost powerless slave women is hard to come by. Delaware court records tell us much about the criminal activity of slaves, free blacks, and whites; but because enslaved blacks were not allowed to testify against whites, court records say almost nothing about the rape of slave women by whites. And yet patterns in other slave states, the corrupting influence of unchecked power, and the presence of many mulattoes all point to at least some cases of sexual exploitation. By 1850 about 9 percent of Delaware's nonwhite population was categorized as mulatto.[53] In addition, many other Delawareans of mixed blood were incorrectly categorized as negro or white.

On the other hand, the presence of so many mulattoes cannot be blamed entirely on white males taking advantage of power relationships to satisfy sexual drives. As elsewhere in the South during the eighteenth century, a number of mulatto children were produced by liaisons between enslaved black males and white females, many of whom were indentured servants. The disproportionately large ratio of male to female slaves in Delaware during the first half of the eighteenth century may partly explain the numerous interracial unions of the period. Moreover, the familiarity that came from enslaved black males and indentured white females working together in the same fields and shops, suffering together under the same master, and living together on the same farm or plantation often resulted in physical and emotional intimacy.

An example of where this intimacy might lead was noted in 1699 in Sussex, when Adam Johnson's white "servant woman" was seen "lyeing commonly with the said Johnson's Nigroe man as man and wife." The earliest extant record of the birth of a mulatto child sired by a Delaware slave took place in Kent County in the same year, when Peter was born to Alice Bryan, a white indentured servant, and a "Negro man named Jack." Four years later in Kent, Anne Wade, who was serving John Walker as an indentured servant, and Peter, who was one of Walker's slaves, were the parents of a mulatto child.[54] Initially, the punishment of white female and black male parents of mulatto children was based on the fact that their union produced a bastard rather than because the child was a product of miscegenation. The punishment of Wade, for example, was the same twenty-one stripes "on the bare back well laid on" as for a white Kent County woman who bore a bastard sired by a white man in 1706. Indeed, compared to neighboring Maryland, early Delaware seemed relatively liberal on the issue of miscegenation.[55]

By 1726, however, so many of the colony's white women had given birth to mulatto children that the legislature decided to severely punish miscegenation. Awaiting any white woman who bore a bastard mulatto was a £10 fine, thirty-nine stripes "on the bare back well laid on," and a two-hour stay in the pillory. If she was an indentured servant and could not pay the fine, five more years were added to her servitude. The slave father received the same number of lashes and then was forced to stand in the pillory for two hours, "with one ear nailed there unto, and cropped off." The mixed-race offspring was to be put out to servitude by the county court until he or she reached the age of thirty-one. By comparison, the 1726 law punished less harshly the mother and father of a bastard white child by giving each parent the choice of receiving twenty-one stripes or paying a £3 fine. Nothing was said about the illegitimate white child. But the legislation of 1726 also took a stand against white men having sexual relations with female slaves by requiring those guilty to endure twenty-one stripes and pay a £20 fine.[56]

The harsh provision that mandated thirty-one years of servitude for any mulatto child sired by a slave was rarely enforced after midcentury and was officially dropped in 1795, but another serious problem for these children soon surfaced. Many masters and mistresses of white indentured mothers routinely, but illegally, claimed ownership of their white servants' mulatto offspring. To free them from a life of bondage—after all, their mothers were not slaves—legislation was enacted in 1760 that gave illegally enslaved mulatto children the right to petition the Court of Common Pleas for their freedom.[57]

Despite harsh punishments mandated by the legislature, the issue of interracial sex between white women and male slaves would not go away. By the 1790s, however, white female indentured servants were no longer very numerous in Delaware. Increasingly, interracial sex was now a union between free but usually poor white women and both free and unfree black males. In 1796 in Sussex, for example, a "very poor white woman" was found guilty of giving birth to two mulatto children contrary to the "Act against adultery and fornication." Her guilt was established by the testimony of another poor white woman who previously had been found guilty of the same offense. In 1807, to put a lid on a potentially explosive situation, the General Assembly reaffirmed that both white men and women and black men involved in miscegenation—black females were not mentioned specifically in the legislation—would face stern punishment, and that interracial marriages were "absolutely void and of no effect."[58]

A fourth factor that worked against family integrity was the inability of many enslaved males to contribute consistently to the economic welfare of their wives and children. In marriages between free blacks or between free whites, the wife's dependence on her husband for income and property gave her added incentive to work hard to preserve the monogamous relationship. Although a male slave periodically might help out in his wife's vegetable plot, or fashion a piece of crude furniture for her cabin, or even give her small gifts of money that he had made in the underground slave economy, it was her master, rather than her husband, who was the primary provider for her and her children's material existence. In short, the strong economic incentive that played a crucial role in holding together both white couples and free black couples was simply not present in slave unions.

Despite these powerful centrifugal factors, in some cases love, commitment, and devotion to family survived the slave experience. In 1821, Sarah overcame her fear of enslavement in another state and successfully petitioned a Kent County court to allow her to join her husband Jacob, who was being sold to a Maryland master. (Because Jacob was deemed dangerous to the community by the courts, he could be legally sold out of state.[59]) In 1813, Henry M. Ridgely of Dover offered to sell Frank to John Banning of Little Creek Hundred. Although Banning's property was only a few miles from Dover, Frank knew that being sold would mean separation from his wife, so he braved Ridgely's wrath by objecting strongly to the sale. Frank's intransigence delayed it long enough to cause Banning to purchase a slave elsewhere and thus allowed him and his wife to remain together in Dover.[60]

It was more than just mutual love and affection between sexual partners, or between parent and child, that held together a number of slave families in the face of so many destructive forces. Particularly crucial in maintaining close ties was a sense of family history that bound the past to the present, together with the recognition that the children represented the vital continuum in the story. The actions and thoughts of Kent County slave Solomon Bayley were representative of those blacks who, by emphasizing their roots and hopes for the future, refused to allow slavery to destroy the integrity of the family.

While writing his autobiography in 1824, Bayley noted that his grandmother was "a Guinea woman" who was brought to Virginia in 1690 "or there abouts," at the age of eleven. She was purchased by "one of the most barbarous families of that day; and although treated hard, was said to have fifteen sons and daughters"; she "lived to a great age, until she appeared weary of life." Bayley's mother, who had thirteen children, served the same "cruel" Virginia family until the master and mistress died. Their daughter married and then "brought our" family to Delaware, where Bayley was born. After some years in the state, the mistress died and her husband moved himself and his slaves back to Virginia in 1799. (It was legal for a master who moved out of Delaware to take his slaves with him, as long as they were not immediately sold after leaving.) Despite the law against immediate sale, soon after they arrived in Virginia, members of Bayley's family were sold to new masters in scattered locations, "some to the east, some west, north and south." His father, brother, and sister eventually ended up as slaves in the West Indies, while his mother and youngest brother fled from slavery to the relative safety of New Jersey. In her old age, Bayley's mother moved to Delaware to be near her son and thus reunited him with at least part of his family.[61]

Soon after Bayley accompanied his family to Virginia in 1799, he, too, was sold to another owner. While being transported to his new master's home west of Richmond, he escaped and made his way back to Camden in Kent County, only to be followed by his original master. But working in Bayley's favor was the fact that his sale was illegal under Delaware law. He knew about this law and threatened to take his master to court. Faced with the possibility of losing his slave through litigation, the master offered a compromise which Bayley accepted. For eighty dollars, or a fraction of what he would bring on the auction block in Virginia, Bayley was allowed to buy his freedom. In subsequent years, he purchased the freedom of his wife, two daughters, and a son from their Delaware masters.[62]

Yet, even before buying his own freedom, Bayley had certain hopes and ambitions for himself and his future issue that were inspired by a family history of perseverance. Despite the agony and danger of the Middle Passage from the Guinea Coast of Africa to the New World and the subsequent burden of four generations of slavery in Virginia and Delaware, his family had survived. And that persistence in the face of almost insurmountable obstacles was an inspiration as Bayley's family looked to its own future. (Not surprisingly, after his years of slavery were long past, pride in his ancestral roots caused Bayley to consider visiting the Guinea Coast.[63])

Despite the refusal of the state and most masters, some slaveholders recognized long-standing monogamous relationships as marriage. Typical was Thomas Irons of Kent County, who noted in his 1784 will that Rachel was the mother of two of his young slaves and the "wife of my Negro man named Charles."[64] Even so-called marriages that transcended farm boundaries were sometimes acknowledged, as in the 1811 case of Hannah, who was owned by Nathaniel Hayes of western Sussex but was the "wife of Abram," who lived on another master's farm.[65]

The continued existence of the slave family was also recognized by a few masters through the particulars of work assignments. In 1781, on the Dickinson plantation, the responsibilities for spinning thread for slave garments reflected in part these family relationships. Priscilla and Dinah made up one team of spinners whose work was to provide for themselves and ten other slaves including Pompey, who was probably Priscilla's husband, and Little Pompey, her son, as well as Nanny, who was Dinah's child. None of either Priscilla's or Dinah's immediate family seemed to be a responsibility of the other team of spinners.[66] Moreover, John Dickinson not only recognized the existence of families among his own blacks, but he also took action to support family unity. In 1783, for example, he bought the wife and five children of his own slave, Nathan, from a farmer in Little Creek Hundred.[67] These specific examples, however, are not very numerous. Although conclusive evidence is impossible to come by, the peculiar nature of slavery in Delaware was so uniquely debilitating to family unity that there is little basis for believing that the slave family was a very strong or robust unit.

~

The family was only one aspect of a much broader topic—slave culture. For years, historians have vigorously debated whether or not remembered African traditions were at its very heart. By focusing on pottery as a cultural artifact, we can better understand the nature of Delaware slave culture in the context of that debate.[68]

In Flowerdew Hundred, near Williamsburg, Virginia, archaeological excavations have uncovered a type of slave-produced pottery called Colono Ware. Other examples of this pottery can be found from the Chesapeake south to Georgia. Of particular interest is the fact that the shape of slave-produced Colono Ware generally becomes more African the farther south it is found. In fact, it becomes most African in South Carolina, where the percentage of blacks in the population was highest, the slave units were largest, and the isolation of slaves from masters and other whites was most common. Conversely, as one moves north, the percentage of blacks in the population declined, the size of the slave units diminished, the contact between slaves and whites increased, and the Colono Ware becomes less African. The Colono Ware story serves as an instructive metaphor for the survival of African cultural traits among slaves throughout America.[69]

Just as with Colono pottery, the Africanness of emerging slave culture depended a great deal on three factors: the percentage of blacks in the population, the size of slave units, and the amount of contact with the master or other whites. In the case of Delaware, these three factors caused slave culture to be far less reflective of African traditions than of the conditions peculiar to the world of a slave in the state. A fourth factor in shaping Delaware's slave culture was the ending by the mid-1760s of slave imports directly from Africa. The importation of black bondspeople from any source was reduced to a trickle by the late colonial era and was banned by the state legislature in 1787. (Slave imports in Virginia and Maryland roughly followed a similar pattern and were finally outlawed in 1778 and 1783, respectively.) The dramatic decline in slave imports from Africa meant that by 1775 the percentage of Delaware blacks born in Africa may have approached the Virginia figure of only 10 percent. This drastic diminution in the presence of the African-born meant that Delaware's slaves were quarantined, long before slaves in the Deep South, from the most significant source of African cultural renewal.[70]

The right to name slave children was an exercise in symbolic authority, and the name chosen was an indication of cultural hegemony. If enslaved mothers or fathers surrendered to the master the right to name their offspring, then they were relinquishing one of the pillars of parental authority, family dignity, and African tradition. But even if enslaved blacks retained the right to name their children, they were moving away from the culture and memory of Africa if they then chose a European or biblical name.

In most slave states, only a small minority of masters insisted on naming newborns.[71] In Delaware, except for the fact that a few slaves bore classical Greek or Roman names such as Caesar or Pompey, there is little evidence that owners directly interfered, in a significant way, with the right of enslaved parents to name their children. But the names those parents chose seem to testify to the dominance of white culture. To be sure, during the eighteenth century, African names were fairly common. Prior to 1765 there was a sizeable immigration of African slaves into Delaware, and some were allowed to keep their original names or at least Anglicized facsimiles. Subsequently, in a few cases Delaware-born slave children were given African names at birth. But a precise analysis of slave-naming practices is almost impossible because it is so hard to distinguish between Anglicized versions of African names and those that were eccentric or provincial spellings of more traditional English and biblical ones. Was Hagar, for example, simply an English version of Haga, which is Mandingo for daughter, or was it the correctly spelled Old Testament name? Nevertheless, a brief examination of slave names does provide some sense of the dominating influence of white culture by the mideighteenth century.

In West Africa, many children were named for the day of the week or the time of the year in which they were born, while others were named for a geographic place or for certain specific character traits. An examination of 1,415 slave names found in Kent and Sussex County wills from 1702 to 1787 indicates that in Sussex, Cuff (day name meaning Friday), Cuba (day name meaning Wednesday, or place name), Paris (place name), and Fillis (losing one's way in Mandingo) were the most common African names. In Kent, Fillis joined Glasco or Glasgow (place name) and Mingo (short for Mandingo?) as the most popular African names. And yet by adding other names that seem African such as Kinner, Sambo, Ummi, Tamer, Quash (Sunday), and Cudge (Monday) to such seasonal names as Easter and Winter and to such place names as Dover, York, London, and Dublin—those names that did not sound English, Scots-Irish, biblical, or classical were categorized as African—"probable" African names accounted for only 10 percent of the combined total of Kent and Sussex slave names in Delaware wills at this time. (In North and South Carolina, and in Philadelphia, the percentage with African names was about the same or only marginally higher for the eighteenth century.[72])

By contrast with African names, classical names were forced on a few slaves by masters in a clear exercise of symbolic authority. By far the most popular was Caesar, followed at some distance by Cato, Pompey, Cyrus, Scipio, and Nero. But these classical names were not very common among the state's enslaved African-Americans for the years from 1702 to 1787. Indeed, only 5 percent of the combined total of Kent and Sussex County slaves bore such names during this period. (For North and South Carolina, and Philadelphia, the figure was significantly higher.[73])

The remaining 85 percent of the names examined were typically Anglo-Saxon, Scots-Irish, or biblical. The latter became more common in the late eighteenth century, thus reflecting the increasing influence of Christianity. In Sussex, where more than seven hundred names were analyzed, the leading names and the number of times used were as follows:

Males	*Females*
Peter, 16	Rose, 20
Sam, 14	Fillis or Phillis, 17
Caesar, 12	Esther, 16

George, 11   Sarah, 15
Isaac, 10   Sal or Sally, 14
Jacob, 10   Rachel, 14

In Kent, the leading names and the number of times used out of more than six hundred slave names examined were as follows:

Males	*Females*
Peter, 15	Hannah, 15
Jack, 13	Nan or Nancy, 15
Caesar, 11	Kate, 14
Isaac, 11	Rachel, 13
Charles, 11	Sal or Sally, 11
Daniel, 9	Fillis or Phillis, 8

Among the most common names, only Caesar and, perhaps, Fillis were not English, Scots-Irish, or biblical.[74]

In other slave states, there is some indication that newly born children were rarely given their mother's name, occasionally given their father's name, and commonly given the name of extended kin. But in Delaware, evidence on namesake patterns is inconclusive. Probate records for Kent and Sussex indicate that daughters were rarely named for their mothers. It is far more difficult to figure out whether or not children were named for their fathers or extended kin because, as noted earlier, black children usually lived in slave units separate from their fathers and their more distant relatives. With no last names to establish blood connections, name tracing of slave children to fathers or other kin living elsewhere is nearly impossible. An exception is the Dickinson plantation near Dover, where a study of some thirty-two children of slaves indicates that only three bore the name of either of their parents.[75] Those few children who were named for a parent living in the same unit were generally distinguished from their namesakes by prefixes indicating size, age, or color. Little Pompey was the son of Big Pompey, while Young Sarah was the daughter of Old Sarah. A mulatto child might be called Yellow Cate to separate her from her darker mother, Black Cate.

While every Delaware slave had a given name, only a few had surnames that were recognized by their masters until the nineteenth century. In almost every case, the surnames of enslaved blacks were not the same as those of their present masters.[76] Did the rejection of the master's surname represent a symbolic declaration of independence by the slave? The nebulous nature of the evidence makes it risky to offer more than a cautious "maybe."

~

Even more central to West African culture than naming patterns was the role played by religion. As with Christianity, African religions relied heavily on public expression and ceremony to reinforce private perceptions. Sacred rites often used parts of plants and trees peculiar to West Africa to draw viewers into the community's spiritual belief system. Clearly, public ceremonies and rituals were essential if African religious beliefs were to be sustained over a period of time.

In the New World, the institution of slavery usually banned large gatherings of unfree blacks. Denied public celebration of their African beliefs and finding themselves in a radically different botanical setting that was unable to provide the sacred elements used in their rites, African-American slaves experienced, according to Jon Butler, a "spiritual holocaust." By the Revolution, he maintains, slavery had destroyed most of the African religious heritage in most parts of the English mainland colonies. Even evidence of healers, conjurers, sorcerers, and witches among eighteenth-century American blacks, according to Butler, is rarely encountered by researchers.[77] His "spiritual holocaust" theory is intriguing and deserves to be tested against specific developments in Delaware.

By 1763 the Anglican Church, the nominal faith of most residents of the colony, had an opportunity to harvest some black souls for white Christianity, but only a small number of slaves were enticed into the Anglican fold. Although there were a number of reasons for this failure, one of the most obvious was the fact that there were too few Anglican priests to serve even the white population. Unlike bordering Maryland, Delaware had no established church during the period of English rule; and, without tax support, its Anglican pulpits were difficult to fill. Indeed, through much of the late colonial period there were only three Anglican clergymen in all of Delaware—one for each county—and as late as 1775 there were only five Church of England clergy in the entire colony.[78]

Since there were not enough men of the cloth to meet the spiritual needs of the Anglo-Saxon population, saving the souls of the "heathen" African-Americans was a very low priority for most Church of England clergy. Nevertheless, a few Anglican clerics, spurred on in part by instructions from the Lord Bishop of London, did make an effort. William Becket, rector of St. Peter's, Lewes, wrote in 1726 that he had baptized "some" slaves in eastern Sussex, and he reported two years later that he had christened "several" blacks since coming to Sussex. In 1748 in Appoquinimink Hundred in southern New Castle County, the Reverend Philip Reading noted that "betwixt twelve and twenty" slaves were constantly at service; indeed, he had, concerning the conversion of slaves, "some glimmering of hope."[79]

Most of the news concerning unfree blacks was not encouraging, however. In 1728, Becket thought that "the greatest part" of the slaves in Sussex "do yet remain unbaptized, and (it is feared) uninstructed." A year earlier in the town of New Castle, the Reverend George Ross had complained that "very little care is taken" to instruct slaves "in religion." Twenty-one years later, Reading labeled the efforts to convert slaves "truly deplorable."[80] A particular problem, according to Reading, was the slaveholder himself, who was often "destitute of common humanity." Because masters' "hearts are set upon gain," they did not allow even their own children to leave work for religious instruction. "What then can be expected in behalf of a poor slave from such as want natural affection even to their own flesh and blood?"[81]

Another problem noted by Reading in the 1740s was the inability of white clergy to communicate with unfree blacks. Because so many slaves had been born and raised in Africa, a significant number had considerable difficulty in speaking or understanding more than a rudimentary kind of English. To Reading, their "wild confused medley of Negro and corrupt English" made them "very unintelligible except for those [whites] who have conversed with them for many years." But even if the language gulf could be bridged, to the frustrated clergyman there remained the issue of "slow apprehension." Reading observed that blacks "seem to be a species quite different from whites, [they] have no abstracted ideas, [and] cannot comprehend the meaning of faith in Christ" and the other basic precepts of Christianity.[82]

At this point, however, Reading admitted that part of the difficulty lay in the stubborn unwillingness of slaves born and raised in Africa to accept the Christian message. These Africans continued to resist pressures to convert by clinging to some shards of their traditional faith despite whites' entreaties to give up "superstition and idolatry." A particular example, noted Reading, was the "Keromantees" from "Guinea," who sometimes committed suicide in the belief that at death they would be transported back to their homeland to live again as free men and women.[83] When, during the second half of the eighteenth century, the generation of African-born slaves gradually died off, so, too, did memories of West African religious rituals and ceremonies. And with the death of these West African religious memories there developed, in the next generation of enslaved Delawareans, a willingness to look to white Christianity to fill the spiritual void and to give some meaning to lives in bondage.

Despite an apparent openness to Christianity on the part of blacks, Quakers and Presbyterians were even less successful than Anglicans in serving their spiritual needs. Although the Society of Friends hardened its opposition to slavery as the colonial period came to a close, some Quakers continued to own slaves. Moreover, even when Quaker meetings in the state took an unequivocal stand against slavery during the Revolution, there was little enthusiasm among Friends for the religious proselytizing of African-Americans. Evangelizing, after all, was not a priority of eighteenth-century Quakers, and there is no evidence that any enslaved Delawareans attended their meetings during the late colonial period. As for the Presbyterians, their churches were scattered throughout the state but were most concentrated in northern New Castle County, where there were few unfree African-Americans. This lack of contact with blacks and the unwillingness to take a clear stand against slavery resulted in few unfree blacks attending Presbyterian services.[84] Moreover, there is no evidence of slaves joining any of the Presbyterian churches in Delaware prior to the Revolution.

By the close of the colonial period, many enslaved Delawareans were ready for, but had not yet found, a new religious faith. They were looking for a spiritual home that was critical of slavery, offered solace to the oppressed in an understandable and dynamic manner, and generally welcomed them. Presbyterianism continued to be too geographically removed and too theologically ambivalent on the issue of slavery to attract them. Although increasingly the champion of enslaved African-Americans, the Society of Friends was too emotionally reserved and too uninterested in proselytizing to appeal to many Delaware slaves. As for Anglicanism, its continued shortage of clergy, its passive acceptance of slavery and the status quo, and its religious services that lacked fire and emotion all combined to make it a less-than-compelling option. Elsewhere in the South, enslaved African-Americans were often drawn, particularly during and after the Revolution, to Baptist services. But in Delaware throughout the slave era, Baptist preachers and congregations were so few that they were unable to offer a viable religious alternative to unfree blacks.[85]

It was at this propitious moment, at the end of the colonial period, that Methodism arrived in Delaware and offered both blacks and whites a spiritual message that challenged the institution of slavery and other elements of the status quo in emotional services that struck a strong responsive chord. Taking their antislavery cue from John Wesley, the English founder of Methodism, itinerant preachers rode through the state attacking slavery and other elements of the gentry's value system. Significantly, Methodist preachers also praised many of the personality traits associated with the humbler classes; and they spoke in a compelling style that appealed simply, clearly, and persuasively to biracial audiences attuned to the spoken rather than to the written word.

As one former slave pointed out, the Methodists were not "so high-flown that we were not able to comprehend their doctrine."[86]

The slaves responded to the Methodists' message because of its content, tone, and inclusive nature and because they were committed to saving black souls. Moreover, by stressing the conversion experience more than religious instruction, Methodism made itself easily accessible to illiterate slaves—and the slaves, joined by free blacks, enthusiastically answered the call. Often they responded to emotional appeals by white preachers with outbursts that were godsends to frustrated circuit riders unable to stir lethargic whites. Above all, both slaves and free blacks appreciated Methodism because, as Richard Allen pointed out, "the Methodists were the first people that brought glad tidings to the colored people."[87]

So compelling was this message that by 1810 almost one in four of Delaware's adult African-Americans—both free and unfree—had become Methodists, while thousands of others attended Methodist worship services and camp meetings. In fact, Methodism proved so attractive that more than 90 percent of both the free and enslaved black Delawareans who attended religious services from the Revolution to the Civil War did so in that denomination's chapels and churches.[88]

For analytical purposes, it is impossible to distinguish between free and unfree black Methodists because they were grouped together in membership statistics. However, comments by clergymen indicate that both groups turned out in large numbers and were about equally attracted to Methodist preaching. Indeed, at times both enslaved and free blacks seemed even more attracted to Methodism than whites. In 1790, when about 25 percent of the state's Methodists were African-Americans, the percentage of whites and blacks who had officially joined the church was approximately the same. Twenty years later, 38 percent of Delaware's Methodists were black. Because blacks remained at between 20 and 25 percent of the state's population during most of the slave era, it is clear that by 1810 a considerably higher percentage of African-Americans than whites had joined the Methodist Church. Like white Methodists, black Methodists were concentrated in Kent and Sussex counties. In 1810, for example, less than 10 percent of the state's black Methodists lived in New Castle County.[89]

Delaware's slaves supported Methodism with their hard-earned money as well as with their enthusiastic attendance. Although they represented the state's poorest residents, many of them somehow scraped together a few shillings or pennies to help itinerant circuit riders meet living expenses. Richard Allen remembered that slaves would often "divide" their small profits from raising their own vegetables "among white preachers of the Gospel."[90] Masters were often amazed at this enthusiasm. In one case, a slave owner in southwestern Sussex gave an elderly female her freedom because "she had too much religion." In 1801, during a service at Moore's Chapel in southwestern Sussex, free and enslaved blacks became so excited that they brought the gallery crashing down on whites below. Two years later, Asbury Methodist Church in Wilmington blamed African-Americans for broken benches, while in 1814 the white trustees of Barratt's Chapel in Kent County had to repair damages caused by free and unfree blacks during worship.[91]

The black style of worship, which included enthusiastic dancing, jumping, and vocal responses, has usually been attributed to African cultural and religious roots. Indeed, Albert J. Raboteau's study of slave religion maintains that among American slaves the gods of Africa may have given way to the God of white Christianity, but the African style remained alive.[92] Butler challenges that view by arguing that the roots of the slaves' worship style are found not in any social memory of Africa but in their exposure to the emotionalism of the Scottish and English evangelical services that were brought to America in the eighteenth and early nineteenth centuries. In short, because of the "spiritual holocaust" that cost them their religious heritage, Butler maintains that American slaves incorporated little that was undeniably African into their newly acquired Christian faith. As a result, in the late eighteenth century "African-American Christianity paralleled its white counterpart far more closely than would ever be true again."[93] An evaluation of the specifics of Butler's thesis requires an even closer look at the religious life of enslaved Delawareans.

Slave owners were of two minds concerning their bondspeoples' attraction to Methodism. On the one hand, the antislavery stance of Wesleyan preachers caused masters to speculate uneasily about the impact of sermons on their bondsmen and bondswomen. Moreover, through Methodist preaching, Bible readings, and hymns, slaves would see the parallel of their own difficult journey to the trials and tribulations of the ancient Israelites. The enslavement of the Hebrews in Egypt and their eventual deliverance from bondage through the intercession of a righteous God was not lost on the sons and daughters of Africa who were also held in bondage in a distant land. Not only did the Methodist message carry hope for this world, but it also promised liberation and equal treatment for blacks and whites when the souls of the dead faced final judgment. Clearly, this message was a very empowering one. Perhaps that was the concern of the owner of Theophilus Collins of Lewes, who in 1858 brutally attacked his slave for attending a Sunday night worship service against his wishes.[94]

On the other hand, Methodist sermons praised hard work and honesty and promised a heavenly reward for those who led a righteous life in Christ. Owners could view that sort of message as an opiate fed to enslaved blacks to cause them to labor hard, refrain from stealing from their masters, and accept their bondage with patience. Moreover, the Methodist sermon often idealized such deferential characteristics as patience, love, gentleness, sensitivity, humility, and submissiveness. If a slave listened closely to the preacher, he might turn into an ideal servant. Indeed, Richard Allen's master, Stokeley Sturgis, was convinced that religion made better bondspeople of his blacks and "often boasted of his slaves for their honesty and industry" after they had converted to Methodism.[95]

In truth, Methodism reinforced the slaves' self-esteem and its corollary, a strong desire for freedom, while paradoxically encouraging the very character traits that were so pleasing to masters. A case in point was the same Richard Allen, whose conversion evidently made him a better slave, at least from Sturgis's perspective, but it also stimulated his desire to be free and increased his confidence that freedom was coming. And that freedom was constantly on his mind because to Allen, even under "a good master," slavery was "a bitter pill."[96]

The celebratory nature of slaves at worship has usually been cited to make the point that black Methodism was demonstrably different from white Methodism. But in the late eighteenth century, despite the fact that blacks seemed more emotional and responsive at worship, the actual differences between black and white Methodists in Delaware were more a matter of degree than kind. This relative closeness between the two races on matters religious was demonstrated over and over again by the approval by white Methodists of the preaching of such leading black Methodists as Allen and former slave Harry Hosier. The record shows that both men were popular with white as well as with black audiences all over the state. In fact, so impressed with Hosier was the Oxford-educated Methodist leader Dr. Thomas Coke that, after accompanying him on a successful preaching trip through Delaware and the Eastern Shore in 1784, he wrote that his black companion was "one of the best preachers in the world."[97]

In singing, too, there was not a great difference between the two races at worship. At Methodist services, African-Americans sang the hymns of Charles Wesley rather than the spirituals and gospel music that later would contribute to the distinctiveness of black church services. Governor Richard Bassett, the state's leading lay Methodist of the late eighteenth and early nineteenth centuries, loved to hear "the colored people sing," not because they possessed an exotic sound or a very different rhythm but simply because "there was no sweeter music."[98]

If African-American Methodists had praised God in song in a manner unfamiliar to white ears, or used a preaching style dramatically different from that of white preachers, or delivered a message that seemed theologically alien to white sensibilities, then they would have lost their white audiences and the approval of the white clergy. And that is just the point. In singing, in preaching, in theology, and in responding to the Word, Delaware's enslaved Methodists closely modeled themselves after white Methodists during the late eighteenth century. While the former may have been more celebratory than the latter in their singing, their preaching, and their response to the Word, again the difference was more a matter of degree than kind. In summary, the evidence suggests that the Butler thesis, which maintains that American slavery led to the loss of almost all of the African religious heritage, seems to be valid when applied to Delaware. Is that really surprising? Religion, after all, is a form of cultural expression. As a recent study of early American culture makes clear, "People at the top have an immense advantage in influencing cultural forms. To believe otherwise is to misunderstand the nature of power."[99]

In one aspect of their religious experience, however, Delaware slaves were not content to simply model themselves after their white coreligionists. In their most important contribution to Methodism, they gave this white-led faith some sense of what it meant to be underprivileged and exploited. During the late eighteenth century, the large numbers of slaves who turned out for Methodist preaching sensitized a generation of white Methodists to the burdens of bondage experienced by their black brothers and sisters in Christ and strengthened the abolitionist sentiments already present in the hearts of circuit riders. Francis Asbury, who had been forced to seek refuge in Kent County during the Revolution, was particularly affected. In 1778 he was so pleased with black responses to his preaching in Delaware and on the Eastern Shore that he abandoned any equivocation on slavery by deciding that Methodists must support abolitionism or suffer God's displeasure.[100]

As it increasingly took on the trappings of the dominant church in Kent and Sussex during the early nineteenth century, Methodism became less concerned with the plight of enslaved blacks and slowly began to retreat from some of its more radical principles. Indeed, the softening of its stand against slavery in the early nineteenth century was duly noted by both slaves and free blacks and eventually caused a significant decline in the percentage of blacks who were Methodists.[101] Reflecting some years later on this change and on his days as a slave in Kent County in the 1770s, Richard Allen recalled how grateful he was in those early years to have "heard a Methodist preach." But he was troubled by the direction that white Methodism was taking in the early nineteenth century. Clearly voicing his disappointment with its weakened position on slavery and on other important early issues, Allen proposed that all Methodists should ask "for the good old way and walk therein."[102]

During the late eighteenth century, "the good old way" had been dominant in Delaware Methodism in part because of the support and the peculiar perspective contributed by the likes of Allen and a multitude of other enslaved blacks. And that support and peculiar perspective were not inspired primarily by memories of Africa but rather by needs and insights shaped by the interaction of African-Americans with the institution of slavery and white society. The evidence indicates that the religion of Delaware's unfree blacks, in the late eighteenth century, was an example of the African-American social experience triumphing over the African social heritage. Indeed, the primary force in shaping slave religion proved to be Methodism as practiced in the state of Delaware rather than remembered ceremonies and rituals as performed on the continent of Africa.

As in the other slave states, the culture of enslaved African-Americans in Delaware remained primarily oral because most slaves were illiterate. To the state government and to masters, the dangers posed by unfree blacks who could read or write were obvious: literate slaves would become increasingly discontented with their lot after reading antislavery literature. Moreover, literate slaves could forge passes and even organize rebellions. For these and other reasons, masters generally refused to educate their slaves. One Sussex slave pointed out in the midnineteenth century that although he was better treated by his master than many, he "never had any privileges to learn to read."[103]

Despite these barriers, a small minority did learn to read and write. In all probability they were taught by the master's children, by other slaves, or even by their own master or mistress. Some even may have taught themselves. One example was Absalom—later known as Absalom Jones, the prominent black leader in Philadelphia—who was born a slave in Cedar Creek Hundred, Sussex County, in 1746 or 1747. When he was very young, he was brought into his master's home where he was able to avoid the field work that was the lot of most slaves. Wanting to learn how to read and write, Absalom bought himself a primer and tried to persuade any literate person he encountered to instruct him. Evidently, by the time he was taken by his master to Philadelphia at the age of fifteen, he could read.[104]

Of the Delaware slaves listed as fugitives in the *Pennsylvania Gazette* from 1739 to 1785, approximately 10 percent were literate.[105] But because literate slaves usually were more tempted to run away than those who could not read or write, the general literacy rate among the state's slaves during the eighteenth century was probably closer to 5 percent. During the nineteenth century, the percentage of slaves who

Absalom Jones (1746–1818) by Raphaelle Peale. *Courtesy of the Delaware Art Museum, Wilmington.*

could read and write may have approached 10 percent, reflecting in part the higher literacy rate of the entire Delaware population.

Although hard statistics are impossible to come by, in all probability a slightly higher percentage of Delaware slaves than those farther south were literate. This strong likelihoood reflects the closer proximity, on a constant basis, of these slaves to literate whites. Farther south, the larger slave units meant greater isolation by most African-Americans from those white children and adults who could teach them to read and write. In addition, by the midnineteenth century, a number of slaveholding states specifically prohibited the instruction of slaves in reading and writing.[106] That step was never taken by Delaware. Despite a greater opportunity for literacy than elsewhere, the barriers to education remained so insurmountable to the overwhelming majority of Delaware's unfree blacks that a typical slave of the late antebellum period was described as being "destitute of the knowledge of spelling, to say nothing of reading."[107]

~

The close proximity to their masters must have been socially suffocating to most enslaved Delawareans. Perhaps sensing that their bondsmen and bondswomen needed some breathing room, many owners permitted them overnight visits to distant friends and relatives that might last up to three days during slack work periods. On some occasions, unfree blacks were even allowed to travel out of state. In 1764, for example, a slave from Newport, New Castle County, was permitted to visit friends in Philadelphia as long as he returned in two or three days.[108] Such trips more than a few miles away from the home farm usually required a pass from the master. Joe, for example, who walked from the town of New Castle to the northern part of Christiana Hundred in 1775, carried such a pass.[109] Freedom to travel and to visit across the Delaware landscape made it possible for slaves to congregate in large numbers, much to the chagrin of paranoid whites. Of particular concern was election day, when unfree blacks poured into town with or without their masters to take part in the festivities. In 1798, to head off such large gatherings, the General Assembly barred all slaves who lived in the countryside from coming into town on election day. In 1825 the same restriction was extended to slaves who lived in town; if they did not leave for the day, their master had to pay a two-dollar fine.[110]

In addition to all of Sunday and perhaps part of Saturday—harvesttime was an exception—enslaved Delawareans were not expected to work on a number of holidays including days around Christmas and New Year's. Typical may have been the bondsmen and bondswomen on a Sussex farm near Milton, who went "a Christmasing" on December 31, 1789, and did not return from visiting friends and relatives until January 4. While enslaved in nearby Talbot County, Maryland, Frederick Douglass observed that these holiday celebrations served the interests of the masters because they acted as "safety valves, to carry off the rebellious spirit of enslaved humanity."[111]

Although we know very little about these slave celebrations and other social gatherings, there is no doubt that music often played a central role. One of the primary reasons that slaves were attracted to Methodism was the fact that hymn singing was a significant part of the Wesleyan religious experience. Until the midnineteenth century, most black and white Methodists sang a capella because early Methodism associated musical instruments with frivolity and moral decadence. Fiddles particularly were rejected because "they revived memories that were associated with sin."[112] However, many enslaved Delawareans ignored Methodist warnings and became proficient on the European fiddle. But unlike slaves in states farther south, few made and played such African instruments as the balafo (a West African xylophone) and the banjo. As in other slave states, some black fiddlers doubtless became fixtures at white dances and other social gatherings. Indeed, their fiddles were so important that a surprising number carried them with them when they ran away. Another European instrument, the fife, was mastered by Peter, a hired slave near Newark in the early 1780s. Only the drum playing of John, who lived in eastern New Castle County in the 1760s but had spent his youth in the Spanish West Indies, suggests the survival of some African musical roots.[113]

In their leisure moments, enslaved blacks were addicted to the same vices that loomed large in white society. Liquor consumption was especially high among all races and all social classes in early Delaware. Not only was alcohol used as an opiate, as a social catalyst, and as a centerpiece to any celebration, but it also was consumed because it was reputed to possess considerable medicinal value. Even many white churchgoers, including Methodists, routinely drank astonishing amounts of liquor.[114]

Given the permissive social atmosphere of the time, the burden of slavery, and the fact that most masters distilled their own peach and apple brandy and kept it on the premises, it is not surprising that Harry of Sussex was "much given to strong drink," or that slaves Jerry Clark and Charles of New Castle County were "fond of strong liquor." The high consumption of alcohol inevitably led to fatal accidents. In 1825 a drunken slave fell out of a canoe into the Nanticoke River and drowned. The next year another intoxicated slave died from exposure while walking from Millsboro to his master's farm in Indian River Hundred, Sussex County.[115]

Some slaves were particularly prone to profanity. To halt the public displays that offended at least some whites, the legislature enacted a law in 1767 that specifically punished slaves for "profane swearing." But one wonders how effective this kind of legislation could be. It certainly did not deter Joe of New Castle County, who was described in 1771 as a "drunkard, swearer and liar." In addition to cursing and drinking, some slaves chewed tobacco. So dependent was Reedy Island slave Jacob Perkin in 1771 that he was "very apt to ask any person he sees use it for a chew."[116]

~

Whether working or relaxing, African-Americans were constantly reminded of the oppressive nature of slavery. That institution's potential for arbitrary cruelty may be seen in the treatment of Robert, a Kent County slave. In 1800 his owner, Richard Cooper, Esq., handcuffed and chained him alongside a horse and carriage to walk "through water and mire over rocks and ruts from Philadelphia to said Cooper's house one mile below Dover, the whole distance about 76 miles in two days." During the second day, a heavy and constant rain made the road impassable in places. But at least Robert survived his ordeal. Twenty-five years earlier in Sussex, Mingo was murdered by his master, Zachariah Collins. Found guilty of manslaughter, Collins successfully claimed "benefit of clergy" and was set free after his left thumb was branded with the letter "M."[117]

Always aware that they were subject to the whip or to other forms of severe physical abuse, enslaved African-Americans generally responded to their master's commands in a prudent manner. There were, of course, occasions when they refused to obey orders, and this refusal often led to physical confrontations (see Chapter III). Although some of these showdowns between slave and master may have initially altered the power relationship by making the master more willing to accommodate the desires of a particular slave to avoid more trouble, unfree blacks who repeatedly challenged their master's authority were usually legally or illegally sold out of state.[118]

Being prudent, however, did not mean toiling willingly in the master's fields or publicly agreeing with every one of the master's decisions. Expressing covertly their distaste for slave labor were unfree blacks such as Henry of Kent County, who during the 1820s avoided working in the fields by "pretending he was sick." An enslaved African-American might stop short of being confrontational and yet express disagreement by being "fretful and saucy," like Jake in central Sussex in the 1820s, who was adept at giving his master "a good deal of trouble."[119]

Some unfree African-Americans were openly critical of their owners because they viewed the master-slave relationship as a contract requiring reciprocal obligations. In return for labor, the master was expected to provide an acceptable level of food, shelter, and clothing. When he failed to meet those standards, his slaves voiced their disapproval. In 1770 in eastern Kent, for example, the right of unfree blacks to judge whether or not their masters were providing for them in the customary manner was recognized in an agreement between William Snipes and Caesar Rodney. Snipes had leased two of Rodney's slaves,

Ebenezer and Absalom, for five years. The agreement required Snipes "to keep and maintain in good victuals and clothes the above named negroes so that they shall not at any time during the term have reason to complain."[120]

Even decisions by slaveholders on whether or not to sell their slaves might be challenged by the African-Americans involved. In 1776, Caesar Rodney considered selling many of his slaves because he wanted to rent out much of his land. He was away at the time, but his slaves got wind of his intentions and asked how he could sell bondspeople who had "been raised" in his own house and did not want to leave his land. Thomas Rodney, who was looking after Caesar's plantation, wrote his brother about their reaction to the proposed sale. He then advised him to keep his slaves and rent them with the land, rather than "go through the disagreeable feelings that will arise from their petitions and remonstrances on separating and squandering them about to different masters." On hearing of these demands, an angry Caesar replied that his slaves "from their past vile behaviour . . . have no right to expect a favour" from him. Moreover, selling them made better financial sense than renting them with the land. Nevertheless, Caesar left it up to his brother to decide what to do. One guesses, on this issue at least, that the slaves got their way.[121]

Although a few whites may have agreed with Thomas Rodney's assessment that slavery made blacks happy, Delaware's bondsmen and bondswomen regarded it as an oppressive institution, and they desperately wanted their freedom. Even those blacks with "good masters" detested enslavement. Richard Allen described his own master as "a very kind and humane man," and yet he worked overtime to buy his freedom as soon as possible.[122] Particularly revealing were the words and actions of Sarah, George, Mingo, Jonathan, Dinbigh, and Elizabeth, all of whom were former slaves of Quaker Thomas Nock of Kent County. Nock freed his slaves and then, in the early 1780s, provided "restitution" to them in his will. After his death, the Duck Creek Meeting was to decide on the amount of compensation from Nock's estate that was due each of the former slaves. Before a final decision was made, however, the six blacks were brought before the meeting and questioned.[123] Instead of gratefully and humbly accepting whatever the Quakers might decide, they instead expressed their outrage at being held as slaves and made "allegations and demands" for considerable compensation. Only after being awarded a sum total of more than £100 were they satisfied.[124]

Even angrier was James Wenyam, a red-haired Kent County mulatto who ran away from his master in 1746. At the time, England and its colonies were engaging the French and their Indian allies in a struggle for control of North America. To get back at the Anglo-

American society that had enslaved him, Wenyam decided to "go to the French and Indians and fight for them."[125] More than a century later, three fugitives who escaped from Sussex to Philadelphia expressed the same resentment. James Alligood "did not believe in working my life out just to support some body else," while Jacob Blockson left another Sussex master because "I made up my mind that I did not want to be sold like a horse." The third, Andrew Jackson Boyce in eastern Sussex, left his master, "a very mean man to his servants . . . , and I got so tired of him I couldn't stand him any longer."[126]

If Delaware's African-Americans so despised enslavement, why did they not put up a better fight, or at least stage one significant revolt in the 226 years that slavery existed in the state? The relatively low ratio of enslaved blacks to whites and the small size of the slave units played a key role in preventing rebellions, but also important was the fact that by the end of the Revolution, Pennsylvania in general and Philadelphia in particular were seen as havens for discontented blacks looking for freedom. By giving angry slaves the chance to express their opposition to bondage by walking away from it, Pennsylvania acted as a safety valve that may have headed off an explosion.[127]

Notes

*Still, *The Underground Rail Road*, 511.

1. U.S. Census Bureau, Manuscripts, 1860, Delaware.

2. Statistics based on *Negro Population in the United States, 1790–1915* (New York, 1968), 57; U.S. Census Bureau, Manuscripts, 1810, 1840, 1860, Delaware, DSA. Because almost all free blacks in 1790 were either slaves or children thereof of the late colonial period, I have combined free blacks and slaves in 1790 to get an indication of the distribution of slaves among the Lower Counties in 1775.

3. Kolchin, *American Slavery*, 177; Welch, ed., *Memoirs of Mary Parker Welch*, 139. Statistics based on U.S. Census Bureau, Manuscripts, 1800, Delaware. The seven communities examined, in order of size, were:

Town	Total Population	Slaves
Wilmington	4,066	186
New Castle	824	58
Lewes	768	73
Milford	651	63
Duck Creek		
Cross Roads (Smyrna)	593	16
Dover	575	47
Camden	323	8
Total	7,800	451

4. Statistics based on U.S. Census Bureau, Manuscripts, 1800, Delaware.

5. Statistics based on Bushman and Hawley, eds., "A Random Sample," passim; U.S. Census Bureau, Manuscripts, 1800, 1810, 1820, 1830, 1840, 1850, 1860, Delaware.

6. Statistics based on Bushman and Hawley, eds., "A Random Sample," passim; Bendler, *Colonial Delaware Assemblymen,* passim; Sussex and New Castle County estate inventories, passim, DSA.

7. Essah, "Slavery and Freedom in the First State," 69. Essah's figures are slightly lower than those in Lewis C. Gray, *History of Agriculture in the Southern United States to 1860,* 2 vols. (Gloucester, MA, 1958), 1:530–31.

8. Kulikoff, *Tobacco and Slaves,* 330–38.

9. Blassingame, *The Slave Community,* 307; Parish, *Slavery,* 5.

10. Mullin, *Flight and Rebellion,* 51; Kolchin, *Unfree Labor,* 135; George W. McDaniel, *Hearth and Home* (Philadelphia, 1982), 42–43.

11. Bushman and Hawley, eds., "A Random Sample," 61–67; Indenture, June 12, 1784, Logan Papers 33:21, HSP.

12. James Gorrell (1751), Kent County Will Book K, 49, KCCH; *Pennsylvania Gazette,* 5/9/1754, 9/29/63, 6/6/65; Welch, ed., *Memoirs of Mary Parker Welch,* 66.

13. Kolchin, *Unfree Labor,* 135; McDaniel, *Hearth and Home,* 41, 53; Kent County Orphans Court Records, Book C, 270, KCCH; Sussex County Orphans Court Records, microfilm reel no. 761: 126 and reel no. 759: 15, DSA. For dimensions of houses of white farmers of all classes see Orphans Court Records for all three counties, passim.

14. Theresa A. Singleton, ed., *The Archaeology of Slavery and Plantation Life* (New York, 1985), 76.

15. This generalization on the occupants of a slave cabin is based on wills, inventories, and other primary sources from Delaware's three counties, most of which are found in DSA.

16. Bushman and Hawley, eds., "A Random Sample," 390; Boorstin, ed., *Delaware Cases,* 1:138; Herman, *The Stolen House,* 130.

17. Allen, *The Life Experience,* 18.

18. Bushman and Hawley, eds., "A Random Sample," 3; Elizabeth Darby, February 27, 1772, Robert Hill, December 27, 1815, and Ebednigo Elliott, October 25, 1825, Sussex County Estate Inventories, DSA.

19. Schlebecker, *Whereby We Thrive,* 33; *Pennsylvania Gazette,* 9/18/1740, 8/7/55, 1/28/62, 7/19/64, 8/21/75.

20. *Pennsylvania Gazette,* 7/24/1746, 7/31/46, 10/8/47, and passim.

21. Ibid., 7/9/1747, 1/26/64, 7/19/64, 8/16/64, 4/29/75, 8/26/75, 1/7/83, and passim.

22. Indenture between John and Philemon Dickinson and William Howell, March 25, 1767, Logan Papers 23:80, HSP.

23. Kulikoff, *Tobacco and Slaves,* 393; Clemens, *The Atlantic Economy,* 151.

24. June 19, 1781, Land and Business Records, box 9, folder 5, Dickinson Papers, HSP; Bushman and Hawley, eds., "A Random Sample," 61, 113.

25. *Pennsylvania Gazette,* 6/30/1750, 1/3/63; Thomas Flowers, April 20, 1789, Sussex County Estate Inventories, DSA; Thomas L. Webber, *Deep Like the Rivers: Education in the Slave Quarter Community, 1831–1865* (New York, 1978), 13–14.

26. Descriptions of fugitive slaves were taken from notices in the *Pennsylvania Gazette, Delaware Gazette,* and *Delaware and Eastern Shore Advertiser,* passim; *Delaware Gazette,* 2/19/1790.

27. *Weekly Union* (Georgetown), 1/29/1864; Still, *The Underground Rail Road*, 237, 516–17, 533.

28. Fletcher, *Pennsylvania Agriculture*, 226. The vast majority of slave owners had orchards, according to Sussex, Kent, and New Castle County estate inventories and other records in DSA.

29. Hancock, "Descriptions and Travel Accounts of Delaware," 39; Allen, *The Life Experience*, 29; Indenture between John and Philemon Dickinson and William Howell, March 25, 1767, Logan Papers 23:80, HSP; John Truitt (1818), Sussex County Will Book No. 7, 364–65, SCCH.

30. Wood, *Black Majority*, 120; Hancock and McCabe, *Milton's First Century*, 299; Justice, *Life and Ancestry of Warner Mifflin*, 61–62.

31. In Hancock and McCabe, *Milton's First Century*, 299, it is obvious that deer had disappeared from southern Delaware by the midnineteenth century. Savitt, *Medicine and Slavery*, 45–46; John B. Boles, *Black Southerners, 1619–1869* (Lexington, KY, 1983), 91–92.

32. Larkin, *The Reshaping of Everyday Life*, 169–70; Kolchin, *American Slavery*, 113.

33. Calculations based on citations in Wright, ed., *Delaware Newspaper Abstracts*, passim; *Pennsylvania Gazette*, passim.

34. Kolchin, *Unfree Labor*, 134.

35. *Pennsylvania Gazette*, 10/18/1747, 6/6/54, 1/28/62, 10/20/63, 8/24/64, and passim. Billy G. Smith, in "Blacks Who Stole Themselves: Fugitives from Slavery in the Eighteenth-Century Mid-Atlantic Region" (unpublished paper given at the University of Delaware, November 8, 1990), 27, maintains that a lower percentage of fugitive slaves in the mid-Atlantic region than other population groups bore smallpox scars. However, these scars may have been less visible on black than on white skin.

36. *Pennsylvania Gazette*, 6/22/1769.

37. Savitt, *Medicine and Slavery*, 59; Boles, *Black Southerners*, 103; Herman, *The Stolen House*, 214.

38. Boles, *Black Southerners*, 103; Savitt, *Medicine and Slavery*, 64.

39. Boles, *Black Southerners*, 91–92; Savitt, *Medicine and Slavery*, 45; Elijah Evans, January 10, 1826, Sussex County Estate Inventories, DSA.

40. Webber, *Deep Like the Rivers*, 9; Boles, *Black Southerners*, 101; Welch, ed., *Memoirs of Mary Parker Welch*, 147.

41. Klein and Engerman, "Fertility Differentials," 374; Meir and Rudwick, *From Plantation to Ghetto*, 58; Parish, *Slavery*, 57; Boles, *Black Southerners*, 69; John West (1796), Sussex County Will Book D-5, 131, SCCH.

42. Klein and Engerman, "Fertility Differentials," 357–74; Menard, "The Maryland Slave Population," 302.

43. Klein and Engerman, "Fertility Differentials," 369; Elizabeth Brinkle (1741), Kent County Will Book I, 127, KCCH; John Goffarth (1750), New Castle County Will Book G, 401, DSA; Elizabeth West (1746), Sussex County Will Book No. 2, 12, SCCH; Isaac Jones (1784), Sussex County Will Book D-4, 178, ibid.; John Loughland (1773), Sussex County Will Book No. 2, 479–80, ibid.; Ebenezer Carey (1793), Sussex County Will Book D-4, 399, ibid.; Frederick Douglass, *Narrative of the Life of Frederick Douglass, An American Slave* (New York, 1968), 24; Webber, *Deep Like the Rivers*, 11.

44. For an increase in the master's recognition of slave marriages beginning in the late eighteenth century see Sussex, Kent, and New Castle County will books, passim, DSA. For the fact that slave marriages were unrecognized in law throughout the South see Kolchin, *American Slavery*, 123.

45. This assumption is based on the fact that Allen never mentions either of his parents or his younger siblings again. Allen, *The Life Experience*; Carol V. George, *Segregated Sabbaths: Richard Allen and the Emergence of Independent Black Churches, 1760–1840* (New York, 1973), 23–25.

46. Douglass, *Narrative*, 24.

47. Kulikoff, *Tobacco and Slaves*, 330.

48. Catherine Gordon, May 10, 1776, and William Gray, April 30, 1801, Sussex County Probate Inventories, DSA.

49. F. Edward Wright, ed., *Vital Records of Kent and Sussex Counties, Delaware, 1686–1800* (Silver Spring, MD, 1986), 107.

50. Kulikoff, *Tobacco and Slaves*, 371; Sussex, Kent, and New Castle County wills and estate inventories, passim, DSA.

51. The significant distances between slave units can be seen in U.S. Census Bureau, Manuscripts, Delaware, for the entire antebellum era. Census takers usually listed living units in the order in which they encountered them while proceeding down a given road. The distance between them suggests the considerable way that enslaved males were forced to travel within the state to find a suitable marriage partner or to visit their wives and children.

52. George Alfred Townsend, *The Entailed Hat* (Cambridge, MD, 1955), 397.

53. *Negro Population, 1790–1915*, 209.

54. Berlin, *Slaves without Masters*, 6; Horle, ed., *Records of the Courts of Sussex County*, 1110; de Valinger, ed., *Court Records of Kent County*, 146, 278.

55. de Valinger, ed., *Court Records of Kent County*, 279, 343; Essah, "Slavery and Freedom in the First State," 42.

56. *Laws of the State of Delaware*, 1:108–9, 105–6.

57. Ibid., 1:380; 2:1201.

58. *Delaware Gazette*, 5/5/1792; Boorstin, ed., *Delaware Cases*, 1:33; *Laws of the State of Delaware*, 4:112–13.

59. Sarah, 1821, Kent County Slavery Material, 1764–1866, Miscellaneous, DSA.

60. de Valinger, ed., *A Calendar of the Ridgely Family Letters*, 2:172. Scharf, *History of Delaware*, 2:1118, lists John A. Banning as owning 326 acres in Little Creek Hundred, Kent County, in 1816.

61. Bayley, *A Narrative*, 38–41.

62. Ibid., 1–32, 42.

63. Ibid., 40–41.

64. Thomas Irons (1784), Kent County Will Book M, 44, 92, 108, 226, and passim, KCCH; Sussex and New Castle County will books, passim, SCCH and DSA.

65. Nathaniel Hayes, 1811, Nanticoke Hundred, Sussex County Estate Inventories, DSA; Sussex, Kent, and New Castle County probate inventories, passim, ibid.

66. February 28, 1781, Land and Business Records, Dickinson Papers, box 9, folder 5, HSP.

67. July 19, 1782, and January 14, 1783, Logan Papers 28:108, HSP. Slave families in Delaware tended to be less vital and complete than those portrayed elsewhere in the South in Herbert G. Gutman, *The Black Family in Slavery and Freedom, 1750–1925* (New York, 1976).

68. For a brief summary of the debate and some personal observations on its development see Kolchin, *American Slavery*, 40–49.

69. James Deetz, "American Historical Archaeology: Methods and Results," *Science* 239 (January 22, 1988): 362–67. For some reason, not much slave-produced Colono Ware has been found in Georgia, which may reflect the relatively late introduction of slavery to that colony. See also Leland Ferguson, *Uncommon Ground: Archaeology and Early African America, 1650–1800* (Washington, DC, 1992). There is also a type of Colono Ware made by Native Americans, but its social history is not germane to this discussion.

70. Although the state constitution of 1776 prohibited the importation of slaves, it was not until the law of 1787 that there were teeth in the ban. Munroe, *Colonial Delaware*, 189–90. For general figures on slave imports and on the percentages of slaves who were African-born, outside of Delaware, see Kolchin, *American Slavery*, 79, 38, 49.

71. Kolchin, *Unfree Labor*, 218; Boles, *Black Southerners*, 42. Allan Kulikoff, in *Tobacco and Slaves*, 326, disagrees with Kolchin and Boles by intimating that masters were more directly involved in the naming process.

72. Kent County Will Books, 1702–1788, passim, KCCH; Sussex County Will Books, 1702–1788, passim, SCCH. New Castle County wills were not used because a large number for the period are missing and the remainder may not be a representative sample. For brief discussions of African naming practices see Wood, *Black Majority*, 181–86; Kulikoff, *Tobacco and Slaves*, 325–26; and Gutman, *The Black Family*, 185–201. An analysis of 258 slave names in Philadelphia during the colonial period indicates that 11 percent had an African or an Anglicized form of an African name. See Nash, *Forging Freedom*, 81. For North Carolina see Kolchin, *American Slavery*, 45.

73. In Philadelphia during the colonial period, of the 258 slave names examined, some 16 percent were classical. Nash, *Forging Freedom*, 81. For the Carolinas see Kolchin, *American Slavery*, 45–46.

74. Kent County Will Books, 1702–1788, passim, KCCH; Sussex County Will Books, 1702–1788, passim, SCCH. For discussion of Fillis as an African name see Kulikoff, *Tobacco and Slaves*, 325.

75. Kent and Sussex County estate inventories, passim, DSA; James Stewart, file 64, no. 9, Rose Cottage, Bureau of Museum and Historic Sites, Dover.

76. Bushman and Hawley, eds., "A Random Sample," 18; John Newell (1759), Kent County Will Book K, 216, KCCH; John Short (1817), Sussex County Estate Inventories, DSA.

77. Jon Butler, *Awash in a Sea of Faith: Christianizing the American People* (Cambridge, MA, 1990), 157–59.

78. Munroe, *Federalist Delaware*, 44. For a history of the Anglican Church in the colony see Nelson W. Rightmeyer, *The Anglican Church in Delaware* (Philadelphia, 1947).

79. Hancock, "Descriptions and Travel Accounts of Delaware," 37, 39; C. H. B. Turner, ed., *Some Records of Sussex County*, 185.

80. Hancock, "Descriptions and Travel Accounts of Delaware," 37, 32, 38.

81. Ibid., 39.

82. Ibid.

83. Ibid., 39; Albert J. Raboteau, *Slave Religion: The Invisible Institution in the Antebellum South* (New York, 1980), 32.

84. Leonard J. Trinterud, *The Forming of an American Tradition: A Reexamination of Colonial Presbyterianism* (Philadelphia, 1949), 207.

85. Williams, *The Garden of American Methodism*, 92–94.

86. Ibid., 111–18; Allen, *The Life Experience*, 30.

87. Williams, *The Garden of American Methodism*, 111–18, 143–46; Allen, *The Life Experience*, 30.

88. Statistics are based on figures in *Minutes of the Annual Conferences of the Methodist Episcopal Church for the Years 1773–1828* (New York, 1840) under "Philadelphia Conference," passim.

89. Ibid.

90. Allen, *The Life Experience*, 29–30.

91. Williams, *The Garden of American Methodism*, 114, 115.

92. Raboteau, *Slave Religion*, 43–92.

93. Butler, *Awash in a Sea of Faith*, 153–62, 248–49.

94. Still, *The Underground Rail Road*, 516–17.

95. Williams, *The Garden of American Methodism*, 110; Allen, *The Life Experience*, 17.

96. Allen, *The Life Experience*, 17–18.

97. Williams, *The Garden of American Methodism*, 143–46.

98. Henry Boehm, *Reminiscences, Historical and Biographical of Sixty Years in the Ministry* (New York, 1865), 429.

99. Bushman, *The Refinement of America*, 405.

100. Francis Asbury, *Journal and Letters of Francis Asbury*, 3 vols., ed. Elmer Clark (Nashville, 1958), 1:273, 274, 582. For Asbury's opposition to slavery during the Revolution, which was later edited out of his journal, see Frank E. Maser, "Discovery," *Methodist History* (January 1971): 35.

101. Williams, *The Garden of American Methodism*, 111–14.

102. Allen, *The Life Experience*, 30.

103. Still, *The Underground Rail Road*, 105.

104. Nash, *Forging Freedom*, 67.

105. *Pennsylvania Gazette*, 1739–1785, passim.

106. Kolchin, *American Slavery*, 129.

107. Still, *The Underground Rail Road*, 490. For a discussion of slave literacy in the South see Genovese, *Roll, Jordan, Roll*, 561–66; Webber, *Deep Like the Rivers*; and Janet D. Cornelius, *"When I Can Read My Title Clear": Literacy, Slavery, and Religion in the Antebellum South* (Columbia, SC, 1991).

108. *Pennsylvania Gazette*, 1/26/1764.

109. Ibid., 5/17/1775.

110. *Laws of the State of Delaware*, 3:9–10; 4:415.

111. Hancock and McCabe, *Milton's First Century*, 42; Henry (1837), Negro, Sussex Coroner's Inquest, DSA; Frederick Douglass, *Narrative of the Life of Frederick Douglass: An American Slave*, ed. Benjamin Quarles (Cambridge, MA, 1960), 106–7.

112. Williams, *The Garden of American Methodism*, 156–57; Adam Wallace, *The Parson of the Islands* (Baltimore, 1906), 193–95.

113. *Pennsylvania Gazette*, 9/6/1750, 2/4/55, 10/1/67, 7/26/84, 6/24/62; *Delaware and Eastern Shore Advertiser*, 6/15/1795, 10/15/94.

114. Williams, *The Garden of American Methodism*, 151–55; William Morgan, "William Morgan's Memoir of His Own Life," 6, 7, 14, 16, DSA.

115. *Pennsylvania Gazette*, 10/1/1767, 1/20/73, 1/22/83; *Delaware Gazette*, 9/28/1783; Martin (1825–26), and Henry (1837), Negro, Sussex County Coroner's Inquest, DSA.

116. *Votes and Proceedings of the House of Representatives of the Government of the Counties of New Castle, Kent and Sussex, upon Delaware, 1765–1770* (Dover, DE, 1931), 127–31; *Pennsylvania Gazette*, 1/10/1771.

117. Report, May 9, 1800, folder 1, Brian Papers, HSD; Special Court for Negroes, 1775, Court of Oyer and Terminer, Sussex County, DSA. For an explanation of "benefit of clergy" see Chapter VI, note 24.

118. Welch, ed., *Memoirs of Mary Parker Welch*, 147–50.

119. Ibid., 151; Petition of George Cubbage, Kent County, 1820, Slavery Material, 1764–1866, Miscellaneous, DSA.

120. Articles of Agreement, December 15, 1770, box 18, folder 8, Caesar Rodney signer, H. F. Brown Collection, HSD.

121. Thomas Rodney to Caesar Rodney, April 26, 1776, box 6, folder 9, Caesar Rodney Collection, HSD; Harold B. Hancock, ed., "Letters to and from Caesar Rodney," *Delaware History* (Spring–Summer 1983): 209–10.

122. Allen, *The Life Experience*, 15, 18–19.

123. Thomas Nock (1782), Kent County Will Book K, 254–55, DSA.

124. Ibid.

125. *Pennsylvania Gazette*, 7/31/1746.

126. Still, *The Underground Rail Road*, 511, 510, 518.

127. Nash, *Forging Freedom*, 138–39.

V

The Long Road to Freedom

Slavery is nearly extinct in Delaware owing to the operation of a
system of laws tending all to its gradual abolition.
    —John M. Clayton to Josiah Randall, February 26, 1844*

During the late seventeenth century, some of Delaware's African-
Americans could look forward to freedom after serving their white
masters for a specified number of years. By the early eighteenth century, however, the sometime practice of temporary servitude had been
abandoned. Now, all black male and female servants, and all children
of black female servants, were considered slaves for life. Only
manumission by their masters could legally end this lifetime of bondage. During the years from 1713 to 1775 a few masters freed one or
more of their slaves, but the evidence suggests that in Delaware, as
well as in neighboring Maryland, less than 5 percent of the black population was free during the late colonial period.[1]

The American Revolution and the postrevolutionary era marked a
dramatic increase in the number of slave manumissions in the state.
Although it is impossible to provide exact figures, manumissions
caused enslaved blacks to decline from an estimated 95 percent of
Delaware's African-Americans in 1775 to 70 percent in 1790 and to
only 24 percent by 1810.[2]

Slave manumissions had increased dramatically throughout most
of the Upper South during the late eighteenth century, but no other
southern state matched Delaware's rate. It was the only state south of
the Mason-Dixon Line to experience a numerical decline in its slave
population from 1775 to 1810. During those same thirty-five years,
Delaware easily outstripped New York and New Jersey in manumitting its slaves. By 1810, when 76 percent of Delaware's blacks were
free, the corresponding figure for New York was 63 percent and for
New Jersey only 42 percent. Of all the eastern states south of New

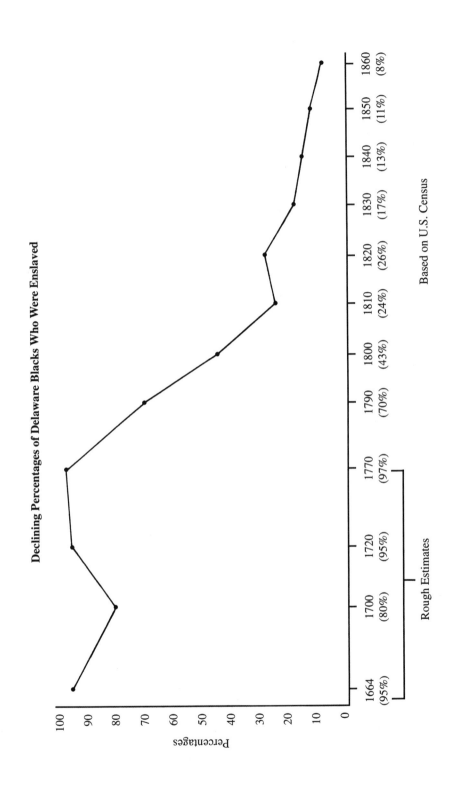

Declining Percentages of Delaware Blacks Who Were Enslaved

Percentages

100
90
80
70
60
50
40
30
20
10
0

1664
(95%)

1700
(80%)

1720
(95%)

1770
(97%)

1790
(70%)

1800
(43%)

1810
(24%)

1820
(26%)

1830
(17%)

1840
(13%)

1850
(11%)

1860
(8%)

Rough Estimates

Based on U.S. Census

England, only Pennsylvania had a higher percentage of its African-Americans free from the bonds of slavery.[3] What is particularly remarkable is that Delawareans freed such a large percentage of their slaves despite the fact that, unlike the residents of Pennsylvania, New York, and New Jersey, they were never required by state law to do so. All manumissions were voluntary acts by individual slaveholders, but so numerous were they that in 1850 a Wilmington newspaper observed that Delaware "has more free colored in proportion to its population than any state in the Union."[4]

Because free blacks were so few in number in the early eighteenth century, they were generally ignored by the colonial legislature. Of the handful of masters who did free their slaves, some manumitted only aged and crippled ones because they were seen as economic liabilities. (At least a few Delaware slave owners continued this practice throughout the antebellum years.) Incapable of supporting themselves once free, these old and lame African-Americans soon became indigent and a burden to the three county governments. By 1731 there were enough impoverished aged and crippled free blacks in Delaware to cause all three county governments to complain. In that same year the legislature responded by requiring masters to reimburse the appropriate county government for the costs of providing for those indigent blacks who had been their former slaves. In 1740, to head off future problems of this nature, the legislature further required that each master provide an indemnity bond of £30 to the appropriate county government for each slave manumitted who was either over thirty-five years old or in poor health.[5]

In that year the legislature also took its first real look at free blacks and did not like what it saw. It perceived them as unwilling to work and therefore "an evil example to slaves." Because they represented a threat to the efficiency and stability of slavery, the number of future manumissions had to be seriously curtailed. But it was not until 1767, when slavery was at its height in Delaware, that the legislature took further action by demanding that slaves of all ages and conditions be covered by individual indemnity bonds of £60 before being legally manumitted. The new bond requirement made all but the most committed masters think twice. A Kent County Quaker wanted to free his blacks just prior to the Revolution but did not because of the "oppressive law in force relative to the freeing of Negroes."[6]

During the 1770s and 1780s some slaveholders simply avoided paying the bonds by freeing their slaves without filling out any official manumission documents. Nevertheless, to the growing number of abolitionists, the indemnity requirement was a significant impediment to even more manumissions. By 1785 these abolitionists were complaining to the state government. In 1787, with abolitionist sentiment now a strong force in Delaware, the required indemnity bond for manumitted slaves between the ages of eighteen and thirty-five was dropped by the legislature. Although after 1787 the indemnity bond requirement for manumitted slaves under the age of eighteen and over the age of thirty-five was probably ignored, it was officially continued until 1819.[7]

Joining the state government in placing barriers in the path of masters wanting to free their slaves were neighboring whites who were fearful that manumission would give free blacks more liberty to rob and steal, and to influence in other negative ways their own enslaved blacks. Angry neighbors exchanged cold glances and hot words with masters intent on immediately freeing their slaves and pointed to such free blacks as Martin Doherty of Kent County, who in 1822 not only stole for himself but also seduced "the negroes and servants of the neighbors into the commission of crime." Indeed, the argument that manumissions would turn loose in his neighborhood a horde of thieves caused Quaker abolitionist Warner Mifflin to delay freeing his own slaves.[8]

Owners who wanted to free their slaves often angered heirs. Even after the 1787, 1789, and 1797 legal restrictions on out-of-state sales seriously limited the potential market value of Delaware slaves, unfree blacks continued to represent a valuable legacy. In 1816 in southwestern Sussex County, for example, a male slave between sixteen and thirty-four was worth one hundred fifty dollars, while a yoke of oxen was worth twenty dollars and an acre of land was expected to bring only one dollar.[9] It was upsetting to prospective heirs to learn that the slaves whom they were to inherit were about to be manumitted by parents or other relatives. At times, efforts by heirs to persuade owners to reconsider manumission must have been very intense.

Despite required indemnity bonds, hostile white neighbors, and angry heirs, a few masters did free one or more of their slaves during the colonial era, but with some apprehension. John Miers of eastern Sussex, for example, manumitted a female in his 1749 will, "provided she behaveth as a free Negro out [*sic*] to do."[10] Occasionally, trepidation was pushed aside by guilt that might not surface until the master was on his deathbed. In 1774 the dying Andrew Caldwell of Kent County had just finished drawing up his will, which, among other provisions, manumitted his slave Jack. On seeing his bondsman across the room, Caldwell called out to him from his bed in a tired but emotion-laden voice, "Poor old Jack, you are free, you are a free man."[11] But despite the actions of masters such as Caldwell and Miers, manumissions were rare in the late colonial period.

The Revolution marked a dramatic increase in manumissions for a number of reasons. The wartime disruption of the international market for corn and wheat, along with the earlier abandonment of tobacco and its attendant hill-and-hoe agriculture, caused slavery to be less profitable than in former years. As a result, the value of Delaware slaves declined during and immediately after the war.[12] The changing agricultural economy, combined with the ban on interstate sales of slaves, further limited the market value of these bondspeople during the late eighteenth century and throughout the antebellum years. The substantially lower market value of enslaved Delawareans, when compared to that of slaves in Virginia or in any other southern state, partially explains why the manumission rate in the years from 1775 to 1810 was far higher in Delaware than in any other state with a significant slave population.[13] Freeing a slave in Delaware was a much smaller financial sacrifice than freeing one in Virginia or South Carolina.

More than economic imperatives lay behind the extraordinary number of manumissions between 1775 and 1810. The new ideas of the Enlightenment, which swept through much of Anglo-America during the eighteenth century, proved attractive to many Delawareans as well as to other whites living in the Upper South.[14] Not only did the Enlightenment's emphasis on natural rights and individual freedom help spark support for the Revolution, but it also caused some Delawareans and other Americans to examine seriously for the first time the institution of slavery. How could one denounce the attempts of George III to enslave English colonists while ignoring the enslavement of blacks by those same colonists? Antislavery petitioners to the state legislature jumped on that very fact in 1786 by quoting directly from the Declaration of Independence "that all men are created equal; that they are endowed by their creator with certain unalienable rights; that among these are life, liberty, and the pursuit of happiness." Clearly, the petitioners added, slavery was "unjustifiable upon any principles of reason or justice."[15]

The specific impact of such abstract ideas as natural rights, however, can be exaggerated. John Dickinson, as much as any Delawarean, was attuned to the principles of the Enlightenment that fueled the Revolution, and he favored the abolition of slavery. And yet, when it came time for him to free a half-dozen slaves in 1781, the motive was quite clear: his six African-Americans had simply become "a burden."[16] If, in many cases, the ideas of the Enlightenment cannot be directly tied to the extraordinary rise in manumissions, they did affect the freeing of blacks in an indirect manner. The concepts of natural rights and individual freedom certainly contributed to the willingness of Anglo-American colonists to take up arms against the mother country. The resulting tension between Patriot and Tory, the persistent coastal raids by the Royal Navy, and the brief occupation of part of New Castle County by the British army in 1777 added up to chaos and confusion in Delaware during the war years. Some African-Americans took advantage of the absence of their masters on military duty and the general turmoil to escape from bondage. Although the actual number who escaped during the Revolution is unknown, the Council of Delaware admitted in 1782 that some of the state's slaves had fled to the British.[17]

Another path to freedom was enlistment in the Patriot forces. Although African-American recruits in state militias or in the Continental Army were generally limited to noncombatant roles, in many states military service by unfree blacks was often rewarded with manumission. Although Delaware did not offer its slaves freedom in exchange for military service, it did follow Virginia's example of letting them serve in their masters' places. Moreover, if a Delaware master wanted to reward his bondsman with freedom for enlisting in his place, then that was a private matter between the two men. Indications are that only a very few Delaware slaves actually served against the British for an extended period and were subsequently freed.[18]

Among many Delaware whites, a more powerful impulse for manumission than changing economic conditions or the ideas of the Enlightenment came from the religious principles of the Society of Friends and the Methodists. But long before these two denominations launched their offensive against slavery, Peter Cornelius Plockhoy led forty antislavery Mennonites from Europe to present-day Lewes in 1663. The previous year he had announced that slavery would not be tolerated in the future Mennonite settlement on the Delaware Bay. After the English took Delaware from the Dutch in 1664, Plockhoy and his fellow Mennonites moved to Germantown, just north of Philadelphia. There is, however, some indication that he was back in the Lewes area in 1700.[19] Although they represent an obscure chapter in the state's early history, Plockhoy and his Mennonite followers were the first white Delawareans to take a clear stand against slavery.

While Quaker meetings were found in all three Lower Counties at the beginning of the eighteenth century, Friends represented only a very small percentage of Delawareans throughout the eighteenth and nineteenth centuries. In Sussex, in 1728, an estimated 3 percent of the population was Quaker; in Kent, in 1743, the estimated figure was only 5 percent. Even in New Castle, where Quakers may have been more numerous, they probably represented considerably less than 10 percent of the population throughout the entire eighteenth century.[20] During the late colonial period, their weekly meetings continued to show signs of vitality in New Castle and Kent, but not in Sussex. It was because of their wealth and standing as merchants, millers, and landowners, rather than their numbers, that Quakers were able to exercise considerable influence over Delaware's economic, political, and social development.

These Quaker meetings were part of the Philadelphia Yearly Meeting and therefore subject to its directives. During the colonial period, both Pennsylvania and Delaware Friends were less than united in the condemnation of slavery. When a Quaker in eastern Sussex in 1749 freed one of his three slaves, few other Delaware Friends followed suit.[21] By midcentury, however, the Philadelphia Yearly Meeting began to put increasing pressure on Delawareans and other Quakers under its jurisdiction both to abstain from the slave trade and to manumit all of their slaves. In 1754, Quakers John Woolman of New Jersey and Anthony Benezet of Pennsylvania mounted a strong attack on slavery before the Philadelphia Yearly Meeting, which in the next year warned Friends against buying or importing slaves. In 1758 it called on monthly meetings to exclude from leadership positions all Friends who continued to purchase and import slaves. In 1766, Woolman visited meetings in parts of Delaware and the Eastern Shore of Maryland, spreading the abolitionist message. Six years later, in 1774, the Philadelphia Yearly Meeting raised to disownment the penalty for buying and selling slaves. And finally, in October 1776, the Yearly Meeting directed all connected meetings to disown Friends who held slaves.[22]

At the time of the 1776 directive, a number of Delaware Quakers, primarily concentrated in Kent County, continued to own slaves. Because some of these people in Kent held far more slaves than their Philadelphia brethren, they were called on to make a significantly greater economic sacrifice. The Duck Creek Monthly Meeting, which included weekly meetings in Kent, part of Sussex, and southern New Castle County, listed at least eleven member families who owned slaves in late 1776. But the Philadelphia Yearly Meeting's directive, as well as its prior urgings, had a considerable impact. The few Quaker manumissions that had marked the early 1770s became a flood tide after 1774. From 1775 to 1783 members of the Duck Creek Monthly Meeting freed 424 African-Americans; and statewide, more than 600 blacks were manumitted by Quakers from 1770 to 1780, primarily in Kent County. During that decade, Quakers probably freed outright or through delayed manumissions between 7 and 10 percent of Delaware's total slave population.[23] By 1784, Friends in the state had granted either immediate or delayed manumission to almost all of their slaves. (Delayed manumission meant freedom for females at age eighteen and males at twenty-one.) The few who continued to hold adult slaves did so because they shared ownership with non-Quakers and therefore lacked the legal right to free the jointly held bondspersons.[24]

Delaware's leading Quaker abolitionist was the same Warner Mifflin, of near Camden in Kent County. Born in 1745 on his father's plantation in Accomack County on Virginia's Eastern Shore, Mifflin grew up in a Quaker family that probably owned more than one hundred African-Americans. At the age of fourteen, he was persuaded by a conversation with one of his father's slaves that the institution was evil and that he should never be a slaveholder. Nevertheless, through marriage and inheritance, Mifflin acquired at least thirty-seven slaves who accompanied him north to Delaware in 1767. Convinced that holding fellow humans in bondage was a "breach of Divine Law," he freed all of his slaves in 1774 and 1775 and then evidently persuaded his father in Virginia to free those one hundred slaves in 1775. Mifflin's timing may have been influenced by the actions of his good friend and fellow Kent County Quaker Govey Emerson, who provided for the manumission of his own bondsmen in a 1773 will. In subsequent years, Mifflin was such a committed enemy of slavery that he became known throughout the United States and Western Europe. In addition to traveling widely to promote the abolitionist cause, he attacked slavery through letters, petitions, and pamphlets that found their way to the General Assembly, other state legislatures, and the U.S. Congress.[25]

In the late seventeenth century George Fox, the English founder of the Society of Friends, had recommended that when enslaved blacks were freed, they should not be sent away "empty handed."[26] Most Quaker slaveholders in Delaware followed Fox's advice. Emerson, for example, arranged for both his male and female slaves to "be learnt to read distinctly" and then given "a good warm suit of cloaths fit to labour in." Mifflin provided his newly freed slaves with livestock and land in return for one-half of their crops. In addition, Mifflin and other manumitting Friends followed Emerson's model by pledging to educate young slaves so that they could read the Bible before freeing them at the "lawful age."[27]

Restitution payments to former slaves for their adult years in servitude were particularly popular among some of these Friends. In 1782, Thomas Nock of Murderkill Hundred, Kent County, explained the general thinking of many Quakers who, because they had held their slaves beyond the "lawful age for white men," had "made a partial discrimination not warranted by the laws of Him who of one blood made all nations of man." In 1784, Jonathan Emerson of Kent County decided that even some of his father-in-law's former slaves deserved restitution payments from his own pocket for their years of bondage after the females had reached eighteen and the males twenty-one. The concern for restitution had been stimulated in 1778 by gatherings of Friends who were former masters and a total of 270 of their former slaves at five different Quaker weekly meetings in Kent County to discuss the willingness of these planters to do further justice to their erstwhile bondspeople.[28]

After setting right their own house, Delaware Friends turned their energies to driving slavery from the state by trying to convince the legislature to take immediate action. Led by Mifflin and several Wilmington Friends and strongly supported by leading Pennsylvania Quakers, they sent petition after petition to the state government in the 1780s and early 1790s. In December 1785, for example, 204 Quakers signed a petition that seven of their number presented to the House of Assembly in January 1786, setting forth "the distressed situation of the Negro slaves in the state; and praying that such relief be afforded them as the natural rights of mankind and the injunction of the Christian religion require."[29] Delaware Friends believed that the slave trade was fundamental to the survival of slavery and that by striking against it, they might deliver a crippling blow to the institution itself. In 1788 a memorial from Quakers was read to the House of Assembly, "praying that effectual provision be made for suppressing the slave trade" as well as "in time to provide the means for the abolition of slavery." Other petitions followed in subsequent years.[30]

These Delaware Quakers realized that they were not alone in their crusade and that allies were important in persuading the state government to act. In their 1785 petition, they had acknowledged that "many religious persons among us of different denominations" have manumitted their slaves.[31] To unite with people of other denominations in the antislavery crusade, Friends took the lead in organizing ecumenical abolitionist societies in Dover in 1788 and in Wilmington in 1789. Joining these abolitionist societies were the state's numerous Methodists, who often worked in tandem with the far less numerous Quakers to seriously weaken the institution of slavery. Indeed, the lofty idealism of the Quaker reform impulse combined with the earthy pragmatism of Methodism to forge a formidable alliance. It was a particularly beneficial alliance for Quakers because some Methodists, unlike members of the Society of Friends, were willing to run for elective office despite the risk of spiritual contamination implicit in the pursuit of public power. Once elected to office, Methodists did much to aid the antislavery cause.

By the end of the Revolution, Methodism's views on slavery already had been strongly influenced by the Quaker perspective. John Wesley, the English founder of Methodism, hardened his antislavery stance after reading a persuasive abolitionist pamphlet by Benezet. While in seclusion in Kent County in 1778, Francis Asbury, America's most important Methodist preacher, decided that his sect must follow the lead of the Society of Friends and support abolitionism.[32]

Although the Methodist antislavery drive depended strongly on the teachings of Wesley and the leadership of Asbury and other circuit-riding preachers, no Methodist was more important in the fight against human bondage in Delaware than Richard Bassett. In public life, the laconic Bassett—Methodism, after all, encouraged economy of speech—was best known for being the first chief justice of the Court of Common Pleas, a state legislator, a delegate to the U.S. Constitutional Convention, a U.S. senator, and the governor of Delaware. In politics he was a Federalist with a strong zeal to reform society. Born into a Cecil County, Maryland, gentry family in 1745 (the same year that Mifflin was born in Virginia), Bassett moved to Dover in 1770 to practice law. During the Revolution he was converted to Methodism and soon emerged as that faith's leading layman in the state.[33] As a devout Methodist, Bassett tried to restrict excessive drinking and conspicuous displays of wealth, and he wanted to reform the casual approach to family unity that characterized the age. Although his attempts to introduce legislation to tax liquor and expensive carriages and to more tightly regulate the process of marriage proved unsuccessful, his antislavery efforts did succeed.[34]

After freeing his own slaves—we do not know how many—Bassett used persuasion and his considerable political and legal skills to lead an attack on slavery and to champion improved opportunities for newly freed blacks. Again and again, he wrote and then signed petitions on behalf of African-Americans such as John of Kent County, who in 1783 was "unjustly held and detained as a slave" by his master. Bassett convinced friends who wanted him to be the executor of their wills to free their slaves. In court, he argued the cases of free blacks such as Cager, who had been illegally transported from Delaware to Maryland as a slave in 1795.[35] But it was in exercising his influence with the legislature that Bassett's antislavery sentiments had their greatest impact. It was he who introduced the 1787 state law that dealt a staggering blow to slavery in Delaware by prohibiting the sale of enslaved African-Americans to the Carolinas, Georgia, or the West Indies. Like many Quakers, Bassett and other Methodists were convinced that restrictions on the interstate slave trade would severely limit the viability of the institution.[36] In the case of Delaware, this perception proved correct.

Bassett's ultimate goal, however, was to abolish slavery completely rather than merely to cripple it. To this end he joined with his friend Warner Mifflin in 1788 to found in Dover the Delaware Society for Promoting the Abolition of Slavery. The state Constitutional Convention of 1792 offered a golden opportunity to abolish the "peculiar institution" in Delaware. Probably inspired by Pennsylvania's gradual manumission law of 1780, Bassett proposed to the Convention that the new constitution declare that no person could be born a slave in Delaware after a specific date. Opposition to this proposal was immediate and intense, and the final copy of the state constitution of 1792 said nothing about slavery. In subsequent years, Bassett continued to work hard for abolition. His obstinacy irritated a number of slaveholders including Thomas Rodney, who was so incensed over Bassett's support for "the immediate freedom of the Negroes" that he labeled his conduct "vile."[37]

Other leading Methodists such as Revolutionary War hero and Wilmington port collector Allen McLane, Kent County sheriff and legislator Andrew Barratt, Kent County banker and Delaware Supreme Court justice Isaac Davis, and Wilmington schoolteacher John Thelwell joined the antislavery campaign. In Sussex, where the antislavery impulse was weaker than farther north, the formation of a short-lived abolitionist society in 1809 was primarily the work of Methodists. William Morgan, a Sussex lay preacher, even took his antislavery

Richard Bassett (1745–1815). *Courtesy of the Historical Society of Delaware, Wilmington.*

campaign to Yorktown, Virginia, where he briefly lived during the early nineteenth century. But in Virginia, where "that desperate thing called slavery spoiled all," his outspoken attacks on human bondage caused him to be considered "an enemy to the country," and he returned to Sussex.[38]

Urged on by their faith, most Delaware Methodists freed their slaves during the years from 1775 to 1810; but, because the followers of Wesley did not emulate Quakers in keeping denominational records of manumissions, it is impossible to estimate how many African-Americans were freed by them. Nevertheless, because of the large population of Methodists in the state, it is probably safe to say that the number exceeded the Quaker total.

Methodist manumissions of adult slaves were of both the immediate and the delayed variety, with freedom under the latter condition usually promised within two to five years. Unless they had a free black parent who could take care of them and provide them with a home, slave children usually received delayed manumissions from Methodist masters, which meant that freedom from bondage would not come until they reached their early twenties. Typical was Methodist Raynear Williams of southern Kent County, who manumitted nine slaves in 1789. Those over twenty-one were given immediate freedom, while those under that age continued in bondage until they reached twenty-one.[39] Unlike Fox, who had directed Quaker manumitters not to allow blacks to walk away from slavery "empty handed," Wesley said nothing on this issue. As a result, Methodists were less prone than Friends to present newly freed blacks with tools, clothing, or money. Moreover, there is no record of their following the lead of some Quakers in providing restitution to newly freed slaves for their adult years spent in bondage.

Although Methodists were willing and even eager to admit both free and unfree blacks to membership—by contrast, the Society of Friends generally did not allow blacks of any category to join a meeting until Philadelphia Quakers led the way in 1796—the antislavery sentiment of the followers of Wesley may have been less intense and was certainly less lasting than that of the Quakers. By commiting itself to greatly increasing its membership among whites during the early nineteenth century, Methodism was forced to deemphasize those radical principles such as abolitionism which, if held too closely, might limit growth. By 1820 the denomination in Delaware had toned down much of its antislavery rhetoric, and church members who still owned slaves were no longer under great pressure to free them. (Farther south, most Methodists had abandoned their abolitionist stance by the beginning of the nineteenth century.) By contrast, nineteenth-century Quakers in Delaware and elsewhere chose to remain true to their late eighteenth-century stance on slavery and on other issues, which meant that the future growth of the Society of Friends would be limited.

Letting go of earlier principles such as abolitionism was easier for the state's Methodists by the early nineteenth century because memories of a more persecuted past were rapidly fading. When Methodism first entered Delaware at the end of the colonial era, its itinerant preachers were often greeted with hostility and its lay members with ridicule. During the Revolution the pacifist stand of many Methodists led to further persecution. Out of these collective experiences developed a real empathy for others who were abused and persecuted. This heightened sensitivity helped make it possible for the white followers of Wesley to sympathize particularly with enslaved African-Americans. By the second decade of the nineteenth century, however, such empathy was no longer central to the consciousness of most white Delaware Methodists.[40]

Before losing some of their enthusiasm for the abolitionist cause, the state's Methodists freed most of their own slaves and worked with Quakers to help convince masters who were from other faiths, or who were unchurched, to free theirs. At least as important, the two denominations were successful in pushing hard during the late eighteenth century for laws banning the sale of slaves beyond Delaware's borders. These legal restrictions were what one of the state's most successful politicians, John M. Clayton, had in mind when he wrote in 1844 that "slavery is nearly extinct in Delaware owing to the operation of a system of laws tending all to its gradual abolition."[41]

Some Presbyterians were also sympathetic to the plight of unfree blacks. In 1789, for example, one of the *Delaware Gazette*'s "Presbyterian readers" supported a gradual manumission policy that was first proposed by the Presbyterian Synod of New York in 1787–88, which hoped to encourage "those habits of industry" among slaves prior to manumission so that, once freed, they could become useful citizens. Because they tended to live in the rolling hill country of northern New Castle County, the least hospitable region to slavery in Delaware, few of the state's Presbyterians owned slaves. But some who did, freed their slaves in the late eighteenth and early nineteenth centuries.[42]

Episcopalians were more apt to hold slaves than Presbyterians, in part because they were more concentrated in "flat Delaware" where slavery was most common. During the late eighteenth and the first few decades of the nineteenth century, the Protestant Episcopal Church avoided taking a stand on the issue, but individual members did occasionally attack human bondage. Again in 1789, in the *Delaware Gazette*, an Episcopalian repeatedly criticized slavery. While many continued to hold slaves into the antebellum period, others freed their bondsmen. According to her 1802 will, Lewes Episcopalian Sarah Tingley freed her five slaves and left them her entire estate.[43]

~

Opposition to slavery in Delaware was also generated by abolition societies. Although their membership was always quite small and their meetings were poorly attended, they kept after the state legislature and continually reminded the general public through letters, lectures, petitions, pamphlets, and broadsides of the evils of the "peculiar institution." The first such society, the Delaware Society for Promoting the Abolition of Slavery, founded in Dover in 1788 by Mifflin, Bassett, and others, was closely patterned after the Pennsylvania Abolition Society. Within a year it was sending petitions to the legislature demanding the enaction of laws to end slavery and to protect blacks in other ways. The last extant record of the Dover group mentions that it was one of two Delaware abolition societies represented at the Convention of Abolition Societies in Philadelphia in 1795. Evidently the Dover society disbanded soon afterward.[44]

In 1788 or 1789 the Delaware Society for the Gradual Abolition of Slavery, also patterned after the Pennsylvania Abolition Society, was founded in Wilmington. In 1799 it, too, was disbanded, only to be reestablished the next year as the Delaware Society for Promoting the Abolition of Slavery and for the Relief and Protection of Free Blacks and People of Color, Unlawfully Held in Bondage. Its membership was overwhelmingly Quaker but also included a few Methodists, Presbyterians, and Episcopalians from northern Delaware. The society's petitions to the state government generally demanded gradual emancipation by legislation similar to the Pennsylvania plan of 1780 as well as more severe laws to prevent the kidnapping and sale of free blacks into slavery and a clarification of the laws concerning voluntary manumissions.[45]

In 1801 the Wilmington society attempted to establish sister abolition societies downstate to be made up of Methodists. Except for the previously mentioned Sussex society, which was in the process of formation in 1809 and probably lasted only a few years at best, these efforts bore no fruit. After 1807, support for the Wilmington group declined to the point where, during the next decade, a year or two might go by without a meeting. Indeed, there was only one meeting from June 8, 1811, to January 1, 1816. Weakened by an inactive recent past—in July 1818 a motion was made to disband the organization—and unable to attract a strong membership base, the Delaware

Abolition Society limped through the 1820s and 1830s. No records exist to indicate that it lasted beyond 1838.[46]

Although these abolition societies were often short-lived and not well supported by the general populace, they did prod the consciences of Delaware's politicians and other citizens. Moreover, much of the energy of these societies, particularly the Wilmington-based one, was focused on protecting the interests of African-Americans after they were freed. (These activities will be examined in Chapter VI.)

~

Initiatives taken by the slaves themselves played a key role in increasing the number of manumissions. While it is impossible to verify conversations between slaves and masters, certainly many blacks broached the subject of eventual freedom to their owners. The small size of Delaware's slave units led to such close contact between slave and owner that discussions of this nature were inevitable. One way to grant a slave's desire for freedom and yet meet the master's need for compensation was to give an individual the opportunity to buy his freedom. In 1728 in Sussex, for example, Joseph Ferdinando "hath lately purchased his freedom."[47] But it was not until the second half of the eighteenth century, when the hiring out of slaves became more common, that more than a handful of blacks could accumulate enough money to do so.

Although being hired out was viewed by many slaves as preferable to being sold, unfree blacks probably saw forced labor for someone other than their master as a violation of customary treatment. And that break with tradition seems to have given them the opportunity to negotiate over how much, if any, of the hiring-out income they might keep. From their share, a number of enslaved African-Americans such as Daniel, a blacksmith living southeast of Dover, purchased their freedom. Richard Allen, the state's most famous slave, hired himself out on weekends during the Revolution to cut wood, make bricks, and haul salt, and he was allowed to apply most or all of this income to the price of his freedom.[48]

The laws prohibiting the sale of slaves beyond the state's borders kept a lid on the value of Delaware's bondspeople, causing the freedom price to be considerably less than in other southern states. In 1800, for example, Samuel of Sussex County was offered his freedom for $200, while a comparable field hand in Virginia would probably have paid $350.[49]

On occasion, a master's will provided that a slave be hired out until he or she earned the freedom price. Generally, the option of purchasing freedom was incorporated into the will to satisfy the bondsperson's strong desire for freedom while also protecting the financial interests of the master's heirs. In northeastern Sussex in 1795, for example, an owner's will provided London with freedom if he could come up with £21.4 for the heirs. In some wills the slave had a deadline, as in the case of Charles of Sussex, who in 1788 was given "just two years and six months" after his master's death to pay his freedom price of £26.18. In others, such as the one written in Kent in 1784, the masters asked that their slaves pay only the manumission bond required by state law. But for most slaves, it was very difficult to come up with the freedom money. As a letter writer to the *Delaware Gazette* pointed out, for those enslaved blacks who were worked long hours by their masters and thus had no time to earn money from outside employment, it was simply impossible.[50]

For some African-Americans, the purchase of their own freedom was only the first step down the often long and costly road to freedom for their entire family. In the early nineteenth century, Solomon Bayley of Kent County purchased freedom for himself and then in subsequent years for his wife, two daughters, and a son, but Bayley was a skilled cooper and could command higher wages than most free blacks. For others, even at Delaware's relatively depressed slave prices, the purchase of relatives was well beyond their means. Occasionally, however, a slaveholder might drop the price to more closely reflect the ability to pay. In 1791, for example, Abraham was charged only $25 for his wife Minty.[51]

Those few who could afford to buy the freedom of a wife or child did so through installment payments over a number of years, but purchasing family members in this way did not lead to immediate freedom. Although the newly purchased bondspersons moved in with the black husbands or fathers who were buying them on time, they legally remained enslaved to white masters until the final payment was made. And, even after the final payment, some blacks continued to be listed as slaves. Indeed, unless the free blacks who purchased relatives were willing to grant them freedom in a documented manner, wives and children continued in slavery, but now under black masters who were their husbands or fathers as well. This peculiar development may partly explain why nine free blacks were listed as slaveholders in the state in 1830.[52]

By the early nineteenth century, a majority of Delaware owners had freed their slaves, but the state government's insistence that most recorded manumissions be accompanied by a security bond encouraged many masters to grant freedom through a verbal statement rather than through a written document. Inevitably, verbal manumissions created problems that were very unsettling to both blacks and whites.

Freedom based on the spoken rather than the written word did not provide blacks with a solid legal foundation for a stable future. If a master subsequently changed his mind or died, an ostensibly free black was almost defenseless against the reenslavement efforts of the master or his heirs. In addition, a black freed only by a verbal commitment was very vulnerable to the kidnapping raids of white profiteers intent on smuggling blacks to southern slave markets. Although some masters—particularly in Sussex in the eighteenth century—might argue that they were illiterate and therefore incapable of writing a manumission document, they had access to hired copyists, called scriveners, to put words to paper.[53]

While African-Americans were unhappy about freedom based only on a verbal promise, many whites felt threatened by the large number of unregulated enslaved blacks who roamed the rural landscape. In 1786 "sundry inhabitants of Sussex" complained about the "many idle and evil disposed slaves" who pretended to be free and wandered at will. Moreover, slaves from the other two counties and from other states travelled freely through Sussex under the same pretense.[54] Clearly, many whites wanted the demarcation line between unfree and free blacks drawn more precisely, while African-Americans desired that their freedom be guaranteed by a written document. In 1797 the General Assembly partially met the needs of both groups by insisting that all future manumissions were invalid unless they were in writing, signed and sealed by the master in the presence of "competent and credible witnesses" and systematically recorded. No legal action protecting a slave's manumission could take place unless these criteria were met.[55]

The requirement of 1797 made it easier to prove or disprove the status of African-Americans roaming the countryside while forcing masters to put all future manumissions in writing. This change led to dramatic increases in documented manumissions. In Sussex, which held almost one-half of Delaware's slaves by the late 1790s, one deed book recorded a fourfold increase in annual manumissions after 1797 and continued at that level until 1830.[56]

Most African-American children who were manumitted were granted delayed rather than immediate freedom, and this led to considerable confusion about their status during the interim. While awaiting the promised freedom date, would the children continue to be treated as slaves, or would they be treated as apprentices? The distinction was important because, by custom, masters were obligated to provide a basic general education as well as vocational training to their apprentices—but not to their slaves. Members of the Society of Friends usually treated these young African-Americans as apprentices.[57] It is less clear how non-Quakers treated them. While some Methodists and others made provisions for vocational training and a basic education during the interim, most manumitting Delaware masters emulated Richard Abbott of Sussex, whose 1787 will provided for the freedom of Patience and Edmund when each reached the age of twenty-one. But prior to their freedom, the two were "to remain in their usual subjection." This pattern of "usual subjection" was reinforced in 1810 when the General Assembly declared that until the promised date of freedom arrived, an unfree African-American who was subject to delayed manumission was "deemed and taken to be a slave."[58]

~

During the late colonial period, Kent County's population included at least as many slaves as Sussex and nearly one and one-half times as many as New Castle County. By 1810, however, Kent had only 30 percent as many as Sussex and 68 percent of the New Castle total. Clearly, Kent had taken a commanding lead in manumitting Delaware's unfree blacks. But why Kent rather than Sussex to the south or, more logically, New Castle County to the north?

Certainly, economic factors played an important role. Slavery seemed far more compatible with the cultivation of corn, which was Sussex's staple crop by the mideighteenth century, than with wheat, which along with corn was the main cash crop in Kent. But New Castle County was even less dependent on corn and more dependent on wheat than Kent, and yet it, too, significantly trailed Kent in numbers of manumissions. Actually, the more rapid decline of slavery in Kent than elsewhere had more to do with timing than anything else. The critical question was: Who owned slaves, and when? Most of the Quaker slaveholders lived in Kent during the late colonial period. When Delaware Friends manumitted their slaves during the Revolution, the impact was far greater on Kent than on New Castle or Sussex. Moreover, the example of John Dickinson, a nonpracticing member of the Kent Quaker gentry, had considerable impact. By the end of 1786 he had freed at least fifty-eight African-Americans.[59]

During the Revolution, Methodism became a dominant force in Kent County but was at least two decades away from a similar position in Sussex and at least one-half century away from making significant inroads into much of New Castle County. It was during the Revolution and the decade that followed it that the Methodist antislavery impulse was most intense and the pressure on old members and new converts to manumit their slaves was most explicit. By the first decade of the nineteenth century, when the Methodist influence in Sussex approximated the level that it had reached in Kent two decades earlier, the intensity of the manumission impulse was declining. In short, Kent County experienced Methodism in its earliest, most anti-slavery phase, while Sussex and eventually New Castle inherited a more mature faith, less inclined to challenge the status quo by declaring the holding of slaves an apostacy.[60]

In addition, in Kent far more than elsewhere in Delaware a substantial number of slaveholding gentry were converted to Methodism. In 1783 a Methodist preacher noted that in central Kent County some of the converts "were wealthy and in the higher circles of life." They followed the example of their Quaker neighbors and freed significant numbers of African-Americans. By contrast, the slaveholders of Sussex and New Castle County tended to be primarily Episcopalian or unchurched during the late eighteenth century and therefore were less inclined to answer either the Quaker or the Methodist call for manumission.[61] Finally, Kent easily led the other two counties in manumissions because it was the home of Delaware's two greatest abolitionists of the eighteenth century, Quaker Warner Mifflin and Methodist Richard Bassett.

Ignited by Kent County's early leadership in the antislavery movement and by the expression of strong abolitionist sentiments by concerned Wilmington residents, a vigorous debate on the merits of slavery got off to an early start in Delaware. But because the number of slaves declined so rapidly from 1775 to 1810, the controversy tended to take on a slightly different configuration than in other southern slave states. Although quite heated in the late eighteenth century, arguments over slavery in Delaware became slightly less confrontational and vitriolic than those in the rest of the nation during the late antebellum period.

The state's abolitionists turned early to portraying Africa, prior to the transatlantic slave trade, in "Edenic" terms. Africa was "a considerable territory" where its native people "enjoyed their freedom," stated a Quaker petition to the General Assembly in 1785. But then "the avarice of professed Christians" created a demand for black slaves, which in turn "encouraged" Africans "in oppression and tyranny over one another."[62] Abolitionists pointed out the destructive impact of slavery on African families and the horrors of the transatlantic crossing. In 1789 one Delawarean maintained that mortality during the passage from the Guinea Coast to North America was 30 percent. After surviving the terrible loss of family and friends in Africa and disease and death in the holds of slave ships, Delaware's African-Americans faced the rest of their lives under the arbitrary authority of oppressive masters. Even a kind master dispensing good treatment could not, according to this abolitionist, "remove the injustice" of slavery.[63]

The best summary of the abolitionists' view was expressed in 1817 by the Wilmington-based Abolition Society of Delaware: "The Africans, who were brought from their home in floating dungeons to our

shores, wore out the vigor of their lives to acquire wealth for our fathers: to us have descended the fruits of their toil and we are their
debtors."[64] In addition, it was argued, slavery corrupted the masters.
In 1789 a Delawarean pointed out that "the virtuous yeomanry of New
England should be our pattern rather than the effeminate and debauched
slave holders of southern states." That theme continued to be sounded
throughout the antebellum period, and slaveholders such as future
Governor William H. Ross of Seaford were contemptuously described,
in 1850, as no better than "proprietors of human cattle."[65]

It was not until the late antebellum era, however, that the state's
abolitionists began to speak out on the negative effect of slavery on
poor whites. In 1850 they noted that "slavery makes labor disgraceful
by associating with it the degraded condition of the slave: so that at
last idleness comes to be more honored than honest industry." What
this meant to the work ethic of the poor whites was clear. In the midst
of slavery they were "striken with poverty but unwilling to work."
Ignorant and "despising" knowledge, poor whites "stand before our
eyes incontestably the legitimate progeny" of slavery. There was no
question, according to the abolitionists, that slavery degraded everyone who came in contact with it. Moreover, there was a noticeable
decrease in the population of the parts of Delaware "most afflicted by
slavery." This argument that the "peculiar institution" corrupted white
society and prevented whites from reaching their full potential as productive citizens was commonly used by abolitionists throughout the
North and the Upper South in the late antebellum period.[66]

The counterattack by proslavery forces was vigorous and pointed,
but it did not respond to all of the abolitionists' charges. Proslavery
Delawareans rejected the Edenic view of Africa by maintaining that
even before the transatlantic slave trade, the continent was in constant
turmoil, chaos, and war. In 1789, for example, this view was supported
by a letter in the proslavery *Delaware Gazette* from a purported African chief that spoke of the constant wars in West Africa prior to the
coming of white men.[67]

Contrary to the abolitionist view, proslavery spokesmen insisted
that slaves in Delaware were well treated. As one writer argued in
1789, the master protected his bondspeople from "hunger, thirst, cold
and nakedness." Moreover, the proslavery view maintained that before abolitionist propaganda reached them, slaves were "happy" and
could be found "singing or laughing at work, or frolicking in their
quarter."[68] Preying on the growing uneasiness of whites over the increasing numbers of free African-Americans who ranged across the
rural landscape, proslavery forces worked particularly at stirring up
white fears of miscegenation. Manumission, they argued, led inevitably to assimilation, which in turn would lead to sexual relations be-

tween the races. In 1789 a letter writer to the *Gazette* asked who among us would give "their daughter in marriage" to the sons of slaves and "choose the partners of your beds and confidants of your bosoms from among their daughters."[69] An abolitionist immediately replied in the same newspaper that marriage was, after all, "a matter of taste." In a society in which both blacks and whites were free, in the joining of sexual partners "everyone would be left to the choice of his own fancy." Then, in a fascinating aside, he spoke about the commonly accepted standard of beauty. While he admitted that shade of color was a factor in the ideal, he called on his readers to "recollect the complexion of the celebrated Cleopatra, so captivating to the Roman eye, the hue of which approached nearer the African, than to that of our own." Nevertheless, the vast majority of whites probably agreed with a supporter of slavery who wrote in the *Gazette* in 1789 that "there are confessedly different grades in the human species" and that none of us would want blacks to share in our councils or "marry in our families."[70]

As the nineteenth century progressed, Delaware's proslavery forces defended their cause by appealing to the racial prejudices and fears of whites. In focusing most of their energies on playing the race card, they ignored the more sophisticated argument, increasingly popular in other southern states, that slavery was superior to the free labor system of the North because it better served the interests of both blacks and whites. Rather, its Delaware apologists primarily concentrated on the potential threat to whites posed by free African-Americans because they insisted that black-skinned people were part of an inferior, barbaric race that would not change its nature over time. In 1850 the *Gazette* challenged anyone to recall "the name of a negro who has ever written a page worthy of being remembered." The newspaper went on to maintain that since the time of the Greek historian Herodotus, some 2,300 years ago, the African "has been a stranger to civilization." Furthermore, the *Gazette* claimed, one had only to look at Haiti, which under black control was "readily relapsing into barbarism," to doubt the ability of people of African descent to act civilized.[71]

In preying on the growing white fear of manumitted blacks, the proslavery forces struck a specific chord that spoke particularly to the economic concerns of the least affluent whites. After the Whig-controlled General Assembly "almost abolished slavery" in 1847, the *Gazette* argued retrospectively that Delaware had narrowly averted a disaster because such a measure would attract both fugitive and free blacks from adjoining states in such numbers that negroes would steal jobs from poor whites. Clearly, job security was an issue that had considerable resonance with the white lower classes. That same warning was repeated in a broadside in 1862, which also called for a meeting of all those "who believe in the superiority of the white race over the

black race and who are opposed to any equality of the races, person-
ally, socially, and politically."[72]

To weaken abolitionism, proslavery voices tried to discredit the
strongest supporters of the antislavery movement during the late eighteenth century. They portrayed Delaware's leading antislavery spokesmen as those same Tories who had backed the British Crown during
the Revolution—in an obvious attempt to label the Quakers and, to a
lesser extent, the Methodists as traitors to the Republic because so
many of them were pacifists during the struggle for independence.
One letter writer, however, did not let these charges go unchallenged.
In 1789 he replied in the *Gazette* that he was not a Quaker but an
Episcopalian. Moreover, he was not a pacifist but instead had been
an active rebel during the Revolution; and yet he was an enemy of
slavery.[73]

~

While Delaware's whites debated the issue of abolition, some impatient African-Americans simply walked away from bondage and
followed the North Star to freedom. A small but significant enough
number escaped from their masters to put a strain, according to a few
midnineteenth-century observers, on the continued viability of the institution in Delaware. In 1863 a downstate newspaper noted that slavery had not fared very well because "the number of fugitives has
been proportionably greater" than in states farther south.[74]

During the late colonial era, fewer than one hundred enslaved
African-Americans were listed as runaways in area newspapers. If we
project that there may have been as many as eight thousand slaves in
Delaware in 1770, the evidence suggests that fugitive slaves were
very uncommon prior to the Revolution.[75] The reason is twofold: prior
to 1765 a majority of the state's slaves were born in Africa, and many
continued to have difficulty in speaking English. Because fluency in
English was crucial to surviving as fugitives, Africans who remained
uncomfortable with the language were reluctant to flee from bondage.
Even more significant was the fact that, prior to the Revolution, a
fugitive slave was hard pressed to find a safe haven because even the
northern English colonies practiced slavery. Thus, faced with very poor
prospects, almost all of Delaware's bondspeople rejected flight as a
reasonable option prior to 1775.

By the time of the Revolution, the slave population of Delaware
was overwhelmingly New World-born and thus far more comfortable
with English. Moreover, the chaos of the war years made flight relatively easy. Even more important was the fact that during the Revolutionary era and in the three decades that followed, all of the states

north of Delaware abolished slavery by mandating either immediate or gradual manumission. Pennsylvania, for example, mandated gradual abolition in 1780. Clearly, the northern states now offered a far more hospitable haven for fugitives than in the late colonial era.[76]

Even in the postcolonial period, however, the number of Delaware slaves who ran away remained relatively small. From 1786 to 1795, for example, only fifty-two blacks were listed as fugitives from slavery in area newspaper notices.[77] While the average of five fugitives per year more than doubled the figure for the late colonial period, these statistics are not very impressive when we consider that there were almost nine thousand slaves in the state in 1790. An examination of fugitive slave notices in nineteenth-century newspapers indicates that, with the exception of the years immediately before and during the Civil War, the annual number of fugitive slaves in Delaware rarely exceeded, and was most often considerably less than, the figures of the 1786–1795 period. In short, even after 1775, when the opportunities for fugitives dramatically improved, the number who chose flight was very small, probably representing less than 5 percent of the state's total slave population. One might argue that the newspapers carried notices on only a fraction of runaways. But given the value of each slave, those who were successful in escaping their masters for more than a week or two and were thought to be heading north to freedom were generally listed by their owners in area newspapers.[78]

Another reason for Delaware's relatively small number of fugitive slaves was that, prior to running away, African-Americans had to weigh the blessings of freedom against the loss of family and friends. Becoming a runaway usually meant never again seeing parents, spouses, children, other kin, and lifelong comrades. As Frederick Douglass pointed out, "Thousands would escape from slavery . . . but for the strong cords of affection that bind them to their families, relatives and friends."[79] Black women were particularly reluctant to steal away to the North because they had to leave behind their children. Moreover, the old, the lame, and the very young were physically ill equipped to face the formidable hardships and dangers that generally accompanied the flight to freedom. Thus, the prime candidates for fugitive slave status in Delaware, as elsewhere in the South, were young men with few family commitments or responsibilities. Of the fifty-two slaves in the state who fled from their masters from 1786 to 1795, some 90 percent were males with a median age of twenty-two. The 10 percent who were female had a median age of twenty-seven. At least 11 percent of all of the fugitives were mulattoes, while only one runaway was clearly born in Africa. No children or elderly people were in the group. In almost every case, fleeing slavery was an individual act.[80]

$600
REWARD!

ABSCONDED from the subscriber, on the night of Saturday, the 6th instant, a negro man, named

JAMES WRIGHT.

He is about 25 years of age ; about 5 feet 7 or 8 inches high; rather trim built, and suppose would weigh about 150 lbs. He has thin lips, white teeth, rather flat nose, white eyes and rather blacker than ordinary. Had on when he left, a dark Cassimere dress frock coat, and supposed, large plaid Cassimere pants, clothes good--Monroe shoes.
I will give $100 reward if arrested in Sussex County ; $200 if arrested out of Sussex County in either case to be delivered to me, or secured in Jail in this State, so that I can get him again.
Seaford, Sussex Co., Del., May 8, '54.   CHAS. WRIGHT.

ABSCONDED!

From the subscriber, on the night of Saturday, the 6th inst., a negro man, named

James Martin,

He is about 5 feet 7 or 8 inches high, weighs about 160 lbs, close built, and a fine looking negro. Has black eyes, large flat nose, large mouth, and very black. Had on when he left a fured hat, thin summer shoes, and took with him a quantity of clothing. I will give $100 reward if arrested in this county, or $200 if arrested out of this county, in either case to be delivered to me or secured in jail in this State, so that I can get him.
Seaford, Sussex County, Del., May 8, '54.   HUGH MARTIN, Sr.

ANOTHER.

Absconded from the subscriber on the night of Saturday the 6th inst., a negro man named

Edward Handy.

He is about 35 years of age, about 5 feet 10 inches high, flat head, flat face, broad forehead, large flat nose, large white eyes and large mouth. He is rather sensible and of pretty good address, lisps when he speaks, and sets himself well back, taking a perfect state when walking.
I will give $100 reward if arrested in this county, or $200 if arrested out of this county, in either case to be delivered to me or secured in jail in this State, so that I can get him.

Notice of runaway slaves, Seaford, 1854. *Courtesy of Claudia Melson.*

For Delaware slaves who were determined to run away, nearby Pennsylvania in general and Philadelphia in particular were the favorite destinations. In 1791, Simon from Sussex, Sall from Kent, and Jonas from New Castle County found refuge in Philadelphia. A later example was Prince, who at nineteen escaped from his Smyrna master in 1820 and made it to Philadelphia only to be captured. Within three weeks of returning to his home farm, Prince led two teenage black males to freedom. To their angry master it was clear that the three fugitives were "headed for Philadelphia."[81]

In their flight from bondage, enslaved Delawareans were often aided and encouraged by fellow slaves. In 1801 in Kent County, Isaac was charged with enticing neighboring slaves to run away to the North and freedom. Indeed, his mistress predicted that neither her own nor her neighbor's bondsmen would remain at home unless Isaac was removed from the state.[82] Even more helpful were free African-Americans. At a fairly early date, the colonial assembly was aware that some free blacks were turning their homes into sanctuaries for runaways. In 1740 it placed heavy fines on any free African-Americans who harbored slaves without permission from the owners.[83] But the practice of free blacks aiding fugitives persisted in Delaware until slavery was abolished in 1865. In some cases, free blacks were kin to the fugitives they helped. Titus Anderson of Mispillion Hundred in southern Kent, who escaped from his master in 1806, was subsequently sheltered by his free relatives in the "lower part" of the county for a number of years. In 1824, Harry Boyer ran away from his master with the intention of catching a boat for Philadelphia, only to be captured while awaiting passage at his uncle's home at Barker's Landing, near the mouth of the St. Jones River.[84]

The clandestine nature of aiding fugitive slaves restricts to a handful the number of free African-American participants who can be identified. In Wilmington, during the midnineteenth century, they included black laborers Comegys Munson and Severn Johnson, mulatto laborer Joseph Walker, and black brickmaker Henry Craig. Joseph Hamilton of Wilmington offered his home as a "regular stopping place" for slaves fleeing to Pennsylvania. Abraham Shadd, a mulatto shoemaker who also lived in Wilmington, was a leading abolitionist and undoubtedly helped fugitives from Delaware and other slave states escape to the North. In Camden, just south of Dover, William Brinkley aided fugitive slaves. Some free blacks even went so far as to persuade slaves to make a run for freedom. Jesse Manlove of Dover Hundred, Kent County, talked Jane White of the same hundred into escaping north in 1837.[85]

Acting as conductors on the Underground Railroad, free blacks aided escaping fugitives from both Delaware and other slave states by guiding them along the freedom trail, providing them with food and shelter, and obstructing the attempts by white authorities to apprehend them. In 1856 free blacks in Wilmington tore down handbills that offered rewards for the capture of a group of fugitive slaves who had recently escaped from Maryland's Eastern Shore.[86] Leading the fugitives from the Eastern Shore in 1856 was Harriet Tubman, who had been born about 1820 or 1821 near Bucktown in Dorchester County, Maryland, about twenty miles west of the Sussex County line. In 1849 she had escaped from her master and made her way north to Philadelphia. In subsequent years she made a number of trips back to Maryland to guide many family members and other enslaved African-Americans north to freedom. Evidently, on her return trips to Pennsylvania, Tubman led escaping slaves northeastward along the Choptank River into Kent County, Delaware, where her small bands of refugees found temporary shelter at Underground Railroad stations located in or near Camden, Dover, Blackbird, Odessa, Middletown, New Castle, or Wilmington. There is no solid evidence, however, that Tubman led any Delaware bondspeople north to freedom.[87]

It took considerable courage for these free blacks to aid runaway slaves because, if caught, they were subject to harsher legal as well as physical retribution than were white abolitionists. In 1848 free black Samuel Burris observed that "helping slaves to regain freedom . . . in the State of Delaware is a crime next to that of murder, if committed by a colored man."[88] He was speaking from personal experience. Burris had been born a free man in Delaware, but he subsequently moved to Philadelphia from where he sometimes ventured south of the Mason-Dixon Line to aid fugitive slaves. In January 1847 he was in Kent County, where he helped Isaac and Alexander make a successful escape. In June of that same year he was back in Kent trying to help Maria Matthews of Dover Hundred flee north via steamboat. Matthews, however, was captured and returned to her master, and Burris was arrested and jailed in Dover for aiding her aborted escape and the successful escapes by Isaac and Alexander.[89]

Burris was found guilty on both counts, fined five hundred dollars plus costs, kept in jail in Dover for ten months, and sentenced to be sold into slavery for fourteen years after his jail term expired. Abolitionists from Pennsylvania and northern Delaware rallied to his cause by raising some money that was turned over to Isaac Flint, a white Quaker abolitionist from Wilmington who was not well known in Kent. In 1848, after Burris had served his ten-month sentence, Flint proceeded to Dover in the guise of a slave trader to be present when he was placed on the auction block. Prior to the sale, Burris was examined "from the soles of his feet to the crown of his head" by traders. After observing their technique, Flint then gave Burris an equally careful examination to protect his own identity.[90] During the bidding that followed, a Baltimore slave trader made the highest offer, only to be bought off by Flint. The disguised abolitionist then made the winning bid while Burris girded himself for fourteen years of slavery in the Deep South. As soon as he was turned over to Flint, he was told that he was free and was then rushed away to his Philadelphia home, where his anxious wife and children waited. Burris never again ventured south of the Mason-Dixon Line.[91]

The Underground Railroad, an elusive but very real network of local havens and willing guides—Quakers, other whites, and free blacks—to aid fugitives in their flight to freedom, represented a series of "stations" and "conductors" that were solidly in place in Kent and New Castle counties by the midnineteenth century. Because of the need for secrecy (its purpose, after all, was illegal), the Underground Railroad in Delaware, as elsewhere in antebellum America, was an institution whose record is a slippery amalgam of fact and fiction. What is clear, however, is that most of the slaves who used it to escape to the North were not from Delaware but from Maryland and states farther south. The small number from Delaware simply reflected the state's very small slave population by the midnineteenth century.[92]

White Quakers from Wilmington who played a significant role in the Underground Railroad included the previously mentioned Isaac Flint as well as Daniel Gibbins, Benjamin Webb, and his two sons Edward and William. Active Friends from southern New Castle County included John Hunn of Middletown and John Alston and Daniel Corbit of Odessa. In Kent County, Ezekiel Jenkins of Camden was the best-known Quaker supporter of the Underground Railroad. The most widely celebrated of all, however, was Thomas Garrett of Wilmington, who was probably the inspiration for the heroic Quaker Simeon Holliday in Harriet Beecher Stowe's *Uncle Tom's Cabin*.[93]

Garrett was born into a Quaker family in Upper Darby, Pennsylvania, in 1789. When he was fourteen, an attempted kidnapping of a free black female who worked for his family sensitized him to the plight of African-Americans. In 1822, Garrett moved to Wilmington, where he became a merchant. By 1830 he was actively aiding runaway slaves. Although a member of the Wilmington Meeting at Fourth and West Streets, he joined with other strong abolitionists to form the Progressive Meeting at nearby Kennett Square, Pennsylvania, in 1853. (Sojourner Truth, a former slave and leading abolitionist, spoke and sang at their first session.) Although it was located just over the Pennsylvania border, the Progressive Meeting included a number of like-minded Delawareans who also were active in the Underground Railroad, which stretched south from the Pennsylvania line to the heart of Kent County.[94]

In his final accounting after the Civil War, Garrett reported that he had helped twenty-seven hundred fugitive slaves escape to the North. Many, if not most, received food and shelter in his own home at

221 Shipley Street in Wilmington.⁹⁵ Although the overwhelming majority were from Maryland and other slave states, Garrett was particularly happy when they were Delawareans. In 1854, eight fugitive slaves arrived in Wilmington seeking help on their journey north. Garrett noted, "The best of it is for our little state, they were all natives of Delaware."⁹⁶

The decision to try to go north to freedom not only meant leaving behind kin and friends but also running the gauntlet of civil authorities and their bloodhounds before reaching Pennsylvania or, in a few

Thomas Garrett (1789–1871) by Bass Otis. *Courtesy of the Historical Society of Delaware, Wilmington.*

cases, New Jersey. Escapees had to be on constant alert because the Fugitive Slave Act of 1793 allowed masters and their hired slave catchers to enter free states to capture runaways. The subsequent Fugitive Slave Act of 1850 made it even more difficult for fleeing African-Americans by directing federal authorities in northern states to return them to their southern owners. Many blacks were convinced that the only really safe haven left was Canada.

Just how hard it could be to escape from Delaware is demonstrated by the case of Minus of North West Fork Hundred, Sussex County. In 1857 he made three attempts, only to be recaptured each time by parties of mounted men inspired by the offer of a "considerable reward." But some fugitives, such as Sam, were able to reach Pennsylvania despite close pursuit. Although chased by the Kent County sheriff and his posse with bloodhounds, Sam made it to Daniel Corbit's house in Odessa. With pursuers close on his heels, he wiggled through a narrow passage to the attic of the hip-roofed mansion where he hid while the posse searched the house. The door to the attic passage was discovered, but the sheriff and his men decided that it was too small for Sam to crawl through and left. At dusk, Sam was given a change of clothes by the Corbits and began walking north on the road to Pennsylvania.[97]

The road north to freedom was a dangerous one. Although, like Sam, most fugitives tried to hide during the day and travel at night, any white person who encountered an African-American had the right to make a citizen's arrest on the suspicion that the black man or woman was a runaway. From the homes of Wilmington abolitionists the final dash into Pennsylvania was fraught with suspense and, in at least one case, with an exchange of gunfire. The railroad trains and the wagon bridges across the Brandywine River, which led north to Philadelphia, were carefully watched. Garrett and other abolitionists responded by often sending fugitive slaves north to Chester, Pennsylvania, by steamboat or northwest by land to the home of Isaac and Dinah Mendenhall at Longwood, about ten miles northwest of Wilmington, just over the Pennsylvania line.[98]

Not only did these fugitives have to be on the lookout for suspicious whites, but they also had to deal with an occasional black conductor on the Underground Railroad who might betray them for money. In 1857, for example, free black Thomas Otwell of near Milford decoyed eight escaping slaves from Dorchester County into the Kent County jail in Dover at 4:00 A.M. The fugitives, however, fought off the sheriff, broke out of jail, captured Otwell (who begged for his life), and then made it to Pennsylvania thanks to dependable black conductors and Garrett. A year later, four other escaping slaves, probably from the Eastern Shore, were betrayed by free black Jesse Perry near

the state line.[99] Although Otwell's and Perry's victims were Marylanders, fugitives from Delaware realized that they had to remain alert or
else they, too, might be betrayed.

The relatively small percentage of Delaware slaves who ran away
from their masters prior to 1850 increased as the Civil War approached.[100] Once war began, enslaved blacks continued to escape in
larger numbers, with many joining the Union Army. In January 1864,
for example, an estimated fifty African-Americans from Delaware were
mustered in Wilmington to report for induction: "Nearly all of these
men were former slaves." One of the inductees had been handcuffed
and confined to an outhouse by his master, but he escaped to report
while still in handcuffs. The increase in runaways caused a downstate
newspaper to comment in 1863 that the number of slaves "is rapidly
diminishing." In 1864 a catalog made the exaggerated claim that
"nearly all the [male] slaves in the state, from [age] fifteen to sixty-
five have enlisted" in the Union Army, but it was closer to the truth in
maintaining that "the state is now practically free."[101]

To be "practically free" of slavery in 1864 was a far cry from the
society that existed in the late colonial period. Although it was not
willing to legislate an end to slavery, Delaware's state government did
exercise considerable influence over its decline from its vital years in
the mideighteenth century through its final demise dictated by the
Thirteenth Amendment in December 1865. From 1767 to 1865 the
actions of the state government reflected a deep ambivalence. Clearly,
Delaware's political leaders were troubled about the morality of slavery; indeed, alive in the memories of some was a time when slave
children were "companions in childhood." But, just as clearly, these
political leaders were strongly influenced by their own and their con-
stituents' growing racism and the reluctance, implicit in government
officials in a very conservative state, to abandon the old order. The
troubled consciences of the legislators were reflected in the willingness of the General Assembly to instruct the state's congressional delegation in 1819 to vote against the extension of slavery into any new
states added to the Union. In subsequent years the General Assembly
passed resolutions against the annexation of Texas, which wanted to
enter the Union as a slave state, and against the extension of slavery
into the territories gained from the Mexican War, yet it refused to act
decisively to end slavery in Delaware once and for all.[102] In short, the
state's politicians and jurists were never quite willing either to completely eradicate slavery by law or to grant it the legislative and judicial support necessary to pump new life into its moribund body. This

indecision reflected the division among whites over which model to follow: the Pennsylvania model of freedom or the Maryland one of slavery.

During the late eighteenth and very early nineteenth century, when so many voices were raised against slavery, Delaware came close to legislating the abolition of human bondage. The first real restriction on the growth of slavery was introduced into the colonial assembly in 1767 when Caesar Rodney and other Kent County representatives proposed that imported slaves be taxed. After heated debate in the House of Assembly, the proposed import tax was defeated. Its supporters responded to their defeat by demanding the addition of a clause "totally prohibiting the importation of slaves" to a bill aimed at regulating unfree blacks. The "prohibiting" clause was defeated by a nine-to-seven vote, but the issue would reappear in 1775 and 1776.[103] Thus, in 1767, some legislators were intent on ending the flow of unfree African-Americans into Delaware, while others wanted to maintain the traffic. On the surface it looked like the first great clash in the legislature between supporters and opponents of slavery, but the reality was quite different.[104]

Because the leaders on both sides were slaveholders, the only important determinant in the debate seemed to be geography. The seven legislators who favored the slave-import ban included one from New Castle and Sussex and all five of the Kent delegation. Four of the nine opponents of the ban were from Sussex, with the other five from New Castle. A probable explanation is that the more established Kent planters had a surplus of slaves by 1767 and were anxious to sell them to farmers in undeveloped sections of Sussex and southern New Castle County, where there was still a strong market for unfree blacks. An import ban would help keep prices high by eliminating the only competing source of supply. (The ban against slave imports into the Chesapeake region during the late eighteenth century was also supported by the more established slaveholders.) Farmers and planters in the relatively undeveloped parts of Sussex and southern New Castle, however, were concerned about increasing their supply of slaves at bargain prices, and they considered the continued importation of even a small number of unfree blacks to be advantageous to their interests.[105]

The issue surfaced again in 1775, and this time a majority of the members of the House of Assembly supported an import ban, only to have Governor John Penn veto it within a few days of its passage. (Evidently, by 1775 there no longer was a demand for new slaves in southern New Castle and Sussex.) With the cutting of political ties to the Penn family and the British government in 1776, Delaware turned to drafting a state constitution. Reflecting the majority sentiments of 1775, the new constitution of 1776 banned the importation of slaves into the state. But only specific legislation could provide the necessary teeth for the constitutional ban to work, and that was not forthcoming until 1787.[106] By the latter date, however, the importation of slaves was really a moot issue because for almost two decades only a handful had annually entered the state.

Other attempts to affect slavery through legislation continued through the 1780s. In 1782, President (Governor) John Dickinson asked the state legislature to halt sales that would cause individual blacks to be "cruelly separated" by great distances from "near relatives." He also asked the legislature to end the requirement that all masters pay a security bond for any blacks that they freed. It refused, however, to pass either proposal. In 1785, Methodist Allen McLane, then a representative from Kent County, introduced a bill "for the gradual abolition of slavery." After considering it in the 1785 and 1786 sessions, the House of Assembly took no action.[107] Of far greater consequence was the previously mentioned legislation passed in the late eighteenth century that made it illegal to sell slaves out of state. Although this legislation dealt Delaware slavery a crippling blow, it did not end racial bondage in the state.

Rising abolitionist sentiment provided the impetus for the introduction of a series of other antislavery measures in both the legislature and at the state Constitutional Convention of 1792. In 1789, for example, the use of Delaware ports by slave ships and for the outfitting and equipping of any ship used in the slave trade anywhere was outlawed by the General Assembly.[108] After an unsuccessful attempt to have the state constitution of 1792 abolish slavery, the abolitionist forces turned their energies to convincing the General Assembly to end the institution in Delaware. In 1796, 1797, and 1803, bills to abolish slavery were introduced into the General Assembly but never received enough support to become law. In 1803 a bill to abolish slavery gradually was killed when the Speaker of the state's House of Representatives broke a tie by voting against the measure. The House vote of 1803 reflected increasing geographic polarization over slavery, with five of six Sussex County legislators opposing abolition. Over the next two years, petitions for the "gradual abolition of slavery" were introduced and supported in the General Assembly by New Castle County signatories and legislators, only to be blocked by the actions of Sussex legislators.[109]

Although from 1803 to 1847 the public debate over slavery was less vitriolic than in the late eighteenth century, it still continued to spark controversy. But during those years, members of the state's House of Representatives and Senate skillfully avoided a public vote on this extraordinarily volatile issue. In 1845, for example, a bill "for the gradual abolition of slavery" was read in the House, only to have action on it "indefinitely postponed."[110] But voting on the issue could not be indefinitely postponed. In 1847 an abolition bill was assigned to a committee for further consideration and subsequently was reported on favorably to the full House. The committee's rationalization for the need to end slavery in Delaware, however, reflected the growing racism of the nineteenth century rather than a genuine concern for the welfare of unfree African-Americans. It also testified to the growing influence of the "modern" mentality, anchored in the northern part of the state, that placed considerable value on economic efficiency. The roots of this "modern" mentality can be traced to some of the principles underlying the emerging industrial capitalism, which argued that slavery, like government regulations, was an artificial hindrance to the free and efficient production of goods and services. What slavery eliminated was the possibility of self-improvement among workers, which in turn removed their main incentive for productive labor. To the emerging leaders of Wilmington's growing industrial and commercial enterprises, the economic inefficiency represented by slavery in more "traditional" downstate Delaware was simply anathema.[111]

Despite insisting that slavery was a mild and gentle institution, the House committee strongly recommended its abolition because the real harm in slavery was not in what it meant to the African-American but its impact on the state's economy. The committee maintained that "the careless, slovenly and unproductive husbandry visible in some parts of our state, undoubtedly result mainly from the habit of depending on slave labor. It is no longer a debatable question that slave labor impoverishes, while free labor enriches people." The House then passed an abolition bill by a twelve-to-eight vote, which would have freed all African-Americans born into slavery after 1850. When it was sent to the Senate, however, a one-vote margin caused consideration of the bill again to be "indefinitely postponed."[112] Thus ended the last major effort in the General Assembly prior to the Civil War to abolish slavery in Delaware.

Although slavery in the state increasingly was a moribund institution, the proslavery forces continued to defend its legitimacy and even took steps to try to reinvigorate it. In 1832, 1837, and 1851, in hopes of giving slavery more stability by making it more profitable, proslavery advocates unsuccessfully tried to have the General Assembly erase the laws of 1787, 1789, and 1797 so that Delaware slaves might be sold "into any state in the Union."[113] These proslavery forces grew increasingly concerned that an abolition bill might be passed by the General Assembly at some future date. Attempting a preemptive strike at the state Constitutional Convention of 1852, they demanded long-term protection for slavery. Democratic party leader and delegate James A. Bayard proposed that a clause guaranteeing the existence of slavery be included in the new constitution, but his proposal was rejected because of opposition led by Quaker Daniel Corbit of Odessa and Methodist lay preacher Truston P. McColley of Milford.[114]

The last major attempt in the General Assembly to end slavery was initiated from Washington, DC, during the Civil War. In the fall of 1861, with the North and the South locked in deadly combat, President Abraham Lincoln proposed to Delaware Congressman George P. Fisher a plan that would compensate the state's masters from federal funds if they would free their remaining slaves. Lincoln hoped that if compensated emancipation was shown to work in Delaware, it could easily be extended to the other loyal slave states of Maryland, Kentucky, and Missouri and then to the Confederacy. The president was convinced that his plan was the "cheapest and most humane way of ending this war and saving lives."[115]

Fisher then arranged a meeting between Lincoln and Republican Benjamin Burton of Indian River Hundred, Sussex County, whose twenty-eight bondspeople made him Delaware's leading slave owner. After listening to the president's plan, Burton assured him that the state's farmers would free their remaining bondsmen and bondswomen for a fair price. (Burton was dead wrong.) Congressman Fisher returned to Dover and, with the help of fellow Republican Nathaniel P. Smithers, drew up a bill to be presented to the General Assembly that would immediately free all Delaware slaves over the age of thirty-five, and all others by 1872. Compensation to owners was to be set by a local board of assessors, with the payments averaging about $500 per slave—considerably more than a prime male field hand was worth, and five times the value of a typical slave in the state. Payments to owners were to come out of a pool of $900,000 that would be provided by the Republican-controlled U.S. Congress. At the time there were less than eighteen hundred enslaved African-Americans in the entire state, and 75 percent were in Sussex, with the highest concentration in the Nanticoke River basin.[116]

There was a serious problem—President Lincoln and his Republican party were unpopular throughout most of Delaware. Republicans were called "nigger lovers"; and Lincoln, because of his dark skin, was charged with being confused about his own racial identity. In the election of 1860, Lincoln ran third in the state behind John Breckinridge and John Bell and received only 24 percent of the vote. Moreover, despite their historic support for the Union—theirs was the first state to ratify the U.S. Constitution—Delawareans were suspicious of any federal policy that might interfere with the sovereign rights of their own state government. A resolution introduced in the General Assembly in 1862 in response to Lincoln's compensated emancipation proposal pointed out that "when the people of Delaware desire to abolish slavery within her borders, they will do so in their own way, having due regard to strict equity." Furthermore, "any interference from without" was regarded as "improper" and was "hereby repelled."[117]

Few Delaware politicians argued that slavery was crucial to the economy. Rather, they spoke of states' rights and party advantage as reasons to oppose Lincoln's compensated emancipation plan. Even U.S. Senator Bayard, a committed enemy of the Republican party, admitted that in Delaware, "slavery does not exist as a valuable source of prosperity." Nevertheless, he opposed Lincoln's plan because its rejection by the General Assembly would "kill Republicanism in Delaware."[118]

Underneath the states' rights rhetoric and the maneuvering for party advantage lay the deep concern that the official end of slavery would be followed by equality for African-Americans and even by considerable black-against-white violence. Republicans were accused of attempting "to place the Negro on a footing of equality with the white man." One Delaware newspaper observed that Lincoln's emancipation plan was but "the first step; if it shall succeed, others will follow tending to elevate the Negro to an equality with the white man or rather to degrade the white man by obliterating the distinction between races." Samuel Townsend, a Democrat, preyed on the fear that free blacks were even more dangerous than slaves and predicted that the end of slavery in Delaware would add two thousand more to the state's already large free black population of twenty thousand. He warned that "in a short time," free African-Americans "might equal the white population and cause a massacre."[119] Townsend and many others hostile to emancipation and to equal rights for free blacks portrayed white Delaware as riding on the back of a tiger from which it dared not dismount. Even the state's Republicans, who were abolitionists, shared with their Democratic opponents a real concern about the increase in unregulated blacks that would be produced by emancipation. Republican Congressman Fisher even went so far as to talk of colonizing overseas not only the small numbers of remaining slaves but also the state's entire African-American population.[120]

In the end, Lincoln's compensated emancipation plan, drawn up by Fisher and Smithers and introduced into the General Assembly in early 1862, was never officially voted on. The two men canvassed the members of both chambers only to find that while the president's plan would probably pass in the Senate, the House would reject it by the margin of one vote. Fisher and Smithers then withdrew the bill. A decisive Democratic victory in the election of late 1862 ended any chance that an emancipation plan would be approved in the General Assembly in the near future.[121]

In 1862 the only significant victory for Lincoln's supporters in Delaware was the election of William Cannon of Sussex County as governor. During the remaining years of the Civil War, Governor Cannon and the Democrat-controlled legislature were constantly at odds. In January 1865 he proposed the speedy end to slavery in Delaware by the passage of emancipation legislation, but his recommendation was treated with contempt by the General Assembly. In the next month, on February 7, the governor submitted to it the Thirteenth Amendment to the U.S. Constitution, which called for the end of slavery everywhere in the country, but the General Assembly refused to ratify it because it violated "the reserved rights of the several states."[122]

Lincoln's Emancipation Proclamation and the subsequent flight of enslaved African-Americans from their owners ended slavery throughout most of the Confederacy by April 1865. Of the four slave states that remained loyal to the Union, Missouri and Maryland legislated an end to human bondage during the Civil War. By contrast, Kentucky and Delaware continued officially to tolerate slavery for seven months after General Robert E. Lee's surrender at Appomattox Court House, Virginia. The actual number of African-Americans still held in bondage in Delaware declined to only a few hundred by late 1865, but whites in the state stubbornly held on to the "peculiar institution."[123] Slavery was ended in Delaware and Kentucky in December 1865 by the Thirteenth Amendment. At last, despite the opposition of the General Assembly, the decaying carcass of slavery was finally put to rest.

Notes

*John M. Clayton Correspondence, HSD.

1. The less than 5 percent figure is an estimate based on colonial-era manumissions found in wills for all three Delaware counties and in other primary sources. In neighboring Maryland, about 4 percent of African-Americans were free in the late colonial period, according to Richard S. Dunn, "Black Society in the Chesapeake," in Ira Berlin and Ronald Hoffman, eds., *Slavery and Freedom in the Age of the American Revolution* (Charlottesville, VA, 1983), 62.

2. Calculated from figures in *Negro Population, 1790–1915*, 57; and D. G. Beers, *Atlas of the State of Delaware* (Philadelphia, 1868), "Tables."

3. *Negro Population, 1790–1915*, 57. The percentage increase or decrease in slave populations by state from 1790 to 1810 was: New York, –29; New Jersey, –5; Pennsylvania, –79; Delaware, –53; Maryland, +8; Virginia, +34; North Carolina, +67; and South Carolina, +83.

4. *Blue Hen's Chicken*, 3/18/1850.

5. Munroe, *Colonial Delaware*, 187; *Laws of the State of Delaware*, 1:214. For an indication that old or crippled slaves continued to be manumitted because they were economic liabilities see *Laws of the State of Delaware*, 5:399.

6. *Laws of the State of Delaware*, 1:214, 435–36; Ann Holiday, March 25, 1775, Deeds of Manumission, Duck Creek Monthly Meeting, 1774–1792, 16, Historical Society of Pennsylvania (hereafter HSP).

7. *Laws of the State of Delaware*, 1:435–36, 2:886, 5:399–402; Deeds of Manumission, Duck Creek Monthly Meeting, 1774–1792, 13, 16, 87 and passim, HSP; Munroe, *Colonial Delaware*, 187.

8. Petition, 1822, Kent County, Slavery Material, No. 2, 1764–1866, Miscellaneous, DSA; Letter from "Humanus," *Delaware Gazette*, 10/24/1789; Justice, *Life and Ancestry of Warner Mifflin*, 79.

9. John Clowes, Esq., 1769, and James Buchanen, 1789, Sussex County Estate Inventories, DSA; Levin Thompson, Dagsboro Hundred, and Gedion Badley, Samuel Bailey, Joseph Cannon, Little Creek Hundred, Sussex County Tax Assessment Books, 1816, ibid.

10. John Miers (1749), Sussex County Will Book No. 1, 409, SCCH.

11. Andrew Caldwell (1774), Kent County Will Book L, 163, DSA.

12. Based on figures from scattered Delaware estate inventories, 1775–1789, DSA. Slaves throughout the Upper South declined in value during most of the period from 1775 to 1789; Berlin, *Slaves without Masters*, 27n.

13. See note 3.

14. Kolchin, *American Slavery*, 63–67.

15. Petition to General Assembly, 1786, Slavery Folder No. 1, HSD.

16. Flower, *John Dickinson*, 200.

17. Ibid.; April 20, 1778, Revolutionary War, Box 32A, Folder No. 1, H. F. Brown Collection, Box 22, File 5, HSD; *Minutes of the Council of the Delaware State from 1776 to 1792* (Dover, 1886), 755.

18. Berlin, *Slaves without Masters*, 19; Hancock, *Delaware Two Hundred Years Ago*, 13; Bill of Sale, 1791, Kent County, Slavery Material, No. 2, 1764–1866, Miscellaneous, DSA.

19. C. A. Weslager, "Lewes, III," in *Papers Given at the Lewes Historical Society's Cultural and Historical Seminar of Lewes, 1978 and 1979* (Lewes, DE, 1979), 25; Fletcher, *Pennsylvania Agriculture*, 116; Munroe, *Colonial Delaware*, 56, 63; Leland Harder, "Plockhoy and His Settlement at Zwaanendael," *Delaware History* 3 (March 1949): 138–54; John Kipshaven (1700), Sussex County Will Book No. 1, 34, SCCH.

20. C. H. B. Turner, ed., *Some Records of Sussex County*, 186, 224, passim. The percentage for New Castle is an educated guess based on the readings of numerous primary sources.

21. John Miers (1749), Sussex County Will Book No. 1, 409, SCCH.

22. Nash, *Forging Freedom*, 26; Williams, *The Garden of American Methodism*, 8.

23. Nash and Soderlund, *Freedom by Degrees*, 92; Nash, *Forging Freedom*, 26; Wright, ed., *Vital Records for Kent and Sussex Counties*, 32; Levi Spencer (1770), Sussex County Will Book No. 2, 395, SCCH; Wright, ed., *Vital Records of Kent and Sussex Counties*, 73; Jonathan Ozbun (1773), Kent County Will Book L, 143, DSA; Deeds of Manumission, Duck Creek Monthly Meeting, 1774–1792, 100–101, 122 and passim, HSP; Essah, "Slavery and Freedom in the First State," 100. The 7 to 10 percent figure is based on an estimated total population for Delaware in 1770 of between thirty thousand and forty thousand. Of that total, my estimate is that 20 to 25 percent were enslaved. According to Deeds of

Manumission, Duck Creek Monthly Meeting, 1774–1792, passim, HSP, the number of Quaker manumissions in central Delaware was as follows:

Years	Slaves Freed
1775	111
1776	44
1777	55
1778	77
1779	50
1780–1783	87
Total	424

24. Deeds of Manumission, Duck Creek Monthly Meeting, 1774–1792, passim, HSP; Nash and Soderlund, *Freedom by Degrees*, 87, 98.

25. Justice, *Life and Ancestry of Warner Mifflin*, passim; Malone, ed., *Dictionary of American Biography*, 6:608–9; Deeds of Manumission, Duck Creek Monthly Meeting, 1774–1792, 2, HSP.

26. Zilversmit, *The First Emancipation*, 57.

27. Govey Emerson (1773), Kent County Will Book L, 133–34, KCCH; Justice, *Life and Ancestry of Warner Mifflin*, 85; Deeds of Manumission, Duck Creek Monthly Meeting, 1774–1792, Frontispiece, 2, 14, 15, 22, 23, 29, 31, 34, 36, 38, HSP. For specific references to young slaves who were freed as apprentices see Deeds of Manumission, Duck Creek Monthly Meeting, 1774–1792, 35, 69, 110, HSP.

28. Thomas Nock (1782), Kent County Will Book L, 254–55, KCCH; Jonathan Emerson (1784), Kent County Will Book M, 24–25, ibid.; Justice, *Life and Ancestry of Warner Mifflin*, 141.

29. Bushman et al., eds., *Proceedings of the House of Assembly*, 305; Petition from Quakers, December 27, 1785, Legislative Papers, DSA.

30. Bushman et al., eds., *Proceedings of the House of Assembly*, 538, 855–57.

31. Petition from Quakers, December 27, 1785, Slavery folder No. 1, HSD.

32. Williams, *The Garden of American Methodism*, 112; Asbury, *Journal and Letters of Francis Asbury*, 1:273–74.

33. Williams, *The Garden of American Methodism*, 112; Maurice A. Hartnett, "Richard Bassett: Patriot or Tory?" *Delaware Lawyer* 6 (Fall 1987): 30–35; Roger A. Martin, *A History of Delaware through Its Governors, 1776–1984* (Wilmington, DE, 1984), 80–89.

34. Bushman et al., eds., *Proceedings of the House of Assembly*, 398–99.

35. Indentures, Petitions for Freedom, 1701–1799, Kent County, Slavery Material, passim from 1781 to 1789, DSA; Charity Alfred (1781), 18, and Thomas Collins (1784), 189, Kent County Will Book M, KCCH; Boorstin, ed., *Delaware Cases*, 1:181–82, 479–80; 2:416.

36. Munroe, *Colonial Delaware*, 189–90; Bushman et al., eds., *Proceedings of the House of Assembly*, 398, 428, 438; Williams, *The Garden of American Methodism*, 163.

37. Bushman et al., eds., *Proceedings of the House of Assembly*, 880, 917; Hartnett, "Richard Bassett," 35; Williams, *The Garden of American Methodism*, 165; Munroe, *Federalist Delaware*, 159 n.218.

38. Williams, *The Garden of American Methodism*, 165, 164; William H. Williams, *A History of Wesley U.M. Church* (Georgetown, DE, 1978), 11; Petition from the Delaware Society for Promoting the Abolition of Slavery (1787),

No. 051, reel no. 10, Legislative Papers, DSA; Morgan, "William Morgan's Memoir," 220, DSA.

39. Raynear Williams (1789), Folder, Slavery Material, passim, DSA; Sussex County Will Books, passim, SCCH; Kent County Will Books, passim, KCCH; New Castle County Will Books, passim, DSA.

40. Williams, *The Garden of American Methodism*, 32–35, 39–49, 167–68.

41. John M. Clayton to Josiah Randall, New Castle, February 26, 1844, John M. Clayton Correspondence, HSD.

42. *Delaware Gazette*, 2/7/1789; Samuel Paynter the elder (1767), Sussex County Will Book No. 2, 330–31, SCCH; Wright, ed., *Vital Records of Kent and Sussex Counties*, 138; Elizabeth Dushane (1790), New Castle County Will Book N, No. 1, 234–36, DSA; Thomas Evans (1796), New Castle County Will Book O, 192, ibid.

43. *Delaware Gazette*, 8/12/1789, 10/7/89, 11/7/89; Josiah Ash (1788), New Castle County Will Book M, I, 300, DSA; Sarah Tingley (1802), Sussex County Will Book No. 6, 265, SCCH.

44. Monte A. Calvert, "The Abolition Society of Delaware, 1801–1807," *Delaware History* 20 (October 1983): 299–300; Essah, "Slavery and Freedom in the First State," 138–39; Petition from the Delaware Society for Promoting the Abolition of Slavery (1787), No. 051, reel no. 10, Legislative Papers, DSA.

45. Calvert, "The Abolition Society of Delaware," 300–302; Abolition Society of Delaware Minute Book, 13, 21, 23, 29, 34, 37, 113–14, Papers of the Pennsylvania Abolition Society, HSP.

46. Calvert, "The Abolition Society of Delaware," 305–6, 317–19.

47. John Roades (1728), Sussex Deed Book F, No. 6, 296, DSA.

48. Nathaniel Luff to John Dickinson, October 25, 1800, John Dickinson Papers, DSA; Barbara C. Smith, *After the Revolution*, 165–66; Allen, *The Life Experience*, 19; Mary Cannon (1816), Sussex Deed Book No. 7, 184, SCCH.

49. Betsy Hill (1800), Sussex County Will Book D-5, 141, SCCH; Franklin and Moss, *From Slavery to Freedom*, 108.

50. Ann Waller (1795), 141, and Isaac Watson (1788), 261, Sussex County Will Book D-5, SCCH; 1791 Bill of Sale, Kent County, Slavery Material, 1764–1866, Miscellaneous, DSA; Vincent Loockerman the elder (1784), Kent County Will Book M, 63, KCCH; *Delaware Gazette*, 10/7/1789.

51. Bayley, *A Narrative of Some Remarkable Incidents*, 17–18, 25–32.

52. Carter G. Woodson, *Free Negro Owners of Slaves in the United States in 1830* (Washington, DC, 1984), 11 and passim.

53. Among Kent County scriveners in the second half of the eighteenth century was Richard Butler. See Kent County Will Book L, 101, KCCH.

54. Petition to General Assembly from Sundry Inhabitants of Sussex County (1786), reel 0560, Legislative Papers, DSA.

55. *Laws of the State of Delaware*, 2:1321–22.

56. Sussex County Deed Book, 1682–1844, Index, Grantee, Sussex County Recorder of Deeds, DSA. From 1779 to 1796 only 139 manumissions were recorded in the Sussex Deed Book for a yearly average of 7; and from 1797 to 1830 a total of 987 manumissions were recorded for a yearly average of 28. Additional manumissions were recorded in will books.

57. Deeds of Manumission, Duck Creek Monthly Meeting, 1774–1792, 110, 35, 69, HSP; Minutes of Duck Creek Monthly Meeting, 1: 465, Papers of the Pennsylvania Abolition Society, ibid.

58. Richard Abbott (1787), Sussex County Will Book D-4, 271, SCCH; *Laws of the State of Delaware*, 4:338–39. For a discussion of the legal status of

children born prior to the law of 1810 while their mothers awaited the day of freedom promised in delayed manumissions see Negro Ben Jones vs. Edward Wooten in *Reports of Cases Argued and Adjudged in the Superior Court and Court of Error and Appeals of the State of Delaware* (Dover, DE, 1837), 77–86.

59. Book Y-1, Kent County Deeds, 17, KCCH.

60. Williams, *The Garden of American Methodism,* passim.

61. Ibid.; Thomas Ware, *Sketches of the Life and Travels of Rev. Thomas Ware* (New York, 1842), 80.

62. Petition to the General Assembly from the People Called Quakers, December 12, 1785, Slavery Folder No. 1, HSD.

63. *Delaware Gazette,* 9/30/1789.

64. Minute Book, Abolition Society of Delaware, 134, Papers of the Pennsylvania Abolition Society, HSP.

65. *Delaware Gazette,* 9/12/1789, 12/17/1850.

66. *Blue Hen's Chicken,* 3/8/1850; Kolchin, *American Slavery,* 190; Berlin, *Slaves without Masters,* 184.

67. *Delaware Gazette,* 8/2/1789.

68. Ibid., 9/23/1789.

69. Ibid., 9/23/1789.

70. Ibid., 10/14/1789, 9/19/89.

71. Kolchin, *American Slavery,* 194–97; *Delaware Gazette,* 10/4/1850.

72. *Delaware Gazette,* 10/8/1850; Broadside, July 25, 1862, Georgetown meeting, HSD.

73. *Delaware Gazette,* 9/23/1789, 10/7/89.

74. *The Weekly Union,* 12/25/1863.

75. *Pennsylvania Gazette,* 1730–1757, 1763–1766, for example, listed only forty-six fugitive slaves from Delaware.

76. Slavery was abolished in Vermont by its constitution of 1782, in Massachusetts by judicial opinion in 1783, and by gradual emancipation acts in Pennsylvania (1780), Rhode Island (1784), Connecticut (1784 and 1787), New York (1799 and 1817), and New Jersey (1804).

77. Figures compiled from Wright, ed., *Delaware Newspaper Abstracts,* 1, passim.

78. Ibid.

79. Quoted in Blassingame, *The Slave Community,* 198.

80. Statistics taken from Wright, ed., *Delaware Newspaper Abstracts,* passim; *Delaware Gazette,* 11/12/1791; *Delaware and Eastern Shore Advertiser,* 9/10/ 1794. The fifty-two Delaware runaways seemed to reflect fugitive patterns in other states. See, for example, Mullin, *Flight and Rebellion,* 40.

81. *Delaware Gazette,* 4/26/1820; Nash, *Forging Freedom,* 138.

82. Sally Rust Petition (1801), Kent County, Slavery Material, No. 2, 1764– 1866, Miscellaneous, DSA.

83. *Laws of the State of Delaware,* 1:215.

84. Ezekiel Anderson (1823) and George Cubbage (1825), Kent County, Slavery Material, 1764–1866, Miscellaneous, DSA.

85. Priscilla Thompson, "Harriet Tubman, Thomas Garrett, and the Underground Railroad," *Delaware History* 22 (Spring–Summer 1986): 14–18; Harold B. Hancock, "Mary Ann Shadd: Negro Editor, Educator, and Lawyer," ibid. 9 (April 1973): 14–18; Thomas Garrett to J. Miller McKim, June 2, 1860, Garrett Papers, vol. 4, HSD.

86. Thompson, "Harriet Tubman," 16. In 1868, Wilmington abolitionist Thomas Garrett recalled Harriet Tubman leading to freedom some sixty to eighty

slaves "from the neighborhood [Dorchester County, Maryland] where she had been held as a slave." However, he says nothing of her leading African-Americans from Delaware to freedom. James A. McGowan, *Station Master on the Underground Railroad: The Life and Letters of Thomas Garrett* (Moylan, PA, 1977), 153.

87. Thompson, "Harriet Tubman," 1–21.

88. *The Liberator*, 6/30/1848.

89. Still, *The Underground Rail Road*, 772–75; Deposition (1847), Indictments (1847), Kent County Court of General Sessions, DSA. For a slightly different version of Burris's experience see *Blue Hen's Chicken*, 11/12/1847.

90. Still, *The Underground Rail Road*, 772–75; *Blue Hen's Chicken*, 5/12/1848.

91. Still, *The Underground Rail Road*, 774–75; *Blue Hen's Chicken*, 5/12/1848.

92. The assumption that most runaways who used the Underground Railroad were from other slave states is based on scattered references in the Garrett Papers, HSD.

93. Thompson, "Harriet Tubman," 3, 10–11; McGowan, *Station Master on the Underground Railroad*, 7, 50; John A. Munroe, "The Negro in Delaware," *South Atlantic Quarterly* 56 (1957): 431.

94. *Laws of the State of Delaware*, 5:151; McGowan, *Station Master on the Underground Railroad*, 25–26; Thompson, "Harriet Tubman," 10–11.

95. Thompson, "Harriet Tubman," 11; Thomas Garrett to Samuel May, Jr., November 24, 1863, Garrett Papers, HSD; McGowan, *Station Master on the Underground Railroad*, 79.

96. Thomas Garrett to William Lloyd Garrison, Wilmington, November 11, 1854, Garrett Papers, HSD.

97. W. H. Ross to Hon. Edward Wooten, Seaford, September 8, 1857, Edward F. Wooten Folder, HSD; An Incident in the Corbit Mansion (n.d.), Slavery (General), IV, ibid.

98. Garrett to Garrison, Wilmington, December 5, 1850, Garrett Papers, HSD; McGowan, *Station Master on the Underground Railroad*, 75, 115 and passim; Alexander M. Ross, *Recollections and Experiences of an Abolitionist* (Temecula, CA, 1991), 67–71.

99. McGowan, *Station Master on the Underground Railroad*, 95, 139, 101–2.

100. U.S. Census Bureau, Manuscripts, 1860, Delaware, Slave Schedules, seems to indicate that a very large percentage of the remaining Delaware slaves were fugitives on the eve of the Civil War. However, I am very cautious about using the Slave Schedules because it is unclear whether the check marks after listed African-Americans actually indicate a fugitive status. Moreover, the Slave Schedules do not include New Castle and Kent counties and at least one of the hundreds in Sussex. If the check marks are accepted as an indication of runaway status, then the sum totals of the other nine Sussex hundreds indicate that 27 percent of listed slaves were fugitives in 1860.

Hundred	Slaves	Slaves Who Were Fugitives
Broad Creek	200	21
Little Creek	220	70
North West Fork	320	74

Baltimore	85	27
Dagsboro	109	47
Indian River	103	24
Broad Kill	142	33
Lewes-Rehoboth	67	36
Cedar Creek	44	20
Total	1,290	352

101. *Weekly Union*, 10/28/1863, 1/1/64, 10/9/63, 10/16/63, 12/4/63, 1/22/64; *Argosy*, 254, Slavery Folder No. 4, HSD.

102. John M. Clayton to Josiah Randall, New Castle, February 26, 1844, John M. Clayton Correspondence, HSD; John G. Dean, "The Free Negro in Delaware: A Demographic and Economic Study" (Master's thesis, University of Delaware, 1970), 4.

103. *Minutes of the House of Representatives of the State of Delaware, 1765–1770* (Dover, DE, 1931), 125–28; Munroe, *Colonial Delaware*, 187.

104. *Minutes of the House of Representatives, 1765–1770*, 128; Bendler, *Colonial Delaware Assemblymen*, passim.

105. *Minutes of the House of Representatives, 1765–1770*, 128; David Brion Davis, *Slavery in the Colonial Chesapeake* (Williamsburg, VA, 1993), 23–24; Kolchin, *American Slavery*, 79.

106. Claudia L. Bushman, Harold B. Hancock, and Elizabeth M. Homsey, eds., *Proceedings of the Assembly of the Lower Counties on Delaware, 1770–1776* (Newark, DE, 1986), 177, 179, 180; *Laws of the State of Delaware*, 1:89; 2:886; Kolchin, *American Slavery*, 79.

107. Bushman et al., eds., *Proceedings of the House of Assembly*, 59, 288, 305, 309, 314, 330, 341.

108. *Laws of the State of Delaware*, 2:884–85, 943.

109. Munroe, *Federalist Delaware*, 160; *Journal of the House of Representatives of the State of Delaware* (Dover, DE, 1803), 66–67; Harold B. Hancock, *The History of Nineteenth Century Laurel* (Laurel, DE, 1983), 255. The *Journal of the House of Representatives* (1804), 26, 49, (1805), 34, 36, 39, 42, 43, 45, 48, 49–53, 55–56 indicate the growing disagreement over government-mandated abolition along geographic lines. By the early nineteenth century the only Sussex legislator in favor of gradual abolition was Caleb Rodney. I am indebted to John A. Munroe for the latter citations from the *Journal of the House of Representatives*.

110. *Journal of the House of Representatives* (Wilmington, DE, 1845), 140, 199.

111. *Journal of the House of Representatives* (Wilmington, DE, 1847), 195–97. For a discussion of "modern" versus "traditional" mentality see Richard D. Brown, *Modernization: The Transformation of American Life* (Prospect Heights, IL, 1988). For a brief discussion of slavery and capitalism see Kolchin, *American Slavery*, 67–68, 173.

112. *Journal of the House of Representatives* (1847), 196–97; Hancock, *The History of Nineteenth Century Laurel*, 258. H. Clay Reed, "Lincoln's Compensated Emancipation Plan," *Delaware Notes* 7 (1931): 65 n.32, maintains that the 1847 bill proposed freeing all children born after 1860. A copy of the actual bill of 1847 is not in the Delaware State Archives.

113. *Delaware Gazette*, 2/18/1851; Reed, "Lincoln's Compensated Emancipation Plan," 65 n.31.

114. Munroe, *History of Delaware*, 123.

115. *Sunday Star* (Wilmington), 2/9/1919

116. Ibid.; Reed, "Lincoln's Compensated Emancipation Plan," 36–39; Harold B. Hancock, *Delaware during the Civil War: A Political History* (Wilmington, DE, 1961), 106–7; Dean, "The Free Negro in Delaware," 3. A male field hand who was eighteen years old was worth about $350 in Delaware in 1853; William Brown (1853), Sussex Inventories, DSA. The average value of a slave in the state in 1862 was $100, according to the *Delaware State Journal and Statesman*, 2/4/1862. The $500 average compensation price is reported in the *Sunday Star*, 2/9/1919, as $400.

117. Hancock, *Delaware during the Civil War*, 30; *Journal of the House of Representatives, 1862* (Dover, DE, 1862), 230–40.

118. Hancock, *Delaware during the Civil War*, 109–10.

119. *Delawarean*, 9/6/1862, 2/1/62, 11/1/62.

120. Reed, "Lincoln's Compensated Emancipation Plan," 48; Hancock, *Delaware during the Civil War*, 109.

121. Munroe, *History of Delaware*, 140; Reed, "Lincoln's Compensated Emancipation Plan," 52.

122. Oversized Proclamations, February 7, 1865, HSD; Hancock, *Delaware during the Civil War*, 154–55.

123. Scharf, *History of Delaware*, 1:361.

VI

"A Mongrel Liberty,
A Mere Mock Freedom"

They [Delaware's free blacks] are truly neither slaves nor free: being subject to many of the disabilities and disadvantages of both conditions, and enjoying few of the benefits of either.
—William Yates, 1837*

By 1860 the once-clean air over Wilmington was daily fouled by black smoke spewing from the stacks of recently built factories along the Christina River. The Industrial Revolution was transforming part of northern Delaware from an agricultural-based to a manufacturing-based economy. The rise of manufacturing had a considerable impact on the state's demographic patterns. Although its overall population growth from 1790 to 1860 fell considerably short of the national average, new jobs created by new companies caused a substantial increase in the northern part of the state. In 1790 only 33 percent of Delaware's population lived in New Castle County; by 1860 it was 49 percent. Wilmington was the key to this growth. While the rest of New Castle County experienced a one-third increase from 1840 to 1860, the city's population increased two and one-half times, from 8,367 to 21,258. In 1810 only one in fifteen Delawareans lived in Wilmington, but fifty years later the figure rose to one in five.[1]

The industrial development and population explosion in the northern part of the state heralded a new social order impatient with traditional patterns that stood in the way of business efficiency and technological innovation. By the eve of the Civil War, a rational and ordered capitalism gave direction to life north of the Christina. But south of the river, in flat Delaware, there were few signs of real change. The dramatic decline of slavery did lead to some minor transformations of the rural landscape and to a significant alteration in labor relations, but the old social order, which supported a hierarchical society based on landholdings as well as considerations of race, class, and gender, showed little sign of stepping aside for the new one.

The area south of the Christina River grew far more slowly than northern New Castle County during the antebellum era (1800–1860) because the downstate region did not offer significant economic opportunities to either blacks or whites. Factories were conspicuously absent, while played-out agricultural land was considerably less productive than the farmland in northern New Castle County. In Kent and, more particularly, in Sussex there was a strong attachment to older farming methods and to the planting of traditional crops that helped keep in semipoverty most of those who worked the land. In 1847, Governor William Tharp pointed out that the land had fallen into the hands of a few large proprietors who turned over its cultivation to "a dependent tenantry who had no sufficient interest in its permanent improvement" and therefore neglected "its proper care and management." This state of affairs was reflected in the comparative value of Delaware farmland in 1860, with New Castle County leading the way at fifty-four dollars per acre, followed by Kent at fourteen dollars and Sussex at nine dollars.[2]

~

Delaware, Maryland, South Carolina, and Louisiana were the only slave states of the antebellum era without a legal racial definition that distinguished blacks from whites. As a result, the classification of Delawareans by race was left to the intuitive judgment of whites. Using this arbitrary method, census takers during this period determined that free blacks were a significant portion of the state's population and that they reached a high of 22 percent in 1840, when about nine in ten African-Americans were free.[3]

In general, free blacks lived where they could find work. Although some were drawn to job opportunities offered by Wilmington's thriving economy, the overwhelming majority continued to play out their lives, as had most of their parents, in rural Delaware. In 1800, 84 percent of free African-Americans lived in the countryside, 10 percent in small towns and villages, and 6 percent in Wilmington. By 1860 a still very high 75 percent lived in a rural landscape, 14 percent in small towns and villages, and 11 percent in Wilmington. Only in the rolling hills of northern Delaware was the rural free black population insignificant, amounting to only 3 percent of the total population in 1860.[4]

The scarcity of African-Americans in the Piedmont played a decisive role, according to one source, in changing the economic history of the state. In the late 1890s, Samuel Bancroft, Jr., a leading Wilmington industrialist, wrote that the Du Pont Company had been established along the banks of the Brandywine River (Creek) in Delaware in 1802 rather than on the Mattaponi River in Virginia because its émigré founder, Eleuthère Irénée du Pont, did not like blacks and Virginia had a large black population. When du Pont informed Thomas Jefferson of his intention to locate his gunpowder factory in Delaware rather than in Virginia, Jefferson is supposed to have replied: "We shall have them all back in Africa within twenty years." But du Pont was not convinced that would happen and chose instead a site in the Brandywine Valley, a few miles northwest of Wilmington, for his powder works.[5] The rest, as they say, is history.

Although free blacks continued to reside primarily in rural settings during the antebellum years, they did not necessarily spend their entire lives on the same farm or even in the same county. Particularly noticeable was the general movement of many free blacks from Kent, and especially Sussex, to New Castle County. In 1790, Kent held 66 percent of the state's free blacks, followed by Sussex with 18 percent and New Castle with only 16 percent. By 1860 the figures had dramatically changed: New Castle led the way with 41 percent, followed by Kent with 37 percent and Sussex with 22 percent.[6]

While a number of free African-Americans such as Richard Allen of Kent and members of the Shadd family of Wilmington moved to Pennsylvania, to other northern states, and even to Canada, most remained in Delaware despite the increasingly hostile attitude of most whites and the continuing danger of being kidnapped and sold as slaves into the Deep South.[7] In the late antebellum years, however, increasing numbers of them left Delaware, with many settling in Philadelphia where, by 1860, at 2,977, they represented 13 percent of the city's African-American population. The increasing free black exodus and a growing white migration from out of state to the Wilmington area caused the percentage of free blacks in Delaware's population to decline from approximately 22 percent in 1840 to between 17 and 18 percent by 1860.[8]

Leading States in Free Black Percentage of Total Population[10]

	1790	1810	1840	1860
Delaware	7%	18%	22%	18%
Maryland	2	9	13	12
Virginia	2	3	5	5
Pennsylvania	1	3	3	2
New York	1	2	2	1

Throughout the Upper South, during the antebellum years, whites feared free blacks even more than slaves.[9] This concern was magnified in Delaware, where free blacks made up a far higher percentage of the total population than in any other state. As previously noted, whites perceived this large free black cohort as a potential threat to domestic tranquility, and they became very uneasy about the prospect of even more free blacks immigrating from other southern states.

Indeed, as early as 1786 there was an unsuccessful attempt in the legislature to bar out-of-state free blacks. In 1807, Governor Nathaniel Mitchell warned that because "some southern states compel their free negroes to emigrate, . . . we may expect a full share of these people." The General Assembly responded by prohibiting the migration of free blacks to Delaware, only to repeal the law in 1808. In 1811 a second ban was passed and remained in force until it was repealed in 1831. In 1851 a third ban was enacted and seems to have remained in force through the Civil War. Understandably, only a small number of free African-Americans moved to Delaware during the antebellum period, a fact that was reflected in the homegrown nature of the state's free black population. In 1850, for example, only 6 percent of free African-Americans were born out of state.[11]

There was a demographic gender imbalance among free blacks in northern Delaware. Because Wilmington, like most antebellum American cities, offered more jobs for black females than for black males, women made up 57 percent of the city's free black population in 1840.[12] This surplus of females was drawn from the rest of New Castle County, leaving nearby rural areas with more black males than females. But farther south, in Kent and Sussex, most areas were gender balanced.[13]

George M. Frederickson maintains that "racism, although the child of slavery, not only outlived its parent, but grew stronger" after the institution's demise. In Pennsylvania, "a strong race prejudice developed among white people after most of the negroes were free."[14] The Delaware experience with racism supports Frederickson's statement and parallels the Pennsylvania model. From the very beginning of slavery in Delaware, whites perceived significant differences between themselves and black Africans (see Chapter III). But racial prejudice and the resulting colonial regulations, based on skin color alone, were relatively mild by later nineteenth-century standards. Subsequently, however, the degradation of blacks in bondage, the fading of white ethnic differences, and the demeaning statements about blacks by supporters of slavery all contributed to growing prejudice against African-Americans. Paradoxically, at the same time that most of white Delaware was hearing and believing increasingly unfavorable stereotypes, the majority of the state's blacks were adjusting to the first few years of freedom after decades in bondage. The number of free blacks increased so rapidly that by 1800 their 13.5 percent of the total population made Delaware the first state in the Union with a significant percentage of free African-Americans. The growing presence of so many free blacks raised white concerns which, in turn, fueled white racism. William Yates, a free black sent by the American Anti-Slavery Society in 1837 to investigate the status of blacks in Delaware, reported that "strange as it may seem, there is an extensive and moral fear of free colored people pervading the community."[15]

Whites were particularly uneasy over a perceived change in the nature of African-Americans after manumission. At first, explained the *Delaware Gazette* in 1826, emancipated blacks retained the habit of deference toward whites "which had been formed in slavery." However, "the fear and deference and sometimes affectionate regard for white people . . . are wearing by degrees; time is planting other feelings in their place." Free African-Americans were seen as increasingly less docile and potentially more dangerous than they were under slavery. This deep concern caused the General Assembly, in 1827, to support the voluntary removal of free African-Americans from the state because it was "essential to our safety"; and, twenty-four years later, to label "the rapid increase of free negroes . . . as a great and growing evil."[16] This escalating concern led white Delawareans to impose a series of draconian laws or black codes that could only be rationalized by further attacking the character, honesty, and work ethic of free blacks.

The dehumanizing impact of the state's black codes was clear to Yates. In 1837 he wrote that Delaware's "free people of color are only nominally free." Because of the "wretched system of laws which have been enacted in regard to them," free African-Americans in the state were "neither slaves nor free: being subject to many of the disabilities and disadvantages of both conditions, and enjoying few of the benefits of either." The General Assembly enacted laws, Yates insisted, that were "designed to degrade, to crush and to render them ignorant and powerless." In doing so, it categorized all free blacks "as worthless, as liars and unfit to be trusted."[17] An examination of the state's specific legislative and judicial decisions concerning free people of color generally supports Yates's observations.

During the colonial and revolutionary periods, custom barred Delaware's free African-Americans from voting. With the increasing number of manumissions that characterized the late eighteenth century, the suffrage rights of free blacks were more specifically addressed. In 1792 a newly adopted state constitution clearly excluded all African-Americans from voting by restricting suffrage to tax-paying white males. The ban was reaffirmed by the General Assembly in 1863. In barring free blacks from voting at an early date, Delaware was joined

by both Maryland and Virginia. To the north, however, it was a different story. In neighboring Pennsylvania, for example, some free blacks
continued to vote until a constitutional amendment in 1838 finally put
an end to the practice.[18]

Most white Delawareans were convinced that a dramatic increase
in crime would follow the manumission of blacks from the restraining
bonds of slavery. The Wilmington Union Colonization Society seized
on this paranoia to rally support for its own agenda of sending blacks
to Africa. In 1827 it sent a petition to the General Assembly pointing
out that exporting newly manumitted blacks to their ancestral homeland would head off a crime wave.[19] Scattered newspaper accounts
and court records suggest that crimes committed by free African-
Americans were common. A writer to the *Delaware Gazette* charged
in 1789 that free blacks stole more than did even poor whites. In 1847
the *Blue Hen's Chicken* reported that "rogues" from Philadelphia, New
York, and Baltimore combined with the state's "colored population"
to account for most of the crime in Delaware.

From April 1835 to April 1840 the Kent County Court of General
Sessions handed down some 253 indictments, of which 102, or 40 percent, were of African-Americans. Blacks made up about 31 percent
of the county's population in 1840; and, because almost all were
free, these figures indicate that a slightly higher percentage of free
blacks than whites were indicted in Kent County from 1835 to 1840.
While one can make the point that newspapers were hardly objective
sources of information, that indictments were not final judgments of
guilt, or that the disproportionately higher number of black indictments may have been simply a product of the era's racism, the evidence does suggest, but does not prove, that free blacks were slightly
more prone to what the white community labeled "criminal" activity
than were other Delawareans. But the evidence also suggests that the
dramatic increase in black crime, which many whites had anticipated
with the manumission of large numbers of African-Americans, did not
materialize.[20]

The specific nature of free black crime reflected much about the
living conditions of its perpetrators. According to the records of the
Kent County Court of General Sessions for the same five-year period,
84 percent of all free black indictments were for criminal acts against
whites, with assaults accounting for only 18 percent of black-on-white
crimes. By contrast, assaults represented 33 percent of black-on-black
crimes and 100 percent of white-on-black ones. These figures indicate that indicted crimes by blacks against whites were primarily aimed
at stealing material goods while, in crimes by blacks against blacks
and by whites against blacks, other goals were more important. Blacks
stealing primarily from whites rather than from other blacks simply

testified to their desperate need, which was reflected in the tendency of thefts of food to increase in winter when many free blacks had very little to eat.[21] Because they had no political voice and because they were the objects of rising racism and were blamed for most of the crime in the state, Delaware's free blacks were singled out for rough treatment by constables and sheriffs. In 1838 a Wilmington newspaper admitted that the city's law enforcement officers treated blacks "with more harshness than whites and very often arrest them for offenses which would not be noticed in whites."[22]

Nor were free African-Americans granted equal rights before Delaware's courts. Unlike slaves, free people of color had always been tried by the same courts that judged whites, but the presiding court officers and juries were always all white. During the late seventeenth century, free blacks had probably testified in court in the same manner as whites. For most of the eighteenth century, however, custom and common practice barred black testimony against whites.[23] In 1793, in a startling departure from past practices, Judge Richard Bassett allowed the testimony of a free black against a white defendant. Six years later, recognizing that a "great injustice and many inconveniences" to whites as well as blacks resulted from the exclusion of black testimony, the General Assembly decided that free African-Americans could testify against whites, but only if "white testimony is unavailable." In addition, under no circumstances was a free black allowed to testify against a white man for siring an illegitimate child.[24] These remaining restrictions continued to give people of color only very limited legal protection from a great variety of crimes committed against them by whites during the antebellum era.

Despite the obvious inequities, certain legal rights of free blacks who were victims of crime were protected. By the late eighteenth century, coroners' inquests were routinely held when either enslaved or free African-Americans died.[25] Moreover, the courts indicted a number of whites who victimized free blacks during the antebellum years.[26] Just as with slaves, free African-Americans who were charged with criminal activity did not automatically face kangaroo justice when brought before Delaware's courts. In fact, there is some indication that their legal rights, once they entered the court system, were carefully preserved. In 1845 in Kent, for example, Ann Bolden was accused of stealing corn. When brought before a justice of the peace, she was informed "that she was not bound to answer anything, and that she was at all events not bound to convict herself." By the late antebellum era, free counsel was routinely assigned to both enslaved and free African-Americans as well as to poor whites if they could not afford an attorney. Because of such careful judicial practices, some free blacks were found innocent after being indicted for serious crimes.

In 1826, for example, Henry Armstrong of Christiana Hundred was charged with breaking into the home of a white woman and raping her, but the New Castle County Court of Oyer and Terminer found him not guilty.[27]

Even when found guilty, free African-Americans sometimes were given relatively mild sentences. In 1859 in Kent County, Mary Burris was convicted of arson, but because "of insanity" she was not sentenced. Nineteen years earlier, free mulatto Robert Hughes of northern Kent had assaulted a white constable, but the case was settled by Hughes's apologizing and then paying court costs. The principle of "benefit of clergy," which was claimed under Anglo-Saxon law by murderers to avoid execution for their crimes, was granted on occasion to blacks as well as to whites. During the early antebellum period, free blacks James Miller, Prince Tilghman, and Lucinda Murray of Kent and Jacob Battel of New Castle County were convicted of murder, but then each was given "benefit of clergy"—an "M" for murderer was branded on their left thumbs and those who could pay court costs were subsequently released. (At least one of the murder victims was white.) But if, like Murray, convicted murderers who were given "benefit of clergy" were too poor to pay, then they were sold into servitude (in her case for five years) to meet court expenses.[28]

Court sentences of whites and free blacks were, in many cases, the same. Black and whites found guilty of murder or rape were usually executed. When John Morris, a free African-American, was sentenced to be hanged in 1792 for the rape of a white woman in Kent County, his punishment was identical to that of white rapist George Parker of the same county some fifteen years later. Also receiving similar punishments for similar crimes in Kent were free black Abraham Gunnage and white John Smith, who were hanged for burglary in 1803 and 1793, respectively.[29] But even if the courts followed legal protocol when trying free blacks, severe limitations on their right to testify, as well as the fact that justices of the peace, judges, and jury members held the same negative perceptions of African-Americans commonly held by other whites, made equal treatment of blacks and whites before the bench almost impossible in antebellum Delaware.

The tradition of selling convicted persons into servitude had long been practiced under Anglo-Saxon law. As late as 1826 the General Assembly listed a wide range of crimes for which both whites and blacks could be sold into servitude for a number of years. In 1830, William Clow, a Kent County white man who was found guilty of horse stealing, was fined, locked in a pillory for an hour, given thirty-nine lashes on the bare back "well laid on," and then sold into servitude for seven years to pay the fine and court costs. In the same year and in the same county, James Williams, a free African-American convicted of stealing money, was fined, given twenty-one lashes "well laid on," and then sold as a servant for up to seven years to pay the fine and court costs.[30]

Similar sentences, however, often fell short of equal justice. In 1837, Yates pointed out that although guilty whites might be sold into servitude, "public opinion neutralizes the law" because convicted whites were often purchased by friends or relatives for only a "nominal" sum, and no service was expected. By contrast, the sale of "a colored man" was "real," and it was often used as "a door to smuggle him off to perpetual bondage." Amid the increasing racism of the antebellum period, even the pretense of equal sentencing was abandoned. In 1839 the General Assembly ended the sale into servitude of convicted whites but continued that of convicted blacks.[31]

The treatment of debtors was another example of increasing racial discrimination. Since colonial times, debtors in Delaware were sold into temporary servitude rather than sent to prison, and the auction price was used to satisfy their creditors. In 1827 the General Assembly required that whites of both sexes and black women debtors be required to give their consent before they could be sold. Black male debtors, however, could continue to be auctioned off into temporary servitude without their consent.[32]

From the beginning of European settlement, the right of white Delawareans to bear firearms was considered a fundamental freedom. Despite considerable reluctance to allow slaves to carry firearms, some were permitted to use guns for hunting game birds and wild animals. For free blacks, owning firearms was not challenged until well into the nineteenth century. According to an 1812 law, for example, free African-Americans, along with slaves and whites, were to be punished for "discharging firearms within villages," but there was no suggestion that their right to bear arms should be restricted. Nat Turner's slave rebellion in 1831 in Virginia changed all that because it greatly intensified white paranoia throughout the South.[33] In 1832 the Delaware General Assembly reacted by making it illegal for free blacks "to have, own, keep or possess any gun, pistol, sword or any war-like instrument whatsoever." For those free African-Americans who depended on hunting birds and small mammals for food—deer by then were almost extinct in the state—exceptions might be made. In 1835 the General Assembly decided that these exceptions were subject to annual renewal. However, in 1863, in the midst of the Civil War, even this small loophole was closed, and all free blacks were denied the right to possess guns "of any kind." The General Assembly further tightened the screws on personal freedom in 1845 by prohibiting the sale of alcohol to free blacks and by barring them from selling liquor.[34]

The legal right of free blacks to acquire property had been challenged by some Delaware whites in the last decade of the eighteenth century. John Dickinson, although an abolitionist, was a spokesman for the group. (They were probably inspired by a plan circulated in Virginia in 1790 that aimed at driving free blacks from that state by denying them the right to buy or inherit land.) At the Delaware Constitutional Convention of 1792, Dickinson proposed that the new constitution contain the words: "None but white persons shall hereafter be capable of becoming freeholders within this state." His proposal directly contradicted a 1787 law, passed while Richard Bassett was an influential member of the legislature, which guaranteed the right of free blacks to acquire and hold private property. Bassett was appalled by Dickinson's attempt to restrict further the already limited economic opportunities of free African-Americans, and he mounted an effort to block the proposal at the convention. In the end, it was turned down by an eighteen-to-seven vote of the delegates.[35]

When Warner Mifflin heard about Dickinson's constitutional proposal, he was enraged. He wrote that Dickinson's "conduct respecting the blacks . . . induced one to believe that he was as great an enemy to the cause of righteousness as was in that body [the convention]." What particularly bothered Mifflin was that Dickinson was incorrectly perceived by most Delawareans as both a Quaker and a sympathetic champion of the interests of African-Americans. He fired off a letter to Dickinson admonishing him that "those that come nearest to the truth and were not in it, and profess it, were its greatest enemies."[36]

In 1851 the legislature again entertained a proposal to stop all African-Americans from acquiring "any real estate, other than such as they now hold." Although, just as in 1792, the attempt was foiled, it was clear to Delaware's free people of color that their right to buy new property and even to hold on to old property was subject to the capricious whims of a legislature increasingly willing to ride roughshod over their rights.[37]

Large gatherings of African-Americans made white Delawareans nervous. The 1798 legislation that banned nonresident slaves on election day from visiting towns where votes were cast also applied to free blacks.[38] The alarming news from Virginia in 1831 caused Delaware to place increasing restrictions on gatherings of free African-Americans throughout the year. In 1832 the General Assembly made it illegal for more than twelve free blacks or mulattoes to hold meetings that lasted beyond 10 P.M. in winter unless "three respectable white men" were present. Sensitive to the potential of black preachers to encourage and even lead an uprising—Turner had been a preacher—the legislature barred all blacks who entered the state from preaching unless they first were licensed by a Delaware judge or justice of the peace. In 1851 the ban against certain black public gatherings was extended to include political meetings "of any party" and camp meetings. Black attendance at white camp meetings, however, was allowed.[39]

Growing racism led to increasing efforts to segregate free blacks so that whites did not have to associate with them, but legal racial separation in antebellum Delaware was not as complete as it would become in the rest of the South with the introduction of Jim Crow laws in the late nineteenth century. Because free blacks represented a smaller percentage of the total population of antebellum Delaware than they would of the former Confederate states in the late nineteenth century, extreme racial segregation seemed less necessary and less practical. However, during the late eighteenth century, most Delaware churches restricted free blacks and slaves to the back pews or to the balconies. By 1800 the Kent County Poor House was routinely placing whites and free blacks in separate buildings. Moreover, marriage between blacks and whites, the most intimate and threatening of interracial associations, was declared illegal by the General Assembly in 1807. During the first two decades of the nineteenth century, a few African-Americans joined whites in attending state-assisted schools where aid was dispensed on the basis of the number of students attending, but in 1821 the General Assembly specifically denied state aid for African-American students. Since free blacks were generally too poor to pay tuition, this law forced the few local schools that were integrated to close their doors to blacks and ended any semblance of state-aided education for African-Americans. Only educated guesses can be made about racial separation in other areas of Delaware's public life prior to the Civil War. In all likelihood such public meeting places as taverns and hotels were segregated, but there was probably less racial separation in public transportation.[40]

Although the increasing numbers of free blacks were seen by whites as a serious threat to domestic tranquility, a black presence was necessary to cultivate the soil and to carry out essential domestic chores. As Yates pointed out, because "there is no other source" of labor, Delaware "is dependent upon them."[41] Even the large number of white employers who constantly complained about the work ethic of their African-American employees admitted their dependence on free blacks "for assistance in the cultivation of their fields, and their domestic concerns."[42]

Among white employers, there was considerable worry that black migration to Pennsylvania and to other northern states might drain

Delaware of its much-needed labor pool.[43] Farmers and businessmen repeatedly turned to the legislature for help in keeping free blacks at home. In 1807 the General Assembly decided that African-Americans spending more than two years out of state would be fined more than thirty dollars on their return. Those unable to pay would be sold into servitude for up to seven years. In 1811 the permitted time was reduced to six months, in 1849 to sixty days, and in 1863 to five days. Only sailors and watermen were exempted.[44] The purpose of this legislation was to make free people of color think twice before leaving because, once out of state, they would face arrest, fines, and years of servitude if they decided to return.

The decline of slavery in Delaware changed the relationship between white landowners and black workers. Contract negotiations now replaced masters' directives. As both blacks and whites struggled to understand the implications of this change, it became clear that the extensive interracial contact that had marked slavery was a thing of the past. Just as in the post-Civil War South, the narrow, exclusively economic plane of this newly created "labor for wages" relationship opened up a wide social gulf between blacks and whites in antebellum Delaware.[45] Replacing paternalism, which sometimes caused a number of masters to think of their slaves as "my people," was a new attitude that viewed free blacks as mere pawns to be exploited for economic gain.

If the complaints of white employers are to be believed, free blacks were not willing to abide by the new rules. They were accused of not responding to job offers or, once employed, of capriciously disappearing when fields needed harvesting. In 1841 white petitioners to the General Assembly maintained that the state "was filled with complaints" and that "there is scarcely a farmer or a house keeper among us who has not experienced grievances." The difficulties were "mainly attributed to the great number of lazy, irresponsible, lawless and miserable free negroes and mulattoes." Free blacks were further described as "having no permanent interest to fix them to our soil, and being by their indigence rendered irresponsible to the obligation of contract."[46] The problem was that white employers were often dealing with black laborers whose work habits had been shaped by slavery. Thus, the priorities of some of these free blacks more closely resembled those of a subsistence-oriented peasantry than a well-disciplined rural proletariat. As elsewhere in the antebellum South, many free blacks were less interested in working an extended period of days for relatively low pay than in tending their own gardens or in fishing in nearby rivers and bays. Moreover, when they did engage in wage labor, they viewed it as a temporary expedient rather than a long-term commitment.[47]

Should free blacks be allowed to sit idly by while crops needed to be planted, cultivated, and harvested and domestic work needed to be addressed? Those who depended on free black labor did not think so and soon were questioning the right of blacks to reject the enticements of contract labor. Employers argued that this labor was so vital to Delaware's economic health that it had to be regulated, controlled, and even coerced by the state. But, initially at least, the state remained out of the labor contract process and treated it as an individual matter between former slaves and prospective employers.

Increasing complaints about idle and undependable black labor, however, finally caused the legislature to act. In 1849 the General Assembly made it illegal for free blacks to be unemployed while also being poor. Since most black laborers were very poor indeed, this legislation made intentional idleness by blacks a criminal act. Whites were encouraged to spy on them for signs of unemployment and were rewarded with three dollars for every idle free black without "a necessary means of support" who was "not of good and industrious habits." The local justice of the peace then ordered the county sheriff to sell the offending person to work "in the capacity of a servant" until the next January 1, for wages agreed to by the employer and the justice of the peace, and "good and sufficient food, lodging and clothing." In an ominous sentence that conjured up the image of the master and his whip, the General Assembly gave to the white employer the right "to enforce his or her [black's] obedience to lawful commands by moderate corrections and by suitable and sufficient means."[48]

When January 1 rolled around, the black servant was given only thirty days to find new employment, or once again he would be sold into servitude until the next January 1. This procedure was to be repeated every year unless he found employment in January, or until he became too old or crippled to work. Although many free blacks in other areas of the Upper South signed very restrictive labor contracts that lasted for a year or more during the antebellum years, Maryland, with its large free black population, was the only other state to allow sheriffs to sell idle free blacks into a form of bondage that was not very far removed from slavery.[49] As in the former Confederate states immediately after the Civil War, freedom in antebellum Delaware and Maryland was followed by an attempt by those in power to extract involuntary or coerced labor from those formerly enslaved.

Once sold into this new form of servitude for a year, it was very difficult to break out. Only by finding new employment in midwinter for their basically agrarian skills could Delaware's free blacks liberate themselves from this annual cycle of state-coerced bondage. But finding white planters willing to take on new hands in January, when the demand for farm laborers was low, was not easy. No doubt, white farmers and other white employers recognized the black laborers' desperate plight and took advantage of it. More African-Americans than usual were hired for a season's work in January, but at very low wages wholly dictated by white employers because these laborers no longer had any negotiating clout. They could not reject job offers because rejection would only lead to their being sold into a form of labor that resembled temporary slavery, for up to a year at a time. The terms of employment caused a further decline in the already low standard of living of many free black laborers. It was no wonder that increasing numbers of them left Delaware for the North during the late antebellum period.

The labor law of 1849 and the other antebellum black codes that regulated the lives of free blacks systematically eliminated most of the few rights and "priviledges" that they had inherited from the eighteenth century. As the free black population grew in size, Delaware's legislature increasingly committed itself to denying it the same basic prerogatives that were considered sacrosanct for whites. The General Assembly's growing disdain for the rights of free people of color was best expressed in 1863 when it maintained that a free black should not be allowed to "enjoy any rights of a free man other than to hold property or to obtain redress in law or in equity for any injury to his person or property."[50]

Throughout antebellum America, the severity of state restrictions on the rights of free blacks was directly proportionate to the percentage of free blacks in the total population. In Maryland, for example, where the percentage was significant, although always considerably short of the Delaware figure, a series of laws increasingly limited the rights of free blacks. But, on the whole, Maryland's restrictions seemed less burdensome than those passed by the Delaware General Assembly. Farther south, where only a tiny percentage of the total population was made up of free blacks, there were fewer restrictions on their rights than in either Delaware or Maryland. In South Carolina, for example, where they represented only 2.4 percent of the total population in 1860, antebellum codes for free blacks were relatively mild. In the antebellum North, the states with the lowest percentage in their total population were the ones that placed the least restrictions on the rights of free blacks.[51] In short, because Delaware led the states in the percentage of free blacks, it also led them in the harshness of its legislation.

∼

Growing white racism provided much of the drive behind a movement in Delaware and elsewhere in the nation to ship free blacks back to Africa. The idea of sending them, on a voluntary basis, to a colony in Africa first caught on in New England, where both whites and blacks supported it. But when the idea was proposed in Philadelphia in 1787, it met with opposition from most of the city's free African-American leaders. They were persuaded that the increased abolitionist activities of the time were a good portent for the future of blacks in America.[52] Delaware's slowly evolving black leadership probably took a similar position. After all, the state's strong manumission record and its promising abolition movement offered hope. Moreover, its close proximity to Philadelphia's free black community, which was the largest in any American city, created a natural tendency to follow that city's lead.

In 1816 the colonization movement was boosted by the founding of the American Colonization Society in Washington. In subsequent years, branches were formed in cities from Baltimore to Boston. Representatives of the Society crisscrossed the Upper South, trying to persuade whites to support the cause financially and to encourage free blacks to volunteer to sail for the fledgling state of Liberia. In 1823 the Wilmington Union Colonization Society was formed, as previously mentioned. Affiliated with the American Society, its membership seemed to be made up of Wilmington-area whites who represented several different religious denominations. Evidently, in the 1830s or 1840s the Wilmington organization either changed its name to, or was succeeded by, the Delaware State Colonization Society. Although it did not meet very often, the latter was still in existence in 1853 under the presidency of attorney and educational pioneer Willard Hall.[53]

The General Assembly expressed its support for voluntary colonization in 1825 and again in 1827, when it praised the American Colonization Society and its Wilmington affiliate for "endeavoring to execute one of the grandest schemes of philanthropy that can be presented to the American people." It went on to extol the concept because it offered the "redemption of an ignorant and much injured race of men" by shipping them back to "that genial clime pointed to by the finger of heaven as their natural inheritance." The legislators saw the colonization movement as offering the "amelioration of the condition of free people of color" while "relieving our country from" the racial violence of another Saint-Domingue (Haiti).[54] Despite the verbal support of the legislature and its own considerable posturing, there is no evidence that the Wilmington Union Colonization Society or its successor sent any African-Americans to Liberia.[55] But it did serve as a lightning rod for racial attitudes and feelings as both whites and blacks responded to the idea.

A disparate mix of white Delawareans led the colonization movement. They included abolitionists such as Thomas Garrett who were probably convinced that removing free blacks from the state would defuse one of the major arguments against further manumissions. Other whites such as Hall may have thought that only in Africa would free blacks have a chance to rise above the constraints produced by strong racist feelings in the state and in the nation. But it also is clear that the most common motive behind white support for colonization in Delaware and elsewhere in the Upper South was the desire to get rid of a troublesome minority who "through mischief or open violence would demonstrate that they are our enemy."[56] In short, the Wilmington Union Colonization Society and the Delaware State Colonization Society aspired to be deportation agencies. Their only real accomplishment, however, was to stir up black opposition to colonization.

On January 15, 1817, Philadelphia's African-American leadership called a general meeting of the city's black residents to discuss the issue. The nearly three thousand blacks in attendance registered an overwhelming "no" to the idea of leaving their homes in Philadelphia for the uncertainties of life in the land of their ancestors. They had no interest in going to Africa and were fearful that white authorities might use any black enthusiasm for voluntary colonization as an excuse to coerce all free African-Americans into leaving the country in general and Philadelphia in particular.[57] At a second meeting in August, the city's blacks spoke of their concern that a mass return to Africa would only strengthen slavery by removing from America the free black voices that were demanding an end to unfree labor. The meeting then denounced the American Colonization Society and its newly formed local branch.[58]

The proximity to Philadelphia and its large population of Delaware expatriates caused Delaware's free blacks—especially those in the Wilmington area—to be very much aware of events there in 1817. But for many years after the founding of the American Colonization Society in 1816, Delaware's blacks seemed far more ambivalent than Philadelphia's on the question of returning to Africa. In part, this ambivalence reflected the fact that the Delaware affiliate of the American Colonization Society was not founded in Wilmington, as we know, until 1823. Thus, for six years after an affiliate had been organized in Philadelphia, there was no local colonization society in Delaware to stir the waters. Moreover, the procolonization views of sea captain and shipowner Paul Cuffe, who was frequently in Wilmington, may have done much to neutralize the influence of the anticolonization stand of Philadelphia's black community.

Cuffe was born in 1759 to an Ashanti slave father and a Wampanoag Native American mother. Although a New Englander for most of his life, he and his ships roamed the Atlantic from Canada to West Africa, and he spent considerable time in such Middle Atlantic ports as Philadelphia, Wilmington, and Chestertown, Maryland. Cuffe joined a

Quaker meeting in Wilmington where he "sometimes spoke." He did much more than talk, however, about the need for African-Americans to return to their ancestral land. Largely at his own expense, Cuffe carried a boatload of blacks to English-controlled Sierra Leone because the colonization of nearby Liberia had not yet begun.[59] Although he died in 1817, Cuffe's strong personal commitment to colonization may have exercised a lingering influence on the thinking of many people in Delaware's black community.

Eventually, most of the African-American leadership in Wilmington and elsewhere in the state recognized that the humanitarian ideals professed by the colonization society were often hypocritical, and that the real intent of many, if not most, of its white supporters was to use colonization to racially purify Delaware. In July 1831 at the Mother African Union Church in Wilmington, a meeting of free blacks was held to deal with the issue. The minister, Peter Spencer, shoemaker Abraham Shadd, and former schoolteacher William S. Thomas succeeded in persuading the gathering to reject colonization.[60]

The three black leaders then were elected to draw up a declaration that encouraged African-Americans to stay put and not be seduced by the Dark Continent's siren call. Although the document pointed out that white prejudice and the lack of certain fundamental rights were a heavy burden, it still anticipated a time in which conditions in Delaware and the nation would be more favorable to blacks. As for those whites who were in sympathy with colonization because they perceived it as a means of improving the lot of blacks, they would better serve the cause of justice for African-Americans by turning their energies toward improving educational opportunities.[61]

~

Making a living in a state marked by increasingly restrictive anti-black laws and growing white hostility was a considerable challenge. Although the percentage of free blacks residing in rural areas experienced a modest decline from 1800 to 1860, by the eve of the Civil War about 68 percent of Delaware's employed African-Americans continued to earn their living in the countryside, primarily as farm laborers, farmers, and domestic servants. This pattern was typical of free black employment in most of the Upper South during the antebellum era.[62]

Approximately 85 percent of working free black males in rural Delaware were farmhands in 1860, and they represented at least 37 percent of all such laborers in the state. Some free African-American women also worked as farm laborers during the antebellum period. Near Milton in Sussex in 1861, for example, a white farm boy found himself in the cornfields side by side with free blacks, "the men topping the fodder and the women stripping the blades, and most of the time mumbling a strain of music." But in a pattern reminiscent of the South after the Civil War, rural free black females worked far more often as domestics than as field hands. As the same boy from Milton would later recall, "in most cases" free black men did the field work and free black women were hired to work in the house.[63]

Generally, black farmhands were divided into two types: those who contracted with one farmer for an extended period, and those who labored for a few days or weeks for many different employers during the calendar year. Although the former and their families tended to stay for some time on their employers' farms, the latter moved constantly across the Delaware landscape and may or may not have regarded a specific place as home. (Certainly, the restrictive labor legislation of 1849 forced some peripatetic blacks subsequently to alter their employment patterns.) Somehow, a few free black farm laborers were able to acquire some acres of land and accumulate more than a bare minimum of personal possessions. Two examples in southwestern New Castle County in 1860 were Suel Jefferson and Joseph Henry, who each owned one hundred dollars' worth of real estate and another hundred dollars' worth of personal possessions.[64]

By 1860, 10 percent of rural Delaware's adult free black males were tenant farmers. Their farms ranged from Ezekiel Abrams's 605 acres in Murderkill Hundred, Kent County, down to those of only a few acres on which subsistence crops predominated. In eastern Sussex, which had the highest concentration of such farms of any region in the state, the average black tenant farmer leased about 100 acres but tended to work only about one-half of the leased land. Black tenant farmers could be found everywhere in flat Delaware but, like rural African-Americans in general, were far less common in the rolling hills north of Newark and Wilmington.[65]

Black tenant farmers first appeared in the late eighteenth century, soon after manumissions produced a sizeable free black population. An early example was Stephen Laws of Dover Hundred, Kent County, who in 1797 leased 73 acres and owned eight cattle, five pigs, five horses, seven sheep, and probably raised corn and wheat as his primary cash crops. Although some African-Americans rented farmland with cash, others paid by sharing their harvests with the white owner. Sharecropping, as the latter arrangement was called, seems to have first appeared in black-white relations in Delaware in the mid-1770s, when Warner Mifflin freed his slaves and then provided them with the use of farmland and teams of oxen in return for one-half of their crops. Another example was the 1805 agreement in Sussex by Nearro to give the white landowner one-third of the corn, fodder, and anything else that he raised.[66]

A few black tenant farmers such as Abram Carny of southern New Castle County, who had five hundred dollars' worth of possessions by 1860, were able to accumulate a fair amount of personal property after years of labor on rented land. Still others managed to purchase some farmland while continuing to lease acreage as tenants. On the eve of the Civil War, about 8 percent—some 25 out of the state's 297 African-American tenant farmers—simultaneously owned and rented farmland. But whether cash renters, sharecroppers, or owners of some of the fields that they cultivated, as elsewhere in the Upper South most black tenant farmers reached a level of material well-being that was only a notch above the abysmally low standards experienced by black "laborers."[67] And yet tenantry did represent an important interim step for ambitious African-Americans intent on setting aside capital for the eventual purchase of farmland.

As early as the late eighteenth century, a number of black tenant farmers were increasing their capital by building up their livestock herds, thus opening up the real possibility of farm ownership. In 1797 in Murderkill Hundred, Prince Tilghman owned twenty-three cattle, twenty-five sheep, eight pigs, and five horses, while Baniah Williams had thirteen cattle, twelve pigs, two horses, and two sheep. In nearby Dover Hundred, Peter Patton owned twenty-six cattle, twenty-one sheep, and four horses. By using their livestock or some other source of wealth as a means of economic leverage, as many as 141 Delaware blacks would own their own farms by the eve of the Civil War.[68]

Not all of these successful tenant farmers eventually purchased farms. In 1837, Yates was told that at least some free blacks were not keen to invest their earnings in Delaware land. Two examples were Benjamin and John Francisco, who in the early nineteenth century sharecropped in Kent County, where they built up considerable holdings in livestock. Prior to Yates's visit, the Francisco brothers chose to leave Delaware and invest their money and their future in the free state of Ohio. Still others remained but hesitated to purchase any farmland.[69] Clearly, the increasingly antiblack atmosphere pervading the state discouraged many of them from making long-term capital investments.

The number of Delaware blacks who owned most or all of the farmland that they worked increased as one traveled from north to south during the antebellum era. Moreover, both the number and the size of farms owned by African-Americans increased as the Civil War approached. By 1860, in a remarkable example of succeeding against the odds, almost 5 percent of free adult black males in rural Delaware owned their own farms.[70] On the eve of the Civil War, the average size of the 141 black-owned farms was 67 acres, with the largest in Sussex and the smallest in New Castle County. The great disparity in the value of agricultural land, however, caused black-owned New Castle farms to be more valuable than the considerably larger units in Sussex. In 1860, for example, Sussex farmland was only one-sixth of the value of comparable farmland in the northernmost county. Thus, the low cost of land in Sussex made it far easier for free blacks to acquire farms there than in Kent and, particularly, New Castle County. The only area of Sussex where black farm ownership was rare was in the Nanticoke River Basin, which included almost all of the western part of the county. Despite low land prices, the Nanticoke Basin had only fourteen black-owned farms in 1860, reflecting the fact that the Nanticoke watershed was the last stronghold of slavery in Delaware.[71]

The level of material existence of African-American farm owners varied greatly, from the many who scratched out a living from several barren acres to a very few who were wealthy enough to own substantial acreage and to surround themselves with some of the trappings of the white gentry. No rural African-American matched the refined tastes or the wealth of Levin Thompson, who lived near Laurel. In fact, only a few whites in southwestern Sussex owned more land or exhibited more visible symbols of economic success.

The date and location of Thompson's birth are not recorded, but we know that his parents were Maryland free blacks who probably lived on the Eastern Shore, not far from Sussex County, and that he never experienced slavery firsthand. It is not clear when and why he moved to Delaware, but he purchased 200 acres of farmland east of Laurel in 1794 and, expressing considerable confidence in his own future, called it "Thompson's Beginning." In subsequent years he bought additional parcels as well as a gristmill and sawmill, which were both located four miles southeast of Laurel at the point where Trussum Pond empties into Bald Cypress Branch (James Branch). By 1816, Thompson owned 428 acres to the east and southeast of Laurel in Little Creek Hundred, and 135 acres of cypress timberland farther east in Dagsboro Hundred. By his death in 1816 his holdings ranked him in the top 5 percent of assessed property owners in Little Creek Hundred. His income came from his extensive farmland and stands of timber, the two mills, and his spinning wheels and loom, which produced two hundred yards of linen and sixty yards of woolen cloth each month. Moreover, he lent money at interest to the local white gentry.[72]

In two buildings located near his sawmill and gristmill, Thompson housed thirty-one free blacks. Although he and his wife, Leah, had at least eight children, most of the African-Americans living on his property were probably employees who worked in his mills, on his farms, or at the domestic production of cloth.[73] Obviously, Thompson was a very good mechanic, timberman, miller, farmer, and entrepreneur. Otherwise, he would not have prospered in southwestern Sussex because it was not a promising place, in the early nineteenth century, in which to make one's fortune. Even more remarkable was Thompson's success despite his being both illiterate and black. Two factors help explain his prosperity and, to a lesser degree, that of other landed rural African-Americans despite the formidable obstacles of illiteracy and race.

Success despite illiteracy may be explained by a court case in Sussex in 1837, some twenty-one years after Thompson's death. Free black Noah Burton sued James Rowland, who was white, for payment for a variety of services rendered on thirteen different occasions over a period of two or three years. Burton was illiterate and, because he had not recorded Rowland's obligations in writing, his allegations seemed to lack substantive proof. But Burton produced "a small stick, cut and notched in a variety of ways," which specifically detailed each job done for Rowland as well as the money owed to him by the white man. The court ruled that the method of record keeping was accurate, and Rowland was ordered to pay the sum indicated by Burton's notched stick.[74] Obviously, Thompson and other illiterate black entrepreneurs used a notched stick or some other unwritten means to keep track of

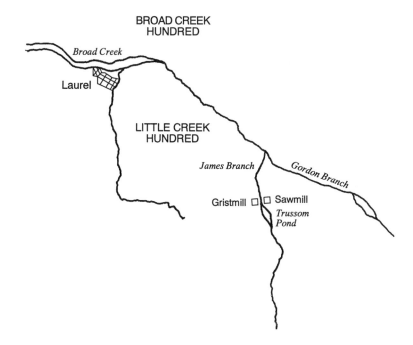

Levin Thompson's mills in southwestern Sussex County.

their own business transactions. In doing so, they employed record-keeping techniques that were also common among illiterate whites.

The race factor was addressed by Thompson's ability to work with whites and to find a powerful white protector. In 1805, when he first became interested in the two mills at Trussum Pond, Thompson was able to purchase only a one-fourth share and thus had to work cooperatively with several white co-owners for nine years. In addition, there is some indication that Isaac Cooper—an important member of the local gentry, a judge in the court system, and the owner of land adjacent to some of Thompson's holdings—took a particular interest in him and acted as his benefactor. Cooper's powerful position discouraged either legal or illegal moves against Thompson by covetous whites.[75]

Judge Cooper must have felt very much at home when he visited Thompson. In the black entrepreneur's yard was a carriage, a vehicle that set off Delaware's gentry from the rest of its rural folk. Inside the large house, Cooper sat in one of his host's Windsor chairs drawn up to an old walnut dining table. He was welcomed with a drink poured into a tumbler from a decanter set near some silver on display. Because free blacks were then allowed to own firearms, Thompson's gun was probably in view.[76]

Thompson's genteel life-style and obvious economic success made him known to whites as well as to blacks throughout Sussex. Although the memoirist Mary Parker Welch was born in 1818, two years after his death, and lived out her childhood at Springfield Cross Roads and in Milton at least sixteen and twenty miles, respectively, northeast of his home near Trussum Pond, such was Thompson's reputation that this daughter of a slaveholder knew many of the specifics of his life and continued to remember them clearly while reminiscing, in the early twentieth century, about growing up in southern Delaware.[77]

Despite success stories such as Thompson's, the standard of living of most black farm owners and their families may not have been appreciably higher than that of most tenant farmers. Indeed, antebellum Delaware's worn-out soil and its inability to compete with the more productive farmlands of the Ohio and Mississippi valleys caused most of its rural people—white as well as black—to undergo a very precarious, hand-to-mouth existence. Bad as times were for rural whites, they were worse for most rural free blacks. Indeed, in 1847 a committee of the state's House of Representatives maintained that "in physical comforts," the condition of slaves was "probably superior to free blacks." Although the report may have reflected the proslavery sentiments of some legislators, it also conveyed some sense of the impoverished conditions faced by most free blacks at the time.[78]

Free blacks did have the option of leaving Delaware to farm the fertile lands of the trans-Appalachian West. Many rural whites from Kent and Sussex had caught the western fever and headed for the Ohio country and the upper Mississippi Valley during the antebellum era. But for most of Delaware's rural free blacks, the lack of capital needed to pay for the trip west and to buy farmland, tools, and livestock made such a venture impossible. Moreover, the likelihood of a cool reception from whites on arrival in the Ohio country and points farther west as well as laws passed in some midwestern states barring black immigration during the late antebellum period caused even those few African-Americans with start-up capital to have serious misgivings about leaving Delaware for the West.[79]

A second option was to move to Wilmington, Philadelphia, or another growing industrial city in the North that needed hundreds of new factory workers. During the antebellum era, increasing numbers of Delaware's rural free blacks did move to Wilmington and, despite the state's restrictive emigration laws, to Philadelphia and to other large northern industrial centers in a desperate search for better economic opportunities. But increasing white racism in the cities and a very high rate of illiteracy among the black emigrants excluded them from almost all desirable jobs.[80] By the end of the period, Delaware's growing racism, its stagnant rural economy, and the limited economic prospects offered by emigration elsewhere left little reason for hope among most rural free African-Americans as they reflected on a bleak future for themselves and their children.

On the eve of the Civil War, 904 free African-Americans of both sexes—perhaps 14 percent of the state's employed blacks—worked in Delaware's towns and villages. One-half, overwhelmingly female, were "servants," "domestics," or "washerwomen." The other half were totally male, and two-thirds of these were categorized as "laborers." In the case of both female "servants" and male "laborers," the jobs were often of short duration, thus causing many in both groups to be constantly on the move from one community to another or back and forth to the countryside.[81] The remaining 247 African-American men, who represented one-third of working free black males in towns and villages in 1860, labored at a variety of jobs. By far the largest group was the seventy-six sailors who lived primarily in the southern communities of Milford, Milton, Lewes, Seaford, and Laurel. The high number of black sailors was typical of the entire antebellum era. In 1826 a Wilmington newspaper noted that "many" of Delaware's African-Americans "are employed navigating the waters of our own and the adjoining states." Because the railroad south from Wilmington did not finally connect with Delmar on the Sussex-Maryland border until 1859, the movement of bulk cargo to and from southern Delaware continued to depend upon water transportation until the eve of the Civil War. Evidently, African-American sailors played a central role in facilitating this vital traffic by river, bay, and ocean. Still other black males toiled as waiters, cooks, and gardeners, and still more as carriage and wagon drivers, and the latter also looked after the horses and mules that pulled those vehicles.[82]

In 1860 only a very small percentage of free blacks in the state's towns and villages were in skilled trades such as carpentering, coopering, brickmaking, butchering, and blacksmithing, and they were all males. In Dover and in the town of New Castle, for example, less than 3 percent of working black males and less than 2 percent of all working free blacks could be categorized as skilled according to their job listings in the U.S. Census of 1860.[83] Only in Milton, in eastern Sussex, did skilled artisans represent a significant percentage of working African-Americans. Although twenty-four males were employed as either laborers or sailors in 1860, there were also one mason, one blacksmith, two carpenters, two shipcarpenters, and one cooper. Approximately 22 percent of the town's working black males and between 16 and 17 percent of all employed (including self-employed) free blacks were listed as skilled artisans.

By far the wealthiest was Elisha Prettyman, a sixty-two-year-old carpenter who supported a wife and four children. On the eve of the Civil War, he owned two thousand dollars' worth of real estate and five hundred dollars' worth of personal property, which ranked his household above 83 percent of all households in Milton. Although Prettyman's holdings were comparable in value to those of white artisans, some of the town's most successful merchants were, according to this measure, seven to forty times wealthier.[84] Prettyman had done as well as a black man could in antebellum Milton. To do any better required moving from artisan to merchant, attorney, or physician, but these occupations were simply off limits in a place where the state-aided schools refused to educate blacks and at a time when growing racial intolerance made whites unwilling either to help finance or patronize black merchants or professionals.

Wilmington, Delaware's only city, was home to just 11 percent of the state's free blacks in 1860, but its 1,126 employed and self-employed free blacks represented 18 percent of the state's working free African-Americans.[85] Following a similar gender pattern of employment found in many American cities, 53 percent of Wilmington's working blacks were female and only 47 percent were male by the eve of the Civil War. Throughout the antebellum period, more African-American females than males found work in the city, but employed and self-employed black males were more numerous in the rest of Delaware.[86]

Although the overwhelming majority of Wilmington's income-earning free blacks were "unskilled" domestic servants or laborers throughout the years from 1800 to 1860, the percentage of black workers employed in skilled and semiskilled positions was higher than in the rest of Delaware and considerably higher among Wilmington's males than females.[87] In 1814 about 30 percent of the city's employed or self-employed black males were holding down semiskilled or skilled positions; in 1860 the figure was about 26 percent.[88]

In 1860 fully 20 percent of Wilmington's working black males were in semiskilled occupations, with thirty-two waiters, twelve brick-yard workers, nine porters, and eight wagon drivers heading the list. Conspicuously missing in this industrial boomtown were black mill and factory workers. Apparently, much of the pressure to deny African-Americans employment opportunities in the flour mills along the Brandywine as well as in the factories along the Christina came from white mill and factory workers. At the Price flour mill in 1862, for example, a strike by white employees lasted until a free black worker was dismissed.[89]

Only about 6 percent of the city's working black males were "skilled" artisans in 1860, down from 14 percent in 1814. On the eve of the Civil War, twelve brickmakers, six blacksmiths, and five cordwainers (shoemakers) led the list.[90] The percentage decline in black artisans from 1814 to 1860 supports the contention that, during the late antebellum period, whites in the Upper South and in the North systematically excluded free blacks from many of the skilled trades. But this pattern does not fit the small town of Milton, where the percentage of working black males who were "skilled" artisans increased from 10 percent in 1850 to 22 percent in 1860.[91]

Despite the migration to other states and Canada by a number of ambitious African-Americans in the late antebellum years, enough remained behind in Wilmington to form a very small but determined black middle class—there were no free blacks wealthy enough to comprise an upper class—that included artisans, barbers, and other small-scale entrepreneurs together with teachers and clergymen. In all, this diverse black middle class amounted to between 6 and 7 percent of the city's working male African-Americans. Among its richer members in 1860 were Robert Graves, a forty-year-old tailor with three thousand dollars' worth of real estate and one thousand dollars in personal property, and Michael Sterling, a seventy-two-year-old blacksmith with three thousand dollars' worth of real estate and two hundred dollars in personal property.[92] The key to the rise of this small black middle class was the concentration in Wilmington of a significant free black population with purchasing power.

By contrast with black males, only a few of Wilmington's black working women, such as nurses, seamstresses, and cooks, held positions that could be labeled either semiskilled or skilled during the antebellum years. In 1860 the city's skilled and semiskilled free black women accounted for less than 2 percent of its black female work force. The unskilled, who made up the remaining 98 percent, included almost 600 domestic servants, 138 washerwomen, and 21 who both washed and ironed.[93]

~

Although poverty or semipoverty was the usual experience for most of the state's free blacks, a surprising number did own real estate by the late antebellum period. In 1850, according to Loren Schweninger, some 446 black Delawareans were property owners—these included farmers, businessmen, and home owners—with New Castle County leading the way with 194, followed by Kent with 132 and Sussex with 120. In general, the distribution of black property holders was proportional to the number of adult free African-Americans in each county. From 1850 to 1860 the number of these property holders more than doubled to 1,059. In 1850, 10 percent of Delaware's free black males, age twenty-one years or more, were property holders; by 1860 at least 20 percent owned property. The latter figure was slightly higher than in either Virginia or Maryland in 1860.[94]

Among African-American property holders in the antebellum South, mulattoes were a special case. (In this study, "blacks" and "mulattoes" are combined under the label black or African-American because no distinctions between blacks and mulattoes were made under Delaware law.) In the Deep South, they generally received better treatment than other slaves, were more likely to be manumitted, and, once free, tended to own considerably more property than darker people of color. In much of the Upper South, however, preferential treatment of mulattoes over darker African-Americans was less evident.[95] In Delaware, mulattoes seem to have fared better in some ways but not in others. They were less likely to be enslaved during the antebellum years. As late as 1850 mulattoes made up between 9 and 10 percent of the state's total African-American population but accounted for less than 4 percent of its enslaved population. In 1850 mulattoes made up 10 percent of the state's black property holders, which roughly reflected their share of the nonwhite population. Although they were no more likely to own land than were other free people of color, in the mean value of their individual real estate holdings they did lead their darker contemporaries by almost 50 percent in 1850.[96]

African-Americans who were born in another state and then moved to Delaware had a significantly greater likelihood of land ownership than those born here. In 1850 only 6 percent of Delaware's African-Americans were born out of state, but they represented 17 percent of the black property owners. The overwhelming majority of born-out-of-state black property holders were from Maryland. About 67 percent of Delaware's black property holders were illiterate, and 90 percent were male.[97] By acquiring real estate, these property holders of 1850 were continuing a pattern pioneered by a few blacks during the colonial era and by a larger number in the late eighteenth century. One example of a late antebellum property holder was Jake ("Jigger") Bell, who acquired land three miles west of Lewes in eastern Sussex. About 1840 he began selling off building lots to other African-Americans and then donated a plot of land for the construction of a church. The resulting all-black community was named Belltown and still stands today as a reminder of the state's first African-American real estate developer.[98]

As already noted, in assessing the material well-being of Delaware's free black community during the antebellum era, one is initially struck by the widespread poverty. In 1837, *The African Repository* was probably accurate when it observed that the living conditions of free blacks were "nearly as bad as that of the slaves."[99] But, as this brief examination of property-owning African-Americans indicates, poverty was not the only free black experience. To the Delaware Anti-Slavery Society, the economic success of some free blacks was not surprising because when they "are treated well, they do well." The evidence indicates, however, that the state's free blacks were rarely, if ever, "treated well" and that those who did acquire a house, some acres of farmland, and some modest personal possessions did so despite living in a place and time where their skin color guaranteed that they would enjoy, in Yates's words, only "a mongrel liberty, a mere mock freedom."[100]

Notes

*Hancock, ed., "William Yates Letter of 1837," 208.

1. Statistics used in computations are found in John A. Munroe, *History of Delaware* (Newark, DE, 1979, 1984), Appendixes E, F, I; Williams, *The First State*, 73. For a sense of white population movement to Wilmington from Kent and Sussex see *Blue Hen's Chicken*, 9/24/1847.

2. *Journal of the Senate of the State of Delaware* (Wilmington, DE, 1847), 58; *Delaware Republican*, 11/11/1860. For a sense of how much more prosperous New Castle County was than Kent and Sussex see Hancock, *Delaware during the Civil War*, 3–8.

3. Berlin, *Slaves without Masters*, 160 n.39; Dean, "The Free Negro in Delaware," 13–14. Statistics are based on figures from U.S. Census Bureau,

Manuscripts, 1840, Delaware, Wilmington; and Beers, *Atlas of the State of Delaware*, "Tables."

4. Dean, "The Free Negro in Delaware," 13–14; U.S. Census Bureau, Manuscripts, 1800, 1860, Delaware, Brandywine, Christiana, and Mill Creek hundreds. As soon as census takers reached the flat areas of southern Christiana and Mill Creek hundreds, the number of free blacks increased appreciably and their percentage of the population approached the statewide figure for free blacks.

5. Samuel Bancroft, Jr., to the Hon. John B. Gordon, Wilmington, February 14, 1897, Bird-Bancroft Collection, vol. V, Box 15, HSD. A third site under consideration by du Pont was at Passaic Falls, New Jersey. But this site, because of potential gunpowder explosions, was too close to heavily populated areas. Du Pont's subsequent willingness to be involved in the efforts to send free blacks to Africa also could be an indication of a deep prejudice against blacks. Scharf, *History of Delaware*, 766. Efforts by other white Delawareans to purify the state of free blacks through a colonization movement are taken up later in this chapter.

6. Beers, *Atlas of the State of Delaware*, "Tables"; U.S. Census Bureau, Manuscripts, 1810, 1860, Delaware.

7. Beers, *Atlas of the State of Delaware*, "Tables."

8. Ibid.; Richard R. Wright, Jr., *The Negro in Pennsylvania: A Study in Economic History* (Philadelphia, n.d.), 210. From 1820 to 1840 the state's free black population increased by 30 percent, but from 1840 to 1860 an obvious surge in free blacks leaving Delaware limited the in-state increase to only 15 percent.

9. Berlin, *Slaves without Masters*, 188–89.

10. These percentages are based on raw data taken from *Historical Statistics of the United States*, Part 1 (Washington, DC, 1975), 24–36; and *Negro Population, 1790–1915*, 57.

11. Proposed Bill, 1786, reel no. 7, Legislative Papers, DSA; *Journal of the House of Representatives* (1807), 13; *Laws of the State of Delaware*, 4:108, 221, 400–403, 8:245, 10:591; Beers, *Atlas of the State of Delaware*, "Tables." *Negro Population, 1790–1915*, 63, provides raw figures for the computation of Delaware free blacks born out of state.

12. U.S Census Bureau, Manuscripts, 1840, Delaware, Wilmington.

13. U.S. Census Bureau, Manuscripts, 1840, Delaware, New Castle County, individual hundreds; Kent County, individual hundreds; Sussex, individual hundreds.

14. George M. Frederickson as quoted by David Brion Davis in "The Ends of Slavery," *New York Review of Books* (March 30, 1988), 28; Turner, *The Negro in Pennsylvania*, vii; Ira V. Brown, *The Negro in Pennsylvania History* (University Park, PA, 1970), 22. For another view that white racism replaced mere prejudice in the South when whites were forced to confront the implications of emancipation see Winthrop Jordan, *White over Black: American Attitudes toward the Negro* (Chapel Hill, NC, 1968). Jordan's view is discussed in James Campbell and James Oakes, "The Invention of Race: Rereading White over Black," *Reviews in American History* 21 (March 1993): 172–83.

15. Hancock, ed., "William Yates Letter of 1837," 208.

16. *Delaware Gazette*, 12/19/1826; *Laws of the State of Delaware*, 7:158, 10:591.

17. Hancock, ed., "William Yates Letter of 1837," 208, 209.

18. Munroe, *History of Delaware*, 49, 83; *Laws of the State of Delaware*, 12:333; Berlin, *Slaves without Masters*, 8, 91; Brown, *The Negro in Pennsylvania History*, 22.

19. Justice, *Life and Ancestry of Warner Mifflin*, 97; *Delaware Gazette*, 12/29/1826; Hancock, "Not Quite Men," 163.

20. *Blue Hen's Chicken*, 12/24/1848. Impressionistic evidence on free black crime can be found in such scattered legal sources as the records of the Courts of Oyer and Terminer, county coroner's inquests, and county Courts of General Sessions, DSA, as well as in Delaware newspapers. Specific figures for Kent County for the years 1835–1840 are found in the Kent County Court of General Sessions, Papers, DSA. Kent County population statistics are from Delaware summaries found in a variety of sources.

21. Indictments, Kent County Court of General Sessions, 1830–1847, Papers, DSA. A few examples of free blacks indicted for stealing food in winter are found in ibid.: Stephen Gales, Daniel Clarkson, James Ellsbury (1832), Daniel Millis, Simon Summers (1838), George Biswick (1841), and Isaac Cannon (1844).

22. *Blue Hen's Chicken*, 10/13/1838.

23. Horle, ed., *Records of the Courts of Sussex County, 1677–1710*, 468, 481, 919.

24. Boorstin, ed., *Delaware Cases*, 1:479; *Laws of the State of Delaware*, 3:80–81.

25. Dick (1768), French Peter (1782), Solomon (1805), Jacob (1826), Ador (1827), Richard Nutter (1832), Henry (1837), Caesar Carey (1847), Sussex County Coroner's Inquest, DSA.

26. Boorstin, ed., *Delaware Cases*, 2:478; Kent County Court of General Sessions, passim, DSA.

27. Ann Bolden (1845), Recognizances, Kent County Court of General Sessions, DSA; Samuel Calaway (1854), Session Dockets, 1757–1951, Sussex County Court of Oyer and Terminer, ibid.; Henry Armstrong (1826), Court Dockets (1826), New Castle County Court of Oyer and Terminer, ibid.; Unice Thorn, Court Dockets, 1751–1848, Kent County Court of Oyer and Terminer, ibid.

28. Mary Burris (1859), Session Dockets, 1751–1939, Kent County Court of Oyer and Terminer, DSA; Robert Hughes (1840), Recognizances, Kent County Court of General Sessions, ibid.; James Miller (1795), Court Dockets, 1751–1848, and Prince Tilghman (1810), Lucinda Murray (1823), Court Papers, 1798–1939, Kent County Court of Oyer and Terminer, ibid.; Jacob Battel (1802), Session Dockets, New Castle County Court of Oyer and Terminer, ibid.

According to Henry Campbell Black, *Black's Law Dictionary* (St. Paul, MN, 1979), 144, "benefit of clergy" exempted medieval clergy from the jurisdiction of the secular courts. In subsequent years it came to mean, in Anglo-Saxon law, that clerks and others who could read might be allowed by the courts to join the clergy in pleading exemption from the death sentence. The plea was made by the defendant only after conviction, and it could be granted or withheld by the secular court that prescribed the death sentence. In Delaware, the legal concept of "benefit of clergy" had become rather bastardized by the early nineteenth century and was requested by both literates and illiterates after being convicted of a crime punishable by death. "Benefit of clergy" was finally abolished by Parliament in England in 1827, and the practice seems to have disappeared in Delaware by the midnineteenth century.

29. John Morris (1792), George Parker (1807), Session Dockets, 1751–1939, Kent County Court of Oyer and Terminer, DSA; Abraham Gunnage (1803), Court Dockets, 1751–1848, and John Smith (1793), Session Dockets, 1751–1939, Kent County Court of Oyer and Terminer, ibid.

30. *Laws of the State of Delaware*, 6:708–13, 716; William Clow (1830), James Williams (1830), Sentences Folder, Kent County Court of General Sessions, DSA.

31. Hancock, ed., "William Yates Letter of 1837," 211–12; *Laws of the State of Delaware*, 9:257.

32. Berlin, *Slaves without Masters*, 225–26.

33. Ibid., 189; *Laws of the State of Delaware*, 7:125, 4:522–23; Herman, *The Stolen House*, 80.

34. *Laws of the State of Delaware*, 8:180–81, 333, 12:332; Harold B. Hancock, "Not Quite Men: The Free Negroes in Delaware in the 1830s," *Civil War History* 17 (December 1968): 325.

35. Bushman et al., eds., *Proceedings of the House of Assembly*, 879–80; Berlin, *Slaves without Masters*, 105; *Laws of the State of Delaware*, 2:887.

36. Justice, *Life and Ancestry of Warner Mifflin*, 104.

37. Hancock, "Not Quite Men," 325; *Delaware Gazette*, 2/18/1851, 3/11/51. For attempts to limit the right of free blacks to hold property elsewhere in the South see Loren Schweninger, *Black Property Owners in the South, 1790–1915* (Urbana, IL, 1990), 63–65.

38. *Laws of the State of Delaware*, 3:9–10.

39. Ibid., 8:181–82, 10:592.

40. *Delaware Gazette*, 12/29/1826; Williams, *The Garden of American Methodism*, 83, 111; Scharf, *History of Delaware*, 2:1036–37; Hancock, ed., "William Yates Letter of 1837," 210; *Laws of the State of Delaware*, 6:86; Williams, *The First State*, 129. Delaware's practice in the early twentieth century of integrating its public transportation system but segregating its restaurants, theaters, and hotels probably had its roots in the antebellum era. For the twentieth-century practice of segregation see Munroe, *History of Delaware*, 225–26.

41. Hancock, ed., "William Yates Letter of 1837," 214–15.

42. Petitions, 1841, Legislative Papers, Negroes and Slavery, DSA.

43. See census statistics in Beers, *Atlas of the State of Delaware*, "Tables," for evidence of increasing black emigration from Delaware from 1840 to 1860.

44. *Laws of the State of Delaware*, 4:108–10, 400–403, 9:319–20, 12:330.

45. Kolchin, *American Slavery*, 220.

46. Petitions, 1841, Legislative Papers, Negroes and Slavery, DSA.

47. Berlin, *Slaves without Masters*, 62. In nearby Maryland a similar pattern of employer dissatisfaction with free blacks appeared both before and after the Civil War. Fields, *Slavery and Freedom on the Middle Ground*, 158–66.

48. *Laws of the State of Delaware*, 10:414–16.

49. Ibid.; Berlin, *Slaves without Masters*, 226; Fields, *Slavery and Freedom on the Middle Ground*, 79. In Delaware and in other southern states some black codes may not have been strictly enforced. While it is impossible to be sure how vigorously the law of 1849 was enforced, the monetary reward offered to whites probably encouraged a greater degree of active prosecution than for some other state black codes throughout the South. For labor contracts with free blacks in other southern states see Berlin, *Slaves without Masters*, 223–24. For a discussion of involuntary labor after emancipation see Wilhemina Kloosterboer, *Involuntary Labour since the Abolition of Slavery: A Survey of Compulsory Labour throughout the World* (Leiden, Netherlands, 1960).

50. *Laws of the State of Delaware*, 12:333.

51. Fields, *Slavery and Freedom on the Middle Ground*, 35; Berlin, *Slaves without Masters*, 194; Litwack, *North of Slavery*, 69.

52. Ibid., 172; Nash, *Forging Freedom*, 101–4.

53. Essah, "Slavery and Freedom in the First State," 162–63; *The African Repository* (Washington, DC, 1846), 43; *The African Repository* (Washington, DC, 1853), 314.

54. *Laws of the State of Delaware*, 6:571, 7:157–58.

55. At least one Delawarean did make his way to Liberia, although there is no indication that he was aided by any Delaware-based colonization society. In 1852, William S. Anderson of Wilmington set sail for Africa. After a few years in Liberia, he was elected to the lower branch of the legislature for one term. In subsequent years he became a successful merchant and an owner of considerable property. In 1872, at forty-three, Anderson was murdered on the streets of Monrovia, the capital. Scharf, *History of Delaware*, 2:661.

56. Hancock, "Not Quite Men," 321; *Delaware Gazette*, 2/21/1826, 12/29/26. For a discussion of white motives behind the colonization movement in the Middle Atlantic states see Nash, *Forging Freedom*, 233–35. Other notable white Delawareans who supported colonization included E. I. du Pont. See Scharf, *History of Delaware*, 2:766, 1:560.

57. Nash, *Forging Freedom*, 237–39.

58. Ibid., 239–41.

59. Lamont D. Thomas, *Rise to Be a People: A Biography of Paul Cuffe* (Urbana, IL, 1986), 101–4; *Wilmington Morning News*, 11/18/1961; *Sunday News Journal*, 3/1/1992.

60. Hancock, "Not Quite Men," 330; *The Liberator*, 9/24/1831; William Lloyd Garrison, *Thoughts on African Colonization* (Boston, 1832), 36–40; Lewis V. Baldwin, *The Mark of a Man: Peter Spencer and the African Union Methodist Tradition* (Lanham, MD, 1987), 22–23.

61. Hancock, "Not Quite Men," 330; Garrison, *Thoughts on African Colonization*, 36–40.

62. The percentages for Delaware are estimates based on figures in Essah, "Slavery and Freedom in the First State," 187; and Dean, "The Free Negro in Delaware," 48–50. For the rest of the Upper South see Berlin, *Slaves without Masters*, 218.

63. Dean, "The Free Negro in Delaware," 48–50; Hancock and McCabe, *Milton's First Century*, 299, 301.

64. Dean, "The Free Negro in Delaware," 48–50; U.S. Census Bureau Manuscripts, 1860, Delaware, Appoquinimink Hundred, 27, 74.

65. Dean, "The Free Negro in Delaware," 50, 58, 56, 54, 52. While Dean calculates that those who lived on tenant farms and those who lived on their own farms together made up 20 percent of the rural free black population of Delaware in 1860, my calculations place the figure at 15 percent.

66. Laura Gehringer, "Analytical Summaries of 1797 Tax Assessments of Kent County Hundreds"; Justice, *Life and Ancestry of Warner Mifflin*, 85; Herman, *The Stolen House*, 125.

67. U.S. Census Bureau, Manuscripts, 1860, Delaware, Appoquinimink Hundred, 26; Dean, "The Free Negro in Delaware," 51; Berlin, *Slaves without Masters*, 224.

68. Gehringer, "Analytical Summaries of 1797 Tax Assessments of Kent County Hundreds," passim; Dean, "The Free Negro in Delaware," 46.

69. Hancock, ed., "William Yates Letter of 1837," 215; Hancock, "Not Quite Men," 325; Kent County Assessment Lists, Little Creek Hundred (1804) and Duck Creek Hundred (1804), DSA.

70. Dean, "The Free Negro in Delaware," 57–58; Essah, "Slavery and Freedom in the First State," 190–91. The 5 percent figure is mine and is based on a

rough estimate of the number of rural free black males over twenty-one years of age (approximately 3,000) and the number of black-owned farms (141) in Delaware in 1860.

71. Dean, "The Free Negro in Delaware," 58–64. For evidence of the concentration of slavery in the Nanticoke Basin on the eve of the Civil War see U.S. Census Bureau, Manuscripts, 1860, Delaware, Slave Schedules.

72. Boorstin, ed., *Delaware Cases*, 1:655–56; Levin Thompson, Sussex County Will Book No. 7, 75–77, SCCH; Sussex Deed Book R, No. 17, 269, DSA; Sussex Deed Book, Patents, T No. 19, 509, ibid.; Sussex Deed Book Z, No. 24, 273, ibid.; Sussex Deed Book A B, No. 25, 103, ibid.; Sussex Deed Book A D, No. 27, 318, ibid.; Sussex Deed Book A E, No. 28, 251, 425, ibid.; Sussex Deed Book A H, No. 31, 210, 366, ibid.; Sussex Deed Book A K, No. 33, 54, 180, ibid.; Sussex Deed Book A L, No. 34, 46, ibid.; Sussex Deed Book A M, No. 35, 216, ibid.; Dagsboro Hundred (1816), Little Creek Hundred (1816), Sussex County Assessment Books, ibid.; U.S. Census Bureau, Manuscripts, 1810, Delaware, 308; Levin Thompson, February 1816, Tha-Thom Folder, Sussex County Estate Inventories, DSA.

73. U.S. Census Bureau Manuscripts, Delaware, 1810, 307, 308; Sussex Deed Book A M, No. 35, 216, DSA; Levin Thompson (1804), Sussex County Will Book No. 7, 75–77, SCCH.

74. Samuel Harrington, ed., *Reports of Cases Argued and Adjuded in the Superior Court and the Court of Errors and Appeals*, 4 vols. (Dover, DE, 1841), 2:288–89. I am grateful to Bernard Herman of the University of Delaware for first calling my attention to the "notched stick" case.

75. Sussex Deed Book A B, No. 25, 103, DSA; Sussex Deed Book A D, No. 27, 318, ibid.; Sussex Deed Book A K, No. 31, 366, ibid.; Sussex Deed Book A K, No. 33, 180, ibid.; Boorstin, ed., *Delaware Cases*, 1:9, 652–55. For the important role played by white sponsors or protectors of free blacks elsewhere in the antebellum South see Schweninger, *Black Property Owners in the South*, 87–90.

76. Levin Thompson, Tha-Thom Folder, Sussex County Estate Inventories, DSA.

77. Welch, ed., *Memoirs of Mary Parker Welch*, 145.

78. *Journal of the House of Representatives of the State of Delaware* (Wilmington, 1847), 196.

79. For westward migration from Delaware see Williams, *The Garden of American Methodism*, 72–73. For a sense of how unwelcome free blacks were in the Midwest see Litwack, *North of Slavery*, 70–73 and passim.

80. Litwack, *North of Slavery*, 153–60, and passim for the lack of economic opportunities for free blacks in northern cities. For Wilmington see list of occupations of each employed free black in U.S. Census Bureau, Manuscripts, 1860, Delaware, Wilmington. Not one black is listed as a factory worker.

81. Dean, "The Free Negro in Delaware," 67–68; U.S. Census Bureau, Manuscripts, 1860, Delaware.

82. U.S. Census Bureau, Manuscripts, 1860, Delaware; *Delaware Gazette*, 1/20/1826.

83. Dean, "The Free Negro in Delaware," 67–68; U.S. Census Bureau, Manuscripts, 1860, Delaware, Town of New Castle, Dover.

84. U.S. Census Bureau, Manuscripts, 1860, Delaware, Milton.

85. Ibid., Wilmington. The difference between the percentage of free blacks living in Wilmington and the percentage of employed free blacks living in Wilmington reflects both the greater access to jobs for black females in the city

than in rural Delaware—hence a higher percentage of black females who were employed—and the fact that a higher percentage of Wilmington's free black population was of working age than in the rest of the state.

86. U.S. Census Bureau, Manuscripts, 1860, Delaware, Wilmington.

87. Ibid. In general, I have found the U.S. Census of Wilmington for 1860 to be a more accurate guide to types of jobs held by free blacks than the various Wilmington city directories.

88. *Wilmington Directory, 1814* (Silver Springs, MD, n.d.), 17–19; U.S. Census Bureau, Manuscripts, 1860, Delaware, Wilmington. Placing jobs in the categories of "unskilled," "semiskilled," and "skilled" is a rather arbitrary exercise at best, and the figures should all be looked at as approximate rather than precise. The employment figures are a summary of a compilation of 1,126 individual jobs held by Wilmington blacks according to the U.S. Census Bureau, Manuscripts, 1860, Delaware, Wilmington. In general, I have categorized such working people as domestic servants, laborers, porters, and washerwomen as "unskilled." I have labelled such working types as coachmen, wagon drivers, whitewashers, sailors, sawmill workers, waiters, and brickyard workers as "semiskilled." I have applied the label "skilled" to tailors, blacksmiths, brick makers, cordwainers, soap makers, and the like.

89. U.S. Census Bureau, Manuscripts, 1860, Delaware, Wilmington; Harold B. Hancock, "The Industrial Workers along the Brandywine, 1840–1870" (unpublished paper, Eleutherian Mills Historical Library [now Hagley Library], Wilmington, DE), 32–33.

90. U.S. Census Bureau, Manuscripts, 1860, Delaware, Wilmington.

91. Ibid.; *Wilmington Directory, 1814*, 17–19; U.S. Census Bureau, Manuscripts, 1850, 1860, Delaware, Milton; Hancock and McCabe, *Milton's First Century*, 115–23.

92. U.S. Census Bureau, Manuscripts, 1860, Delaware, Wilmington.

93. Ibid.

94. Professor Loren Schweninger of the University of North Carolina at Greensboro has generously shared with me his unpublished summaries of Delaware free black landholders based on figures from U.S. Census Bureau, Manuscripts, 1850, Delaware. Hereafter, the source of these figures will be referred to as Schweninger, "Notes." For the number of black property holders in 1860 see Schweninger, *Black Property Owners in the South*, 159. The 10 percent figure for black males who were real estate owners in 1850 and the minimum figure of 20 percent for 1860 are mine, based on the estimate that of the state's 18,073 free blacks in 1850, less than 4,500 were males age twenty-one or over, and on a similar estimating procedure for 1860. For a summary of black property holders in the antebellum South see Schweninger, *Black Property Owners in the South*.

95. Berlin, *Slaves without Masters*, 178–80; Kolchin, *American Slavery*, 82–84; Schweninger, *Black Property Owners in the South*, 287.

96. U.S. Census Bureau, Manuscripts, 1850, Delaware.

97. Schweninger, "Notes"; "Communication from the Delaware Society to the Convention of 1796," Pennsylvania Abolition Society Papers, Pennsylvania Abolition Society Manuscript Collection, HSP.

John Johnson, one of the first significant black property holders in Delaware, owned an island in Rehoboth Bay in Sussex County in the late seventeenth century. He was even called a "planter" by contemporary court records. Welch, ed., *Memoirs of Mary Parker Welch*, 144; Horle, ed., *Records of the Courts of Sussex County, 1677–1710*, 857.

Gabriel Jackson of Wilmington was a late eighteenth-century property owner of some note. He and his son, Gabriel, Jr., were shipcarpenters of considerable reputation. James Gibbons to the Pennsylvania Society for the Abolition of Slavery, October 16, 1787, Pennsylvania Abolition Society Manuscript Collection, HSP, as reprinted in Catts, "Slaves, Free Blacks, and French Negroes," 44–45; Montgomery, *Reminiscences of Wilmington*, 251–52.

98. Jeanette Eckman et al., *Delaware: A Guide to the First State* (New York, 1938), 494; *Sussex Post*, 8/10/1988.

99. *The African Repository* 13 (1837): 315.

100. *Blue Hen's Chicken*, 3/18/1850; Hancock, ed., "William Yates Letter of 1837," 208.

VII

A More Independent People

And it is hereby further provided that none but persons of colour
shall be chosen as trustees of the . . . church.
—Deed of Ezion Methodist Episcopal Church, 1805*

In the increasingly hostile world of antebellum Delaware, free
African-Americans were constantly buffeted by powerful forces beyond their control. Discriminatory state laws and impoverishing economic conditions threatened to drive even the most optimistic blacks
to the brink of hopelessness and despair. Denied the right to a public
education, to equal rights before the law, to bargain freely with employers, to hold desirable jobs, and to vote, free blacks turned to their
families for physical and psychological nurturing during this time of
adversity.

With freedom, many of the conditions that were detrimental to the
formation and vitality of African-American families in Delaware disappeared. Once free of the shackles of bondage, most black men and
women set up households together and raised children who knew their
fathers as well as their mothers. By 1850 about 80 percent of the state's
black property holders lived in stable, two-parent families.[1] But these
were the black elite and, far more than those without property, might
be expected to belong to such stable households.

The strong drive to form two-parent families was found, however,
among free blacks of all income levels. In 1830 some 92 percent of all
free black households (those living apart from white households) in
Appoquinimink and St. Georges hundreds in southern New Castle
County had present a male and a female adult at ages appropriate to be
man and wife.[2] For the entire state, the percentage of independent free
African-American households that contained both two parents and their
children was probably in the 75 to 85 percent range found in Patience

Essah's study of the three representative hundreds of New Castle (New Castle County), Duck Creek (Kent County), and Cedar Creek (Sussex County) for the years 1820, 1840, and 1860. But in Wilmington, with its surplus of free black females, two-parent families with children were less typical, ranging from 58 to 68 percent of independent African-American households for the same period. The enhanced position of the male in these newly formed households was reflected in the common practice of naming sons after fathers, a practice that the evidence suggests may have been less common under slavery.[3]

Surnames were important to family building. The precise origins of most black surnames in Delaware and elsewhere in the South remain a mystery, but a few can be traced to specific slave owners. On occasion, Delaware manumission documents such as masters' wills required that certain blacks adopt their owner's surnames as a condition for freedom.[4] Once in a while a freed African-American would voluntarily choose the last name of a particularly kind master, but that was rare. In general, even those blacks who had very good feelings about their former masters declined to take their surnames. Typical was Richard Allen, who described Stokeley Sturgis as "a very kind and humane man," but after manumission Richard chose Allen rather than Sturgis for his last name.[5]

By 1800 some 58 percent of Delaware's African-Americans were free; and, with freedom, almost all had adopted surnames. There were 555 different last names used by free black households in 1800, but only 250 were used by five or more households. Heading the list of the most popular ones was Miller, which was the choice of seventeen black families, followed by Caldwell, Jackson, and Jones, each the choice of eleven families. Other surnames taken by at least eight black families were Draper, Gibbes, Laws, Lewis, Lowber, Sammons, and White. In general, the most popular black surnames in 1800 also tended to be common among the state's white families. These choices reflected the enthusiasm of newly freed bondspersons for familiar white names, as long as they did not belong to their former owners. Refusing to adopt the names of their former masters but taking other white surnames was a pattern repeated by newly manumitted blacks throughout the antebellum South.[6]

Adding a surname helped these manumitted African-Americans to close a chapter of their personal history in which most masters had denied the existence of the slave family. By taking last names, newly freed blacks affirmed that the family existed among them and would be central to their future in Delaware. Moreover, by adding surnames, they were giving notice that they now were ready to participate in society as fully human beings. Although whites might be unwilling to accept African-Americans as peers, their surnames were a testimony to their emerging dream of equality.

A major and immediate concern to newly established free black families was housing. Although the state's vacated slave cabins could serve as dwellings for some African-American farm laborers and their dependents, there had never been a large number of such cabins in Delaware; moreover, most of those remaining at the beginning of the nineteenth century were in poor repair. To meet the urgent need for additional housing, a new type of structure called the "colored house" began to appear in the rural landscape. Cheaply built and owned by white farmers, these houses were usually located at some distance from the homes and outbuildings of whites. The "colored house" continued to be a familiar sight in Delaware in the twentieth century.[7] Although most rural African-Americans set up independent households soon after manumission, a significant minority continued to live in white homes during the antebellum years: almost 28 percent in 1800, and a slightly diminishing percentage thereafter.[8]

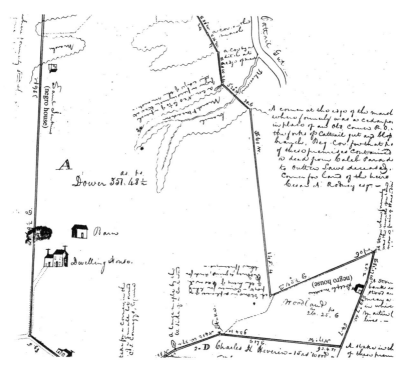

Plat showing two negro ("colored") houses in eastern Kent County, 1830s. *Courtesy of Kent County Court Records Depository, Dover.*

In towns, villages, and in the city of Wilmington, a majority of free blacks lived in independent households in scattered clusters of cheaply constructed homes, often on the outskirts and in the least desirable locations. The large concentration of African-Americans found today in the heart of Wilmington did not exist during the ante-bellum period, when the scattered black population varied from 10 to 20 percent of the city's total. But just as in the countryside, some single blacks in villages, towns, and the city lived in white households where they were employed as domestics and laborers.[9]

Economic realities often made it difficult for free families of color to hold together. In fact, a few families were so impoverished that they were forced to sell some of their children into temporary servi-tude. The practice had its roots in the late eighteenth century, and the family of Nathan and Abigail Phillips of Jones Neck, Kent County, is one example. The couple and at least five of their children had once been John Dickinson's slaves. Evidently, freedom brought poverty and caused Nathan to sell thirteen-year-old Curtis and twelve-year-old Reuben to Dickinson for eight and nine years, respectively, in 1793. In return, Nathan received five shillings and "other valuable consider-ations" and the two boys were to be trained as servants.[10]

Like Curtis and Reuben, a number of free African-American chil-dren became apprentices during the antebellum era. Ostensibly, ap-prenticeships offered young men and women of both races the opportunity to develop a skill or learn a trade while also being taught by their masters to read and write. In Delaware, as in many other slave states, there are indications that apprenticeships for free black chil-dren were not the same as those for whites. As noted elsewhere, the former were more commonly apprenticed than the latter to the lowly occupations deemed proper for blacks, such as farming and domestic work. Moreover, most masters did not teach black children how to read and write. Some even stated at the outset that their black appren-tices would not be made literate. Ten-year-old Elizabeth Rodney was apprenticed for eight years in 1820 to learn domestic work, and it was agreed that she was to receive "no schooling."[11]

While many young African-Americans left their homes to serve apprenticeships with family approval, there were others who were forced to do so by state law. In 1811 and again in 1827 the General Assembly empowered the local justices of the peace and the guard-ians of the poor, upon the testimony of a constable that a certain black family was too poor to support its children, to "bind" them "out" as apprentices until the males reached the age of twenty-one and the fe-males eighteen. These coercive measures remained in force in Dela-ware until 1915. The involuntary binding out of free black children supplied cheap labor for the state's farms, homes, and businesses, but at the cost of breaking up black families.[12]

~

In its struggle to survive, the African-American family found a strong ally in the black church. Methodism, which was the faith of almost all of Delaware's "churched" people of color in the antebellum period, promoted family unity as a keystone to Christian morality. During the early nineteenth century, "a tradition arose" in the Methodist Episcopal Church to "turn out all free members that lived together as man and wife without being married." This insistence on an "official" marriage had an impact on many free blacks. One example was Methodist Solomon Bayley of Kent County, who was living with a female slave while buying her freedom. Because he was not married in the eyes of the Church, Bayley "grew uneasy" and, under pressure from a white minister, committed himself to a marriage ceremony.[13]

During the antebellum years, Methodism moved from its eighteenth-century tolerance of a modest amount of drinking to the perception that the consumption of alcohol threatened the integrity of the family. Some Delaware free blacks who attended Methodist services became convinced that the consumption of alcohol was evil. Bayley was a cooper, and many of the wooden barrels that he made were used to store and ship whiskey. Bothered by his Methodist conscience, he gave up coopering for the far less remunerative life of a farm laborer.[14]

The percentage of Delaware free blacks who were members of the white-controlled Methodist Episcopal Church dramatically declined after 1810 in response to increasing institutional racism. Even more than in the late eighteenth century, African-Americans were relegated to the galleries or back pews of Methodist churches and were allowed to receive Communion only after all of the whites had been served. On occasion, even the segregated gallery could be taken from them if an overflow of whites needed room. At Barratt's Chapel near Frederica in Kent County, for example, a service became so crowded in 1842 that "it was deemed proper to request the coloured people to vacate the gallery for the whites."[15]

Adding even more to black frustration was the fact that in Delaware, as across the South, Methodism was far less critical of slavery in the antebellum period than it had been in the late eighteenth century. Indeed, as we know, some of the state's Methodists in good standing with their church were slaveholders; and yet, to many African-Americans, "the Methodists were the first people that brought glad tidings to the colored people."[16] That memory and the continued attraction of the Wesleyan message of hope were enough to hold the allegiance of some of Delaware's free black population despite insensitive and insulting treatment by their white Methodist brothers and sisters. Nevertheless, from 1814 to 1860, African-Americans dropped from 37 percent to 8 percent of the total membership of the Methodist Episcopal Church in Delaware.[17]

Even those blacks who remained loyal Methodists grew increasingly restive under the suffocating restrictions placed on them by the white-led denomination. Not only were blacks segregated in worship, but their ambitious young men with talent for spiritual leadership found that any position of authority except that of the unordained local preacher was closed to them. Always, it was clear, the control of mixed-race congregations would rest in the hands of the white preacher and the white laity; and always, it was equally clear, blacks would be restricted to the galleries or the back pews. Very rarely would gifted African-Americans be given the opportunity to preach the Gospel from sanctuary pulpits.

It was against this background of growing frustration with exclusive white control that a revolt took place in Asbury Methodist Episcopal Church on Third and Walnut streets in Wilmington. At the end of the eighteenth century, African-American members of Asbury began to assert their independence by holding their own services in black homes and in shady groves at the edge of the city while simultaneously attending services at the church. At Asbury, where they made up about one-half of the membership, blacks were relegated to the balcony during Sunday worship but were allowed to hold class meetings on the main floor of the sanctuary at other times. (Class meetings were gatherings of a small number of Methodists—perhaps ten to thirty—intent on sharing with each other the joys and sorrows of their spiritual journeys.) Adding to blacks' discontent was the fact that their two local preachers, Peter Spencer and William Anderson, were prohibited from speaking from Asbury's pulpit.[18]

Racial tensions reached the boiling point in 1805 when church trustees accused black members of breaking benches and of not cleaning up after holding class meetings in the sanctuary. They then ordered all African-Americans to restrict any future class meetings to the balcony. This ultimatum was the last straw, and Spencer, Anderson, and forty black members left Asbury to found an all-black Methodist Episcopal church about six blocks away on Ninth and Walnut streets. They named their new church Ezion for the port of Ezion-Geber, where King Solomon kept his warships. Built of stone with the financial help of local whites, including some members of Asbury, the

Ezion building was about the same size as the older church. More important, Ezion had its own board of trustees, class leaders, and lay preachers. In short, Spencer, Anderson, and their followers were now convinced that "we could have the rule of our church." But in order to remain within the Methodist Episcopal Church, Ezion had to accept as chief minister the same white pastor who had been appointed to serve Asbury. Despite this setback, Ezion's members did establish the first all-black church congregation in Delaware.[19]

By 1818, Harmony Methodist Episcopal Church, a few miles east of Millsboro in Sussex County, had become the second all-black Methodist Episcopal congregation in the state. Before the end of the Civil War, eight other all-black Methodist Episcopal congregations were formed: two in New Castle County, two in Kent, and four in Sussex. Evidently, Israel, located just south of Belltown in eastern Sussex, was specifically built for and by mulattoes.[20] Although blacks usually initiated their withdrawal from racially mixed congregations, there is no evidence that white Methodists actively opposed the process.

White acquiescence may have been shaped by the realization that all-black congregations, with their own preachers and trustees, were a necessary compromise to keep at least some African-Americans from leaving the fold. As each successive annual membership report pointed out, the Methodist Episcopal Church was losing much of its earlier appeal. Obviously, dramatic new steps were required to hold on to the diminishing numbers of Delaware blacks. But separate congregations based on skin color also appealed to whites because of the rising racism of the era. In 1866, for example, white members of Mount Calvary Church in Concord, in central Sussex, locked out the black members because they no longer wanted to worship in the same sanctuary with blacks.[21]

By the 1850s the all-black congregations in the Methodist Episcopal Church still lacked the right to choose their own ministers and were still subject to the white ministers appointed by the Philadelphia Conference. To address this and other common issues, a series of meetings of black local preachers representing all-black congregations from both Delaware and the adjoining states was held during the 1850s and early 1860s. Finally, in 1864 the all-black Delaware Conference of the Methodist Episcopal Church was formed with the power to appoint and ordain ministers. This development guaranteed that all-black congregations in Delaware as well as on the Eastern Shore of Maryland, in southeastern Pennsylvania, and in New Jersey now would be served by ordained black ministers appointed by a black conference.[22] With persistence and courage, free blacks from Delaware united with

those from surrounding areas to force white Methodists to acknowl-
edge their right to autonomy within the Church.

While the organization of all-black congregations and the formation of the Delaware Conference protected the dignity of African-
Americans in worship, it also opened a widening gap between the
religious experiences of blacks and whites in the state. Before the es-
tablishment of all-black congregations, blacks and whites were usually in close proximity to each other during worship. Despite segregated
seating, each group heard and saw the other during services, and each,
no doubt, was strongly influenced by the example of the other. If
African-Americans became so enthusiastic that they made white
worshipers uncomfortable, then the minister might admonish them to
follow the more sedate pattern of behavior exhibited below by their
white brothers and sisters in Christ. But the exuberant celebration of
faith from church balconies, or from behind the preacher's platform at
camp meetings, sparked some white Methodists to be less inhibited
and more demonstrative. In short, there is some indication that, at
times, the mix of black and white worshipers made for good spiritual
chemistry.[23]

During the early antebellum period, Methodist class meetings were
occasionally integrated affairs that might even be held in the homes of
African-Americans. (By the late antebellum period they were always
segregated.) Just as at worship services, the mix of races could produce heightened spiritual feelings. Probably the best known of these
interracial class meetings was held on October 16, 1822, at the home
of free blacks Isaac and Betsey Carter, about two miles from Odessa
in southern New Castle County. Levi Scott, a curious white apprentice cabinetmaker, showed up that evening at the Carters' home and
was converted. Subsequently, Scott became a Methodist minister and
then a bishop while Isaac and Betsey Carter slipped back into
anonymity. But Scott never forgot the Carters and the many other
African-Americans who played a key role in both his own spiritual
development and in the shaping of early Methodism. He became
one of the white clergy who strongly supported the formation of all-
black congregations in Delaware and the creation of the Delaware
Conference.[24]

Ironically, Scott's efforts to preserve black dignity through black
autonomy formally ended any future possibility in the Methodist Episcopal Church of the kinds of interracial religious services and class
meetings that were responsible for the launching of his own spiritual
journey. But increased black autonomy also meant that many of
Delaware's African-Americans were now free in the Church to pursue
a form of worship and an expression of piety that seemed appropriate
and relevant to their particular needs and inclinations.

~

Prior to the formation of the Delaware Conference, many of Delaware's blacks withdrew from the Methodist Episcopal Church to join one of the completely independent African-American denominations. Back at all-black Ezion in Wilmington, white paternalism created constant tension. In late 1812 a dispute erupted between the congregation's black leadership and white pastor James Bateman, who had been appointed by the Philadelphia Conference, over who exercised ultimate authority. When Spencer, Anderson, and other prominent blacks rejected Bateman's claims, the white minister summarily dismissed Ezion's trustees and class meeting leaders without so much as a hearing. The question of control over the appointment of a minister and the ownership of Ezion's physical plant then was taken to court. Spencer and the others were wary of the Delaware legal system. Even if they won an initial judgment, they could only expect that decision to be challenged in further litigation that could go on endlessly. Moreover, the court proceedings were already costing money and time, neither of which they could afford. Believing that they had no other choice, Spencer, Anderson, and most of the other blacks left Ezion to form a totally independent black Methodist church.[25]

In 1813, with some help from wealthy Quakers, Spencer and his followers erected the African Union Church—it was also called Old Union, the Union Church, the Union Church of Africans, and the African Union Methodist Church—between Eighth and Ninth on French Street in Wilmington. Under Spencer's leadership, it declared that it was Methodist but not Methodist Episcopal. With that declaration, "Old Union" became the first really independent black Methodist church in the United States. At the end of 1813 the African Union Church had become the nucleus of the country's first independent black denomination by adding congregations in Pennsylvania and New York. By the time that Spencer died in 1843, there were thirty-one congregations in Delaware, Pennsylvania, New York, and New Jersey that were connected to the African Union Church. Records from 1837 indicate that all five of the Delaware congregations were located in New Castle County. By that date, about one in every four New Castle County blacks attended services at one of the churches connected to Spencer's independent black Methodist movement. His African Union Church eventually became the parent of the African Union Methodist Protestant Church and the Union American Methodist Episcopal Church.[26]

Because of his importance, more needs to be said about Spencer. According to his biographer, Lewis V. Baldwin, Peter Spencer was born a slave in Kent County, Maryland, in 1782. When his master died, Spencer was manumitted and then moved to Wilmington in the mid- or late 1790s. There, he received a basic education in a private school and then commenced to make his living as a "laborer" or as a mechanic. But whatever he did, he must have been good at it because, by his death, he had accumulated enough money to own several houses in Wilmington.[27]

Although little is known of his family beyond the fact that Spencer was married at least once, it is clear that he viewed family and church as twin pillars of a meaningful and moral life for African-Americans. In addition, the sanctity of the home and the teachings of the Bible could also lead people of color to greater economic success. To Spencer, a strong family and a committed church encouraged their members to be honest, frugal, hardworking, and to abstain from the use of alcohol. He believed that these traits plus economic cooperation among African-Americans would gird blacks for survival in a basically hostile world. And as hostile as Delaware and the rest of the country were to African-Americans, it was better to remain here in the hope that conditions would get better than risk moving to Africa. Spencer also understood that education was power, and he advised each of his congregations to establish Sabbath schools to combat illiteracy.[28]

The significance of Spencer's life was recognized by even the white press. On his death in 1843, the *Delaware State Journal* noted that "few persons vested with the authority which he held would have walked so humbly and exercised so tender and liberal a sway over those under his direction. He was influential, yet not proud; he was powerful, but not dictatorial or tyrannical; he was wise, kind and parental, giving his superior energies to the amelioration of his associates and the advancement of his church." The *Delaware Gazette* characterized Spencer as "a practically good man" who "exercised much influence over the colored population of this section of the country."[29]

Spencer's legacy includes the annual Wilmington celebration known as Big August Quarterly, or simply Big Quarterly. Both Quakers and Methodists had held yearly meetings to assess the past, quicken spiritual life in the present, and lay plans for the future. Spencer probably took his idea for an annual gathering of black Methodists from one or both of these examples. Begun in 1814 by Spencer and set to take place on the last Sunday in August, Big Quarterly became, according to Baldwin, the first major black religious festival in the United States. The focus was on the day's religious service at Spencer's African Union Church, but the gathering soon took on broader social and cultural dimensions.[30]

Thousands of African-Americans from all over the Delmarva Peninsula and from Pennsylvania and New Jersey descended on Wilmington for religious renewal and often week-long visits with relatives and old friends. Although most of them were free blacks, a large number of slaves were permitted by their masters to attend Big Quarterly. Particularly noticeable were the considerable numbers of Philadelphians, many of them Delaware expatriates. In 1845, for example, an estimated one thousand black residents of the Quaker City attended Big Quarterly. In 1867 almost five thousand African-Americans from Delaware and the surrounding states were present and, no doubt, made white Wilmington uneasy. But the large crowds that showed up for Big Quarterly gave those attending a sense of who they were and whom they might become. For one Sunday in late August, they were immersed in the celebration of black spiritual and cultural life.[31]

Beginning with 1843, the year that Spencer died, a salute to the founder of Big Quarterly and the African Union Church was added to the festivities. Marching to the cemetery behind the Union Church on French Street, the celebrants placed a wreath on Spencer's grave. In later years, to the tune of "John Brown's Body," they often sang:

Peter Spencer (1782–1843). *Courtesy of Dr. James Newton, University of Delaware.*

"Father Spencer's body lies a-moldering in the clay, Father Spencer's body lies a-moldering in the clay; His church is marching on."[32]

In addition to Spencer's movement, a second independent black Methodist denomination, led by former Kent County slave Richard Allen and calling itself the African Methodist Episcopal Church, played an important role in the lives of many Delaware blacks during the antebellum period. Allen was born in 1760, the property of attorney Benjamin Chew, who had moved to Philadelphia from Kent County in 1754. Because Chew continued to maintain land and slaves in Kent County that he had inherited from his father, Samuel Chew, it is possible that Allen was born in Kent and quite probable that he spent some of his early years there as well as in Philadelphia.[33] In the 1760s or early 1770s he and his family were sold to Stokeley Sturgis, whose holdings were a few miles northeast of Dover. At the age of seventeen, Allen was converted to Methodism. The earlier sale by Sturgis of both of his parents and most of his siblings probably left the lonely slave with a deep longing for the sense of family and community that the Methodist class meeting provided. Shortly after his conversion, Allen began to hold prayer meetings in his master's house and then persuaded Sturgis to open his home to Methodist preachers such as Francis Asbury and Freeborn Garrettson. In 1780, persuaded by Methodist preaching that slavery was wrong, Sturgis offered Allen the opportunity to buy his freedom.[34]

After six years in which he worked enough to purchase his freedom and also preached on Methodist itinerant circuits from South Carolina to New York State, Allen settled in Philadelphia. In 1786 he became the spiritual leader of African-Americans who attended St. George's Methodist Episcopal Church in Philadelphia, where he often conducted dawn services. Among those who attended these early services was the recently manumitted Absalom Jones, who had spent his first fifteen years of slavery in Cedar Creek Hundred in northeastern Sussex County. Together, Allen and Jones established the Free African Society in Philadelphia in 1787. As Gary Nash points out, "The society was quasi-religious in character from the beginning," functioning as a self-help organization that supported and promoted spiritual uplift, self-definition, and advocacy for black rights. Furthermore, the Free African Society offered vital training for blacks in leadership skills.[35]

In subsequent years, racial slights caused the two former Delaware slaves to leave St. George's and, because of differing religious sensibilities, to go their separate ways in organizing all-black congregations in Philadelphia. Allen founded Bethel Methodist Episcopal Church, which moved into its new building in 1794. In that same year, Jones organized St. Thomas Protestant Episcopal Church. But

Allen wanted even more freedom from white control, and in 1816 he cut all ties with white Methodism by helping to found the totally independent African Methodist Episcopal denomination and became its first bishop. Jones, by contrast, remained the leader of an African-American congregation that continued its ties with the white-controlled Protestant Episcopal Church.

During the antebellum period, at least twelve African Methodist Episcopal (A.M.E.) congregations were established in Delaware. But

Richard Allen (1760–1831). *Courtesy of the Moorland-Spingarn Research Center, Howard University, Washington, DC.*

unlike the concentration of Spencer's followers in New Castle County, Allen's congregations could be found throughout the state. As early as 1822 some A.M.E. preachers were active among blacks in the Smyrna area of northern Kent County. Evidently, they were successful because there was an A.M.E. congregation meeting at Hopkins Landing, not far from Smyrna, in 1824. Within three years there was another congregation in the heart of Sussex in Milton. By 1838, New Castle County had its first A.M.E. church, located about one and one-half miles southwest of Newark. Seven years later, Bethel A.M.E. Church in Wilmington was established.[36] The large number of A.M.E. congregations indicates that a significant percentage of Delaware's African-Americans practiced black Methodism as shaped by Allen's leadership. Clearly, whether measured by the black congregations that made up the newly created Delaware Conference of the Methodist Episcopal Church or those aligned with one of the totally independent black denominations founded by Spencer or Allen, by 1865 the African-Americans at worship were freer from white control than at any other time in Delaware history. As a result, black Methodism was well on its way to developing its own distinctive version of the Wesleyan faith.

Many Delaware free blacks believed in the reality of a supernatural world at odds with orthodox Christianity. Still others integrated their faith in Christ with a belief in the occult.[37] Because practitioners and believers in non-Christian cosmologies did not keep records of their spiritual activities, however, it is difficult for historians to catch even a glimpse of the occult practices that were probably widespread among the state's African-Americans. Of course, belief in magic, conjuring, and witchcraft was not confined to blacks. The acceptance of a non-Christian spiritual world was also very much alive among a large segment of the white population. As a result, early Christianity in Delaware and elsewhere in the country worked hard to purge the faith of ancient folk beliefs in the supernatural that were strong on this side of the Atlantic as well as in Europe and Africa. But these efforts failed to rid much of white society of these "superstitious" practices. The problem was that many whites were unchurched, and they therefore were untouched by the attempt to disabuse Delawareans of a worldview that endowed animals with magical powers and allowed humans to conjure up both good and evil spirits. As one antebellum observer noted, the white lower classes in Sussex "were steeped" in these kinds of beliefs.[38]

During the late eighteenth century, most black Delawareans lost touch with the specifics of the traditional spirit world of their African

ancestors (see Chapter IV). And yet many African-Americans continued to share with many whites a broad belief in the efficacy of magic
and conjuring. During the antebellum era, much of Delaware became
polarized over such occult practices. Whites and blacks with some
education, genteel refinement, and a strong commitment to Christianity usually scoffed at magic and conjuring as merely one more mark
of heathenism. To a large segment of blacks and whites, however, animals with magical powers and human beings able to call up both good
and evil spirits were very real. So, too, was the need to share with
others the astonishing events that reflected this magical world.

The spirit world that many whites shared with African-Americans
was heavily influenced by European folk beliefs that were filtered and
reshaped over time by the American and the Delaware experience. A
case in point was the traditional European veneration of the salamander
as a creature with unusual attributes and powers, which evidently became part of the cosmology of free blacks in southern Delaware.[39] In
fact, some African-American storytellers took considerable pleasure
in using the salamander to introduce incredulous young whites, who
had been brought up to doubt the reality of the non-Christian supernatural world, to the world of occult phenomena. Jake Jack, a free
African-American who lived in central Sussex during the early nineteenth century, delighted in telling the daughter of a slave master and
her young friend that he frequently saw salamanders at an iron furnace in Millsboro, where they scrambled over the red-hot coals or dived
into the molten iron "like so many crocodiles into a pond." The salamanders were so cold "that several of them thrown into a furnace would
extinguish the fire." Jack's story was cheerfully verified by other
African-American witnesses.[40]

Although they may have been more European than African in
derivation, the superstitious beliefs and practices of some antebellum
African-Americans made many of Delaware's white legislators uneasy. Eventually, the General Assembly outlawed certain occult ceremonies that recognized spirits and forces contrary to orthodox
Christian theology or to perceived rational sensibilities. As a result,
free black Priscella Gibbs of northern Kent was indicted for "conjura-
tion" and "fortune telling" in 1844.[41] But the cosmology of Gibbs and
of many other antebellum free blacks was such an integral part of their
cultural identity that its beliefs and practices could not be ended by
legislation.

For a brief period during the late eighteenth century, some
African-Americans who were native to northern Delaware were ex-
posed to beliefs in occult phenomena that were more specifically
African than European. During the early 1790s a slave revolt in Saint-
Domingue (Haiti) forced many French planters to flee with their slaves

to seaports along the Atlantic coast of the United States. The number of both masters and slaves who landed in Delaware is unknown but, by 1794, French households in the town of New Castle included twenty-five black servants and slaves, and six years later there were at least forty slaves in French households in Wilmington. Although most, if not all, were from Saint-Domingue, the total was well short of one hundred, and most did not remain very long in Delaware. By 1800 many had left with their masters for France or the West Indies, and by 1810 only a handful of blacks from Saint-Domingue remained in northern Delaware.[42]

Before leaving, however, this small number of Caribbean blacks shared with Delaware-born blacks from the Wilmington area a cosmology of African derivation that had been kept alive in the West Indies. This vision of a spirit world, in its specifics at least, was different from the folk beliefs of lower-class whites. But because the West Indian purveyors of African cultural practices were so few in number and remained in northern Delaware such a short time, they were not a really significant factor in shaping the religious perceptions and practices of most African-Americans in the state.

~

Under slavery, black Delawareans experienced such an extraordinary amount of white interference in most aspects of their daily lives that their evolving culture could neither maintain much of the social inheritance of Africa nor create a new system of values and mores that was largely independent of the norms of white culture. The state's antebellum free black culture also reflected little that was African, unlike the slave culture of the late eighteenth century, but it was clearly distinctive from that of whites. A key factor in shaping this distinctiveness was the far greater independence from white interference enjoyed by most African-Americans after manumission. Central to this increased independence was the replacement of slavery with contract labor. Although the restrictive labor legislation of 1849 tempered some of this new economic independence, in freedom most blacks were socially and even economically far less subject to white control than they were under slavery. Also contributing to this new freedom was the construction of "colored houses" some distance from the homes of white farmers, the founding and growth of autonomous or independent black churches, the formation of two-parent black families that lived apart from white families, and the concentration in Wilmington of a sizeable free African-American population that comprised an almost autonomous community unto itself. Moreover, scattered across the rural countryside by the late antebellum period were small groups of houses that formed tiny, all-black communities such as Star Hill, south of Dover, and Belltown, west of Lewes.[43]

Demonstrating free black cultural autonomy were black festivals such as Big Quarterly and smaller social outings that became more common over time. In 1847, for example, a Wilmington newspaper reported that "the [black] barbers of our city had an excursion to Penns Grove [New Jersey] on Monday last. They were accompanied by a band. There were a large number of both sexes who enjoyed themselves exceedingly."[44] Furthermore, black fraternal clubs were organized in Wilmington during the antebellum era. In 1848, at Seventh and Locust streets, African-Americans finished constructing an Odd Fellows' Hall. Within the year the three-story brick building was the site of regular meetings of the black Odd Fellows, Masons, and Sons of Temperance. By the same year such Wilmington-based groups as the Daughters of Smith, which was connected with Bethel A.M.E. Church, and two chapters of the Colored Daughters of Temperance were meeting with the goal of encouraging religion, reducing the consumption of alcohol, and promoting morality. While these goals seemed to reflect white middle-class values, they were independently arrived at by blacks intent on improving the lives of other African-Americans in Delaware. The social improvement organizations that were specifically female also enabled African-American women to meet together far from the censoring eyes of black men.[45]

Some of these attempts to create social improvement and self-help societies faced opposition from the state government. In 1820 the African Benevolent Association of Wilmington was organized to spread knowledge, suppress vice, and inculcate "every virtue that renders man great, good, and happy." Petitions of incorporation were rejected by the General Assembly in 1823 and 1825, forcing the association to function without a charter. In 1830 free African-Americans in the town of New Castle founded the Sons of Benevolence, but their request for a charter from the General Assembly also was rejected.[46]

Despite being chronologically further removed from Africa, Delaware's free blacks of the antebellum period were more open to African cultural practices than were the slaves of the late eighteenth century. There is, for example, some indication that the "ring shout," an African dance ceremony, was used in services at Spencer's African Union Church in Wilmington and that other dances rooted in the past were performed at Big Quarterly.[47] These dances may have been part of the legacy left behind by the blacks from Saint-Domingue, or they may have been introduced by some of the out-of-state African-Americans who attended Big Quarterly.[48] But overall, Delaware's free blacks were more likely to salute their African origins by rushing to join independent black churches and other organizations that proclaimed "African" in their titles than to commit themselves to a cosmological and cultural perspective with specific roots in the Dark Continent.

Delaware's diverging and evolving free black culture was a response to increasing white racism and to gradually expanding black autonomy. It was produced by a people who insisted on their right to human dignity and human expression while at the same time reacting realistically to the considerable constraints imposed on them by whites. Simply put, in the shaping of the state's antebellum free black culture, conditions in Delaware provided the hammer and even the anvil. By contrast, because of its continuing contact with European values, ideas, and traditions, the state's white culture was far less shaped by the Delaware experience.

Free African-American culture expressed its divergence from white culture through distinctive singing, preaching, and congregational responses during religious services at independent and autonomous churches, in the evolution of a unique spoken version of vernacular English, in the development of a powerful oral tradition, in the preference for specific foods, in the fondness for a certain style of cooking, and through a commitment to a number of other social mores and practices that set blacks apart from the white world.[49] But just as different economic and educational levels produced variations in white culture, so did free black culture also vary according to the economic standing and literacy level of its participants.

～

In 1837, William Yates noted that "the free people of color in Delaware are in a most dreadful state of destitution in regard to schools." All tax-aided schools had been officially closed to African-Americans by the third decade of the nineteenth century. There was one privately funded school for blacks in Wilmington, sponsored by the Delaware Abolition Society, and two schools in Kent County near Dover, supported by a fund established by Samuel Fisher, a Philadelphia Quaker with Kent County ancestors. The two Kent County schools, however, were able to meet for only three months of the year. There were also "three or four" Sabbath schools connected with black churches that instructed African-Americans; two were in Wilmington.[50]

The pioneer in establishing formal instruction for blacks in the state was John Thelwell, a white, one-eyed Wilmington Methodist, who was the town crier and "a school master of some note."[51] As early as 1801, Thelwell was donating part of his Sundays to instruct young blacks in reading, writing, and arithmetic. His activities drew the support of the Abolition Society of Delaware, which agreed to pay him a small fee for his services in 1802. Abolition Society members also visited homes in Wilmington's black community to persuade parents to send their children to Thelwell for instruction and then offered their own services as volunteer teachers. The only school for blacks in the entire state continued to meet on Sunday afternoons until 1807, when the schedule was changed to weekday nights. Although it is not clear how regularly the city's school for African-American children met over the next few years, the time of instruction was probably changed to daytime hours. Initially, fewer than twenty black children attended, but by 1817 the figure had risen to forty-five boys and girls. For most of the years from late 1807 to 1816 the instructors hired were African-Americans.[52]

There were optimistic reports concerning Delaware's only school for blacks. In 1804 the conduct of the children was "orderly and attentive evincing in general a capacity and disposition to profit by the opportunity." By 1816 the efforts of the students were "silently but certainly undermining the prejudice which has existed unfavorable to their capacities." But there were limitations that had to be acknowledged. In 1817, despite the fact that in the last five years "500 scholars have learned to read and 300 to write, and a considerable number have acquired a sufficient knowledge of arithmetic to enable them to keep accounts," the students did not spend enough time in school "to go much beyond a knowledge sufficient to read and write."[53] Yet the Abolition Society continued to be optimistic about the endeavor, proclaiming that the supporters of the school eventually would see their efforts crowned with success when "the sable skin shall not be peculiarly the cover of ignorance and the plea for oppression." Thanks to the Wilmington school and to efforts in the future, there would come a time when "the enlightened sons of Africa shall rejoice in the uninterrupted enjoyments of liberty and equal privileges with their white brethren." The school was incorporated in 1822 as the African School of Wilmington and continued to employ black faculty members from out of state, such as John W. Adams and William S. Thomas. But the student body did not grow, and in 1839 there were only thirty-nine children in regular attendance.[54]

Throughout the antebellum period, educational opportunities for Delaware's African-Americans continued to be severely restricted. Although in 1865 there were seven schools for blacks in the state, all had to depend on private funding, and together they annually enrolled only about 250 students. Thus, only about 3 percent of free black Delawareans over five and under sixteen years of age were attending school during 1865. Five of the seven black schools were in New Castle

County: three in Wilmington, one in Newport, and one in Odessa. Because the two remaining schools were in central Kent County, there was no school for African-Americans in all of Sussex.[55]

The location and limited number of black schools as well as the restricted number of days that many of them were in session were reflected in literacy statistics. In Broad Creek Hundred in southwestern Sussex, only 5 percent of the free black population age twenty and over could read and write, according to the 1860 census. By contrast, in Wilmington, where there had been schools for African-Americans for some time, 35 percent of the same cohort was proclaimed literate. (By comparison, literacy among free blacks in neighboring Maryland seems to have been considerably higher during the late antebellum period.) Because the Delaware General Assembly continued to deal with black education in an irresponsible manner after the Civil War, illiteracy continued to plague the African-American community. As late as 1890 only one-half of Delaware blacks, ten years or older, were literate, according to the U.S. Census Bureau.[56]

~

As we know, most free African-Americans in the state lived in constant fear that they or members of their families would be seized by white kidnappers and sold to slave masters in the Deep South. Although kidnappers did abduct some enslaved blacks, they preyed more often on free blacks because they then did not have to fear the wrath of angry masters. In 1787 and 1793 the General Assembly passed laws for the punishment of kidnappers, and in subsequent years some were arrested and convicted. In 1817 the Abolition Society of Delaware reported that four kidnappers had been sentenced, and it entertained "a hope that some severe examples of punishment for kidnapping that have lately taken place may lessen the number of piratical violaters of the liberties of their fellow men." A later example was Isaac Updike, who in 1847 was convicted, whipped, fined one thousand dollars, and sentenced to two years in prison for abducting free blacks.[57]

The most famous kidnappers were Patty Cannon and her son-in-law, Joe Johnson, who lived four miles west of Seaford in the hamlet of Johnson's Cross Roads (now Reliance), on the Sussex border with Maryland. In the early nineteenth century, the Cannon-Johnson gang of cutthroats routinely abducted free blacks, along with some slaves, and sold them into bondage to southern traders who in turn shipped them to Georgia, Alabama, Mississippi, and Louisiana. The gang seized its victims on Maryland's Eastern Shore, in Delaware, and as far north as Philadelphia and then dodged back and forth across the Delaware-Maryland line to frustrate law-enforcement officials bent on arresting its members. An example of kidnapped free blacks was a mother and her baby: "The pair had been in bed when three members of the Cannon-Johnson gang broke into her cabin. One man held her down while another pulled a noose around her neck to keep her from screaming. The third assailant blindfolded her and she was done for. Her only comforts were that the baby went with her and she had been able to bite off a piece of her blindfolder's cheek during the fray."[58] While the actual number of enslaved and free blacks kidnapped by the Cannon-Johnson gang and others is not known, it is clear that their raids spread terror through the free black community of Delaware and probably spurred some of them to move north to Pennsylvania, to some other free state, or to Canada.

In 1822, in Georgetown, Johnson was convicted of kidnapping blacks and was "publically whipped on the bare back with 39 lashes, well laid on," and then was forced to stand "in the pillory with both ears nailed thereto." In 1829, Cannon was arrested and indicted for murdering one and perhaps two slave traders—evidently, she killed them to steal their money—as well as a number of African-Americans. While waiting for trial in the Sussex County jail in Georgetown, she allegedly took poison and ended her own life. Joe Johnson and his brother, Ebenezer, were also indicted for murder but escaped arrest by fleeing the Delmarva Peninsula for the Deep South.[59]

Kidnapping continued to plague Delaware throughout the antebellum years because abducting free blacks was very profitable. Clearly, observed the Abolition Society of Delaware, this nefarious activity attracted "men whom avarice has changed into demons." The reluctance by some state officials to take action also contributed to the practice. As early as 1802 the Abolition Society complained because kidnapping was "so disgracefully prosecuted." In 1816 it further maintained that the courts, the legislature, and certain attorneys were all "aiding this inhuman traffiking." The Abolition Society worked hard to right the situation through petitions and protests to the General Assembly and by hiring counsel to fight for the release of free blacks who had been kidnapped, but more often than not its efforts met with frustration.[60]

In 1800 a ring of kidnappers was accused of selling several hundred African-Americans in Virginia after having abducted them in Delaware. (The numbers were probably exaggerated.) In 1809 white abolitionists in Sussex complained about "the cruel and inhuman practices of kidnapping free negroes." Because of the rising value of slaves in the Deep South, abductions continued throughout the antebellum period and caused the General Assembly to legislate particularly harsh punishments for kidnappers in 1826. But subsequent indictments indicate that the problem continued until the Civil War.[61]

During the war most kidnappers found their lucrative southern markets closed. But this shutdown did not mean that free blacks were now secure from raids by whites intent on doing them harm. In central and southern Delaware, roving gangs intimidated, harassed, and assaulted members of the free African-American community. Nocturnal visits to black homes by white thugs, the burning of black churches, and the threatening of black ministers and other leaders with physical violence were commonplace. One example of harassment took place in Seaford, where three former Confederate soldiers from downstate— many in Sussex County had joined the Confederate cause—led a band of whites who interrupted a black church service, searched members of the congregation for weapons, and then broke out several windows of the building. Former Governor William Ross of Seaford, who owned a large farm with at least fourteen slaves in 1860, was accused of being one of the ringleaders. A Union officer, after taking part in an investigation in Sussex a few months after the end of the Civil War, noted that blacks in the southern part of the state needed federal protection because "their churches are burned, their schools broken up, and their persons and property abused and destroyed by vicious white men with impunity; and their appeals to the civil authorities are utterly disregarded."[62]

In northern Delaware, it was not much better. Black girls were often stalked or verbally abused by "a certain set of dandy white bucks." In 1848 in Wilmington, white mobs attacked three houses inhabited by African-Americans; in two of the three attacks, the houses were destroyed. One white mob assaulted a home on Tatnall Street on a hot August evening and "fired volley after volley of stones into the house," forcing the black residents to flee with some of their furniture. A Wilmington newspaper warned that "this course of things must be stopped or none of the houses inhabited by colored people will be safe." Evidently, no arrests were made.[63]

~

In early March 1864 the death of Comfort Mifflin, a free black female "in the neighborhood of 100 years," received unusual attention in a Georgetown newspaper. Although illiterate and relegated to servile work, Mifflin had been able to save enough to acquire one hundred dollars' worth of real estate and twenty-five dollars' worth of personal property by 1860. But it was her memory for past events rather than her material possessions that attracted notice. The newspaper claimed that Mifflin's recollections were "such as to bring to light many incidents long lost to our town and county."[64]

And what memories they must have been! When Mifflin was born in Sussex during the late colonial period, almost every African-American in Delaware expected a lifetime in bondage. It is not clear when and under what circumstances Mifflin received her freedom, but, like many newly manumitted African-Americans, she set up a household with a free black of the opposite sex and proceeded to have children. (One of her offspring was named Moses after her husband, Moses Mifflin.[65]) Busy as she was raising a family and working outside the home, Mifflin evidently developed a keen awareness of many of the events that shaped the history of both black and white Delawareans in the century preceding the Civil War. In addition to the decline of slavery, she also witnessed the increasing racism of the antebellum years that led to the oppressive race-based legislation passed by the General Assembly and to the many physical attacks on blacks by whites. But she also noticed that not all free blacks passively accepted the increasing hostility. While some simply left the state and others expressed their frustration behind the protective walls of family and church, a few blacks occasionally went public with their anger. Not surprisingly, because they were the best educated and most seasoned in leadership, members of Wilmington's black community usually led these protests.

In addition to encouraging and aiding slaves bent on escaping from their owners, Delaware's free African-Americans found other ways to strike out at slavery. Abraham Dores (Dorcas) of Wilmington, for example, left one hundred dollars to the Abolition Society of Delaware in 1825. But far more public were the actions of Abraham Shadd of Wilmington, who in 1831 became the local subscription agent for William Lloyd Garrison's abolitionist paper, *The Liberator.* Two years later, Shadd held an office in the American Antislavery Society. By the late 1830s the city's black community was annually making a statement about unfree labor by celebrating on August 1 the abolition of slavery in the British Empire.[66]

The black codes passed by the General Assembly in response to Nat Turner's rebellion in Virginia in 1831 and the increasing racism of the late antebellum era drove some literate blacks to take a public stand in writing. In late 1832 and again in early 1833, in response to the law of 1832 that severely restricted the right of free African-Americans to bear arms and to assemble, eight similarly worded protest petitions were drawn up, signed, and then delivered to the state government by free blacks. The petitioners did not claim the full protection of the Declaration of Independence and the U.S. Constitution, but they were confident that in addressing race relations, the General Assembly at least would be guided by the spirit of those two documents. The petitioners further pointed out that the law of 1832 had "a demoralizing effect on free people of color." In 1849, Kent County blacks signed another petition, this time against the requirement that African-Americans carry a pass signed by a white man before they could leave the state. Four years later, a free black petition maintained that the series of antiblack laws passed by the General Assembly during the antebellum years were "heavy and hard to be borne in this enlightened age and land, where the hand of oppression is stayed from all except our unfortunate race."[67]

Petitioning was an option for those African-Americans who were literate. But for the vast majority, who could not read and write, opposition to racist legislation was expressed by simply ignoring specific government regulations. In 1838 it was noted that despite the restrictions against blacks possessing guns and assembling together, both regulations were regularly flouted. Even in the "streets and public square of the capital of the state, . . . negroes of every description not only own and carry guns at will, but are often seen with the very muskets belonging to the state." Moreover, it was observed that blacks held both religious and other kinds of meetings "without molestation; and are allowed to meet and act as they please, disturbing the peace, by noisy assemblies at the corners where they will often remain the greater part of the night in crowds singing, dancing and yelling, to the annoyance of quiet people."[68]

As she lay dying in her home near Georgetown in 1864, Comfort Mifflin's thoughts must have ranged back over these and other events as she reviewed the triumphs and tragedies that marked the African-American experience under slavery and freedom in Delaware. Perhaps no public event was more satisfying for her to recall than the one that had just taken place only a short distance from where she dozed. During the Civil War, 954 Delaware blacks enlisted or were drafted into the Union Army; they represented 8 percent of all the state's soldiers who fought for the North. More than 300 other Delaware blacks enlisted in the Union Navy. While some of these soldiers and sailors were fugitives from slavery, most were free men. In the first few days of March 1864, only a little more than a week before Mifflin died, eight black army recruits from Lewes arrived in Georgetown. They were so happy to be fighting for the Union "that their inner feelings gave way in shouts of hallerlujerums, which was sung at the top of their voices as they rode through town in their wagon."[69]

The excitement of the moment was predicated on more than fighting for the abolition of slavery. The eight Lewes recruits were confident, despite recent attempts at intimidation by many whites, that better days for African-Americans were just ahead. Perhaps it was for the best that Mifflin died at this point in Delaware history because, despite the increasing racism of the late antebellum years, the apparent success of the Union forces in the Civil War offered her and other African-Americans some grounds for hope. Had she lived longer, her hopes only would have been dashed by the subsequent refusal of the General Assembly to ratify the Thirteenth, Fourteenth, and Fifteenth amendments to the U.S. Constitution.[70]

Even more prophetic was the resolution by the Democrat-led General Assembly in 1866, which declared:

> The immutable laws of the Creator have affixed upon the brow of the white races the ineffaceable stamps of superiority and that all attempts to elevate the negro to the social or political equality of the white man is the result either of an unwise and wicked fanaticism or a blind and perverse infidelity, subversive of the ends for which this government was established, and contrary to the doctrines and teachings of our fathers.[71]

These particularly negative perceptions of people of color were more deeply rooted in the minds and hearts of white Delawareans at the end of the antebellum period, when almost all of the state's blacks were free, than in the mideighteenth century when slavery was flourishing. This intense racism became part of the heritage of twentieth-century Delaware and provided the rationale for the ongoing mistreatment of African-Americans. Indeed, unfavorable stereotypes of blacks continued to be so pervasive in the hearts and minds of successive generations of white Delawareans that more than a century would pass before some of the hopes and dreams for equal treatment that lay behind the joyful "hallerlujerums" of 1864 were realized.[72]

Notes

*Deed Record of the Property of Ezion Methodist Episcopal Church, June 25, 1805, New Castle County Recorder of Deeds, Wilmington.

1. Schweninger, "Notes."

2. The raw figures that these percentages are based on come from Bruce Bendler, "Securing the Blessings of Liberty: Black Families in Lower New Castle County, 1790–1850," *Delaware History* 25 (Fall-Winter 1993–94): 245.

3. Essah, "Slavery and Freedom in the First State," 181–84; Bendler, "Securing the Blessings of Liberty," 247.

4. Sussex County Deed Book A B, No. 25, 315, DSA; Sussex County Deed Book A K, No. 33, 54, ibid.

5. Rachel Hickman (1790), Sussex County Will Book D-4, 402, SCCH; Mitchell Kershaw (1815), Sussex County Will Book No. 7, 127, ibid.; Jackson, ed., *Delaware Census Index for 1800*, 16. For Richard Allen's perspective on Stokeley Sturgis see Allen, *The Life Experience*, 15, 18–19. Gary Nash has discovered that Allen did not adopt his last name until after manumission. See Manumission Book A, 2, Papers of the Pennsylvania Abolition Society, HSP.

Among the few who did take their master's name were the slaves of William Ross of Seaford.

6. Jackson, ed., *Delaware Census Index in 1800*, passim; Berlin, *Slaves without Masters*, 51–52. A search of wills, manumission deeds, and other primary source material indicates that almost all former Delaware slaves decided not to take their former masters' surnames. While by 1800 the overwhelming majority of these free African-Americans chose traditional surnames, a number also chose last names that did not exist in white Delaware in 1800. Some of these uniquely black surnames were only slightly different from white ones, and the differences may have been the result of the era's untrained census takers interviewing illiterate free blacks, who probably had no idea of how the name they chose was spelled. When the census takers subsequently copied their notes on government forms, there was considerable margin for error.

A few free African-Americans may have taken such last names as Plumonnis, Oronoka, Elapage, and Songo simply because they liked the sound. Others were recorded as not yet having chosen a surname. The 1800 census was selected for surname analysis over the censuses of later years because, due to the manumission pattern in Delaware, more free blacks most recently had chosen a surname in 1800 than would do so in the next sixty years.

7. Hancock and McCabe, *Milton's First Century*, 301, 303. For plats showing the location of the "colored house" see Delph Martin, Negro Martin, and Negro Peter, Kent County Orphans Court Plats, Kent County No. 1, 81, 88, 89, Kent County Orphans Court Records, Register in Chancery, KCCH.

8. Essah, "Slavery and Freedom in the First State," 182.

9. The cluster patterns of free blacks in towns, villages, and the city of Wilmington can be seen in U.S. Census Bureau, Manuscripts, 1830, 1840, 1850, 1860, Delaware, passim. For Wilmington, in addition to the above, see Carol Hoffecker, *Wilmington, Delaware: Portrait of an Industrial City* (Charlottesville, VA, 1974), 7.

10. Hug Durborrow to John Dickinson, July 19, 1782, Logan Papers, 28:108, HSP; Indenture, May 15, 1793, Logan Papers, 37:27, 28, ibid.

11. Berlin, *Slaves without Masters*, 226; Elizabeth Rodney, February 4, 1820, Du Humel Papers, Negroes, HSD. In general, apprentice agreements for blacks did not mention the education requirement.

12. *Laws of the State of Delaware*, 4:469, 7:97–98; Elizabeth Godwin, "The History of Poor Relief Administration in Delaware" (Ph.D. diss., University of Chicago, 1938), 80–87.

13. Bayley, *A Narrative of Some Remarkable Incidents*, 26–28.

14. Ibid., iv.

15. William C. Jason, "The Delaware Annual Conferences of the Methodist Episcopal Church, 1864–1965," *Methodist History* 4 (July 1966): 28; Andrew Manship, *Thirteen Years Experience in the Itinerancy* (Philadelphia, 1856), 21–22.

16. Allen, *The Life Experience*, 30.

17. *Minutes of the Philadelphia Annual Conference of the Methodist Episcopal Church for 1861* (Philadelphia, 1861), 17–18; *Minutes of the Annual Conferences of the Methodist Episcopal Church for the Years 1773–1828*, 244.

18. Baldwin, *The Mark of a Man*, 11–12; idem, *"Invisible" Strands in African Methodism* (Metuchen, NJ, 1983), 38–41; Williams, *The Garden of American Methodism*, 115–16; Asbury Methodist Episcopal Church, 5:passim, DSA.

19. Baldwin, *The Mark of a Man*, 12; Scharf, *History of Delaware*, 2:730; Asbury Methodist Episcopal Church, 5:passim, DSA; Baldwin, *"Invisible"*

Strands in African Methodism, 41–43; Williams, *The Garden of American Methodism*, 116. The size and building material used in the construction of Ezion is mentioned in Elmer T. Clark, ed., *The Journal and Letters of Francis Asbury*, 3 vols. (Nashville, TN, 1958), 2:501.

20. Frank Zebley, *The Churches of Delaware* (Wilmington, DE, 1947), passim; Scharf, *History of Delaware*, 1063, 1221. According to Zebley, black Methodist Episcopal congregations founded by 1861 included: Ezion (Wilmington, 1805); Harmony (east of Millsboro, by 1818); St. James (Georgetown, by 1840); Carlisle (west of Dover, 1849); Whatcoat (Dover, by 1852); Wesley (southeast of Milford, by 1853); Israel (south of Belltown and west of Lewes, by 1853); Bathsady (south of Newark, 1859); and Mount Calvary (Portsville, Sussex, 1861).

21. Mildred G. West, "History of Mount Calvary A.M.E. Church, Concord, Delaware" (unpublished paper in my possession), 3.

22. Jason, "The Delaware Annual Conferences of the Methodist Episcopal Church," 26.

23. The generalizations in this paragraph are based on information in Williams, *The Garden of American Methodism*, 114, passim; Robert Todd, *Methodism on the Peninsula* (Philadelphia, 1886), 172–237.

24. James Mitchell, *The Life and Times of Levi Scott, D.D.* (New York, 1885), 18, and passim.

25. Baldwin, *The Mark of a Man*, 14; idem, *"Invisible" Strands in African Methodism*, 43–45; Scharf, *History of Delaware*, 2:729; Williams, *The Garden of American Methodism*, 116; Folder No. 5, M.E. Black, Federal Writers Project, Church Records, DSA; Asbury Methodist Episcopal Church (Wilmington), 5:passim, ibid.

26. Baldwin, *The Mark of a Man*, 5, 14–15, 19, 46; idem, *"Invisible" Strands in African Methodism*, 46–48; Williams, *The Garden of American Methodism*, 116; Baldwin, *"Invisible" Strands in African Methodism*, 121; summary of U.S. Census Bureau, Manuscripts, 1840, Delaware, New Castle County. For a detailed account of the African Union movement and subsequent schism see Baldwin, *"Invisible" Strands in African Methodism*.

27. Baldwin, *The Mark of a Man*, 2, 5; Scharf, *History of Delaware*, 2:730.

28. Baldwin, *The Mark of a Man*, 3–4, 34–41.

29. *Delaware State Journal*, 8/1/1843; *Delaware Gazette*, 8/4/1843.

30. Lewis V. Baldwin, "Festivity and Celebration: A Profile of Wilmington's Big Quarterly," *Delaware History* 19 (Fall-Spring 1981): 197–206. Because slavery was dying in Wilmington's black hinterland by 1814, the overwhelming majority of African-Americans attending Big Quarterly were free rather than enslaved.

31. Ibid.

32. Ibid., 202.

33. Nash, *Forging Freedom*, 95; Scharf, *History of Delaware*, 537. For the Kent County holdings of Samuel Chew, perhaps the state's largest slaveholder, see Kent County Probate Inventories, DSA.

34. Williams, *The Garden of American Methodism*, 145; Nash, *Forging Freedom*, 95.

35. Nash, *Forging Freedom*, 95.

36. Williams, *The Garden of American Methodism*, 118; Zebley, *The Churches of Delaware*, passim.

37. Many black church members in Delaware were also believers in the world of hags, witches, and sorcery. These African-Americans seem to have constructed a dual view of the world in which a Christian cosmology lay side by side with a

non-Christian belief in magic, conjuring, and spirits. For a description of this spiritual dualism in South Carolina see Joyner, *Down by the Riverside*, 141.

38. Butler, *Awash in a Sea of Faith*, 243; Welch, ed., *Memoirs of Mary Parker Welch*, 110.

39. Butler, *Awash in a Sea of Faith*, 243. The salamander played a key role in the discovery by Joseph Smith of the sacred golden plates that became the textual basis of the Church of Jesus Christ of Latter-day Saints (Mormons).

40. Welch, ed., *Memoirs of Mary Parker Welch*, 123.

41. Priscella Gibbs (1844), Indictments, Kent County Court of General Sessions, DSA.

42. Catts, "Slaves, Free Blacks, and French Negroes," 56–61, 72.

43. Scharf, *History of Delaware*, 948; Eckman et al., eds., *Delaware: A Guide to the First State*, 493–94.

44. *Blue Hen's Chicken*, 9/3/1847; Scharf, *History of Delaware*, 2:1140.

45. *Blue Hen's Chicken*, 4/7/1848, 9/11/48, 11/26/47, 3/3/48.

46. Hancock, "Not Quite Men," 327 n.39; Essah, "Slavery and Freedom in the First State," 204.

47. Baldwin, *"Invisible" Strands in African Methodism*, 137–40; Graham R. Hodges, *Black Itinerants of the Gospel: The Narratives of John Jea and George White* (Madison, WI, 1993), 13–14; Baldwin, "Festivity and Celebration," 200–201; idem, *The Mark of a Man*, 24.

48. Eckman et al., eds., *Delaware: A Guide to the First State*, 494.

49. For specific examples of spoken black English in Delaware and on the Eastern Shore of Maryland during the antebellum period see the caricatured references in Todd, *Methodism on the Peninsula*, 173–201; and Townsend, *The Entailed Hat*, passim. Oral exchanges were the only means of communication for most free blacks because they were illiterate. One senses, but cannot prove, that "soul food" began to make its appearance in Delaware during the antebellum era. See Baldwin, "Festivity and Celebration," 200.

50. Hancock, ed., "William Yates Letter of 1837," 210–11; *Laws of the State of Delaware*, 6:86; Hancock, "Not Quite Men," 327.

51. Montgomery, *Reminiscences of Wilmington*, 227.

52. Minutes, 1802–1807, Abolition Society of Delaware, November 9, 1802, HSD; Abolition Society of Delaware Minute Book, 10, 11, 36, 56, 90, 128, Papers of Pennsylvania Abolition Society, HSP.

53. Abolition Society of Delaware Minute Book, 36, 90, 128–29, Papers of Pennsylvania Abolition Society, HSP.

54. Ibid., 130; *Laws of the State of Delaware*, 6:338–40; Hancock, "Not Quite Men," 327, 328, 329 n.48, 330.

55. Harold C. Livesay, "Delaware Blacks, 1865–1915," in Hoffecker, ed., *Readings in Delaware History*, 137; Scharf, *History of Delaware*, 1:448. Attendance figures are based on raw data from U.S. Census Bureau, Manuscripts, 1860, Delaware.

56. U.S. Census Bureau, Manuscripts, 1860, Delaware, Broad Creek Hundred, and Wilmington; Fields, *Slavery and Freedom on the Middle Ground*, 39; *Negro Population in the United States, 1790–1915*, 409, 415.

57. *Laws of the State of Delaware*, 2:885, 1093; Abolition Society of Delaware Minute Book, 13, Papers of Pennsylvania Abolition Society, HSP; Thomas Garrett to Governor William Tharp, August 11, 1847, Garrett Papers, HSD. For examples of kidnappers indicted see John Lewis (1837), Levin Calloway (1840), Israel Brinkley (1840), James Whitaker (1840), Isaac Griffin (1841), Kent County Court of General Sessions, DSA.

58. Ted Giles, *Patty Cannon, Woman of Mystery* (Easton, MD, 1965), 36, 30, 20. For a fictionalized description of a Dover raid see Townsend, *The Entailed Hat*, 424–33. The most recent account, based on primary source research, can be found in Carol Wilson, *Freedom at Risk: The Kidnapping of Free Blacks in America, 1780–1865* (Lexington, KY, 1994), 19–37.

59. Giles, *Patty Cannon*, 21, 29, 46, 33–35; *Delaware Gazette*, 4/11/1829, 4/17/29, 4/19/29; Wilson, *Freedom at Risk*, 33. For a fictional treatment of Johnson's trial and punishment see Townsend, *The Entailed Hat*, 287.

60. Abolition Society of Delaware Minute Book, 136, 13, 88–89, 113–14, 136, 74, 34–36, 21, Papers of Pennsylvania Abolition Society, HSP; Berlin, *Slaves without Masters*, 100.

61. Berlin, *Slaves without Masters*, 99; Constitution of Sussex Society for Promoting the Abolition of Slavery, 1809 (property of Sandra Short Lord of Georgetown, Delaware); *Laws of the State of Delaware*, 6:715; Hancock, ed., "William Yates Letter of 1837," 212.

62. Hancock, "Delaware during the Civil War," 87, 166; David Ames et al., eds., *The Ross Mansion Quarter* (Newark, DE, 1992), 10–11; Col. J. M. Wilson to Lt. Col. Catlin, July 18, 1865, War Department, Middle Department, Letters Received, 1865, National Archives, printed in part in Harold B. Hancock, "The Status of the Negro in Delaware after the Civil War, 1865–1875," *Delaware History* 13 (April 1968): 59. William Ross, governor of Delaware from 1851 to 1855, actually was out of the country during most of the Civil War but returned to Seaford at least once during the conflict. Ross's son Caleb joined the Confederate Army and died of disease during the war. Claudia Melson, *Ross Mansion Quarter* (Seaford, DE, 1994), 30.

63. *Blue Hen's Chicken*, 11/5/1847, 4/7/48, 8/11/48.

64. *Weekly Union*, 3/11/1864; U.S. Census Bureau, Manuscripts, 1860, Delaware, Broadkill Hundred, Georgetown, 2.

65. U.S. Census Bureau, Manuscripts, 1860, 1820, 1850, Delaware, Broadkill Hundred.

66. Catts, "Slaves, Free Blacks, and French Negroes," 66; Hancock, "Mary Ann Shadd," 188–89; idem, "Not Quite Men," 327.

67. Petitions (1833), (1849), (1853), Slavery and Negro, DSA; Hancock, "Not Quite Men," 324–25. Hancock and Hite, *Slavery, Steamboats, and Railroads*, 73–74, contains a copy of one of the petitions of 1832–33.

68. *Delaware Register*, 1:1838, as reprinted in Hancock and Hite, *Slavery, Steamboats, and Railroads*, 72.

69. Frederick C. Dyer, *A Compendium of the War of the Rebellion* (New York, 1959), 11, 12; *Weekly Union*, 3/4/1864; James E. Johnson, "Lower Delaware Blacks in the Civil War," *Fully, Freely, and Entirely* (Winter 1944): 4–5. In all, 954 blacks and 11,236 whites from Delaware served in the Union Army during the Civil War.

70. The Thirteenth (ending slavery), Fourteenth (declaring that blacks had the same rights as other Americans), and Fifteenth (protecting the right of black males to vote) amendments were adopted in 1865, 1868, and 1870, respectively. Delaware, however, demonstrated its continued resistance to even the appearance of equal rights by refusing to ratify them until the first decade of the twentieth century.

71. *Laws of the State of Delaware*, 13:87. In his inaugural address of the previous year (1865), Governor Gove Saulsbury took a similar stand toward African-Americans and called for their exclusion from all political and social privileges. See *Journal of the House of Representatives of the State of Delaware*

for 1865 (Dover, 1866), 450. Governor Saulsbury's brother, U.S. Senator Willard Saulsbury, also made some very strong racial statements about the need to keep blacks subordinate to whites. See Hancock, *Delaware during the Civil War*, 109, 129. Both Saulsburys were Democrats.

72. For information on the African-American experience in Delaware from 1865 to the present see Hancock, "The Status of the Negro in Delaware after the Civil War," 57–66; Livesay, "Delaware Blacks, 1865–1915," 121–55; Amy M. Hiller, "The Disfranchisement of Delaware Negroes in the Late Nineteenth Century," *Delaware History* 13 (October 1968): 124–53; Carol E. Hoffecker, "The Politics of Exclusion: Blacks in Late Nineteenth-Century Wilmington, Delaware," ibid. 16 (April 1974): 60–72; Jacqueline J. Halstead, "The Delaware Association for the Moral Improvement and Education of the Colored People: Practical Christianity," ibid. 15 (April 1973): 187–94; Pauline A. Young, "The Negro in Delaware, Past and Present," in Reed, ed., *Delaware: A History of the First State*, 2:581–608. Very little has been written on the history of Delaware's blacks in the twentieth century. The best study that deals only with the present century is Annette Woolard, "A Family of Firsts: The Reddings of Delaware" (Ph.D. diss., University of Delaware, 1994).

Appendix

Population of Delaware, 1790–1860

	Black		White	Total
	Slaves	Free		
1790				
New Castle County	2,562	639	16,487	19,688
Kent County	2,300	2,570	14,050	18,920
Sussex County	4,025	690	15,773	20,488
	8,887	3,899	46,310	59,096
1800				
New Castle County	1,838	2,754	20,769	25,361
Kent County	1,485	4,246	13,823	19,554
Sussex County	2,830	1,268	15,260	19,358
	6,153	8,268	49,852	64,273
1810				
New Castle County	1,047	3,919	19,463	24,429
Kent County	728	5,616	14,151	20,495
Sussex County	2,402	3,601	21,747	27,750
	4,177	13,136	55,361	72,674
1820				
New Castle County	1,195	4,344	22,360	27,899
Kent County	1,070	5,533	14,190	20,793
Sussex County	2,244	3,081	18,732	24,057
	4,509	12,958	55,282	72,749
1830				
New Castle County	786	5,708	23,226	29,720
Kent County	588	5,671	13,654	19,913
Sussex County	1,918	4,476	20,721	27,115
	3,292	15,855	57,601	76,748
1840				
New Castle County	541	6,773	25,806	33,120
Kent County	427	5,827	13,618	19,872
Sussex County	1,637	4,319	19,137	25,093
	2,605	16,919	58,561	78,085

Appendix

	Black		White	Total
	Slaves	*Free*		
1850				
New Castle County	394	7,621	34,765	42,780
Kent County	347	6,385	16,084	22,816
Sussex County	1,549	4,067	20,320	25,936
	2,290	18,073	71,169	91,532
1860				
New Castle County	254	8,188	46,355	54,797
Kent County	203	7,271	20,330	27,804
Sussex County	1,341	4,370	23,904	29,615
	1,798	19,829	90,589	112,216

Selected Bibliography

Manuscripts

Delaware State Archives, Dover, Delaware (DSA)
    Court of General Sessions, Kent County
    Court Orders to Sell Slaves, 1798–1829, Slavery Material
    Court of Oyer and Terminer, Kent County
    Court of Oyer and Terminer, New Castle County
    Court of Oyer and Terminer, Sussex County
    Court for Trial of Negroes, 1749–1788
    Delaware 1850/1860 Slave Schedules
    Dickinson Letters Collection
    Folders, Slavery Material
    Kent County Estate Inventories
    Legislative Papers (including sundry petitions)
    Manumissions, 1780–1865, Slavery Material
    New Castle County Estate Inventories
    New Castle County Wills
    Slavery Material, 1764–1866, Miscellaneous
    Slavery Material, 1805–1865, Petitions for Freedom
    Sussex County Coroner's Inquest
    Sussex County Estate Inventories
    Sussex County Orphans Court Records
    Sussex County Recorder of Deeds
    Sussex County Tax Assessment Records, 1801, 1816
    Sussex County Wills
    United States Census Manuscripts, Delaware, 1800–1860, microfilm
Kent County Court House, Dover, Delaware (KCCH)
    Kent County Orphans Court Records
    Kent County Wills
Sussex County Court House, Georgetown, Delaware (SCCH)
    Sussex County Wills
Historical Society of Delaware, Wilmington, Delaware (HSD)
    Abolition Society of Delaware Minutes, 1802–1807
    Caesar Rodney signer, Rodney Collection
    Garrett Papers
    H. F. Brown Collection
    John M. Clayton Papers

Minutes of the Acting Committee of the Society for the Abolition of
Slavery, 1801–1804
Negroes, Du Humel Papers
Slavery Folders, 1–3
Historical Society of Pennsylvania, Philadelphia, Pennsylvania (HSP)
Deeds of Manumission, Duck Creek Monthly Meeting, 1774–1792
Abolition Society of Delaware Minute Book, 1802–1818, Papers of
Pennsylvania Abolition Society

Typed Copies of Manuscripts

Bushman, Richard L., and Anna L. Hawley. "A Random Sample of Kent
County, Delaware, Estate Inventories, 1727–1775." DSA.
Stewart, James, and Madeline Thomas. "John Dickinson's Negroes."
Unpublished collection based on Logan Papers, HSP. On file at Bureau
of Museums, Dover, Delaware.
Stewart, James, Madeline Thomas, and Laura Simmons. "Kent County
Assessment Records, 1797." On file at Bureau of Museums, Dover,
Delaware.

Newspapers

American Watchman and Delaware Republican (Wilmington)
Blue Hen's Chicken (Wilmington)
Delaware Gazette (Wilmington)
Federal Ark (Wilmington)
Messenger (Georgetown)
Pennsylvania Gazette (Philadelphia)
Weekly Union (Georgetown)

Other Printed Primary Sources

The African Repository 13 (1837): 315.
Boorstin, Daniel J., ed. *Delaware Cases, 1792–1830*. 2 vols. St. Paul,
MN, 1943.
Bushman, Claudia L., Harold B. Hancock, and Elizabeth M. Homsey, eds.
*Proceedings of the House of Assembly of the Delaware State, 1781–
1792*. Cranbury, NJ, 1988.
De Valinger, Leon, ed. *A Calendar of Ridgely Family Letters, 1742–1889*.
Vols. 1–3. Dover, DE, 1948.
———. *Court Records of Kent County, Delaware, 1680–1705*. Washing-
ton, DC, 1959.
Gehring, Charles T. *New York Historical Manuscripts: Dutch; Volumes
XVIII–XIX, Delaware Papers, 1648–1664*. Baltimore, 1981.
Hazard, Samuel. *Annals of Pennsylvania from the Discovery of the Dela-
ware, 1609–1682*. Philadelphia, 1850.

Horle, Craig W., ed. *Records of the Courts of Sussex County, Delaware, 1677–1710.* Philadelphia, 1991.

Horle, Craig W., and Marianne S. Wokeck, eds. *Lawmaking and Legislators in Pennsylvania: A Biographical Dictionary,* Vol. 1, *1682–1709.* Philadelphia, 1991.

Jackson, Ronald V., ed. *Delaware Census Index for 1800.* N.p., n.d.

Journal of the House of Representatives of the State of Delaware. Dover, DE, 1803. Wilmington, DE, 1845, 1847.

Journal of the Senate of the State of Delaware. Wilmington, DE, 1847, 1848.

Laws of the State of Delaware. 12 vols. New Castle, DE, 1797. Dover, DE, 1798–1865.

Minutes of the Annual Conferences of the Methodist Episcopal Church for the Years 1773–1828. New York, 1840.

Minutes of the Council of the Delaware State from 1776 to 1792. Dover, DE, 1886.

Minutes of the Delaware State Senate. Wilmington, DE, 1797.

Minutes of the House of Assembly of the Three Counties upon Delaware, 1740–1742. N.p., 1929.

Minutes of the House of Representatives of the State of Delaware, 1765–1770. Dover, DE, 1931.

Turner, C. H. B., ed. *Some Records of Sussex County, Delaware.* Philadelphia, 1909.

Votes and Proceedings of the House of Representatives of the Government of the Counties of New Castle, Kent, and Sussex, upon Delaware, 1765–1770. Dover, DE, 1931.

Wright, F. Edward, ed. *Vital Records of Kent and Sussex Counties, Delaware, 1686–1800.* Silver Spring, MD, 1986.

———. *Delaware Newspaper Abstracts, 1786–1795,* vol. 1. Silver Spring, MD, 1984.

Memoirs

Allen, Richard. *The Life Experience and Gospel Labors of the Right Reverend Richard Allen.* New York, 1960.

Bayley, Solomon. *A Narrative of Some Remarkable Incidents in the Life of Solomon Bayley, Formerly a Slave in the State of Delaware, North America.* London, 1825.

Douglass, Frederick. *Narrative of the Life of Frederick Douglass, An American Slave.* New York, 1968.

Hayes, Manlove. *Reminiscences.* N.p. or p.d.

Manship, Andrew. *Thirteen Years Experience in the Itinerancy.* Philadelphia, 1856.

Montgomery, Elizabeth. *Reminiscences of Wilmington.* Wilmington, DE, 1851.

Welch, George T., ed. *Memoirs of Mary Parker Welch (1818–1912).* Brooklyn, NY, 1947.

Dissertations and Theses

Catts, Wade P. "Slaves, Free Blacks, and French Negroes: An Archaeological and Historical Perspective on Wilmington's Forgotten Folk." Master's thesis, University of Delaware, 1988.

Dean, John G. "The Free Negro in Delaware: A Demographic and Economic Study." Master's thesis, University of Delaware, 1970.

Essah, Patience. "Slavery and Freedom in the First State: The History of Blacks in Delaware from the Colonial Period to 1865." Ph.D. diss., UCLA, 1985.

Articles

Bausman, R. O., and John A. Munroe, eds. "James Tilton's Notes on the Agriculture of Delaware in 1788." *Agricultural History* 20 (July 1946): 176–87.

Bendler, Bruce. "Securing the Blessings of Liberty: Black Families in Lower New Castle County, 1790–1850." *Delaware History* 25 (Fall-Winter 1993–94): 237–52.

Berlin, Ira. "Time, Space, and the Evolution of Afro-American Society in British Mainland North America." *American Historical Review* 85 (February 1980): 44–78.

Calvert, Monte A. "The Abolition Society of Delaware, 1801–1807." *Delaware History* 20 (October 1983): 295–320.

Christoph, Peter R. "The Freemen of New Amsterdam." *Journal of the Afro-American Historical and Genealogical Society* 5 (Fall-Winter 1984): 109–18.

Cohen, David S. "In Search of Carolus Africanus Rex: Afro-Dutch Folklore in New York and New Jersey." *Journal of the Afro-American Historical and Genealogical Society* 5 (Fall-Winter 1984): 149–56.

Eltis, David. "Europeans and the Rise and Fall of African Slavery in the Americas: An Interpretation." *American Historical Review* 98 (December 1993): 1399–1423.

Hancock, Harold B. "Not Quite Men: The Free Negroes in Delaware in the 1830s." *Civil War History* 17 (December 1968): 320–31.

———, ed. "William Yates Letter of 1837: Slavery and Colored People in Delaware." *Delaware History* 14 (April 1971): 205–10.

Jordan, Winthrop. "American Chiaroscuro: The Status and Definition of Mulattoes in the British Colonies." *William and Mary Quarterly* 19 (April 1962): 183–200.

Klein, Herbert S., and Stanley L. Engerman. "Fertility Differentials between Slaves in the United States and the British West Indies: A Note on Lactation Practices and Their Possible Implications." *William and Mary Quarterly* 35 (April 1978): 357–74.

Main, Gloria L. "Probate Records as a Source for Early American History." *William and Mary Quarterly* 32 (January 1975): 89–110.

Menard, Russell R. "The Maryland Slave Population, 1658–1730: A Demographic Profile of Blacks in Four Counties." *William and Mary Quarterly* 32 (January 1975): 29–54.

Reed, H. Clay. "Lincoln's Compensated Emancipation Plan." *Delaware Notes* 7 (1931): 27–78.

Wax, Darold D. "Quaker Merchants and the Slave Trade in Colonial Pennsylvania." *Pennsylvania Magazine of History and Biography* 86 (April 1962): 143–59.

Books

Baldwin, Lewis V. *The Mark of a Man: Peter Spencer and the African Union Methodist Tradition*. Lanham, MD, 1987.

———. *"Invisible" Strands in African Methodism*. Metuchen, NJ, 1983.

Bendler, Bruce. *Colonial Delaware Assemblymen, 1682–1776*. Westminster, MD, 1989.

Berlin, Ira. *Slaves without Masters: The Free Negro in the Antebellum South*. New York, 1976.

Berlin, Ira, and Ronald Hoffman, eds. *Slavery and Freedom in the Age of the American Revolution*. Charlottesville, VA, 1983.

Blassingame, John W. *The Slave Community: Plantation Life in the Antebellum South*. New York, 1979.

Boles, John B. *Black Southerners, 1619–1869*. Lexington, KY, 1983.

Brackett, Jeffrey R. *The Negro in Maryland: A Study of the Institution of Slavery*. 1889. Reprint, New York, 1969.

Breen, Timothy H., and Stephen Innes. *Myne Own Ground: Race and Freedom on Virginia's Eastern Shore, 1640–1676*. New York, 1980.

Bushman, Richard L. *The Refinement of America: Persons, Houses, Cities*. New York, 1993.

Butler, Jon. *Awash in a Sea of Faith: Christianizing the American People*. Cambridge, MA, 1990.

Carr, Lois Green, Russell R. Menard, and Lorena S. Walsh. *Robert Cole's World*. Chapel Hill, NC, 1991.

Clemens, Paul G. *The Atlantic Economy and Colonial Maryland's Eastern Shore: From Tobacco to Grain*. Ithaca, NY, 1980.

Degler, Carl. *Neither Black nor White: Slavery and Race Relations in Brazil and the U.S.* Madison, WI, 1986.

Ferguson, Leland. *Uncommon Ground: Archaeology and Early African America*. Washington, DC, 1992.

Fields, Barbara J. *Slavery and Freedom on the Middle Ground: Maryland during the Nineteenth Century*. New Haven, CT, 1985.

Fletcher, Stevenson W. *Pennsylvania Agriculture and Country Life, 1640–1840*. Harrisburg, PA, 1950.

Frederickson, George M. *The Black Image in the White Mind: The Debate on Afro-American Character and Destiny, 1817–1914*. Middletown, CT, 1987.

Garrison, J. Ritchie, et al., eds. *After Ratification: Material Life in Delaware, 1789–1820.* Newark, DE, 1988.

Genovese, Eugene D. *Roll, Jordan, Roll: The World the Slaves Made.* New York, 1976.

George, Carol V. *Segregated Sabbaths: Richard Allen and the Emergence of Independent Black Churches, 1760–1840.* New York, 1973.

Gutman, Herbert G. *The Black Family in Slavery and Freedom, 1750–1925.* New York, 1976.

Hancock, Harold B. *Delaware during the Civil War: A Political History.* Wilmington, DE, 1961.

———. *Bridgeville: A Community History of the Nineteenth Century.* Bridgeville, DE, 1985.

Hancock, Harold B., and Russell McCabe. *Milton's First Century, 1807–1907.* Milton, DE, 1982.

Herman, Bernard L. *The Stolen House.* Charlottesville, VA, 1992.

Higginbotham, A. Leon, Jr. *In the Matter of Color: Race and the American Legal Process, the Colonial Period.* New York, 1978.

Hodges, Graham R. *Black Itinerants of the Gospel: The Narratives of John Jea and George White.* Madison, WI, 1993.

Hoffecker, Carol E., ed. *Readings in Delaware History.* Newark, DE, 1973.

Joyner, Charles. *Down by the Riverside: A South Carolina Slave Community.* Urbana, IL, 1984.

Justice, Hilda. *Life and Ancestry of Warner Mifflin.* Philadelphia, 1905.

Kobrin, David. *The Black Minority in Early New York.* Albany, NY, 1971.

Kolchin, Peter. *Unfree Labor: American Slavery and Russian Serfdom.* Cambridge, MA, 1987.

———. *American Slavery, 1619–1877.* New York, 1993.

Kulikoff, Allan. *Tobacco and Slaves: The Development of Southern Cultures in the Chesapeake, 1680–1800.* Chapel Hill, NC, 1986.

Litwack, Leon F. *North of Slavery: The Negro in the Free States.* Chicago, 1961.

McGowan, James A. *Station Master on the Underground Railroad: The Life and Letters of Thomas Garrett.* Moylan, PA, 1977.

McManus, Edgar J. *A History of Negro Slavery in New York.* Syracuse, NY, 1966.

Mullin, Gerald W. *Flight and Rebellion: Slave Resistance in Eighteenth-Century Virginia.* New York, 1974.

Mullin, Michael. *Africa in America: Slave Acculturation and Resistance in the American South and the British Caribbean, 1736–1831.* Urbana, IL, 1992.

Munroe, John A. *Colonial Delaware: A History.* Millwood, NY, 1978.

———. *Federalist Delaware.* New Brunswick, NJ, 1954.

———. *History of Delaware.* Newark, DE, 1979.

Nash, Gary B. *Forging Freedom: The Formation of Philadelphia's Black Community, 1720–1840.* Cambridge, MA, 1988.

Nash, Gary B., and Jean Soderlund. *Freedom by Degrees: Emancipation in Pennsylvania.* New York, 1991.

O'Callaghan, E. B. *Voyages of the Slavers St. John and Arms of Amsterdam, 1659, 1663.* Albany, NY, 1867.

Raboteau, Albert J. *Slave Religion: The Invisible Institution in the Antebellum South.* New York, 1980.

Ruttman, Darrett B., and Anita H. Ruttman. *A Place in Time: Middlesex County, Virginia, 1650–1750.* New York, 1984.

Salinger, Sharon V. *To Serve Well and Faithfully: Labor and Indentured Servants in Pennsylvania, 1682–1800.* New York, 1987.

Savitt, Todd L. *Medicine and Slavery: The Diseases and Health Care of Blacks in Antebellum Virginia.* Chicago, 1978

Scharf, J. Thomas. *History of Delaware, 1609–1888.* 2 vols. Philadelphia, 1888.

Schlebecker, John T. *Whereby We Thrive: A History of American Farming.* Ames, IA, 1975.

Schwarz, Philip J. *Twice Condemned: Slaves and the Criminal Laws of Virginia, 1705–1865.* Baton Rouge, LA, 1988.

Singleton, Theresa A., ed. *The Archaeology of Slavery and Plantation Life.* New York, 1985.

Smith, Barbara C. *After the Revolution: The Smithsonian History of Everyday Life in the Eighteenth Century.* New York, 1985.

Starr, Raymond, and Robert Detweiler, eds. *Race, Prejudice, and the Origins of Slavery in America.* Cambridge, MA, 1975.

Still, William. *The Underground Rail Road.* Chicago, 1970.

Turner, Edward R. *The Negro in Pennsylvania: Slavery, Servitude, Freedom, 1639–1861.* Washington, DC, 1911.

Weslager, C. A. *The Swedes and the Dutch at New Castle, 1638–1664.* Wilmington, DE, 1987.

White, Shane. *Somewhat More Independent: The End of Slavery in New York City, 1770–1810.* Athens, GA, 1991.

Williams, William H. *The Garden of American Methodism: The Delmarva Peninsula, 1769–1820.* Wilmington, DE, 1984.

Wood, Peter. *Black Majority: Negroes in Colonial South Carolina from 1670 through the Stono Rebellion.* New York, 1975.

Wright, Donald R. *African Americans in the Colonial Era: From African Origins through the American Revolution.* Arlington Heights, IL, 1990.

———. *African Americans in the Early Republic, 1789–1831.* Arlington Heights, IL, 1993.

Zilversmit, Arthur. *The First Emancipation: The Abolition of Slavery in the North.* Chicago, 1967.

Index